ORANGE IS THE NEW BLESSING

ORANGE IS THE NEW BLESSING

FROM BUSTED TO BLESSING

NOTHING IS WASTED
GOD CAN REDEEM ALL YOUR MISTAKES

DEBBIE GRIFFITH

Copyright © 2022 by Debbie Griffith
All rights reserved. Written permission must be secured from the publisher or the author to use or reproduce any part of this book, except for brief quotations in critical reviews or articles.

Scripture quotations, as marked, are taken from the New International Version (NIV), New Living Translation (NLT), and Amplified Bible, Classic Edition (AMPC). English Standard Version (ESV), Berean Study Bible (BSB), King James Bible (KJB), New King James Version (NKJV), New American Standard Bible (NASB), Common English Bible CEB), New Century Version (NCV), and The Message Bible (MSG).

ISBN: 979-8-218-07589-7

Front cover design by Nathaniel Navratil.
Cover layout by LACreative.
Good News Glove by Campus Crusade for Christ, Inc.
Author's cover photos by Bethany Tubman Johs.
Page layout by Win-Win Words LLC.

Printed in the United States of America.

To the one, Auntie Ginger, who shared the Good News of the One who gives unconditional love, grace, and forgiveness—our Savior Lord Jesus

THE GOOD NEWS GLOVE

CONTENTS

Foreword   xi
Acknowledgments   xiii
The Beginning: Moving Forward   xvii

"The fruit of the Spirit is Love, Joy, Peace, Patience, Kindness, Goodness, Faithfulness, Gentleness, Self-control."
— Galatians 5:22–23

Addicted to LOVE
1. Orange Is the New Blessing   1
2. I Just Wanna Be Loved   5
3. Addicted to Love   11
4. For Better or Worse   17
5. #MeToo   25
6. Dear Megan, Choose Joy   33

Driven by JOY
7. Run Your Race with Perseverance (and Cancer Sucks)   41
8. Thank God for Laughter and Wine   48
9. The Joy of Life in Deer Season   54
10. My Wrong Direction Redeemed   58
11. Looking in the Mirror   64
12. Take the 'Should' Out of Your Life   68

Serving PEACE
13. Forgiveness Sets *You* Free   81
14. Being Real: 'I Need a Cigarette'   97
15. Earth Is the Bus Stop: Heaven Is Home, Welcoming All   102
16. Hope in the Wilderness of Anxiety   112
17. Do You Know Where You're Going?   122
18. Parenting Isn't for Wimps   129

Prescribed PATIENCE
19. Where's the Verse of the Day?   139
20. Parenting a Pete   145
21. *Attention!* He's Not Finished with You Yet   151
22. The Quarantine Chronicles of COVID   156
23. 'Hope' Spreads Easily Too (like COVID-19)   163
24. 'There'll Be Days Like This,' Mama Said   171

Dependent on KINDNESS

25	Love Serves: *Muchas Gracias*	181
26	Server Girl Blues and Orange	189
27	Pride Goes Before the Fall	195
28	Your Parent Changes but Love Doesn't	200
29	'I Guess I Can Just Pray'	205
30	Release & Replace: The 3 C's to Peace	218
	Part 1: Release Coveting—Replace with Celebrating	221
	Part 2: Release Comparison—Replace with Compassion	223
	Part 3: Release Competing—Replace with Confession	226

Buzzing with GOODNESS

31	The Matter of Loving All	239
32	It's Not Easy Being Green	245
33	Green Beans for Breakfast	256
34	Growing Up with Jesus	262
35	'Look Up Child, There's Hope'	269
36	What Matters Most as a Christian?	276

High on FAITHFULNESS

37	Skipping to Church or Church Skipping?	287
38	Uncle Peter, God Is Greater in Our Weaknesses	302
39	Making Best Friends Wherever You Go	314
40	My Testimony: 'I'm Still Here'	320
41	Choose What You Think On	328
42	Getting to the Other Side	336

Therapeutic GENTLENESS

43	Until We Meet Again	343
44	I'm Keepin' It Real, Jammere	349
45	Embrace Your Inner Loser	355
46	God Is Not Mad at You	364
47	Become Like a Little Child	369
48	The Beauty of God's 'Grace'	374

Craving SELF-CONTROL

49	We're All Addicts	383
50	I Wanna Be Pop-u-lar	391
51	Sinners & Saints: Life Is Short	399
52	One Step at a Time	404
53	Season Finale: Orange Is the New Blessing	414
	Griffith Family 2022	423

FOREWORD

IF I WERE TO SUMMARIZE the message of Debbie's book, it would simply be this: God fits our failures into His future for us. In fact, I would take that statement a step further and say that the thing that qualifies us best for service *is* failure.

I remember being told by a Sunday school teacher when I was young that in order to be an effective witness for Jesus, we need to be good, clean, and nice. So, I grew up assuming that the less sin we have—or the more sin we hide—the more attractive Jesus will be to our neighbor. Our bad behavior makes Jesus look bad and our weakness makes Jesus look weak, so we should always seek to be "good Christians" because the better we are, the better we honor God.

But what I've discovered—and more importantly, what the Bible teaches—is that the exact opposite is true.

Someone once said, "We glorify a water fountain by coming thirsty and drinking deeply." This means that when we are real—by confessing our sins, demonstrating our desperation, acknowledging our neediness, telling the truth about our fears and insecurities and struggles and secrets, admitting that we are selfish and arrogant and controlling and self-righteous and faithless and unforgiving—that is when we bear witness to the world about a Savior who came, not for the righteous, but for sinners.

This is what I love about Debbie's book.

Debbie's honesty about her own failures points us to the God who graciously rescues people who fail because people who fail are all that there are. Refusing to present a Photoshopped version of herself, she discusses her life as it really is. She not only confesses that she is a sinner, but she confesses her sins. And in doing so, she gives the reader a ton of hope.

Trust me, those parts of you that you are most fearful of disclosing—the parts of you that get jealous, the parts of you that are greedy, the parts of you that lust for what you don't have, the parts of you that hate, the parts of you that doubt, the parts of you that thirst for vengeance, the parts of you that are unwilling to forgive, the parts of you that will sacrifice anything for selfish gain, the parts of you that easily betray others in your heart, the parts of you that rage, the parts of you that are painfully insecure—those are the very parts that will be most helpful to people if you admit them. Opening up about your struggles helps people so much more then talking about your strengths. People might be somewhat (and temporarily) inspired when you share your successes with them, but they connect with you and feel less alone when you share your failures with them.

So, thank you, Debbie, for sharing your failures with me. By doing so, you have pointed me to the One who promised to never leave me or forsake me—to the One who always meets my messiness with His mercy, my guilt with His grace, and my failure with His forgiveness.

— Tullian Tchividjian
Pastor of The Sanctuary/Florida and author of more than a half dozen books about Christianity and current issues, including *One Way Love* and *It Is Finished*. He is a grandson of Christian evangelist Billy Graham.

ACKNOWLEDGMENTS

IT'S ONLY BY GOD'S GRACE that this book happened. Over the last fifty-five years I've learned that I'm a Storyteller and a Talker Girl, but a Writer I am not. I am a Child of God and a lover of His Word because He is the Word. Proverbs 3:6 tells me that if I acknowledge God in all my ways, He will direct and make straight my path. Acknowledging God means to care about what He thinks. I care. "So, here I am Lord, send me." God has directed me to share the Good News of His Grace, Redemption, and the Hope of Eternity by sharing my stories of hope and blessings in the messy and hard parts of life.

God receives the glory for this book you hold in your hands, but, of course, I must acknowledge others whom God has placed in my life to give me encouragement, support, and prayers. There aren't enough words to explain my gratitude. I. Can't. Even.

Thank you to all the people who have supported the ministry of *Everyday Matters*, beginning in 2006 with the radio station managers, directors, and listeners. Bruce Christopherson, I thank for giving me the opportunity to have the feature first air on KBHW through Heartland Christian Broadcasters in the town where I live. It's been a huge blessing for me to write and record how God's Word is applicable in everyday life, and to have the feature broadcast on more than one hundred stations in the US, Canada, Australia, and even Norway. This is something we never imagined. Tim Nelson, my producer and "little brother" who has not only helped me become a better communicator, but who is also one of the most fun humans I know, and whose antics and humor made coming into the station each week one of my favorite activities. Mike Worth, The Tech Wizard for the feature, who's an absolute Godsend and has volunteered his time, talent, and engineering for both Matters Mail subscriptions and updating the website each week. He's always "on-call" for my emergency calls. Thank you to Rick McConnell from Monumental Studios in Colorado who now generously produces the feature. My community of people who "show up" and live life authentically and crazily, too, where my family and I have lived for more than twenty-seven years—International Falls, Minnesota (Icebox of the Nation). This Northern Town and its people have taught and given me so much. The International Falls Public Library saw me many days working on the final edits of this book, on the back table with the globe. I was grateful for the quiet and community. Pastor Chris at Gateway Assembly of God Church, with its small congregation but powerful presence of God, witnessed my struggles and surrender at the altar most Wednesday evenings as God moved in me in the final months of writing (which began in the summer of 2017).

I am grateful for the speaking ministry, which began in 2007, and to all the hosts, directors, and attendees of these retreats and conferences. I am in awe of the way God moved throughout Minnesota and the Midwest, from Iowa's cornfields to the beaches of Pensacola, Florida, as well as into the Sweet South of Georgia, Tennessee, and Alabama (grits and pickled beets, y'all). *So* many women at these events have touched and impacted my life, including many who would continually ask me, *"Will you write a book with your stories in it? I want to share the story about you running over the deer."*

Thank you to all the theater people I've worked with, directed, and performed alongside, all throughout the Midwest in various seasons of life. Working as a managing artistic director for a children's theater company for three summers in Moorhead, Minnesota, a high school teacher in Minneapolis and a substitute for years in "The Icebox" also equipped me with lessons on living a life of love. Students, parents, and colleagues taught me so much about how real life and real love work together, with its challenges in teaching, performing, directing, and serving in a restaurant. You are all family to me. Truly.

I am thankful to the wee town and people of Callaway, Minnesota (population 230), where I went to elementary school and the Missouri Synod Lutheran Church (a lot of interesting and good experiences came from that time). I am thankful to the town in which I went to high school in Detroit Lakes, Minnesota, and the small-town love of community and old classmates. The *Detroit Lakes Tribune* gave me the opportunity to write a column for their *Faith* section (beginning in 2015 until the end of 2021). That helped me to connect with an audience of everyday people from all backgrounds of faith and gender. Many of the stories in this book come from columns that I expanded on and my dear "Ron-Man" Wilson, editor of *North Dakota Outdoors*, edited numerous columns and helped give me confidence that I could tell a story in writing.

Thank you to all the Beths and Joshes, who were there when I needed help with editing and communicating clearly. Oh, Lord, thank You for the "Michelle People" who prayed for me through the anxiety of writing and the generosity of Doug and Jamie, allowing me to stay in their Arizona mountain home to work on editing. Mike Towle, my editor, whose patience and understanding helped make this book readable with his skills and suggestions but still let me be me. Of course, I must certainly acknowledge my "dead body" girlfriends (that's a friend you can call at 2:00 A.M. and say, "*I've got a dead body at my house. Come help me,*" and that person comes over and helps—no questions asked). These dear women, (a gal-pal group, fewer than ten), encouraged, supported, laughed, cried, prayed, and helped me carry difficult burdens (and you absolutely know who you are). *Thank you.*

My extended family support, with my brother Jay and four nephews, new niece-editor, and my sister-in-law, Jonell, have been *huge* in their love and support! Lord have mercy! "What would I do without you, Jonell?" Seriously? God is so nice to me. I love my dad, who inspired the love of questions and adventure in me, and my dear mom, the woman who has known, supported, and loved me the longest.

My Cute Husband, Dan, who is the Leader of Love for our family and is rock solid. He's read every story and helped bring clarity to what I was trying to say. Dan shows me unconditional love and is an example of putting others before yourself. "Please, Dan, edit this story now. I need it now." I love and acknowledge our four sons: Marco, Peter, Joey, and David, who are in so many of my stories and who inspire me by the way they have a real and personal relationship with Jesus. *And* to my daughter-in law, Rachel, who is one of the best listeners to a talker-girl like me.

Thank you to a hero of mine, Uncle Stan, for his example as a Servant of Jesus, and to my Auntie Ginger . . . well . . . whoa, she's my mentor, who has given time to me like no other, who loves the messy me, the "model" me, and the mercy of God working in me. She gave hope and humor, insight, focus, support, prayer, and unconditional love since I waddled into her life at age three. We've been the dearest and closest of humans ever since that time, and to her, I dedicate this book.

Again, Thank You, Jesus, for giving me this opportunity to share Your love and grace with others, and Your never-failing love when I was scared and wanted to give up. I praise You. I thank You.

> *"So, we're not giving up. How could we! Even though on the outside it often looks like things are falling apart on us, on the inside, where God is making new life, not a day goes by without His unfolding grace. These hard times are small potatoes compared to the coming good times; the lavish celebration prepared for us. There's far more here than meets the eye. The things we see now are here today, gone tomorrow. But the things we can't see now will last forever."*
> **— 2 Corinthians 4:16-18 (MSG)**

THE BEGINNING: MOVING FORWARD

"But now, this is what the Lord says—He who created you, Jacob, He who formed you, Israel: Do not fear, for I have redeemed you; I have summoned you by name; you are Mine."
— **Isaiah 43:1 (NIV)**

WHAT IF YOUR BIGGEST BLESSINGS come through the hardest, most painful and challenging of circumstances? My first response when in a difficult place isn't to think about the goodness that God will bring. Yet look at James 1:2–4: "Consider it pure joy when you encounter trials of many kinds, because you know that the testing of your faith develops perseverance. Allow perseverance to finish its work, so that you may be mature and complete, not lacking anything." I do want to obey God and most certainly I desire to be mature and not lack the blessings God has for me. I might get busted in life but I want His blessings.

The Greek word for *perseverance* is *hupomone*. Literally, "an abiding under"—*to remain under God!* Now, put that meaning of "perseverance" into the reading of James 1:2–4. "Consider it pure joy when you encounter trials of many kinds, because you know that the testing of your faith develops the ability to remain under God. Remain under God to finish its work, so that you may be mature and complete, not lacking anything." I'm in! How about you? I really try to make a point of saying, "Praise, God, thank God" as a mantra when I'm hit "with a fiery dart" of a difficult circumstance. I'm *trying* to be a first responder to shout out praise rather than shout out my pain.

It's the hardships of life that shape who we are as individuals and the seasons we walk through, no matter the length of them, and they also affect how we live with and for others. I've come to realize that God doesn't bless us just to "bless us." He blesses us so we might be a blessing to love and serve others. I understood who Christ Jesus was in a personal relationship at a very young age and not through organized religion.

I am convinced that had I not known the power of God's Holy Spirit working in me, I would have responded to seasons of depression, anxiety attacks, loss of friendships and dreams, physical health issues, and serious disappointments, in a way that would have led me to despair with the possibility of no longer wanting to live. Don't get me wrong, I still have yelled and lamented loudly and dramatically (theater people, like me, don't need an audience to show drama). I think, too, that I would have numbed my pain with alcohol sooner (rather than wait until I was forty-five years old) and perhaps also looked for any other means but God Himself to "shut down."

Of course, being a wife of thirty-plus years and a mom to our four sons has shaped who I am significantly, but the woman I am inside is because God's Word has dramatically changed me as I aim to "stay the course" by following, obeying, and *applying* His promises into my everyday life.

In 1995 I began the habit of reading the Bible every day even if it was only a verse or two. In 2004 I began to write down one simple Scripture and then any words of encouragement I heard God speak to my heart pertaining to the Scripture. As this habit developed, I began to hear the Holy Spirit prompting, "You're gonna want to memorize this one. You're going to need it, in times when everything and everyone around you seem unstable and crazy."

It's from my journal writing entries that in 2006 I was given the opportunity to write a one-minute feature, *Everyday Matters*, to air on the Christian radio station in International Falls, Minnesota, where I still live. I never expected it would grow to reach thousands while being carried on hundreds of stations in the US, Canada, and even Norway.

The book you now hold in your hands is a collection of journal stories in which I share my seasons of pain—both emotional and physical. It's also a book filled with hope and humor. It's where God showed me, "Nothing is wasted." He can redeem all mistakes.

My receiving a DUI in February 2017 was a game changer. It was hard and humiliating, *but* it launched me into a season of blessings and showed me God's grace in a way I never would have imagined. Grace is the kindness of God poured out upon undeserving people (me), not because of who we are, but because of who He is . . . merciful, patient, and loving toward even the worst of who we are. When we're humble, we can bring hope to another because, "we've been there." C. S. Lewis succinctly wrote, "The load, or weight, or burden of my neighbor's glory should be laid daily on my back, a load so heavy that only humility can carry it, and the backs of the proud will be broken. . . ."[1]

Most definitely the DUI season caused me to humble myself in a new way. Perhaps because it was a public humiliation and when wearing orange in a jail cell (even if it's a good color on you) can shake/wake you up. Yet, I knew in my spirit that I didn't have to live in shame. Shame says you *are* something wrong; guilt says you've *done* something wrong. I was guilty. In submitting more to God, I began to praise Him more. Each morning, before my feet hit the ground, I'd thank God for the fresh mercy He was giving me because,

---

[1] C. S. Lewis, *The Weight of Glory and Other Addresses* (London: William Collins, 2013).

of course, yesterday I had used my allotted and perfect amount. I can't agree more with Tullian Tchividjian, "My life doesn't look like Jesus'—it looks like someone's who needs Jesus."

The nonfiction writing contest I entered and won required that those submitting a piece use the Scripture from Micah 6:8 with a word count no longer than one thousand words. It was a contest held by the Northwestern radio station KTIS in Minneapolis, Minnesota, in March 2017. It was only a month after I had received the DUI charge, but I knew almost immediately that I was to share my story and become vulnerable to help myself and others.

Life continued. Two of our four sons were out of the home, and their love for me, along with my husband Dan, showed how nice God is to me, too, by their graciousness. I also continued as a substitute teacher, retreat/conference speaker, writer for a newspaper column, all while recording the *Everyday Matters* radio feature.

I had nine months of riding my bike to most destinations, and on Minnesota icy roads it was an adventure. Of course, I had friends and my family who gave me rides when I needed. And with each passing day of this season, I saw more and more of God's grace and love in fresh ways. I was provided with new opportunities as others reached out to me and I reached into their lives in a way I couldn't have done previously.

Jesus continued to remind me of His redemption in all things and that I was enough because He was. I was never alone even though I felt lonely at times. I always had hope even though I felt some days were never ending and I sometimes slipped into despair and chose to have a cocktail to numb a bit of the pain but never again would I get behind the wheel.

God repeatedly welcomed me to "look up" when I was down, and He reminded me I was loved for who I was and not for what I did. I was reminded that I don't represent Him well, but He represents me perfectly by what He did on the cross.

The first story in this book's collection is the story that won the contest, and the last one is the "season finale." The Earth experience is hard, but it's not our home, not our final destination. Life is not always good but God always is. Yet, of course, all stories in this life will eventually come to an end, but with death we need not be afraid. "Where, O death, is your victory? Where, O death, is your sting?" (1 Corinthians 15:55). We have the hope of eternity and the real beginning of the perfect story, for those who are in Christ Jesus. Oh, what a day that will be.

Keep on keeping on, Dear Heart. Nothing Is Wasted.

ADDICTED TO LOVE

1
ORANGE IS THE NEW BLESSING

"He has shown you, O mortal, what is good. And what does the Lord require of you? To act justly and to love mercy and to walk humbly with your God."
— **Micah 6:8 (NIV)**

I HAD TO WEAR ORANGE. I like the color. It's in my color wheel as a flattering wardrobe choice. An orange jail jumpsuit, however, was never a choice for me; it was a consequence for my bad choice.

I made a mistake. Who doesn't? I'm a sinner. We're all sinners. The temptation to justify and explain is usually our default position. Yes, I see your list. I see your "reasons why" you needed to self-medicate; you have back pain in your shoulder that is now shooting down your left arm; you failed at getting the position you interviewed for; your dream seems lost; or worse yet you've lost a loved one and, in your grief, you just want some stinkin' relief. Relief takes many forms.

Should you, though, get behind the wheel in your pajamas after having a large adult beverage and drive three miles and back to get a Big Mac and fries to help feed the pain? What if after, you sit privately in your own driveway and stuff your face trying to forget and numb the pain? Does that work?

No. It does not work. You should not do this. But I did. It was not a good choice. Micah 6:8 tells us to "do justice" and, in my situation, God saw to it that I was made right by humbly accepting His orange justice. Thankfully, I *know* He wants our trust in what He did for us in redeeming all our mistakes rather than our trying to justify and solve our problems on our own strength. No amount of personal sacrifice, good deeds, or penance can earn His acceptance or love. It is humbling to share my story, but my hope is that the mercy and love I received may be redemptive and encourage others.

It's important to know that the negative consequences we experience as believers should never be thought of as punishment because Jesus has already been fully punished for our sins. All sin has consequences, and some of those consequences are *really* hard, but they are a part of God's corrective discipline, which comes out of His great love.

I looked at my consequences, and they were hard ones. I cried. I cried for what I had done wrong, for my sin, and for the shame. It was and is painful. I actually wailed, and the next day, when a friend came over, I wailed some more and snot-cried. The only way to describe my friend who purposely left her phone in the car to spend five hours to sit, listen, and love me, is "loving mercy." It's this kind of unconditional love not based on my performance value as a wife, mom, radio person, high school teacher, or speaker girl that I desperately needed. We all desperately need it. We need to know our value and identity come from *whom God says* we are. He says we're created in His image, and He valued us enough, even while in our sin, to die for us. We are not a mistake, even though we make mistakes. Micah 6:8 commands us to walk justly, to love mercy, and to walk humbly with our God. It is not just one; it is all three. We know it when we receive it. And we want to do the same for others.

My jail time news spread (and, believe me, it was a swift delivery of information) throughout my small town of seven thousand the minute the jail roster went up on the internet. The nice thing about living in a small town is when you don't know what in the world you're doing . . . everyone else does. My phone had blown up while I was away. Plus, I had several private messages written with concern, kindness, grace, and so much love that I felt I needed to issue a statement on Facebook. So, I wrote. "Love is kind. Thank you, my friends, for your kindness." In all of what happens, I know my Redeemer lives and takes the parts in us that are broken to teach and bless us. He gives us the grace we need for each day so that in turn we are able to help someone else when they are down. I am not alone. You are not alone. We all need love. We all need kindness.

The Earth experience is hard. We lose focus and isolate even though we know better. When the enemy comes in with his lies and the haters come in with their hate, we must choose to stand strong. There's no truth to the voice that tells you that you'll never be enough, that you're a disappointment, and that your past defines your future. There's no condemnation in Christ. That's why we need to reach out and step forward and say, "Hey, I need to tell you something. I'm scared and I feel alone. I'm hurting. I know what's true, but I can't hear very well because my feelings are screaming at me and blocking all channels of truth." Speak up, even if it's a whisper, because there's going be someone who gets it and just loves you. The sweetest encouragement comes from the fallen who rise again. It reminds me of what late author and speaker Brennan Manning shared: "One of the most healing words I ever spoke as a confessor was to an old priest with a drinking problem. 'Just a few years ago,' I said, 'I was a hopeless alcoholic in the gutter in Fort Lauderdale.' 'You?' he cried. 'O, Thank God!'"[2] When we bring a smile to the face of someone in pain, we have brought Christ to them.

---

[2] Brennan Manning, *The Ragamuffin Gospel* (Colorado Springs, CO: Multnomah Books, 2015).

The experience in orange has been a game changer for me, a severe mercy. Before I left the jail, I asked if I could keep the orange socks as a souvenir. The socks serve as a reminder of God's justice and mercy. I own what happened and because God is real in our pain, I can honestly say, "Orange is the new blessing."

2
I JUST WANNA BE LOVED

"Where can I go from Your spirit? Where can I flee from Your presence? If I go up to the heavens, You are there; If I make my bed in the depths, You are there."
— **Psalm 139:7–8 (NIV)**

WHY CAN'T YOU JUST UNDERSTAND that I'm hurting, and I need to vent, cry, and wail? Don't try and fix me. Let me be my miserable self, okay?

I've had tears streaming down my face trying to explain my hurt, only to get more frustrated that the help I'm offered is to "just calm down," or to be questioned with, "Why are you so crazy?" It would be better if I were told to "get more hysterical," along with, "I don't know why you're so upset, but it's okay."

When I am distraught, I don't necessarily want a solution or to "be fixed." What makes all the difference is to know that I'm loved right where I'm at and especially when I'm most unlovely. It is the deepest ache for all of us to be loved for who we are and where we are. "I just want to be loved," is the deepest cry of most women.

Life can be beastly, and sometimes it's that beast within us that makes life so difficult. That's why the story of *Beauty and the Beast* resonates with us. The fairy-tale ending is real, true, and about being loved no matter what others see on the outside.

For the Beast to be transformed back to his real self, he first must be loved for who he is, which is "beastly." Yet, in just a short time Belle sees past all the ugliness that he and others find hideous because she's able to see a way into his beautiful heart. It's Belle's love and then the Beast's acceptance of her love, which transformshim. He becomes his real and true self and the curse is broken.

It is "a tale as old as time" and one right from the Good Book. We are only transformed when we accept God's love for us as we are in our sinful state of affairs. It's His work on the cross, and His forgiveness and unconditional love that transform us so we can live honestly and freely despite our messy lives.

Those crying fits never do me much good because my husband wants to fix me. Sometimes, I don't really know what's breaking me— or I do and I just want to be loved and accepted in the state I'm in. After thirty-plus years of marriage, I have now found that it's often best if I leave the room and sometimes take a drive, have a long cry, and talk to God. When I come home, we're both calmer. I need to stay grounded in what I know is true, which is "God loves me and God gets me." I have a husband who does, too, but there's no human on this Earth who will perfectly understand and perfectly love me, expect for Christ Jesus, and we're all better off when we come to that realization. God loves with no conditions. He loves, doesn't give up on us, and never leaves us. Nothing from our past, present, or future will surprise or shock Him. And He is always able to fill the ache and void of our hearts. "For your Creator will be your Husband; the LORD of Heaven's Armies is His name! He is your Redeemer, the Holy One of Israel, the God of all the Earth" (Isaiah 54:5, NLT).

I remind the girls I mentor that "God sees the beauty in you. He loves His girl, Susan (insert your own name)." We all need to know we're beautiful and loved despite our past, present, OR future mistakes. But sometimes when we're starving for love, we'll take what we can get. Attention "feels" like love, but it's not real or lasting. Presenting a picture or "look" that attracts physically can feel empowering, but usually it's not about lasting love. But at least I'm desirable, and it's better than being alone, right?

I think deep inside we all know the truest answer is that real love never leaves and gives up on you. Victoria Robinson, author of *They Lied to Us* and an abortion recovery counselor, shared strong advice in a May 11, 2021 Facebook post: "Young women, if you're dating a guy, thinking of dating a guy, or engaged to marry one who constantly puts you down, makes you feel you're not good enough or smart enough, thinks you're beneath him, doesn't like your family or they don't like him, convinces you you're the one who's always wrong, throws up anything you do in your face, belittles you, makes you feel stupid, says you're lucky he's with you, or a coward punk who physically or mentally abuses you, here's a piece of *free* advice. *Run, girl, run.*" But sometimes we do what's familiar and comfortable regardless, if it's healthy. Perhaps it's because we've never experienced or witnessed a healthy relationship or never heard the words, "I'm proud of you. I support you. You're pretty."

Joey, our twenty-one-year-old, sent me a short text recently from his college dorm that read, "I'm fat." I wrote back, "You're handsome." I could see him smiling as soon as he received my encouragement. What we hear and then believe makes all the difference in the way we walk forward with our lives and what kind of attention we are willing to give and receive.

There's such comfort in Psalm 91:1, which I call my 911 verse: "S/he who dwells in the secret place of the Most High will remain stable, fixed under the shadow of the Almighty, Whose power no foe can withstand." (AMPC) Well, I'm in. I need this dwelling place because it's in the secret place of dwelling where God is and where we're safe and secure. It's a place where we can be our most vulnerable.

The world of people, namely the world of people we see on our screens, whether friends, family, or the media world, is one-dimensional. We tend to compare ourselves to them as they vie for our attention. It's a place we go to post and where we try and put on a good face. We don't want to be hurt and judged by the world, so we hide our secrets and maneuver around to come across as having it all together.

For extra security, we try and find someone we can pick apart, poking at their flaws and failings to make ourselves feel better. It's all rot. Yet the lure and glamour of this world is a means for the enemy of our souls to whisper we're not good enough. It can be hard to withstand, especially when we don't know where to run.

We hear, "You need to look like 'this' and perform like 'this' and be more like 'this.'" And we're trying so hard to look like we know our parts and perform so well, when, really, we need to stop and ask ourselves, "What the heck does this image I'm trying to play look like anyway? Can anyone see the real me? Do I know who I am?" Our enemy, the devil, knows our name, but calls us by our sins. Jesus knows our sins, but calls us by our name.

Jesus wants us to stop and rest, so we hear His words, which are true, but we must be vulnerable with our secrets (which He already knows about anyway). We need to come clean and admit our sins, especially the sins of jealousy and pride. Pride is deceitful, and it hides. It's tricky because we don't think we have it. "The pride of your heart has deceived you" (Obadiah 1:3, NIV).

A good test for me to take to see if I'm prideful or jealous is to ask myself the questions, "Am I happy at the success of another, or do I really prefer they fail? Surely, God knows how rotten and undeserving they are?!" But guess what? None of us deserves grace, yet God has grace for us in abundance every day, new and fresh. Yes, just like the song, great is His faithfulness. His mercies are new every morning.

As I get older, I realize more and more how much I need grace, which helps me to give grace. We need to shut down the negative voice in our heads that says we don't deserve real love because of our past mistakes. God welcomes us all to His table to sit and eat. He doesn't welcome sin, but in one swift swoop He can forgive and clean up our mess and set us before a wonderful table of grace. We all have a story and it's refreshing to be real and honest and then hear, "I'm sorry, it's hard. You're going to make it. You're not alone—been there, done that." Waiting on God is hard. I get that, too. I didn't think I'd still be working as a server girl in a Mexican restaurant in my fifties while I was still traveling as a Speaker Girl, but here I was and I'm thankful and I am humbled. Humility is a key to receiving real love.

Crazy as it sounds, I know we've all thought we might just help God along, make a plan without talking (praying) to Him first and then asking Him to bless what we decided. I know it is easier to steer a ship that's moving, but we get there faster when we don't have to be turned around. "In their hearts humans plan their course, but the LORD establishes their steps" (Proverbs 16:9, NIV).

I remember the Post-it note that my husband left on my steering wheel years ago that read, "Debbie is pretty." It stayed stuck on the steering wheel for weeks and so many times when I got behind the wheel feeling crummy, and certainly not pretty, I would smile and think: *Someone loves me and thinks I'm pretty, even when I don't.*

We all just wanna be loved and God loves you right where you're at. In JJ Heller's song "What Love Really Means," we hear the truth sung to us of God's love: "I will love you for you, not for what you have done or what you will become, but I will love you for you."[3] Once you know you're really loved, you can then begin to sincerely love another human in need, because you understand the ache of disingenuous affections.

---

[3] JJ Heller, "What Love Really Means" (official music video), September 29, 2010, https://youtu.be/PgGUKWiw7Wk, viewed May 18, 2021.

Loving yourself through God's eyes enables you to give grace and love to others unconditionally, too. It's so freeing to receive and give God's love. Oh, how I would love to give you a big hug of encouragement right now because I understand that each of us has experienced feeling unlovable. But the honest truth is that you are lovely and loved right in this very moment of time. Trust me on this, but more importantly, trust Him.

3
ADDICTED TO LOVE

*"The Lord: 'I have loved you with an everlasting love;
I have drawn you with unfailing kindness.'"*
— **Jeremiah 31:3 (NIV)**

I MIGHT AS WELL SAY IT.

I'm addicted to love.

I'm a girl of the 1980s, so yeah, Robert Palmer had it right. I want to be loved as I am, *and* I want to love others as they are. I suppose we all do. The problem is when we chase love by running after the feeling rather than the essence. That's why a lot of us bounce from relationship to relationship. We want to "feel" love more than choose it. Love is a choice, a commitment.

I remember a discussion with girlfriends right out of college and the advice was given, "Love when you're ready, not when you're lonely." Another friend, who had been through a few relationships added, "Debbie, you become who you choose to spend the most time with. Choose wisely. I mean, if I line up all my ex-loves in a row, I can see the flow chart of my mental illness."

Advice taken.

In life's journey we all want to be known and loved, and Jesus knows us better than anyone and still loves us. He knows me, my pain, my ache, my disappointments, my shame, anger at myself, and the part of my heart that hasn't fully forgiven others. He knows. *He is* here, waiting to make use of what has happened. He is always on the move. He isn't wasting time, thinking about all the trouble He has with us or how awful we feel about where we are with ourselves and our troubles. God loves us unconditionally.

Jesus chose to love us long before we returned any feelings for Him.

Attention feels like love, but real "love" will not give up on you. Real love is God's love. Feelings are only a small part and come and go. Love is more about making a choice and then sticking with it.

"For better or worse" is declared at weddings, but perhaps not so much anymore. Continually we read about another Hollywood marriage on the skids and then it's over. No more "Old-School/Old Hollywood" style, such as Jimmy Stewart's and Paul Newman's respective marriages.

Newman was well known for his devotion to his wife and family. When once asked about infidelity, he famously quipped, "Why go out for a hamburger when you have steak at home?"

Unfortunately, nobody seems content with their cut of meat anymore. We want to shop around and taste all kinds of things, and when it doesn't feel right we move on. The grass might look greener on the other side but you have to maintain and mow that, too.

What's the big deal? The big deal is that marriage involves so many others, namely children. One of my dear friends, who is in a solid marriage with three children, told me recently that the pastor doing their marriage counseling more than twenty years ago also gave them parenting advice, saying, "The most important thing a father can do for his children is to love their mother and vice versa." I have had both male and female friends leave a marriage due to their unfaithfulness. The eventual aftermath to others is so painful, confusing, and frustrating. I'm a child of divorced parents who were married for forty-four years. There's no pleasant way to say it, but "divorce sucks."

The problem is we've become so feeling-oriented and self-focused. The root of what causes divorce is selfishness. We might know better, but because we want to "feel better" as soon as possible, we chase after being in love rather than being loving.

Hollywood breakups don't surprise any of us, but I was bummed when Jennifer Garner and Ben Affleck announced their divorce after their tenth wedding anniversary. I admire her honesty in her interview with *Vanity Fair*. "It was a real marriage," she revealed. "It wasn't for the cameras. And it was a huge priority for me to stay in it. And that did not work."

Most often we'll hear, "I deserve to be happy," after a relationship breaks, but Jennifer said, "It's not Ben's job to make me happy. The main thing is these kids—and we're completely in line with what we hope for them. Sure, I lost the dream of dancing with my husband at my daughter's wedding. But you should see their faces when he walks through the door. And if you see your kids love someone so purely and wholly, then you're going to be friends with that person."

I applaud them both. I suppose I'm clapping a little longer and louder for Jennifer in all of this because of her transparency. She related, "People have pain—they do regrettable things, they feel shame, and shame equals pain. No one needs to hate him for me. I don't hate him. Certainly, we don't have to beat the guy up. Don't worry—my eyes were wide open during the marriage. I'm taking good care of myself. I didn't marry the big fat movie star; I married him. And I would go back and remake that decision. . . . He's the love of my life. What am I going to do about that? He's the most brilliant person in any room, the most charismatic, the most generous. He's just a complicated guy. I always say, 'When his sun shines on you, you feel it.'

But when the sun is shining elsewhere, it's cold. He can cast quite a shadow."[4]

It makes me sad. Not just for Jen and Ben and their children, but for so many of my friends and family who have had this road of brokenness. It's so hard. It's so sad.

Award-winning music artist Derek Webb is a favorite of mine. I was saddened by his divorce after thirteen years of marriage because of his infidelity. Webb and his wife, Sandra McCracken, were viewed as a power couple in the Christian music industry, successfully reaching both religious and secular audiences. Derek wrote, "The truth is, I cheated. What started as a brief, inappropriate, and quickly confessed connection with a very old friend evolved quickly into something more serious, which was hidden from spouses and friends. It continued in secret for a matter of months, was eventually discovered, and set into motion the consequences that I will now live with for the rest of my life."

Webb explained that he believed lies, which led him to believe even more lies rather than recognize the truth. "This is why temptation is so tempting . . . as much as I wish I could, I simply cannot change what I've done or the resulting consequences. I can only own these despicable actions, which have left me completely devastated and deeply ashamed. Sometimes, no matter how bad you want it or how hard you fight for it, broken things just can't be mended. The only path forward from here is to continue focusing on health and healing, my children and parents, and investing in a safe community."

More than just a confession, Derek talked about the importance of having a handful of safe people in your life with whom you can truly share everything, especially the hardest and most shameful things.

---

[4] Krista Smith, "Exclusive: Jennifer Garner's Frank Talk about Kids, Men, and Ben Affleck," *Vanity Fair,* March 2016, https://www.vanityfair.com/hollywood/2016/02/jennifer-garner-talks-kids-career-ben-affleck, viewed January 13, 2022.

He continued, "I would plead with you to find a small group of safe men or women, friends who will not respond with platitudes of morality, but will instead get down and not only join you but stay with you in your s***, in hopes of helping pull you out. Inevitably, they'll need you to join them in theirs someday."[5]

I want to scream out *in love*, "Listen to what Derek is saying here. Your marriage is worth it. Your future is worth it. There is nothing God can't restore or redeem," but our shame and our mistakes make us feel we can never be free or worthy of love again.

Enough with the feelings, already. I want you to know this: No matter if you're the one searching for love, lost love, or ran to what you thought was love, there's hope. All the Jennifer, Sandra, Ben, and Derek people out there with children, you have to know there is always hope and you're not alone in your marriage struggles. It's such a hard place because you might be feeling angry, hurt, lost, and alone. Your feelings are valid, but there are others like you who've been in your place and they are now walking a little less crooked, with a little more hope because they know, despite what they feel, things do get better. The sun shines again.

I have a close friend who discovered her husband was having an affair after almost thirty years of marriage. The anguish, hurt, and trust broken were devastating. Their children were devastated. *But she knew God was bigger than the affair.* She trusted God to allow her to grieve as she needed, and she also knew God as a Redeemer and Miracle Worker in restoration. Her husband was willing to do what he needed to do to reconcile, and he was truly repentant. He went to individual counseling alone, as so did she. They also did biblical counseling together, using scripture from the Bible as the main

---

[5] "Derek Webb: On Failure, Liturgy, and New Years," *Relevant Magazine*, January 3, 2016, doi:https://www.relevantmagazine.com/life5/derek-webb-failure-liturgy-and-new-years/, viewed January 13, 2022

resource for help (biblical counseling is different than Christian counseling), and they began to heal and restore their marriage. It wasn't easy. And yes, there was a separation time and there were tears, pain, and the past to work through, *But* God in His power and grace worked in their lives to change what He needed them to change and to forgive (not recalling the past and its hurts because even though it's not forgotten, it's forgiven and the recalling of the hurts is buried). Now, their marriage is *back*! Their journey of restoration in having hope and putting trust in Christ, our Redeemer, has been so inspiring and grounded. Now they're even able to counsel and help others where unfaithfulness has taken place.

I have another dear friend whose husband was also unfaithful after thirty-plus years, but because he was unwilling to get help for substance abuse and take any responsibility or work toward change to restore the relationship, they are now in the process of divorce. It is devastating, painful, and gut wrenching. *But* because God is always good, my friend is healing and has hope. She has a new little cottage house that's her own and her only child has a place to come home to when he's on break from college, etc. She is brave and strong. God is faithful. He is redeeming in what seems wasted and she carries on. It's important to know that even if your marriage failed, you're not a failure.

So, listen. I hope you know you're capable and brave and significant even when it feels like you're not. I hope you know that there's redemption and restoration no matter what the brokenness is. I hope you know that Jesus is someone who is more interested in His love taking root in our hearts than tallying our faults. Take it one step at a time, moment by moment. Breathe in. Breathe out. It will get better.

4
FOR BETTER OR WORSE

"Love one another. As I have loved you,
so you must love one another."
— **John 13:34 (NIV)**

It's been two weeks and I haven't taken down the notes taped to the bathroom mirror. The first one reads: "Debbie is pretty and a good mom." The next day another note appeared under the first and it read: "Debbie is pretty again."

My husband, Dan, put them there. Yep, I'm keeping him.

Dan has always called me "Pretty Debbie." Always. He would leave me notes, when we were first dating, stuffed in my tote bag or in some drawer in the town house I shared with three other girls. Sometimes he would write, "VP" (Very Pretty), which I thought was so sweet because it also meant *"very important."* Hmm . . . What?

I still remember Dan looking at me, like I was being the jokester I can be, saying, "But that would be VIP. Hmm . . . what? Oh, right, I get it." I did get it, but I also knew that besides Dan thinking I was pretty, he also thought I was very important. On our ten-year anniversary, he gave me an engraved charm that says, "To my VP Debbie: Very 'Portant/Very Pretty."

Well, good for you, Debbie. I wish I had a husband like that.

You're right. It is good for me. Dan is good for me. But I didn't wish for him. I prayed for him. God has always instructed our four sons, too: "Remember you aren't just marrying the outside, but more importantly you're marrying the inside of that person." I still believe in the same good God that I did on November 17, 1990, when Dan and I had our first date. I believed it when I said, "I do, for better or worse" on June 1, 1991, six months later.

Dan tells our four sons that the most important decision they'll ever make is to enter into a personal relationship with the living God. The second-most-important decision is who they'll marry. Let God choose your spouse. That's what Dan did. He prayed for me. He got me.

Dan was very specific with four things he wanted in a wife: 1) He wanted someone who was pretty, not necessarily pretty to the world, but to him. He even gave God a visual and said, "Someone like this, God" as he referred to a gal on the cover of a brochure at the University of Minnesota, where he was going to school. 2) He wanted a woman who wanted children. 3) He wanted someone who truly loved God and didn't just call herself a Christian or wasn't religious in any way. 4) Dan wanted someone cuddly.

Now I might not be the prettiest gal out there, but as Dan tells it: "When I saw Debbie and asked her out for the first time, I told her she was the prettiest girl I had ever met. I meant it. She was. She is. She's my Pretty Debbie. (And for the record, she looked very similar to the picture I showed God)."

I am glad I have four boys, but my original thought was I'd get married and not have children. I was still planning on Broadway, and I thought having a husband to support me while I auditioned for shows was a good idea. I know. God loves me and I love Him, so I've been changed. I had always thought that marriage was for me, but I was wrong. It wasn't. It is about the other person. My life changed dramatically when I got the memo that true love serves in my marriage, my family, and my life.

I was serious about God when Dan met me. I knew the freedom of having a personal relationship with Him. Sure, I had been confirmed as a good Lutheran girl, but more importantly I knew Jesus was very real and very present in everyday life, no matter what. God loves us for who we are and where we are. Nothing we do or don't do would cause Him to ever withdraw His love.

Our freedom in Christ brings fun into our lives, too. Dan still says, "It's when Debbie came into my life that I began to really have fun. Otherwise, it was just work, school, and work. She was crazy. She still is and she can drive me crazy, but that's one of the fun things I love about her."

The last part of Dan's petition to God was asking for a wife who cuddled. Sometimes, when we're sharing the story about the four specific things Dan prayed for, he leaves that part out. "But request number 4 is the coolest part!" I shout.

Dan's not someone you'd meet and think, "Now there's a man who likes to cuddle." You would meet me and think, "Yep. She cuddles." No matter who you are, I'm likely to hug you when we first meet.

Dan's asking for someone who's cuddly just seemed weird. What guy even uses that word? It wasn't until years later we discovered the significance of his request. But God knew.

When we were dating, Dan was in law school. He'd hang out at the townhouse, at times, and study—*and* he'd rock. I can't describe the bewilderment I felt as I watched him read and rock while he sat on the couch. It was not a rocking couch. Dan rocked hard. It wasn't this gentle-sway-to-the-soft-melody rock. It was like he was on an automatic rocking machine, ready to blast off.

"Ahhh, Dan, whatcha doin'?" I asked the first time it happened. He looked up at me on the landing and said, "Studying."

"Yeah, right, but you're rocking, too."

"I know. It's how I study and read."

So, Dan rocked and read for the first three years of our marriage and then stopped completely after we had our first child, Marco.

One evening, years later, my RN friend, Diane, was explaining to me her work with home health-care visits and how small children often rock to comfort themselves, especially if they are in a broken home and not nurtured or held enough. Dan grew up loved but in a broken home. I remember Dan's mom telling me that he was the only one of her five children who didn't want to be held or cuddled. Wow. It hit. Dan had been rocking as a comfort mechanism for years, but after three years married to a cuddly wife, he stopped. Dan prayed for something he didn't even know he needed, but God knew. That's crazy incredible.

Incredible, too, is that God knew I needed Dan for my husband. Dan isn't perfect, but he's the perfect one for me. We don't need someone to complete us. We just need someone to accept us completely. I don't have to try and be someone I'm not. Dan accepts me as I am.

Here are some good words of wisdom from pastor, author, speaker, and married man of forty-three years, Timothy Keller: "To be loved but not known is comforting but superficial. To be known and not loved is our greatest fear. But to be fully known and truly loved is, well, a lot like being loved by God. It is what we need more than anything. It liberates us from pretense, humbles us out of our self-righteousness, and fortifies us for any difficulty life can throw at us."[6] I know.

Dan and I marked thirty years of marriage on June 1, 2021. We have four sons who are now adults and out of the home (Thanks,

---

[6] Timothy Keller with Kathy Keller, *The Meaning of Marriage: Facing the Complexities of Commitment with the Wisdom of God* (New York: Penguin Books, 2016).

God) and some of those seasons in parenting were brutal to our marriage. Each year it would seem to get better even if it was crazier, but it was more honest, too. We know who we are and who we're not. We also know how much grace we need from God and each other. This parenting thing that might come along in a marriage is huge and it can wreck you and your marriage, but it can also bring on a whole new level of love.

"Debbie is pretty and a good mom," is a note that stayed taped to the bathroom mirror for a very long time. Dan loves me, truly, in the place I'm in right now and reminds me of who I am, even though I don't always behave so well, especially when it came to our strong-willed teenage son, who is dramatically like me.

There are other bumps that God knew would come in our marriage, too. Dan's cancer, my scoliosis surgery, crappy finances, broken friendships and family relationships, my parents' divorce, the death of Dan's parents, my season of anxiety attacks, and the shame we'd have thinking, *I should've done this differently or I shouldn't have done this at all.*

God knew that parenting wouldn't be a cakewalk. He knew before we knew and through every stage He was in step with us. He shows His grace, love, and strength. And right now, it seems that we're actually beginning to understand that He really loves us. He does. It's true.

My friend Kelly is one who has helped many new married couples travel down the road of realistic expectations, because often our expectations are that our pure love will carry us through. Kelly said, "Ohhhhhh, early on in marriage I felt I was in a disaster pit, so I filed for divorce but not before screaming to God; 'Fix my husband!' Wasn't I the perfect wife? And why wasn't my husband seeing this and apologizing for his horrible behavior. With only a few days before the divorce was final, God stopped me. It was while I was reading *A Woman After God's Own Heart* by Elizabeth Elliot when the scales from my eyes began to peel away. God's word to me; 'You let me worry about your husband. We need to talk about you, My daughter.' What? I have issues? I did. *But* through *God*, marriage counseling, and reading the truth I was able to own my own junk, and amazingly my husband owned his. It was humbling but major change happens when we die to self. It's not easy but worth it. I see good fruit from good choices; like going on twenty years of marriage! One of the best choices: Change direction by asking God, 'Change me.'"

The "Change Me" prayer is hard but worth it. Remember, your spouse married a sinner, too, and He knows the struggle you have and He knows how to change your heart, too, if you allow Him. When there's a heart change there's behavior change. And with healthy change there comes freedom to have fun. Dan and I have a lot of super-fun memories with each other. There are movies, pranks, and situations together where we've laughed so hard, we've peed ourselves. Speaking of which. While on our honeymoon in Carmel, California, I asked Dan to pull over because I had to pee. He pulled over thinking I might be sick. When I went to the side of the road and squatted near a tree, he was incredulous.

"Debbie, the Carmel Village is only two miles away."

"I know, but I had to go."

He took a photo. We still have it and I'm still the same Debbie.

We've made a decision to love no matter what. Because, of course, there are dry spells, hard places in life and marriage, but the commitment and covenant we've made is stronger. We try and do right and not make the point of being right even if we are. And we try not to just follow what we feel, which is good because if it was by feelings, we'd be done and I'd be toast.

But honestly, it goes back to being pretty. For me, I need to remember that Dan loves me inside and out, just like Jesus does. This is especially helpful when I'm frustrated and stinking mad and when I don't feel heard or understood.

So, let me share with you the time when I was six months pregnant, with our first son, and I had horrendous acne all over my face. All day I would pick at the "hurt zits" and then "stop and start" with vigorous scrubbing and application of topical creams, and then covering with makeup to camouflage the mess I made. My face would be a scabbed, red disaster by the end of the day. My night-time solution was to put zinc oxide all over my face for soothing and healing. I looked like a clown in bed. But with all sincerity, my husband would look at me and say the same words I heard almost every night, "Good night, Pretty Debbie."

Who does that?

My husband does and, like I said, I'm keeping him. He's mine. I am his. We are in this for better and for worse. We will encourage each other and our sons to love one another and love God above all. Discovering each other's Love Language was helpful too. Author Dr. Gary Chapman's book, *The 5 Love Languages: The Secret to Love that Lasts*, was very helpful. We all need love to be communicated from each of the five languages, (Words of Affirmation, Acts of Service, Physical Touch, Quality Time and Gifts) but knowing what language best shows love to our spouse can really make an impact. Dan and I also work at finding the root issue of an argument, too, because it's usually not as simple as, "You forgot to take the trash out and make the reservation you said you would."

Taking responsibility for our own messes, words of hurt, and giving grace is huge for marriage survival and beauty. I remember having an argument with Dan in a restaurant with another couple present. Because we had taken separate vehicles, Dan seemed to abruptly excuse himself and said, "I need to get going. Thanks for dinner, and I'll see you at home, Debbie." I visited a little while longer and then said, "I need to get going, too, and I need to apologize to Dan."

Now, I believed Dan was most rude but telling him so was hardly going to be worth the battle. Giving grace that I actually felt he didn't deserve because he was interrupting me was exactly the best thing I could have done, and so, too, Dan then apologized to me. However, I didn't expect he would and that's important to note. Apologize out of sincere love and not because you expect the same kind of payment in return. It's also helpful to be genuine around others rather than performing like you have a "perfect" marriage (as *if* anyone does). When we focus on God's love for the other, then our marriage grows beautifully. Ask God to let you see your spouse as He does and then find little ways each day to show simple acts of kindness with compliments. You might not *feel* like doing this but do it anyway out of your commitment to God and your marriage. The results are always worth the effort. You can do hard things or things that feel unfair when it's the Holy Spirit working in you.

I hope people we know and don't know will see something different about my marriage to Dan, not a sappy greeting card image of marital bliss but a genuine commitment to the covenant we made to each other and God to truly love one another until death takes us. My hope is others will want to know more of where our real love and stability comes from.

Jesus works in marriage restoration and wholeness, and it's "pretty" for everyone to look at.

5
#MeToo

*"He comforts us in all our troubles so that we can comfort others.
When they are troubled, we will be able to give them
the same comfort God has given us."*
— **2 Corinthians 1:4 (NLT)**

No matter our age, if we're honest there's this letdown that comes after all the gifts are unwrapped at Christmastime. And if you live in northern Minnesota, you're trying to wrap your head around the fact that the first day of spring is likely to be ushering in another blizzard, or we're still shoveling snow from one that recently occurred. It's not an exaggeration. It's real life in The Icebox of the Nation. Sigh.

But isn't the anticipation of actually giving and receiving a gift, the experience of it all, that brings us the greatest joy? I think the same sort of letdown happens with the unwrapping of people. Each of us is a gift and we all have beauty within, but we're also flawed. When our messes are unwrapped and our ugly behaviors exposed, we disappoint people and ourselves.

Two thousand seventeen brought to the surface some major issues of vulnerable people being used and mistreated wrongly by those who always thought they could get away with it. Powerful media, movie moguls, and those in politics used their power to manipulate and exploit others, and it has left us all a bit shocked and disappointed. The number of victims affected by their actions grows every day. People who publicly champion "women" and then privately exploit and manipulate them is the definition of hypocrisy; it's an unwrapping of facts that hurts and affects us all.

And yet, I, too, am a wretch but for the grace of God. If the spotlight of my poor behavior and choices were exposed for the world to judge, I'd be toast. How true are the words from the former slave trader, John Newton, who wrote the hymn, "Amazing Grace"?

> *Amazing grace how sweet the sound*
> *That saved a wretch like me!*
> *I once was lost, but now am found*
> *Was blind but now I see.* [7]

Whew. Thanks be to God.

Christ pursues us, rescues us, and redeems us. Our choice is to unwrap His gift of grace and know that God is not good to us because we are good, but because He is. So how then can we place limits and conditions on how we forgive? How do we forgive the wretches who prey upon us? How can their families forgive them? How can they forgive themselves?

Today show host Savannah Guthrie asked that question the day Matt Lauer's dismissal from NBC was announced: "How do you reconcile your love for someone with the revelation that they have behaved badly?"[8] And the answer is . . . ? We want actions with

---

[7] John Newton, "Amazing Grace," https://en.wikipedia.org/wiki/Amazing_Grace, viewed May 18, 2021.
[8] Christopher Rosen, "Watch Savannah Guthrie Announce Matt Lauer's Firing," *Entertainment Weekly,* November 29, 2017, https://ew.com/tv/2017/11/29/savannah-guthrie-matt-lauer-fired/, viewed May 18, 2021.

resolutions and sincere change and apologies. We wonder, *What now?* with mixed emotions of anger, sadness, and disbelief.

I think many of us may know that the answer is *love*, but what does that really mean when we are the ones who are hurt? How does that work? What does His love look like in action through us?

Author and radio host Eric Metaxas helped me to process the heartache of good humans with bad actions. "*This*, my dears, is The Human Dilemma. It is the root of all our trouble and all our strife. Not just because of the people we know and love who behave badly, but because of ourselves. How does any human person reconcile his love of himself with the occasional revelation that he has behaved badly, will behave badly, and can't help behaving badly?"[9]

What you have to do if you have behaved badly is to stop (by the grace of God), and don't make excuses or minimize your guilt. Tell someone who knows how to keep their mouth shut and who is a real friend and then fling yourself onto Christ's mercy. It was the adulterous woman who came clean to God, who Jesus said was forgiven, not the religious Pharisee who said within himself that at least he wasn't as bad as that woman. Admit that you aren't who you thought you were and that you often fail. In other words, repent of your sin and change direction.

God longs to restore you just like a parent who loves their child. It is not cheap grace without consequence; it's just that He hung condemned in your place. He has the right to forgive you because He suffered the consequences of your secret sins. You can be totally and completely forgiven.

"He himself bore our sins" in His body on the cross, so that we might die to sins and live for righteousness; "By His wounds you have been healed" (1 Peter 2:24, NIV).

In the Lord's Prayer, I always stop at the part, "And forgive me

---

[9] Eric Metaxas, *Life, God, and Other Small Topics: Conversations from Socrates in the City* (New York: Penguin, 2012).

my sins as I forgive those who sin against me." Nope. I don't want the kind of forgiveness I give. I want God's complete forgiveness. When we confess our bad behavior (our *sin*), Jesus washes us clean and remembers our sins no more. It's not due to any memory failure on His part. God forgives us *for His own sake*: "I, even I, am He who blots out your transgressions, for My Own sake, and remembers your sins no more" (Isaiah 43:25, NIV).

Mockingbird Ministry published a piece entitled, "Love the Art, Hate the Artist?" The author, Abby Farson Pratt, writes, "We never want to be in the same boat with the dirtbag poets and directors and rock stars. But maybe we always have been. Maybe we've been rowing alongside them all this time. They just experienced the misfortune of having the searchlight expose them first. This knowledge—that none of us do good, not even one—doesn't erase that uncomfortable tension when we appreciate the artwork of a monster. Can we separate the beauty of the work from the ugliness of its creator?"[10]

When I was seventeen, I was chosen, along with three other teens in the Midwest, to be a part of a summer stock theatre company of college students. It was 1984 and the first time I was really exposed to wild theatre parties, which involved the classic combo of drugs, sex, and rock and roll. I remember leaving one such party early and then never attending another, but the other female intern, Kelly from Ohio, continued to be invited and continued partying. She did things and had things done to her that were not okay. I cried with her. I said we should go tell the director and stage manager, but they were there, too, and Kelly didn't feel she could. She was ashamed and felt she had contributed and done things she should not have. She "let it go," but I imagine it has always stayed with her on some level.

Kelly's story could have been mine a million times over. I was a

---

[10] Abby Farson Pratt, "Love the Art, Hate the Artist?" November 28, 2017, viewed at https://mbird.com/2017/11/love-the-art-hate-the-artist/

theatre major. I was in hundreds of shows and one film. I saw a lot of "stuff" go down. I had a lot of choices about extracurricular actives that would have made me popular and put me on the inside track and maybe they would have brought me more opportunities. But I want to be clear here. *There is no excuse* for someone to be used, preyed upon, and taken advantage of. And yet, it's also true that we can make choices of whom we hang out with, what events we attend, and how to enter into a situation. My sophomore year in college I entered into counseling through the Chaplain's Services and was helped and encouraged by a vicar, named Justin, who was fifteen years my senior. I was feeling ugly, insecure, and like I just didn't fit in anywhere, not the sorority I had pledged the year previously nor with the theatre gang which were "my people." Justin helped me because he listened and affirmed that I mattered. The problem was that his affirmations extended to him asking me to sit on his lap so he could tell me how special and beautiful I was. This happened during a spring break visit to my family's resort because it was an hour away from another college with which he had business.

The first evening of his visit I was simply chatting with him in his cabin when suddenly he turned the conversation into explaining how truly beautiful I was. Justin wanted to "show me" how much he believed this. Not only was he surprised by my standing up and yelling at him but I was surprised, too. "What are you doing?! What are you saying?! You can't say this to me! You're wrecking everything!"

I ran out of the cabin and immediately woke my mom up to tell her (Justin had specifically told me not to tell my mom as he knew I usually told her everything). He was gone the next morning but had left a cassette tape of songs by Billy Joel (my favorite) wrapped in a map of the US with a circle around Key Largo. The words, "Come away with me" were written in capped letters.

Back at college I reported him to the dean of students. The school then interviewed a few other young women Justin was counseling, only to find out that he had lured them onto his lap and taken advantage of their vulnerabilities and insecurities. A close friend, who knew one of the girls (Sharon), told me later that Sharon was so ashamed she had allowed Justin to violate her that she had become suicidal but didn't know where to turn. When I came forward with my story, and an investigation began, Sharon cried with relief because she wasn't alone. She entered into healthy counseling so she could begin to heal. Vicar Justin was soon released from his position and gone from campus. Oh, how I could empathize with the other women because I, too, was weak and vulnerable, and it was only by the grace and strength of God that I was able to stand up and scream. Attention feels like love and we're all starved for it.

Kathy Lee Gifford, of *Today*, said words that were so comforting in the wake of Matt Lauer's departure from NBC. She sent a text to Lauer as soon as the news broke, affirming him with, "I adore you." She then shared about the time her husband was unfaithful and the hurt his betrayal brought, but also how faith and forgiveness kept her alive.

Gifford said, "When I found out that my husband had betrayed me, you question your own judgment. You question and ask, 'Was everything a lie?' And I think we have to fight against that. Because the man we love and adore is still the man we love and adore. No one is perfect. 'We all sin and fall short of the glory of God,' is what Scripture says. What we need now is forgiveness and mercy for one another, and we don't need taunts and ugliness. We have enough of that in the world. I send out my love to the person, whoever came forward, and to Matt and his family. In my long life the only thing I've been sure of is that only God can heal, only God. There's no bad time to reach out for His help. He guided me throughout my life, through everything.

"There was a man who was an advisor to me and Frank throughout our lifetime. And for a long time, I had my eyes just on me because

I was upset and hurt, which you would normally be. This mentor said to me, 'Kathy if you can't forgive your husband, forgive your children's father. He's the same person, but that's the one you love, the one you believe in.' We're all so broken and we need someone to put us back together. And it is possible. It is so possible."[11]

Girlfriend gets it.

Unwrapping truth, Abby Pratt, with her piece "Love the Art, Hate the Artist?" continued with, "I am willing to stand in this uncomfortable paradox. Yes, there is still a desperate need for justice. We need the LAW, the earthly law, to keep us responsible for our actions and to protect the innocent. I dream of a world in which sexual abusers are actually held accountable. That day is not yet here. We have to scrape by and hold onto the little beauty there is in this world. This is all we have. If we can no longer appreciate the art of monsters, we won't have any art left."[12]

Obviously, you don't have to be a monster to be artistic, but that's the case with many. Also, sexual abusers and abusers of any sort are not high on anyone's social list. We do put them in jail and in many cases make them register.

Religion is simply the law with rules and regulations, but the very first Christmas was the end of religion as we know it, because it was about Jesus, fulfilling the law by His death and resurrection. His sacrifice for our sins meant giving us what we don't deserve and it's called, grace. It's something we receive and something we cannot earn by what we do or don't do. We're all in the sinner's club, but when we receive God's grace and forgiveness, we enter into the Savior's club. A brave person will risk their life to save another, especially someone

---

[11] Gabriella Paiella, "Kathie Lee Gifford Is Ready to Forgive Matt Lauer," *The Cut*, November 29, 2017, doi:https://www.thecut.com/2017/11/kathie-lee-gifford-is-ready-to-forgive-matt-lauer.html

[12] Abby Farson Pratt, "Love the Art, Hate the Artist? "November 28, 2017, viewed at https://mbird.com/2017/11/love-the-art-hate-the-artist/

they love. God did more than that. He came into the world not to "risk" His life, but to give it, to give it as a ransom for all who would accept Him. He understands abuse and He understands shame. It's all grace. Grace trumps.

It's by the grace of God we can say, "I am what I am." We're all messy on some level, but we're all deeply loved despite our messiness. It's our choice to continually unwrap the grace and love God gives us every day so that we, too, might give that same grace to others and live free.

You need His affirmation and love more than anything or anyone else. You also need to know it's not your fault that you were abused or assaulted. The enemy will try and mess with your mind and tell you that you are to blame. Don't listen to him. Listen to Jesus. He can take the muck of it all and redeem it all to help you to bring a message of comfort to someone else. And as Scripture says, "Anyone who believes in Him will never be put to shame" (Romans 10:11, NIV). No more shame, okay? Rest in the love of who He says you are, a unique individual worthy of His unconditional love and grace no matter what you've done or what's been done to you. Unwrap and received the unconditional love He has for you every single day and forevermore.

6
DEAR MEGAN, CHOOSE JOY

"The thief comes only to steal and kill and destroy; I [Jesus] have come that they may have life, and have it to the full."
— **John 10:10 (NIV)**

WE HAVE A FREE WILL TO CHOOSE what we think on *and* our free will lets us choose how we respond.

The topic of free will and choice was written in an email to a girl named Megan. It was part of an ongoing conversation that began around the bonfire of a retreat where I had spoken. We talked about the idea of "deserving to be happy." In going through my files, I came across my letter to Megan, written almost five years ago:

> Happiness is based on what happens to us, which means it is controlled by our circumstances. Joy is a choice, which means it is controlled by our response to what happens to us. Nehemiah 8:10 is so true: 'The joy of the Lord is my strength.' Really? *Yes.* I want to remember that no matter what happens, I can experience joy knowing that I am liked, loved, approved, and accepted because I am centered in Christ. I believe the truth of who He says I am, but do I always? Sometimes I become centered on myself and what I think will make me happy. But the girl you want to be

around is the one whose life is based on the identity she has in Christ and not the girl who wants you to feed her insecurities. The person centered in Christ is more likeable, more attractive, and more real than any self-focused self.

We allow Satan to steal our joy and peace when we become more focused on the people and circumstances that bug us and the 'what-ifs . . . ?' I have to stop myself, all the time, and say; "Debbie, do you trust God more than your feelings right now? Do you expect He will vindicate and address this issue with the person who you got into a "discussion" with on Facebook?" Yes. But . . . this type of thing just happened to me yesterday, and I *knew* that if I opened up, using my words on the keyboard, to respond to the hurtful things being said to me, that not only would I not be able to change this person's mind, but the problem would only get worse. I prayed aloud, "Lord, *talk to* this person, please." I kept my mouth shut and no comments were made. Later I received an apology and a "thank you" for not retaliating. It all comes down to trusting God and waiting on Him. It's about leaning into His strength while knowing there is hope ahead despite what I feel. I love the promise of Isaiah 54:17 (AMPC): "But no weapon that is formed against you shall prosper, and every tongue that shall rise against you in judgment you shall show to be in the wrong. This peace, righteousness, security, triumph over opposition is the heritage of the servants of the Lord; this is the righteousness or the vindication which they obtain from Me, says the Lord." I used to think that the Scripture meant I could "tell someone off" because it does say, "You shall show them to be in the wrong." *But* I know that keeping my mouth shut and letting God defend and avenge me come by trusting His way and not mine. Giving the person another "piece of my mind" never results in reconciliation. Ask yourself this: "Do I want to be right or do right?" You might be right and win the argument but lose the relationship. Is it worth it?

I don't understand how God works and all the 'whys' and I certainly don't have answers to all your questions. But even though I don't know *why*, I know God is the way. For all the ugliness in the world and the people who are trapped in horrific circumstances and those with broken families and relationships, hope might seem far away. Many ask, "If God is real, then why is there such evil in the world?" The answer: "Because we are still here on Earth, and the fight isn't against flesh and blood but against the rulers of the darkness of this world, against spiritual wickedness in high places" (Ephesians 6:12). God could wipe out the evil, but He would have to wipe us out, too. Instead, He sent Jesus to offer us a way to change our nature. That is what is meant by being "born again." We have a choice to continue with a sin nature or be "born again" with a new nature.

We live in a fallen world and it will stay fallen until Jesus comes back the second time when the "Angels will come forth and separate the wicked from among the righteous . . . " (Matthew 13:49). I'd say that, for my part, I don't pray for specific things enough. I've had times God has awakened me to pray for a person who was in danger or hurting. Some names I knew and some I had no idea. God is bigger than the enemy, and the story ahead is eternal hope. Many people stuck in horrid situations are simply praying to survive. They don't dare think that there's ever going to be change or that the hope or desire they have will ever come to pass. *But* prayer changes everything. God is always on the move and aware. There's always hope and a way for all things to be redeemed.

The thing that God desires most from us is a relationship with Him, just like we want with our own children. When we have the security of God's love, we want to do things that line up with what He has for us because He knows best. Proverbs 16:3 (AMPC) is gloriously good: "Roll up your works upon the Lord, commit and trust them wholly to Him, and He will cause your thoughts to become agreeable to His will, and so shall your plans be established and succeed." I memorized that verse a few years ago and it's like, *Yes, that is it!* I want *this*!

Memorizing verses has helped me hear God because *He is The Word*. I try and pray one verse every morning, and for weeks and weeks it will often be the same one.

God is God and He cares about *everything* you feel and care about. He understands and loves you. He never condemns. He is not surprised by what you're going through, and it must pass through Him before it comes to you. So, yeah . . . . tell Him your heart and the needs and wants you have. Ask for wisdom and discernment. He will gladly give them and then expect you'll receive that wisdom (James 1:5–6). Ask for the Holy Spirit to give you strength, too. John 20:22 is a verse I pray all the time: "Holy Spirit breathe on me. Help. Thanks. Amen."

Don't listen to the garbage of the enemy that tells you that you aren't good or thankful enough. You're loved right where you are at and not where you should be. You'll never be where you should be or good enough. Yet, God IS always good. Remember, too, that feelings are indicators but should not be dictators. I think the most helpful and healthy practice is simply to be honest with God. Tell Him, "God, I feel this but I choose to receive the peace You give and not the fear I feel." What happens inside of me isn't so much of a feeling but a *knowing* that God is on the move. Nothing we go through is gonna be wasted with Him. You may still feel crummy, but there's always hope.

Now, back to Megan:

Megan, I know you shared about your sons and the struggle it can be with them. *And*, oh, how I *get that!* But I know I can't live my sons' Christian lives for them. I can ask questions like, "What could I do to make this better for you?" Sometimes I have to apologize and say; "I'm gonna make an effort to change what I can, but it's a two-way relationship. You need to own your own stuff, too, and make the changes God wants you to make." Ask God to talk to them and pray they'll listen to Him. I recently read a tweet from Tullian Tchividjian that read, "Parents: kids will run from law and they will run from grace. The ones who run from law rarely come back. The ones who run from grace almost always come back."[13] *That* is truth.

Bottom line is this: "Let go and let God." Try not to fix and understand "Why?" Try to find the humor or the story of how you "made it through," and this "drama" in your life that you're going through might encourage someone else. I know this is a lot to think about, Megan, but the process of writing you also gave me a lot to think on and apply, too. I'm a sinner saved by grace and I need Him continually.

I'm praying for you. I'm just me, on this Earth journey, too.

Love and God's blessings,

Debbie

---

[13] Tullian Tchividjian, https://twitter.com/TullianT/status/1382381650491871233, viewed May 19, 2021.

DRIVEN BY JOY

7
RUN YOUR RACE WITH PERSEVERANCE (AND CANCER SUCKS)

> *"Therefore, since we are surrounded by such a great cloud of witnesses, let us throw off everything that hinders and the sin that so easily entangles. and let us run with perseverance the race marked out for us."*
> — **Hebrews 12:1 (NIV)**

MY FRIEND WAS DYING OF CANCER.

She knew it. We all knew it.

Not fun.

But if you were around Jill, you would never have imagined for a moment that she was dying because she was too busy living. Jill was fun. You'd walk away from your time with her, however short, with an understanding that you had been in the presence of someone very special. Someone who was more interested in hearing about how you were doing, and who had a story to encourage and make you laugh. Jill radiated the joy in knowing the love of Christ. She was a testimony of who Jesus is, and she knew planet Earth was not her final destination.

Jill took me to lunch at Sandy's Place when she knew that the Earth life for her was short. Sandy's is my favorite restaurant in our little town. This "home-cooked-meal" (hot beef sandwich with real mashed potatoes) restaurant seats maybe twenty-five people, with the little counter at the front. It's always packed at lunchtime. I was my usual five minutes late, but no worries because *everybody* in the restaurant knew Jill, and she was busy making the rounds, smiling and asking how everyone was.

I think the entire town of six thousand people in International Falls, Minnesota, knew who Jill was. Most had probably had a visit from her, received a homemade apple pie, had a venison meal delivered, or a scarf knit for them. Jill happened to be the godparent of our youngest son, David. As long as he was in elementary school, he celebrated his birthday with her frosted sugar cookies cut out in the shape of a balloon with his age iced on top. It was the best and most magical gift an elementary student could have delivered to his class. I felt like "Mom of the Year" just because I knew Jill. Certainly, no one thought for a second that I was the mom who had created the masterpiece cookies, and they were absolute perfection.

Jill also played the piano beautifully. She would be at the front of the church playing for every early morning service. And no matter their denomination, she was likely the pianist at someone's funeral. But I'd say the outdoors is where Jill felt most at home—fishing, hunting, cutting wood, helping build a cabin or a shack—making most of what the day offered with family and friends.

She was famous for bagging a buck nearly every year. I'll never forget meeting her twenty-two years ago, walking into the church basement for an event, when she said, "Honestly, Debbie, I feel more comfortable carrying a gun than a purse." Jill was one of the most feminine and gentle spirits you'd ever meet, unless you're a deer in deer season.

It was clear that Jill loved Jesus and had a relationship with Him. You could see how God was glorified in her sickness, and how she committed to following Hebrews 12:1 and running with perseverance the race that God set before her. Jill was also aware that, "What we see now is temporary, but what is unseen is eternal." She was committed to looking for any and all opportunities to share the hope she had, whether it was with the hair stylist where she got her hair done or the clerk at the gas station.

Jill shared how God was real and there was something to look forward to. There is the hope of heaven, with no more pain, no more tears, a place and time where there is no more brokenness, but where we will be completely whole and restored.

Heaven will be wonderful, purposeful, and fun, too, because while there's no more turmoil there's still something we're given to do that's meaningful with the plans God had in mind before the fall and sin entered in. We aren't angels or souls floating around. We are fully perfected and resurrected just as Jesus is. And while this Earth experience is ever so challenging, we are able to receive the forgiveness, love, and freedom Jesus offers, so we can live securely and confidently as we are and where we are until we go "home."

I still chuckle thinking of our son, Joey, summarizing heaven when he was younger: "Jesus throws the best parties." C. S. Lewis might well agree as suggested by his oft-repeated quote: "There are far, far better things ahead than any we leave behind."

Before we ordered our food at Sandy's Place, I asked Jill if she was experiencing any pain. She said yes, but waved the question away with the hand she was using to massage her shoulder and neck. If it weren't for one of her daughters telling me the depth of her pain, the depth of her illness, I would have never known her deep agony of it all or that the wig she wore and bought online for thirty-two dollars was not her own hair. The ebony color of the wig and style was just like "Our Jill," and a beautiful stark contrast to her brilliant blue eyes.

"Oh, Debbie, I have nothing to complain about. I just keep on," Jill said. "I have so much to be thankful for. God is so gracious and loving. It really is true. His strength is perfected in my weakness. He's got me. I am strong because of Him and I just keep on."

"Keep on" are two critical words to our success in life and especially as followers of Christ. Those two words are personified by the way Jill lived every day. The biblical word for "keep on" is perseverance, the ability to keep on doing the things we've committed to doing, when we feel like it and when we don't. Nothing is more essential to success in the Christian life than perseverance. Faith gets you started; perseverance keeps you going.

Jill continued: "I'll give you an update on my health, but first tell me what God is doing in your life. How are Dan and the boys? What writing projects are you working on? How are your parents? Tell me about your travels and speaking. I want to know everything." I told her one of my travel stories with some of the new and interesting people I had met from other countries. It's always fun to practice my accents, and telling one of the stories out loud for the first time had us both giggling. Jill then shared a story about one of her ten grandchildren on a recent ice fishing adventure. We laughed some more. Laughter is such good medicine.

Jill seemed to get the memo very early on that "Life is not about you." Of course, we all need to get this memo and live in a way that puts others before ourselves *because* supernatural joy, a fruit of the Spirit that God gives believers, is released when we focus on ways to serve and give to others. This was how Jill lived her life, continually giving.

While Jill and I were still at the restaurant, an elderly man named Billy came to our table and expressed much concern in waiting for a report from the doctors. Jill touched Billy's arm and smiled while offering words of hope. I could see some weight being lifted as she talked to Billy while continuing to pat his arm. Jill accepted her cancer as an assignment from heaven. She was diagnosed with melanoma twenty years ago, it invaded her body six years ago, and for three years it had been at stage four. Jill used her time to be a blessing to others.

I would say she was in ministry, ministering and serving others wherever she's at. She was an example of what being a missionary is like every day; no matter what is going on or how we're feeling.

Finally, Jill told me about her last visit to Mayo, but she was most excited to tell me about her doctors and technicians who have been part of her life for the last nine years. There is nothing that can cure her cancer, but her life can be prolonged as long as the tumors don't grow and are managed through various treatments.

"You know, Debbie, this doctor I have at Mayo, she's just wonderful and I'm praying that she gets to know Jesus. During my appointment she had me sit down across from her as she delivered some difficult news about my cancer. I nodded my head that I understood, but apparently the doctor didn't think I really did, so she said, 'Jill, you understand what I'm telling you is serious.' 'Yes, I can accept what you're saying because I know where I am spending my eternity. I'm okay.'"

Her doctor said, "But, Jill, I'm not okay with this. I love you." And she hugged Jill as the tears came.

Wow. Just wow.

Sill told me about sitting in the waiting room as she was scheduled for a scan of some sort. When the technician came out to get her, he said, "Oh, it's you. Let me give you a hug," to which a gentleman in the waiting room replied; "I've been here for years and I've never had that that kind of reception."

It was hard not to put Jill on a pedestal. Her faith and trust in God spoke volumes by the way she carried herself. You think, "I want what she has," not the cancer, but the joy she displayed despite her circumstances. Besides, Jill would kick down any pedestal ever erected for her. She was very clear that it's nothing she's done that merits God's love, His grace and the hope of heaven. "Debbie, I'm human, like everyone else." She's right, but still . . .

It's hard to wrap your head around people like Jill and Mother

Teresa, who don't receive God's love and acceptance by being good but simply by being His kids. I think it's because the world's religions shout at depravity and trumpet good works. If you just do more good than bad, then you merit heaven. Christ says all of your good works are as filthy rags. You are no further away from heaven than Jill or Mother Teresa, and neither is closer than you.

And let's face it, I am glad they're not the standard because they're way ahead of me. No matter how many times we've served at soup kitchens, gone on mission trips, or volunteered our time at a shelter, we can't let those acts of kindness blind us and lull us into a false sense of security that we have no need of repentance. We are all in need of a Savior. We are not born good, we are born broken, but often we let our heroic works of charity shield us from the truth of our inner poverty.

People like Jill and Mother Teresa do and did acts of kindness, which is important in the way we love and honor God. But our good works don't get us into heaven. Only Jesus' sacrifice on the cross and His resurrection do that. That is Good News.

But it's not just Jill's faith that encouraged me in my own walk, it was her perseverance, her attitude to "keep on keeping on" with the commitments of life. Actually, it's the testing of our faith that produces perseverance. Yep, right there in the Bible. The Book of James 1:2-3 says; "Consider it pure joy whenever you face trials of many kinds because you know that the testing of your faith produces perseverance." The Greek word *hupomeno* means "staying power"; the ability to remain under the pressure.

So, here's the question. What do you do when the pressure is on? It's easy to start the race. I can get up and put on my running costume (I'm a theatre major, so it's always a costume) and start the race, but when it gets long and difficult and the muscles start to fatigue and it isn't easy, what do I do? What do *you* do?

Let's try perseverance, remaining under God with the humility to admit our human depravity, receive God's forgiveness, and then forgive ourselves for when we've messed up, instead of obsessing on our past mistakes and trying to do more good works to cover our brokenness. We all need to receive the grace God gives us to change. We need to think on what is good, be thankful, and serve others, and *that* is a memo that is a magnet on my heart. I want to finish strong.

So, right now, stop. Thank God for what you do have. Ask for His strength to run your race with perseverance, strong and focused on serving others to help them run their race. Be a Jill warrior who follows Hebrews 12:1–2; "Let us run with perseverance the race God has set before us." We do this by keeping our eyes on Jesus, the Champion who perfects our faith. Be like Jesus. "And because He's strong, we can keep on."

Note: Jill Wynn Austin, 64, of International Falls, Minnesota, passed away Monday, October 10, 2016, after a long, courageous, and, as she would say, "a victorious battle with melanoma."

8
THANK GOD FOR LAUGHTER AND WINE

"Then He said to them, 'Go your way. Eat the fat and drink sweet wine and send portions to anyone who has nothing ready, for this day is holy to our Lord. And do not be grieved, for the joy of the Lord is your strength.'"
— **Nehemiah 8:10 (NIV)**

I LIKE TO HAVE FUN. One of my mottos has been: "If it's not fun, I'm done." Seriously. With so much drama out there, I like to keep mine on the stage, if possible. When I sat in on board meetings as managing artistic director for the theatre company I worked with, it was not unlike me to randomly stand up and sing a song or tell a story with multiple character voices. Ask the board, ask anyone who knows me. Yep. I'm pretty sure there's humor to be found in any given situation.

Jesus wept. But He laughed, too.

I think because we humans have a sense of humor indicates that God does, too, since we're made in His image. Jesus was fully God and fully man. He wept with compassion and for the pain that we experience because He experienced it, too. Yet, the joy He must have had . . . the laughter, too.

I have this picture of Him sitting by a campfire with the disciples laughing. His head is thrown back and He's slapping His knee, most likely over a prank or joke of Peter's. People wanted to be around Him because He was winsome and not all full of gloom and doom.

Jesus was fun, too. In the Bible, in John, Chapter Two, we can read about the time Jesus restored the festivities while at the same time performing His first miracle. The wedding was in Cana of Galilee, and weddings during that time would last many days. The obligation of the host was always to have plenty of wine on hand. Running out wasn't an option, as it would shame and embarrass the family.

But, you see, this day they did run out. Mary, mother of Jesus, caught the problem before the bridegroom found out, and Jesus (being God) told the servants what to do. It didn't make sense, but they obeyed and 180 gallons of water turned into wine, restoring the party. The wine was so good, the master of ceremony shouted: "Everyone brings out the choice wine first and then the cheaper wine after the guests have had too much to drink; but you have saved the best till now" (John 2:10, NIV).

I mean there could have been so many other things Jesus could have done to prove He was God, yet as His first miracle He chose to turn water into wine. He performed an amazing miracle, actually altering the molecular composition of water.

What makes me crazy is that in some "religious circles," it's questioned whether Jesus transformed water into wine or into nonalcoholic grape juice? But throughout the passage, the Greek word translated as "wine" is *oinos*, which was the common Greek word for *normal wine*—wine that was fermented/alcoholic. (Side note: Our son Marco attended Moody Bible Institute in Chicago. Greek class about killed him but it's great for me.)

So, it's clear that the Greek word for the wine Jesus created is the same word for actual wine. The Greek word for the wine Jesus created is also the same word that is used in Ephesians 5:18, " . . . do not get drunk on wine . . . " Obviously, to get drunk on wine requires the presence of alcohol.

Everything, from the traditions of a wedding feast, to the usage of *oinos* in first-century Greek literature (in the New Testament and outside the New Testament), argues for the wine that Jesus created to be normal, ordinary wine, containing alcohol. There is simply no solid historical, cultural, or contextual reason to side with grape juice.

Those who oppose the drinking of alcohol, in any quantity, argue that Jesus would not have turned water into wine, as He would have been promoting the consumption of a substance that is tainted by sin. In this understanding, alcohol itself is inherently sinful, and consumption in any quantity is sin. That's not a biblical understanding.

Some Scriptures discuss alcohol in positive terms. Ecclesiastes 9:7 instructs, "Drink your wine with a merry heart." Psalm 104:15 states that God gives wine "that makes glad the heart of men." It is the abuse of alcohol, drunkenness and/or addiction, which is sinful. Therefore, it would not have been a sin for Jesus to create a drink that contained alcohol.

Was Jesus promoting gluttony when He multiplied the fishes and loaves far beyond what the people needed? Of course not. Creating a substance that can be abused does not make one responsible when another person foolishly chooses to abuse it. Jesus in no sense encouraged drunkenness. That's not good. It's not fun.

I had a discussion with someone who thought that alcohol should be banned. "We have no need for it, and as a former police dispatcher I had numerous calls come in where alcohol was the cause of deaths and tragic accidents," he said. I get it. It's painful and sad when people make bad choices from something God gives us to enjoy, but it's no longer enjoyable when it's abused. We don't need Cherry Nib licorice, either, but I'm glad it's out there for me to enjoy as one of my favorite candies.

I get it, too, that my husband, Dan, decided as a teen to have nothing to do with alcohol because he witnessed the abuse and upheaval caused by it. I respect that. When we married, it wasn't something he wanted around, and we didn't offer it at our wedding. Yet, today, Dan enjoys a glass of wine or cocktail. I, on the other hand, have used alcohol to numb my pain or to "shut down" when I didn't want to feel the hurt or think about the hard stuff. It's not a good way to "use" alcohol.

I really don't drink to enjoy a social occasion but more so to "escape." It has been problematic. I think sobriety would probably be the best choice for me but I haven't separated myself from the feelings of letting "the drink" control me. There are those very hard moments or seasons of life where I've felt I "need" to drink because I know that some kind of release or peace will take place even if the peace is fraudulent. The consequences of indulgences can lead to many mornings of ache and regret (or evenings if "day drinking" is the choice) and when that happens, I vow with a solemn promise to myself that, *I'll never do that again.* I know well the instruction of Ephesians 5:18: "Don't be drunk with wine, because that will ruin your life. Instead, be filled with the Holy Spirit."

When a person is drunk on alcohol, they feel, think, and act differently. But the exact same thing is true when we are filled with the Holy Spirit—we feel think and act differently. The Christian life is not the result of trying to act like a Christian; that's only frustrating. The secret is developing our relationship with God empowered by the Holy Spirit. As God's Spirit fills us, we better understand who God really is. Our lives are changed from the inside out and good behavior is the end product. But I won't deny the struggle is real, and if it's getting more real and harder to live under the leading of the Spirit, ask for help. I have and I'm sure I will again.

I remember asking our son Joey, who was fifteen at the time, his take on the fermented wine issue. He said, "Mom, the disciples were fishermen. After a long day fishing, they would want the real-stuff kind of beverage. I mean, they were fishermen."

Good point, Joey. I never thought about it that way. But Joey, as well as our other sons, could point out and has noticed when their mom being intoxicated was not a good thing.

I know not everyone who reads this will agree with me. It's okay. I don't have to be right. But I am free. Jesus set me free to be me and I know the joy of who He is, who I am, and who others are, too. I love people. I love laughing, having fun, and helping others to have fun. And yes, thank you, having a glass of wine or a cocktail (or two) can have its place in our lives but it shouldn't be a placeholder for pain and escape.

A friend I met through the Mockingbird Ministry, Erin Jean Warde, has shared her journey with sobriety and is honest about life still being hard, no matter what. Her piece entitled, "Sobriety Broke Me to Pour Me Out" spoke to a place in my heart. After two years of sobriety she wrote, "I experience failure but now show up to that experience with self-compassion while trying to love others out of a deeper space of empathy." It's so true and it's helpful to hear her wisdom, especially as she relates the story of Jesus and the woman who anoints His feet with the expensive perfume:

> In the Gospel of John, Jesus visits Martha, Mary, and Lazarus, the man he had raised from the dead. Mary unexpectedly anoints Jesus's feet with a pound of nard, a costly perfume, wiping his feet with her own hair. Judas protests, crying that she's wasteful, that there are better uses for such an expense. Jesus defends her: "Leave her alone. She bought it so that she might keep it for the day of my burial."
>
> She's seen Lazarus die and live, so she knows a little something about how the presence of Jesus meddles with the breath that sifts through our lungs. It seems she knows any day could be the day we die, any day could be the day we live, every day is a day worth anointing. I got sober, because I wanted my life to be not in a bottle but in a jar—a jar of nard. Something poured out to prepare

myself and the world for the kind of death we believe will give us true life. In the Gospel of Mark, Jesus is anointed with nard and the jar is broken. I love it, because it isn't meant to be put back together. It's meant to be given away entirely. The precious gift cannot be salvaged or hoarded. I wanted my life to be in a jar. Broken to be poured. Not meant to be neatly put back together, because the notion that we are neatly anything is a lie.[14]

Erin Jean shares this beautiful truth, and with it she's free as well as fun. She laughs a lot, too, and maybe even more, in a more real and authentic way, without the booze.

Jesus had a serious mission to accomplish in this world, but He was not one to be somber all the time. He empathized with us completely and felt all of our emotions. Laughter is part of life, and Jesus truly lived.

Christ is risen! Shout, "Hallelujah." He is the Lord of the dance, the dance of the living. He is the risen Lord of glory, who in sovereign authority can say, "Blessed are you who laugh, because you can bring the joy of Christ to others."

Laugh at yourself. Lighten up. Life doesn't revolve around you and your needs. Let's laugh and take in the joy of it all, find the humor in the meeting, friendship, parenting, traffic, art, music, sports, and politics, and all in the presence of the living God. Life isn't always good, but God always is and He gives us laughter, He gives us joy. Laughter means that we have let go in reckless confidence all that ties us to yesterday, imprisons us in our small selves today, and frightens us with the uncertainty of tomorrow. Blessed are you who laugh, because you are free.

Life is about balance, moderation and in so knowing this you can Thank God for laughter and for wine.

---

[14] Erin Jean Warde, "Sobriety Broke Me to Pour Me Out," Mockingbird Ministry, https://mbird.com/2019/06/sobriety-broke-me-to-pour-me-out/, viewed May 19, 2021.

9
THE JOY OF LIFE IN DEER SEASON

"A cheerful heart is good medicine,
but a crushed spirit dries up the bones."
— **Proverbs 17:22 (NIV)**

"HAVE YOU BEEN DRINKING?" Bill asked as we stood on the side of the road, waiting for my husband's Cousin Eddie.

"No," I said. "Why?"

"Well, you just ran over a deer in the middle of the road and you seem too happy, like you don't realize what's just happened. Your van is messed up."

"Nope," I smiled. "I'm not drunk. This is my normal self."

I was driving home from a conference and ran over a deer in the last stretch of highway, seventy miles from home in the "Icebox of the Nation." I did see a man waving his arms at me from the side of the road, but before I had time to process if he needed my help, I had to pull over because my van was farting out pieces of the poor, dead deer the man was trying to warn me about.

"Are you crazy?!" Bill yelled. "Why didn't you stop when you saw me warning you?"

"I dunno. I didn't really process what was going on until just now," I explained.

I knew calling my husband, Dan, might result in him questioning my sanity, too, so I called Cousin Eddie. Eddie lived ten miles from my deer incident and worked at a garage. He would know what to do.

While we waited, Bill again questioned my happy-go-lucky state. "Ya know, when the cops come to examine the situation, they're gonna check to see if you've been drinking."

"Bill," I said, "I'm not hurt and you're not hurt. The deer was already dead. So what if my van's messed up? Getting upset won't change that."

Bill wasn't getting it. He thought I was messed up. When Eddie arrived, he thought it best to call Fletcher, nicknamed Skip, to tow me and my vehicle home. Cousin Eddie assured me it would be okay.

When Skip pulled up, he was in a huge, semi-trailer tow truck, complete with an air horn.

It doesn't get much better than this.

Once my van was loaded onto the trailer, I hopped into the truck with Skip and we were headed home. What happened on the hour-long ride was the beginning of a friendship. Skip shared his family with me, his love for his wife, cooking, and we talked about the message of Jesus. I actually took notes.

Skip stated it simply: "The message of Jesus is to LOVE and forgive others. You can only do that once you realize how bad you really are and accepted His forgiveness. You need to know how much you need God's grace, otherwise you won't be able to give it to someone else."

Preach it, Skip.

When you think about it, Jesus' way and teaching are much harder than any religion. It's easy to like those who like us. But who isn't tempted to direct their own life, take revenge, or get a quick fix, rather than wait on God's method or timing? Leaving the settling of accounts to Him and loving our enemies are not easy propositions to swallow, and they are impossibly unrealistic without understanding the real meaning of Jesus.

Skip has accepted the gift of grace from Christ. I have, too, even though what I feel and see in me is often wrong, unfair, hurtful, and judgmental. And to make it worse, there's always more where that comes from. But again, that *is* why Jesus died for us. He paid my debt and forgives all my sins. When He died, every sin we committed was in the future, so I know even what I do wrong tomorrow can be forgiven.

When we starting talking about love, it was only natural that we talked about our spouses, and Skip shared how he liked to cook and serve his wife all sorts of delicious recipes. I continued my note taking. It was interesting that we both saw love as a sacrifice, and with that sacrifice we actually experience joy.

It's always interesting to talk to others about faith. I have found that many believe there are many roads to God and that true spirituality is simply loving your neighbor and helping the poor. How then do you know when you've given enough? What if Mother Teresa is the standard? If a soldier drapes his body over a grenade to save his friends, we recognize it as a sacrifice. Something we honor, but not something we can earn or for which we can pay him back. To suggest we could, would be an insult to him and his family. The same is true with Jesus draping His body on a cross to pay for our sins. You cannot earn that.

"Blessed are the poor in spirit, for theirs is the kingdom of heaven." When Jesus shares this Sermon on the Mount, I think He is talking about the humble versus the arrogant. The arrogant focus on their position, power, and riches, and the worst of them lord it over others. The humble are thankful and willing to listen. They, like Mother Teresa, do not think they are too great to help others.

My time with Skip wasn't just fun, it actually brought me joy.

People are what life is all about. How we treat others will be the legacy we leave behind. While humans might be our biggest heartaches, they also can bring us incredible joy.

Was it just fun or pure joy? I'll let you decide, but Skip let me pull that air horn at least a dozen times, including the three when we pulled into town at midnight.

I have since had some more crazy adventures with others and with my van. Even in the moment of a frustrating adventure I try and think about the humor of it all and how it will be fun to share the story later. This is extremely helpful. Laughter is the best medicine and sharing it with others is so rewarding. I also assured Skip that I would share his wisdom and recipes with others.

What follows is a delicious apple dumpling recipe using Mountain Dew that Skip said was one of his favorites. My suggestion is to make enough to share with someone and include a note of encouragement. They might need to know how much they matter, and you'll likely rediscover that you receive the most joy when you give unto others.

Mountain Dew Apple Dumplings
2 (8 count) cans crescent rolls
3–4 tart apples
1 1/2 cups sugar
1/2 cup butter
1 teaspoon cinnamon
1 (12 ounce) can Mountain Dew soda

Spray a 13x9 baking dish or pan. Peel and slice apples into 16 pieces. Roll each apple slice in 1 section of crescent roll. Place rolled slices in pan in two rows, put extras along the side. Melt butter, add sugar and cinnamon, and pour over apples. Pour can of Mountain Dew over all. Bake at 350 degrees for 45 minutes.

10
MY WRONG DIRECTION REDEEMED

"We can make our plans, but the Lord determines our steps."
— **Proverbs 16:9 (NLT)**

AT ANY MOMENT I EXPECTED to see Dorothy Gale's house from *The Wizard of Oz* fly by. The wind was blowing so fiercely that I thought my van and I would soon be lifted off the freeway.

Call me crazy, but I thought that after my speaking event in southern Minnesota, I could logically reverse the directions in my mind and head back home to International Falls, Minnesota. It was at the second freeway rest stop when I realized I had driven eighty miles in the wrong direction. I yelled aloud.

Are you kidding me? I don't have time for this. Ahhhhhhhhhh . . . Now I'm over four hundred miles from home.

I got out of the van and screamed into the whipping wind. Then I got back in and thought about my choices.

Life is challenging, but we don't have to focus so tightly on the bad that we cannot find the good. There is a blessing and a lesson in all the challenges, if we only ask God to show us.

I first received this advice from my Aunt Ginger when I was

recovering from scoliosis back surgery in 2003. She encouraged me to view my recovery as a class. I was instructed to look for what I could learn from the trial: the lesson and blessing God had in store for me. I will never forget the postcard I received two weeks into my recovery, which I would describe as a living hell. The card read: "How's class going? I know you're being a good student."

I've had a lot of high-level classes since then. During my courses it's always helpful to discover how others managed their own trials, which often make mine seem like a walk in the park. Corrie Ten Boom shared her story of hiding Jews in her home during World War II, along with her story of being confined in a Nazi work/death camp in 1944. She famously wrote, "God, I can thank You for almost everything but I can't thank You for the lice." She later discovered that the lice infestation kept the guards away from their shelter, which allowed them the opportunity to use the smuggled Bible for studies in the Nazi camp. Amazingly, even the lice served a good purpose.

Here's the thing. For us to receive the lesson and blessing in a trial, and to make it count, we need to ask God to show us what's redeemable. We need to pray and then listen. Often our prayers are ones where we lament about all that is wrong and we list what needs fixing. Just so you know, it's more than okay to do this. God cares about our pain and all that happens to us. (Remember, I chose to scream at the top of my lungs at the rest stop before getting back in the van.) But sometimes we stop praying and give up on God because He didn't answer the prayer like we thought—our sick friend got sicker and the marriage we prayed would stay together ended in divorce. That's hard.

I'm sorry if that's been the outcome for you in a prayer, but please remember this truth in your heart. *God will never give up on you.* Nothing you do or don't will cause Him to withdraw His love. And nothing is too small or too big for Him to look at or take care of. He loves each of us personally and intimately. God rescues us, but more importantly, He redeems us.

There's no fun in complaining and being crabby, so I chose to ask God to show me the "good" of my error in driving the van in the wrong direction for more than eighty miles. It's more than fun to see how He shows up. A simple way to ask God to bless and teach us in the hard place is to simply pray . . . "God, make it count."

So I exhaled, prayed, and got back on the freeway. I had barely started my new journey when I heard this weird flapping sound. I pulled over and saw that the plastic splash-guard-thing on the front left tire was coming unhinged. I figured it didn't look like too much of a problem, and I could drive until I found an exit where someone at a gas station could help me.

I sped on, but it soon appeared that the plastic thing was coming unhinged entirely and I was now dragging a long black plastic piece of "van tongue" down the freeway. Passing motorists pointed and mouthed, "Something is falling apart on your van."

"Yep. I know," I nodded and carried on, albeit a bit slower.

I finally pulled over only because I saw a trucker-man who was trying to fix one of the straps that had come loose on his cargo. My van was parked on the side of the freeway about twenty feet in front of him, so I had time to think about how to explain my situation. But when I got to the man, named Ray, I couldn't quite explain my problem. I simply asked him to follow me.

It was hard not to laugh as we walked to my van. The wind made it not only hard to hear as I tried to explain my problem, but Ray's flannel shirt kept blowing up to expose his belly. Fun is funny. I was having fun.

When Ray saw my problem, he said "I can help you." He walked back to his truck to get tools and returned to remove the entire splash-guard-thing. While Ray lay on the ground working, I talked and talked. I found out everything I could with the time I had. He told me about his travels, marriages, the adventuresome weather he'd experienced, his dreams, and how proud he was of his children. We became fast friends.

When Ray finished, he handed me the "van tongue" and I thanked him a million times over. He told me that it was the first time in fifteen years he had ever been stopped like this to be asked for help.

"It's a good thing it was me and not someone else," Ray assured. "You're a lucky little lady. Not all truckers would have helped you in this way."

I didn't have any cash so I gave him one of the CDs I sell at speaking events. "Here ya go, Ray. This is a CD of short inspirational stories of how God is involved in Everyday Matters," I said. "Perhaps your wife will enjoy it."

I was sitting in the driver's seat and Ray was standing outside my window when I handed him the CD. He looked at it with my picture and name and then looked at me again, startled and said, "You're Debbie Griffith? You're Debbie Griffith on the radio . . . Debbie Griffith?"

"Yes, that's me," I said.

"*I can't believe it,*" Ray continued "I've heard you a dozen or so times while driving on the freeway in my truck. I just can't believe it's really you . . . here . . . right now."

Ray then started to cry.

"I've walked away from God so many times and every time I think He's done with me, something like this happens to remind me He's still got my back."

I then told Ray how I wasn't even supposed to be on this stretch of freeway, and I thought I must have gone at least eighty miles in the wrong direction.

We both were speechless for a second or so.

"*Ray!* This is so cool. God is so awesome. Think about it. God knew you needed to know He hadn't given up on you. He hasn't left you and He loves you like crazy. I'm just so blessed that I got the opportunity to remind you."

I extended my arms out the van window and held onto Ray's arms as I prayed for him. "Dear God, thank You that You showed up today in a powerful way to remind Ray how much You love him. I pray for his wife and family and for Ray to continue to walk toward You and trust all the wonderful things You have for him. *Amen.*"

Ray wiped his eyes, thanked me, and I thanked him a million more times. As he turned back to his truck, I saw him shake his head and mutter, "Debbie Griffith on the freeway . . . wait until the wife hears."

These kinds of everyday life matters bring me such joy, and it makes me think all over again how God wants all of us to know how much He cares about everything we care about. He longs for you to know His great love for you. If I said, "Hey, guess what? God had me meet Harrison Ford on the road so I could pray for him and tell him God loves him." You might think, *Wow, Debbie, that's really amazing.* But it is just as important to God (and to me) that I got a direct route to connect with Ray, the Trucker and I was able to tell him about God's great love. Cool, right?

You'd better believe God's trying to tell you that same thing, too. *He loves you* as you are, right where you are. If it helps, as it has for me, say it aloud throughout the day. "God really loves me."

This is a testimony of God's great love showing that He is always and forever pursuing us. This is a testimony of how something that was so irritating ended up being so much of a blessing. Telling this story reminds me of how God can turn an irritation into something good. He makes it count for the good, which is a promise He gives us in Romans 8:28: "And we know that God causes everything to work together for the good of those who love God and are called according to His purpose for them."

It doesn't mean that all things that happen to us are good, but He does promise that no matter what happens to us, all of it can be used for good. He will make all things count for the good and glory of who He is. Because of His promise, there isn't any suffering or experience we or someone we love,goes through that will ever be wasted. Christ is always there waiting to make creative, redemptive use of all things. Simply pray and ask Him, "God, make it count." The plan you made, even with mistakes and a wrong direction, can be redeemed because He promises to direct you each step of the way.

11
LOOKING IN THE MIRROR

"For now, we see only a reflection as in a mirror;
Then we shall see face to face. Now I know in part;
Then I shall know fully, even as I am fully known."
— 1 Corinthians 13:12 (NIV)

As an eighth-grader looking in the full-length mirror in the "smoker girls" bathroom, I hated how skinny I was. My only curves were curves from my scoliosis. No butt. No boobs. I was completely unaware that anyone was in the bathroom with me until I saw a ninth-grader, Jenny Baker, walk out of one of the stalls. She took a look at me and said, "You don't have to look. You know you're pretty."

Huh?

Now it's called bullying, but in 1980 it was called, "Don't-get-in-the-way-of-the-mean-girl-who-decides-she-hates-you." It was a long year of threats, with Jenny even requesting I meet her behind the football bleachers so she could beat me up. Jenny liked to shove me into Minnesota snow banks as I waited for the bus.

But when the snow began to melt that year, I saw the light—the lights of the theatre, with costumes, props, set designs, and characters.

I found I could sing and act, and I could look in the mirror and see someone I liked to look at because I was someone else.

I also met Susan, a student make-up artist. Susan liked me and I liked Susan, who, it turns out, was a smoker friend of Jenny's. She talked to Jenny and I have no idea what was said. But after that conversation, Susan assured me I never had to worry about bleachers or snow banks again. She was right. I was rescued.

New friends and the "smell of greasepaint and roar of the crowd," however, still did not provide the lasting rescue I wanted, until I met Jesus. I was a girl with anxieties and insecurities. Outward changes and a new identity weren't lasting. Without Him, I would *never* really like what I saw in the mirror because I knew only too well what was inside the "pretty" image Jenny saw. He had to help me see the way He sees me.

It's easier to chase happiness on the outside than on the inside because of the immediate gratification and applause. I really believed my outer appearance, relationships, and successes would bring me happiness on the inside. It is actually the reverse. Peace that surpasses understanding refers to peace despite the outside, not because of it.

We feel our neediness when we stop our busyness and the things we do to anesthetize the pain in and around us. Forgiveness. We all need it. Acceptance. We all want it. Purpose. We all strive for it. I think this is where God comes in. We seek a way to transcend life's disappointments and hurts.

Many religions claim to be the only way, but they cannot all be right. When you study the religions of the world, it is easy to see the uniqueness of Jesus. *He still lives.* He claims to be The Way, not just show the way. There is an enormous difference in religion and the forever-relationship Jesus offers. It's not based on what we do, but what He's done.

All religions require us to sacrifice or do something to please God so we can earn heaven. Most are intolerant of people who disagree.

Some even hate and want to hurt those who disagree. Jesus's message is just the opposite. He says, "Love must be sincere. Hate what is evil; cling to what is good. Be devoted to one another in love. Honor one another above yourselves" (Romans 12:9–10, NIV).

He says, "Love your enemies," not just tolerate them.

What?

The message of Jesus is to *love* and forgive others, which you can only do once you have seen your bad self and accepted His forgiveness. When you think about it, Jesus' way and teaching are much harder than any religion. It's easy to like those who like us and think like us, but who isn't tempted to want to direct their own life and get revenge, or a quick fix, rather than wait on His method or timing?

Being kind to those who spitefully use us, leaving the settling of accounts to Him, and loving our enemies are not easy propositions to swallow. They are impossibly unrealistic without understanding the real meaning of the Good News: Complete forgiveness from God completely changes us.

How does the "changing" take place? Fruit grows quickly in *only* time-lapse photography! Truth needs cultivating. For me it actually starts with my knowing and playing "the CD of truth" in my mind until it becomes more prominent than the old negative CD we were all born with. "God loves me unconditionally. I make mistakes but I am not a mistake."

He proved His love and acceptance *once* and for *all*. He *knows* what we are like behind the image others see. Once this truth begins to "air" regularly, I cannot wait to tell others. Freedom is a magnet, and others will want that "get out of jail free" card.

I am still Debbie, with a slight curve of scoliosis, made less noticeable with the surgery I had as an adult. I am still Debbie who needs to look every day in the mirror and wonder what else I can do to my hair to change my life. I want to not care so much, and there are times I don't, and I walk out in my pajamas to get groceries or record my radio feature at the station. But if I can walk away from the mirror with the *truth* of who He says I am, rather than what I feel or think about me, then I am more excited to talk about it to someone else, regardless of what I know that they don't see. Every day, I have to remember the way He sees me despite my moral failings and missteps and bad hair days.

Jesus loves me, He knows me, my pain, my ache from the loved one I lost, the cancer that came to my Dan, my anxiety attacks and depression, the lies that spread, and the unrealized dream of stardom on Broadway. He knew before I knew. *He is* here, waiting to make creative, redemptive use of what has happened. He is always on the move. He isn't wasting time thinking about all the trouble He has with us, or how awful we feel about where we are with ourselves and our troubles. God loves us unconditionally. End of story.

I don't have all the answers to all the questions, but enough answers to know what will happen to me when I die, and to know the difference it makes now to have peace with God and my neighbor. He gives me strength to live and love, and even death won't end my relationship with Him. He is the path to and for eternity. He is The Way, Truth, and Life, and no one comes to the Father but through *Him*. I am created in His image, and it's His image I want to reflect and see in the mirror.

12
TAKE THE 'SHOULD' OUT OF YOUR LIFE

"Christ has truly set us free. Now make sure that you stay free, and don't get tied up again in slavery to the law."
— **Galatians 5:1 (NLT)**

THINK HOW OFTEN YOU SAY, "I should read the Bible, I should memorize Scripture, I should attend a Bible study, I should lead one." But how often do we say, "I get to read the Bible, I get to memorize words of *life*, I get to attend a Bible study, and I get excited in leading others to know Christ?"

Jesus came, not as a "Kill-Joy," but as a "Give-Joy." He came not with a list of "you should" rules, but instead He came with a list of love, hope, and promises that we can all receive by entering into a relationship with Him. Second Corinthians 3:6 (AMPC) makes it pretty clear why Jesus came to us as God Himself: "He has qualified us, making us sufficient as ministers of a new covenant of salvation through Christ, not of the letter [of a written code] but of the Spirit; for the letter of the Law kills by revealing sin and *demanding* obedience, but the Spirit gives life." Jesus came to fulfill the law and set us, the captives, free. "Be free," I say, "and let God help you take 'the should' out of your life."

Sadly, many Christians are still living with a religious mindset. When Christianity is all about being religious rather than having a relationship with God, we are bound to the slavery of the law. (Christianity without Jesus is just another religion). With a religious outlook we become focused on what we shouldn't be doing, what we shouldn't be thinking, how we don't measure up, how we should be like someone else or how we should have more of "something" but we're always falling short. Many of us, when told, "You shouldn't do this," want to do the opposite. My husband used to say, "Debbie, have a safe trip." I would usually scoff at this as pedantic. Now he knows to say, "Debbie, drive like hell and use your road rage if you have to." I always smile and then proceed on my trip taking the precautions I know I need to take. I mean, haven't we all said (or at least thought) when hearing a bad but fun proposal, "That sounds like a terrible idea. . . .What time?"

It seems in the last few years that more people who identified as Christians are now deconstructing their faith and walking away from Christianity. When I hear this, I get really sad. Are they saying, "Goodbye" to Christ? Maybe what they really mean is they are walking away from religion and rules, and who can blame them? I have to wonder if they ever had a relationship with Jesus, because who in their right mind would walk away from forgiveness, grace, mercy, and unconditional love?" Who could walk away from Jesus once they really knew Him?

When we start thinking I *should* is when we can get stuck in being religious. Some religious circles want you to believe that God can only be reached through rule keeping and good behavior. This "religious spirit" was alive when Jesus walked the Earth, but He died so we could have a close personal relationship with Him and not a religion. Today that same religious spirit still trips people up if they don't know the truth. And even when we know the truth we get tripped up. My friend Sharon wrote me a text after I suggested she read Psalms to help her get out of the depression she was in. "Thank you, dear friend," she wrote, "for pointing me back to Psalms and, boy, did I need Psalm 40:5, "O Lord my God, you have performed many wonders for us. Your plans for us are too numerous to list. You have no equal. If I tried to recite all your wonderful deeds, I would never come to the end of them. You take no delight in sacrifices or offerings."

Sharon further said, "The 'martyr' in me sometimes feels like I need to pay the price for my sin, especially when I sin against another. I try to be extra 'nice' and serve them in excess to somehow make up for my saltiness. God takes *no* delight in that! We can't fix our sin. Only Jesus can." It turns out I needed that Psalms' guidance at the exact moment Sharon sent the text. Remember the Law was given to show people their need for a Savior. Our personal relationship with Christ enables us to walk in freedom and to be loved right where we are at and not how others think we "should" be.

I'm a 1967 baby and I came to know the realness of Jesus when I was seven, in 1974. My Aunt Ginger explained how Jesus is God, and there was a way to have a relationship with Him. I don't recall Ginger giving me a list of "you should" and "you should not" commands. What I recall is her explaining that with Jesus there is hope and a love from Him that will never leave or fail you. She explained that we all enter into the world as sinners and nothing we can do can save ourselves. Jesus came to Earth to pay the penalty for our sins. "The wages (penalty) for our sins is death, but the gift of God is eternal life through Jesus Christ our Lord" (Romans 6:23). The only "work" I needed to do was accept the pardon by accepting Jesus into my life and turn away from living a life of sin. That is something "I should do," explained Auntie Ginger and I did. I prayed and accepted Jesus into my heart.

In a relationship we not only can talk to God and He listens, but He speaks, too. We can hear His voice speak through His Word because He IS the Word. "My sheep hear My voice. I know them and they follow Me" (John 10:27, ESV). I don't look at the Bible as something I "should" read but it's something I get to read. My relationship grows this way because it's a way to have a two-way conversation with God continually. The Bible and Scriptures aren't "self-help" suggestions or "empowerment" tools. I don't memorize Scripture because I have to and there's a chart in heaven with sticker-stars for how much I know or commit to memory. I memorize Scripture because I get to. I need to. His Word keeps me alive.

Every day I have a choice to follow Him, to put my trust in Him rather than in myself and what I think "feels right." I don't always take the route God guides me to, yet He doesn't condemn me when I do stray nor does He condemn me for the feelings I have when I'm hurting. He's always right by my side even when I'm distant. "I know the Lord is always with me. I will not be shaken for He is right beside me" (Psalm 16:8, NLT). I have memorized and repeated that phrase over and over aloud many times and especially when I felt overwhelmed and afraid. Speaking the truth aloud eventually brings peace because Jesus is standing right beside me completely aware. The circumstances might not have changed, but I have.

We all fall short of the glory of God right now—all of us. Accept the fact that you'll never be enough to cure yourself. The sooner you realize it's not about you and that it's all about Him, the sooner you'll understand who you are and what your purpose is until you're Home with Him. You'll enjoy the uniqueness of who you are and others. You can receive God's forgiveness and work on forgiving yourself for what He's already promised to forget. You can grow in your relationship with Christ by reading the Bible even if it's only a verse a day. When this happens, you'll be living in His grace, which you'll realize you so desperately need, so you can't afford to withhold from others. Once you have a heart change, you'll have a behavioral change and it will be gradual change, but also, there's some sliding backward or you're simply being stagnant. That's why I don't say, "I desire to represent Jesus," because I don't represent Him well. He represents me well by what He did for me. He represents me in my successes and failures. He is righteous and my righteousness comes from Him (Righteousness = Right Standing with God). Real change didn't happen in me as a result of being told I needed to change. Real change happened as a result of knowing I was fully known and fully loved by Jesus. That made me want to change. Love changes you—not so for rules that only make demands. My personality relates to this meme I read on Pinterest, "Someone just honked to get me out of my parking spot faster, so now I have to sit here until we're both dead."[15]

Right now, right here in everyday life in my fifties, God is *very* real to me in the "realness" of my brokenness. In my twenties with my theatre degree, I thought I was on my way to becoming a shining star on stage, but that's when my greatest problems were me, myself, and I. Years later, married, with four sons and taking the time to connect to people in everyday life, I found the way to shine bright was by investing in relationships and being honest with others about who I am and how great He is.

A way to peace begins with accepting the truth of myself, the whole truth and not some pretty version of me posted on Instagram. To love others is actually a command from God, but loving humans can be hard. My copy of Brennan Manning's *Reflections for Ragamuffins* has pretty much every page underlined because it's wisdom. Brennan understands: "My struggle to cope with certain people has a simple explanation. They represent those things that I have refused to acknowledge and accept in myself." He continues, "To accept the truth of my brokenness is unbearable, if not impossible, without turning to Jesus. If my vision of myself isn't looking at the mercy and compassion of Jesus, I have to get dishonest, camouflage my warts, and present to you

---

[15] W. (n.d.), "Whisper Quotes, Whisper Confessions, Bones Funny," https://www.pinterest.com/pin/318277898647798437/, viewed April 21, 2021.

a self that is mostly admirable, fault free, and superficially happy." [16]

I want to present to you a real, Everyday Debbie Girl who knows her depravity, but also knows the grace of God and that being honest with myself and others is completely freeing. *Everyday Matters* is the name of the radio feature I write and deliver. I often post the transcripts on Facebook. Recently, I posted a "Tuesday Matters" entitled, "Everyday Personal and Real." I was quite honestly surprised at the many responses I got saying, "*This* is good."

"I think it's my favorite Everyday Matter, Debbie," Stacy said.

"Oh, thank you for posting. I feel better about me," Karen joined in.

"You too, Debbie? Glad I'm not alone," Jenny commented.

Below is the *Everyday Matters* feature that aired on a Monday sometime in April 2021:

Everyday Personal and Real

I've lost weight and I'm overall toned and fit. I feel healthy, too. I've no more debt and even an excess of money (after donating to special relief funds) so I was able to buy some adorable new outfits. My marriage is perfectly perfect, and our four sons know exactly God's direction for their lives.

Don't you feel better knowing how great I'm doing? Probably not, so here's the truth: I can't fit into my everyday jeans, it's a hard road getting out of debt, my marriage takes work, and our sons are all in different places making decisions about their future. *Now* I bet you feel better because you can probably relate on some level. God's real and He wants us to keep it real, too. Pain is personal and Jesus is personal so sharing our pain is a way to help others know they're not alone.

When we enter into community, we can find the one who needs

---

[16] Brennan Manning, *The Ragamuffin Gospel* (Colorado Springs, CO: Multnomah Books, 2015).

to know Jesus personally too. Ya know, others may fail you, but Jesus never will. It's a promise from 1 Corinthians 13 . . . every day.

Walk in love. Ask God to help you take 'the should' out of your life and help others live in the freedom of Christ's love.

Look to the Holy Spirit to strengthen you in being sincerely kind to others and yourself. Everyone you meet is fighting a battle you know nothing about (and sometimes you can't always know why your battle is happening and the emotions you're experiencing with it). Be kind. Kindness is a fruit of the spirit that will always need fertilizing.

One important part of getting 'the should' out of our lives is by not thinking we have to be like someone else with their strengths or thinking we have to have a large number of skills, smarts and strengths to be a good wife, mom, worker, artist or decent human. I was really encouraged when Allie Beth Stuckey's book came out, *You're Not Enough (and That's Okay): Escaping the Toxic Culture of Self-Love.* The book's message is needed in a world where it seems many female "influencers" are telling us how we can be empowered and confident if we simply believe in ourselves, work hard, and reach up and out to achieve our dreams. Many of these "influencers" are giving the "You should do 'this' and you should do 'that' to be successful" message. In the description of Allie Beth's book we read, "Instead of feeling fulfilled, our pursuit of self-love traps us in an exhausting cycle: as we strive for self-acceptance, we become addicted to self-improvement. The truth is we can't find satisfaction inside ourselves because *we are the problem*. We struggle with feelings of inadequacy because we are inadequate. Alone, we are not good enough, smart enough, or beautiful enough. We're not enough—period. And that's okay, because God is."[17]

---

[17] https://www.amazon.com/Youre-Not-Enough-Thats-Self-Love/dp/0593083849/ref=sr_1_1?crid=1RXXH6KJ45EDZ&keywords=allie+beth+stuckey+you%27re+not+enough+book&qid=1644019628&sprefix=allie+bet%2Caps%2C174&sr=8-1

When we're honest with ourselves, we know that no amount of our strong wills and self-determination can remove the stain of sin and selfishness that we're all born with. Sure, there can be success in marketing yourself and performing well, but it's not where true peace is found. I think the "I should do this" is more about trying to perform well and trying to be successful by our own good works. When you take the "I should" out of your life and live with God's representation and validation you're free to live honestly and authentically and that has the greatest influence on others who come in contact with you. I was struck by reading the reviews of women who had read Allie Beth's book and were relieved to know they were "okay" right where God had them because He's enough.

One Amazon reviewer of Stuckey's book, 'J. B.,' wrote,

Allie challenges the widely accepted mantras of self-love, self-affirmation, and frankly self-obsession. But she does this with grace and love for the reader. I was particularly challenged by her discussion on self-forgetfulness. I paused to examine my life. When in my life was I the most happy? When in my life was I the most fulfilled? The truth, which aligns with what Allie wrote, is that I've felt the most joy and the most fulfillment when I was not concerned with myself. This truth is something I never really thought about until reading this book."[18]

Another reviewer with a "special needs" child shared this:

After my child was born with a disability, I suffered pretty severely from postpartum depression. I kept trying to be 'enough' for him, for my husband, and for myself. The days were honestly a blur, and I heard a lot of advice which initially turned me away from God. I was told, "If you just pray enough, God will heal him," or "He isn't healed because you don't have enough faith." I never felt like I was enough because I was in such darkness. This wasn't the life I had

---

[18] https://www.amazon.com/Youre-Not-Enough-Thats-Self-Love/product-reviews/0593083849/ref=cm_cr_getr_d_paging_btm_next_6?ie=UTF8&reviewerType=all_reviews&pageNumber=6

dreamed of or the life that I planned for my child. I spent way too many years searching for happiness within myself and trying to accept my child's diagnosis. I totally bought into the self-love culture and obsessed over working out/self-improvement and drowned my sorrows with wine. It was a miserable and exhausting journey trying to find happiness and fulfillment within myself. Recently I heard the *true* gospel from a friend of mine, and it wasn't until then that I realized I was in desperate need of a Savior. This book has helped me battle countless false teachings that I have heard. It has also eliminated the self-destructive mindset that I had for so long. I'm not enough, and that's okay because Christ is enough. I now know that He is the only way to real joy and happiness.[19]

— Ragan

You hear that "You're enough. You're enough because Jesus is enough." Life is hard but I think it's made a lot harder when you're trying to be someone else, or trying to find fulfillment in yourself and all you can achieve. Plus, our feelings aren't always valid, and we can never "self-help" ourselves to perfection, but Jesus is perfect. Sometimes He uses counselors and doctors to help us stabilize through medication, therapy, or both. Let's get off that draining hamster wheel of trying to "pull ourselves together" so perfectly. Philippians 4:13 tells us we can do all things through Christ who strengthens us, but remember it's all the things God sets before us and not necessarily what we or others decide as "things" that need our attention. Knowing your identity in Christ will be the best start to being at peace with who you are and where you are in life.

Tullian Tchividjian's tweet the other day hit home for me. "God's love is a gift to be received, not a wage to be earned. It is a no-strings-attached present for the hopeless and weak, not compensation for the hardworking and strong." Actually, it's in our weaknesses that God is strongest.

---

[19] Ibid.

I want God's love to define who I am, so others might see He represents me. I hope to always extend grace and empathy toward others and not be known as a giver of "You should" directions. I love reading about Sister Mary Michael O'Shaughnessy, who had a banner in her room that said, "Today I will not should on myself." I want to live with the hope and expectation from Philippians 1:6 (NLT), "I am certain that God, who began the good work within me, will continue His work until it is finally finished on the day when Christ Jesus returns."

Morning by morning new mercies you can receive while walking in love and freedom with who you are in Christ and by taking 'the should' out of your life.

SERVING PEACE

13
FORGIVENESS SETS *YOU* FREE

*"Make allowance for each other's faults,
and forgive anyone who offends you. Remember,
the Lord forgave you, so you must forgive others."*
— **Colossians 3:13 (NLT)**

WHEN IT'S THE SEASON OF CELEBRATIONS, such as Thanksgiving, Christmas, Easter, graduations, and other family get-togethers, and not everyone gathering is on good terms and there's bitterness harbored, these can be some of the most painful events you ever attend. You need grace. You need it because you're going to have to give it to someone who doesn't deserve it, and they might need to give it to you. Without grace you'll want to find the nearest bottle of wine and a location to drink it. My anxiety rages when I see someone who hurt me. Sometimes I become sick to my stomach or rehearse again the hurt scenario.

Alcoholics Anonymous still celebrates the tenet, "Let go and let God." That is where the forgiveness rubber meets the road. I've done it the other way by letting my mouth run wild while pulling others into the drama to strike back at the one who's hurt me. But the wise thing is to shut up. I need to let God in and hear what He has to say.

After twenty-seven years of living in a small town of six thousand, I like to say it's nice. Even when you don't know what you are doing, someone else does. What's not so nice? It's hard to find a place to be alone. I go to the airport. It's a remote location where I can park, sit, talk to God, and sob. Last month I drove to the airport to process, vent, and cry. I eventually found some peace and settled into the back of the van to write in my journal. I was ready to hear what God had for my hurting heart. I was startled when Daryl tapped on the back window.

"Hey, are you okay? What are you doing?"

"Hey, Daryl; this is Debbie Griffith."

"Oh, hey, it's you. What's going on?"

"I know this is weird, but sometimes I just come to the airport to write and reflect. That's what I'm doing right now. It's crazy busy at home, and everywhere else in town I seem to run into someone who knows me."

"Oh, okay. You're sure you're okay?"

"Yes, thanks, Daryl. See you in church on Sunday."

Busted at the airport, but it's a blessing, too. People care and I know if I reach out for help, I can find it. It's sometimes not about me waiting for God to provide, but for me to simply abide in Him and wait, pray, wail as needed, and know that He is always aware and always cares no matter how broken I feel. He's a Redeemer who is always on the move redeeming. Parking at a secluded spot helps me get perspective. I'm able to look out at the horizon and somehow get the bigger picture and remain silent. Of course, this is after a good cry and an "It's not fair" speech to God.

A scenario that recently brought me to the airport lot was learning that someone was talking behind my back, stabbing me with gossip and unkindness. My usual first response is to set things straight by talking to everyone involved and to make sure my side of things is told. That's not the healthy route. Been there, done that. That path only sets in seeds of bitterness, which if allowed to grow become deep roots of unforgiving ugliness that rot our lives. Remember that forgiveness doesn't excuse the other person's behavior. It prevents their behavior from taking over our thoughts.

God is fully aware of what the other person is doing and feeling, just as He is fully aware of what you're going through. He loves you both. Sometimes I need to confess and bring my garbage to the light, but in more recent times I've needed to trust the promise of Romans 12:19 and leave the avenging part to God. "Beloved, never avenge yourselves, but leave it to the wrath of God, for it is written, 'Vengeance is Mine, I will repay, says the Lord'" (ESV). I love reading this verse aloud and thinking how God calls me "Beloved." It's like He knows how hard it is to let go and take the person off my hook and put them on His.

One of the hardest things *ever* is to let the offense drop and not to play the hurt over and over in my mind. When I ask God for wisdom, He continually and clearly speaks. "Wait on Me, Debbie."

After my recent airport "sob and sigh," it seemed like everywhere I turned there was a Post-It reminder of encouragement, such as Exodus 14:14. "The Lord will fight for you; you need only be still" (NIV). I'm not saying it is easy to stop rehearsing the hurt over and over in your head like a nagging melody, but it's so worth it.

You have to make a choice. You have to choose to let all the garbage, hurt, and anger go to God and not think or talk about it. If you are simply saying to yourself, "I'm not going to think about it," good luck. My experience is that it only results in obsessing and remembering even more about the incident. Instead, choose to replace your thoughts with how much God loves you, and literally try and find the funny moments you've had in hard places. I often think about and rehearse a story to tell someone that will make them laugh—to replace the hurtful story I want to share instead. I also want to follow what God's Word directs me to do and then do it! This may mean talking to the person and asking forgiveness, or if I'm not yet ready for that I pray for the self-control to not send "just one more" message, text, or email explaining myself. God's direction is best. I've written scripts and directed myself on ways to make amends and they've always been flops.

But it's helpful to not ignore your hurt. Speak it aloud and express your pain and frustration to God. I tattle on the person to God and talk about what they did wrong and how it's not fair. This helps immensely. God already knows the song of hurt I'm playing, and so my out-loud expression is cleansing (so are tears) and helps clear my head. But then, it's important that I speak aloud to what is true and good to get a new song of hope in my head.

I begin with thinking about Love. It never fails. I go to 1 Corinthians 13 and put "I" in the "love" blank. I am patient, I am kind. I do not demand my own way. I am not irritable. I keep no record of being wronged. I never give up. I never lose faith. I am always hopeful. I endure through every circumstance. Yeah, right. I know that I am none of those things *without* the grace and power of the Holy Spirit working in me. Depending on greater self-effort and strong-willed determination just won't work in freeing us from the bitterness we hold inside whether or not the other person apologizes.

I know it doesn't seem fair. It's hard. But if you think that's tough to apply, go to Luke 6:28. "Bless those who curse you, and pray for those who mistreat you." That's a tough one when what you really want to do is punch their lights out and throw ugly words toward them. But ... God's passionate, crazy love for you promises a blessing when you obey what He calls you to do. When you start to rehearse the hurt simply repeat over and over: "Lord, bless them. Lord, bless them."

So, not only does God tell us to forgive others, but He instructs us to bless them. In this context, the word *bless* means "to speak well of." So, one of our problems is even though we pray and try to forgive those who offend, we turn and curse them or rehash the offense again and again with others.

That will not work.

To work through the process of forgiveness and receive peace, we must do what God tells us to do, which is not only to forgive, but also to bless. One reason we find it so hard to pray for those who hurt and mistreat us is that we tend to think we are asking God to bless them physically or materially like with large cash prizes and an all-expense trip to Disney World for the whole family. The truth is that we are not praying for them to make more money or have more possessions. We are praying for them to be blessed spiritually. What we're doing is asking God to bring truth and revelation about their attitudes and behaviors so they will be willing to turn to God and be freed from their own junk. I mean, honestly, God could bring someone a blessing by way of an illness or hardship. I know many of my own blessings have come through trials. Of course, I'd like to direct God on how to bless someone, but then again He's God and I'm not. He knows each person's heart and how to mend them. It's "trust and obey," like the old hymn says. "for there's no other way to be happy in Jesus, but to trust and obey."

Hating those who hurt you is like taking poison and hoping your enemy will die. Obviously, anyone who did that would only be hurting themselves. Why spend your life angry at people who sometimes don't even know or care you're angry? These people may be totally enjoying their lives while you're miserable. Release them, let the offense go, drop it, and ask Jesus to give you the same attitude toward them as He had toward His enemies. Release the hate you have inside and replace with love. *Only* Jesus has the power to fill you with that supernatural request. It's hard because as Frederick Buechner notes in his book, *Wishful Thinking*, anger can actually be fun:

> *... Of the seven deadly sins,* anger is possibly the most fun. To lick your wounds, to smack your lips over grievances long past, to roll over your tongue the prospect of bitter confrontations still to come, to savor to the last toothsome morsel both the pain you are given and the pain you are giving back—in many ways it is a feast fit for a king. The chief drawback is that what you are wolfing down is yourself. The skeleton at the feast is you."[20]

Okay maybe it's "fun" for a "hot" minute or even a full-heated day to feast on self-pity and rehearse the hurt, but you'll never experience freedom and peace unless you let go and give it *all* to God. Memorize Romans 12:19 ("God will avenge me") so you can hear His promise of vindication. The alternative is more of your obsessive hurtful thoughts on the unfairness of your pain.

I'm kind of obsessed with the Netflix series *The Crown*, which, as I write this, has been produced for four seasons and chronicles the life of Queen Elizabeth II from the 1940s to modern times. The series begins with an inside look at the early reign of the queen, who ascended the throne at age twenty-five after the death of her father, King George VI. It is a drama full of such rich-life stories of love, losses, victories, and faith. Season Two, Episode Six is where Queen Elizabeth meets evangelist Billy Graham. This episode also reveals how the royal family struggles with its relationship to former King Edward VIII, Elizabeth's uncle who abdicated the throne to marry a divorcée and became the Duke of Windsor. That familial struggle becomes increasingly tense as the queen learns the family's dark secret: Her uncle had become friendly with the Nazis during World War II, and even plotted to overthrow his brother. It also suggests he encouraged Germany to bomb England. After learning the shocking details about her uncle, the queen asks Billy Graham open-ended questions about forgiveness.

---

[20] Frederick Buechner, *Wishful Thinking: A Theological ABC* (New York: Harper & Row, 1973).

The Queen: "Mr. Graham, can there be any circumstances where one can be a good Christian and not forgive?"

Graham: "The Christian teaching is very clear on this. No one is beneath forgiveness. Dying on the cross, Jesus Himself asked the Lord to forgive those who killed Him."

Queen: "Yes. But we must remember His words, 'They know not what they do.' That forgiveness was conditional."

Graham: "True, but He still forgave them. God Himself forgives us all. Who are we to reject the example of God?"

Queen: "Mere mortals."

Graham: "We are all mere mortals, that is our fate. But we need not be un-Christian ones. The solution for being unable to forgive is that one needs to ask for forgiveness for oneself, humbly and sincerely, and then one prays for those, one cannot forgive."[21]

But we want to say, "Yes, but . . . excuse me, Mr. Graham, the Queen is talking about collaborating with *Nazis*. Surely there is an exception for Nazis."

I appreciate the thoughts my friend Carrie Willard, a writer for *The Mockingbird Ministry*, wrote in her piece "The Crown, Season 2: Reconciliation and Her Majesty" . . .

> When reconciliation and forgiveness become law, instead of reminders of God's grace toward us, they don't become easier to achieve. And forgiveness does not always mean that we let the wolf back into the chicken coop. That would be cruel to both the wolf and the chickens, and the farmer who has to clean up the mess. We have to be careful when we paint broad brushstrokes

---

[21] Peter Morgan, Netflix: *The Crown*, Season 2 Episode 6: "Vergangenheit." December 8, 2017, https://www.netflix.com/watch/80149010?trackId=13752289&tctx=0%2C0%2C828191549a23e93b93412f8c9197225dc8394f26%3A8f8d9bb37f75017cfda27f6074f647b123235798%2C828191549a23e93b93412f8c9197225dc8394f26%3A8f8d9bb37f75017cfda27f6074f647b123235798%2C%2C, viewed May 21, 2021.

about forgiveness, remembering that the victims of domestic abuse have been told for generations (by the church!) that they should forgive their abusers to keep the peace.

I don't think that it means that we should give up on forgiveness and reconciliation altogether, of course. I think we do need to remember that we need God's help to forgive, and that sometimes God's timeline is not on our calendar. Forgiveness may not always look like we think it should, with everyone hugging and getting a nice cushy government job at the end of the episode. Sometimes forgiveness can also come with some serious heartbreak and firm boundaries, as it did with the Queen and her uncle.

I appreciated this episode so much, for its glimpse into the Queen's struggles to try to piece together a broken family, and looking to Jesus as her guide. The episode showed how deeply unsatisfying it was for the Queen to not have a tidy answer to the problem of her uncle and his misdeeds, and how she still turned to God even when she was not getting the answers that she thought she might want.[22]

That is real life. But, it is a process to forgive and perhaps an even greater process to recognize how quickly and completely God forgives our sins.

An excerpt from Frederick Bauerschmidt's book, *The Love That Is God*, was shared by my friend Josh, whom I learn so much from because he is always leaning in and learning about the grace of God, too. Most of us don't take the time to read all the "good stuff" out there on important subjects such as forgiveness, so I appreciate it when others share what they've read or experienced, and therefore I do the same in my collection of stories. The subject of the following paragraph is about a friend who struggles with the

---

[22] Carrie Willard, *The Crown*, Season 2: "Reconciliation and Her Majesty," Mockingbird Ministry [Web log post], February 14, 2018, viewed at https://mbird.com/2018/02/the-crown-season-2-reconciliation-and-her-majesty/, viewed May 14, 2021.

command of God to "love your enemies." I think we *all* understand this struggle:

> I have a friend who visibly winces whenever the subject of loving enemies comes up. She is someone who has committed to a life of prophetic advocacy for the poor and vulnerable, and who hates hypocrisy and selfishness and willful ignorance of the plight of others. She winces because she knows that loving your enemies truly lies at the heart of Christianity. She winces because she knows that the only love that can encompass even our enemy is the love that has been stretched out and broken open on the cross: love that makes itself vulnerable to the hatred of enemies believing that love is stronger than hate and that life will triumph over death. She winces because she knows that friendship with Jesus means sharing in this crucified love. [23]

With some damaged relationships there's been restoration, and with others I'm still waiting. Nevertheless, I've landed on a good truth: *God can handle it all.* When He asks us to do something, He always gives us the grace and strength to do it. I pass someone who's hurt me in the grocery store and smile. I can say, "God bless them" (under my breath) and mean it even if I don't feel it.

Think on this amazing gift from God: He forgives our sin completely and chooses not to recall them, as far as the East is from the West. Of course, God could recall them (it's not memory failure) and retrieve them or send someone else to get them, but He just chooses not to. I think of my own children. I know they have faults and they are sinners, but I do not like to think about them, and I am very testy with someone who thinks it is their job to remind me of them. I love them. I might be disappointed, and there was often discipline involved with a consequence, but love and grace were not withheld. I pray the Lord's prayer completely differently than I used to. The part where it says, "Forgive me my sins as I forgive others?" Yeah, right. I

---

[23] Frederick Bauerschmidt, *The Love That Is God: An Invitation to Christian Faith* (Grand Rapids, MI: William B. Eerdmans, 2020).

don't want my kind of conditional forgiveness that rehearses an offense again in my mind. I want God's erasing forgiveness. Now I pray the Lord's part on forgiveness like this, "Forgive me my sins and may I forgive others the way You forgive me, completely." *Amen*.

It's really having a funeral for either your sins or forgiving someone else's sin against you. You should bury it and not dig it up again. It doesn't mean you won't feel grief, anger, sadness, denial, and bargaining, but once you bury the hurt, let it stay dead by not resurrecting it by mulling it over again . . . and again. Bury it and don't leave a tombstone to mark the burial because you'll only have the temptation to go back and dig it all up again.

Years ago, I sought counseling over a conflict with a close friend whom I had hurt and offended. She had hurt and offended me, too. It was so painful and I know it was for her as well. Sadly, we both were stuck on the facts of what the other had done, thinking they were far worse than what we ourselves had done. I cried a lot and felt sick to my stomach most days. I shared my hurt with others, which unfortunately extended to a behavior known as gossip. Others picked up my offense, which wasn't theirs to carry, and while it felt helpful at the time it wasn't wise. Eventually we met with a mediator, and it was messier and more difficult than I could have imagined.

There was one point when the friend exclaimed, "Debbie can't be forgiven because she hasn't apologized the right way." I literally thought, "Get thee behind me, Satan," And I actually dropped to my knees and said aloud, "I don't identity with who you say I am." 1 John 1:9 says: "If we confess our sins, God is faithful and just and will forgive us our sins and purify us from all unrighteousness." I then got up and sat back in my chair. There was a stillness and then more discussion and questions from the mediator, but nothing really got settled. It's been years now and there is congeniality and stability and on some level there's reconciliation, but full restoration hasn't happened. In working with others on forgiveness I know, too, that healing can only come when *both* parties are ready to take responsibility for their parts. It's *so* hard. The book the counselor gave me to read during this time was T*he Peacemaker: A Biblical Guide to Resolving Personal Conflict*, by Ken Sande. Most of the pages are underlined. I still have this excerpt written out and in a drawer and I've definitely needed to rely on the wisdom and application of its truth:

> The first stage of forgiveness requires having an attitude of forgiveness, and the second, granting forgiveness. Having an attitude of forgiveness is unconditional and is a commitment you make to God. By His grace, you seek to maintain a loving and merciful attitude toward someone who has offended you. This requires making and living out the first promise of forgiveness, which means you will not dwell on the hurtful incident or seek vengeance or retribution in thought, word, or action. Instead, you pray for the other person and stand ready at any moment to pursue complete reconciliation as soon as he or she repents. This attitude will protect you from bitterness and resentment, even if the other person takes a long time to repent.[24]

Forgiving my dad when I found out he had been unfaithful to my mom was an extremely painful process. It wrecked me. Of course, anyone's infidelity is going to have an effect on not just the one member, but it will touch many others. I sought counseling. I cried out to God. I talked to my only sibling, aunt, sister-in-law, and close and compassionate friends. I did more counseling. I cried a lot. Two years after the news was out, I had a breakdown and needed to go on medication for anxiety attacks that were seeing me fall apart emotionally and physically. Of course, other factors played into this, but I knew the marriage of my parents ending after forty-four years contributed to my struggle.

Eventually, four years after it all happened, my dad agreed to do

---

[24] Ken Sande, *The Peacemaker: A Biblical Guide to Resolving Personal Conflict* (Grand Rapids, MI: Baker Books, 2007).

a counseling session with me in a town that was a two-hour drive for each of us. It was biblical counseling. It was very helpful, and I was at a place to begin letting go and forgiving. It was maybe a year later when my dad came to a cross country meet out of town for our oldest son, Marco. I parked the car and saw my dad from a distance and without thinking I saw my dad whom I loved. I ran to him and almost bowled him over with a hug saying, "You're here. You made it. It's great to see you." I was the young, joyous girl loving on her dad again. Don't get me wrong, it's not like it's been butterflies and bunnies ever since. My dad can be frustrating, just like he can be frustrated with me. But there is no more bitterness. I have let it go. Love never fails and I sincerely love my dad.

What if you're the one who has to give an apology? Here's some great advice when giving a sincere one, "Never let your big *but* get in the way. A sentence coming out of your mouth that goes something like, "I'm sorry I hurt your feelings, but you needed to hear the truth," or "I am sorry you thought I was giving you the money but you're mistaken because you have a spending problem," will not be effective, no matter how true the statement is. The other party will only hear the "but" of your apology. Another example of what not to say would be, "I'm sorry I shared your story with others, LuAnn, and you thought it was gossip, but you hurt my feelings in your Facebook post on difficult people, even though you didn't mention my name." The correct way to apologize would be to say, "I'm sorry I shared your story with others, LuAnn. It was gossip. What can I do to help restore our friendship? Please forgive me." Instead of blaming others for a conflict or resisting correction, we must trust in God's mercy and take responsibility for our own contribution to a conflict. We *must* confess our sins to those we have wronged no matter if they ever confess their part to us. Author, speaker, and Hebrew scholar, Chad Bird shares this: "Forgiveness, like life itself, doesn't have our name scrawled on it. It isn't our property, much less our tool or weapon. Those who sin against us don't owe us an apology. They don't owe us repentance, tears, promises of improvement, vows never to repeat what they've done. Nothing is what they owe.

"When we forgive, we are pressing into the palm of a fellow transgressor the coin of freedom with which Christ has enriched us. We give only what we first received. When the Spirit reveals this to us, we discover what joy it is to bury the hatchet in an unmarked grave. In the same grave we bury the myth of self-forgiveness. We're seeking relief from the last place we should be looking: ourselves. Forgiveness, like medicine, comes from outside of you, from the hand of a healer. When God forgives us in Christ, He gives forgives completely. There's no deficiency. Even if, heaven forbid, others refuse to forgive us, we rest peacefully in the only declaration of release that ultimately matters: the one Jesus Himself gives from His ugly cross of beautiful love. It is the most unexpected pleasure in the world to be loved without condition by a God who makes no demands."

I have the above quote underlined and highlighted in Chad's book, *Night Driving: Notes from a Prodigal Soul*.[25] I need God's grace, strength, and help to change any attitudes and habits that led to the conflict or relationship breakage, and I need to seek to repair any harm I have caused. The bottom line is this: Understanding God's grace, we can come to an understanding that conflict is an opportunity, not an accident. Because we need to realize that success in God's eyes is not really about specific results but of faithful obedience. I understand the blessing of obedience and my own brokenness that without following what He asks, I'm complete toast.

It's so easy to judge others, isn't it? So often when we feel crummy about something inside of us, we find someone else's problems to judge. When we begin to sinfully judge others it is characterized by

---

[25] Chad Bird, *Night Driving: Notes from a Prodigal Soul* (Grand Rapids, MI: William B. Eerdmans Publishing Company, 2017), 64-65.

a feeling of superiority or resentment. Sinful judging often involves deciding what others' motives might be. It reveals the absence of a genuine love. We get together with others to discuss someone's problems when instead we should be praying for them.

A listener named Janet wrote me about this problem and said, "The sad truth is that when we judge someone's heart, perhaps cuz we're angry and hurt, there is often gossip involved. The one judged, becomes what I call 'boxed and labeled' by the accuser and the gossip-hearers." Exactly. God promises us vindication. Isaiah 54:17 reads, "No weapon turned against you will succeed." Wait on God and He we will silence those voices who stand to accuse you unjustly. God promises redemption and vindication. Maybe you won't see that vindication in the timeline you'd like *or* even here on Earth, but God will always keep His promise. Oh, that place when you know the only change that will happen is if you ask God to change you. I've been there, crying in the middle of a dark living room, asking God to forgive me, to change and mold and make me to be more like Him. I didn't ask that He change the other person, but instead I knew the only real solution was that my heart be changed.

I also said aloud, "I choose to forgive her." I didn't feel like giving forgiveness to someone who had really hurt my heart and whom I felt had accused me unjustly. I cried, "It's not fair," and God understood. After about two hours this amazing sensation came over me, like a bath of warm water being poured over my head, and all the hurt and bitterness I had toward this person disappeared. It seemed miraculous. I remember driving to the church to tell my pastor, who was well aware of the struggle, and I exclaimed with great joy, "I've forgiven her, and I have the feelings to go with it!" The question, when our hurt is so large and looming, is always "Can God be trusted?" He can because of His grace and understanding to meet you in the middle of your mess. Humble yourself by swallowing your own pain and pride and look at 1 Peter 5:6: "Humble yourselves under the mighty power of God, and at the right time He will lift you up in honor" (NLT).

I continually go back to the questions in Ken Sande's book *Peacemaker* to reveal the true condition of my heart.

I ask these questions:

What am I preoccupied with? What is the first thing on my mind in the morning and last thing on my mind at night?

How would I answer the question: "If only _____, then I would be happy, fulfilled, and secure"? What do I want to preserve or to avoid at all costs?

Where do I put my trust?

What do I fear?

When a certain desire is not met, do I feel frustration, anxiety, resentment, bitterness, anger, or depression?

Is there something I desire so much that I am willing to disappoint or hurt others in order to have it?

How often have I rehearsed a hurt all day long and gone to bed with it?[26]

I know that's a loaded box of crayons with colorful and honest questions, but if you want to do the real work of letting go and experience freedom in forgiveness, then it's a most helpful route to take. What is the morning wake-up routine you have when you're hurt and burdened with unforgiveness or bitterness? I like to start with "The Prayer with Everything in It" (The Lord's Prayer) along with Ephesians 3:16 (which I memorized from the Amplified Bible Classic Edition): "Grant me out of the rich treasury of Your glory to be strengthened and reinforced with mighty power by the Holy Spirit Himself indwelling in my innermost being and personality." I actually call this the "Sign-Me-Up" verse. Who doesn't want an indwelling of God's power

---

[26] Sande, *The Peacemaker*.

and a transformed personality? Surely, that's a morning wake-up booster stronger than any good coffee.

My airport parking- ot days are numbered, this Earth experience is tough, and it's not our home. But until I'm "home," I'm so grateful He meets me right where I'm at. When it's the season of any family celebrations and you want to cancel, instead ask for His grace. Ask the Holy Spirit to breathe on you (John 20:22). Say aloud, "Jesus I receive the peace you give despite the anxiety I feel" (John 14:27) and "Bless this person who's hurt me" (Luke 6:28). The Holy Spirit can control what's going on inside better than any bottle of wine (or a stiff drink), which is often used as a personal diffuser in family gatherings, but unfortunately it often ends up bringing more drama and escalating a family drama at many of these gatherings. Forgiveness is a process of letting go and letting God make amends. And no matter what season you or I might be in, the best and most freeing gift is to receive and give the grace and forgiveness like God does for us.

14
BEING REAL: 'I NEED A CIGARETTE'

*"The goal of this command is love, which comes from
a pure heart and a good conscience and a sincere faith."*
— **1 Timothy 1:5 (NIV)**

"I've just about had it. I need a cigarette. Do you want to join me?" I ask.

"I thought you didn't smoke?"

"Well, I don't 'really,' but I 'fake' smoke," I reply. "I love it because it lets me take a break from the situation where I can inhale and exhale, regain some focus."

FAKE SMOKING IS FUN, and it's a healthy habit. When I've been in a tense or complicated situation, I will pretend to take a puff out of a cigarette and then I'll exhale. Someone always notices and guffaws or giggles. I usually end up in a conversation about my habit of fake smoking and its benefits. I've had many people open up to me during a "fake" smoke break about their crazy-hard life dramas such as heartaches over their children, marriage, or even an addiction. I simply offer what we all need to hear: "You're not alone and there's hope." Then we inhale and exhale, and try to gain some perspective on the situation. Call me crazy but it works.

Many times, I'd find myself screaming on the inside, *It's not fair!* but as I've stopped screaming and started listening, I've discovered "fake" smoking is a way to connect and bring laughter, empathy, and compassion to someone in need. This is the basic core of *love*. "Love is kind." Everyone we meet is fighting a hard battle, and we all need to know that "this, too, will pass." We need to hear we are loved right where we're at and not where we, or someone else believes "we shouldbe." We all need to let go of 'the should' in our lives and have a cigarette.

I love people. A college friend used to say, "Who has more fun than people"? True. I try to find the fun in every situation I'm in, no matter how painful or hard it is. If it's not fun, I'm done. This means if I can't find the humor in a difficult circumstance it usually means "I'm done" as in, "I'm toast."

Okay, so I'm at T. J. Maxx in Fargo just chatting up a storm with a few people waiting in the checkout line with me. Kelly, who manages behind the counter, notices and says, "Well, you're fun!"

"Well, you're fun for recognizing fun," I reply.

We proceed to talk about things we love and have in common, like the theatre. We list our favorite musicals and, of course, we sing and dance. It doesn't look like we'll have time for a cigarette break but we do have time for a selfie.

"But wait," Kelly laments. "My hair is puffy and I'm chubby."

"Oh, Kelly, stop," I say. "Guys don't get much cuter, except for my husband."

Kelly then tells me about being from Wahpeton, North Dakota, and how his school was home of the Huskies.

"I always had to buy the husky jeans growing up," he tells me. "So as the saleslady was helping my mom and I find the right size, I'd say, 'I just have a little extra school spirit.'

I explode, as only I can, with love. I love people like Kelly. We exchange phone numbers and Kelly ends with, "We'll be besties for the resties."

Once I posted our selfie on Facebook, there arrived a splash of comments from people who recognized Kelly; they all raved about what a great student he was, a committed employee, his fun friendship, and his enthusiasm and his love for others. Clearly, Kelly was making a positive difference in the lives of others. A friend of mine on the East Coast wrote, "Keep doing you! More than ever, we need moments of simple kindness and human connection and letting our silly dilly side out of the bag!"

It's so true. Our lives leave a legacy. How we treat others, not our wealth or accomplishments, is the most enduring impact we can leave on Earth, and "smoking" has connected me to people and their stories in fun and endearing ways.

We need to be our real selves. People in pain need our compassion and time more than our solutions. Solutions have their place, but it's usually after we have crossed the bridge into understanding. The difficult paths we've traveled in pain, confusion, and loneliness are experiences that can be the bridge to let others know they're gonna be okay and they're not alone.

I look at my shopping experiences and outings as opportunities to meet everyday people and find ways to connect and have a conversation with them. Ministry isn't simply about going on a missions trip to Honduras or volunteering to serve meals at a homeless shelter; it's about ministering to the person God puts in front of you. I have a phone with a million selfies with people I've connected with at Target, gas stations, and clothing and grocery stores. I ask God each day, "Who is there that I can minister to?"

I think when I pray this way God does something in me so that I visibly change by the way I smile or make eye contact, and it's an attitude shift in thinking, *How can I serve?* rather than *How can I be served?* Most people receive it as a blessing to be asked questions of where they came from, what their dreams are and simply, "How's your day going?"

Of course, the person I end up connecting with ends up being a huge blessing to me, too. I've heard some of the most fascinating stories from someone helping me find the right size of blue jeans at The Gap. Staying at a variety of hotels throughout the US, I've learned from employees who've come from other countries such as Pakistan, Vietnam, Spain, Africa, and Mexico and heard fascinating testimonies about them personally and their culture. I usually get a phone number from them because, of course, I need to send them the selfie we took.

Some individuals, whom I still keep in touch with, are in locations that are more than two hundred miles from me, such as Fargo, North Dakota. I lived there for three summers directing a children's theatre company, and so Pro-Nail was my go-to for manicures. I knew all the guys and gals who were all Vietnamese, and they knew me. I learned so much about their lives and families. Of course, every time someone was having a baby, they received a gift from me. It's been years since I've lived there but I visit and get my nails done when I can. Lao and the gang all great me as an old friend. I learned so much about their culture and their faith. This is usual for me and not an isolated story in connecting with others. It happens frequently with the personality God's given me. You'd be surprised how many I still am in touch with and who receive care packages from me periodically (because of course I often get a mailing address or I mail to the place of business where I met them). I receive so much joy in giving and thinking about the surprise and fun of the quirky and creative packages I send.

Make it a habit to find time in your day to inhale and exhale and connect with another human being. Find the fun in the mundane of life and help someone else do it, too. Find the gifts you have that make you unique, and then find ways to use and share those gifts. Practice being thankful for what you have instead of whining about what you don't have; you'll be a much wiser and happier individual. Pause. Breathe. Relax. Being real and transparent is beautiful. Relationships are what life is all about.

This is not a dress rehearsal. This is the show.

Live in the now. The habit of being real, being relaxed with who you are and what you have with the occasional needed cigarette break will change your life.

Excuse me; I need a smoke.

15
EARTH IS THE BUS STOP: HEAVEN IS HOME, WELCOMING ALL

> *"For this world is not our permanent home;*
> *We are looking forward to a home yet to come."*
> — **Hebrews 13:14 (NLT)**

"When do you think you'll get here," read the text from Jonell, my sister-in-law. I carefully watched the road curving before me on the last stretch to my family home. She texted again: "Continuing texting, put on some makeup and drive like hell."

Exactly. I smiled and slowed down. Give me rules and I'm likely to do the opposite.

I know, right? You get it. Well, not all of you do because some are helping to rein in some of us who have rebellious attitudes and want to do everything but follow rules. Rules have their place, but rules without relationship lead to rebellion.

I follow God because I know He loves me right where I'm at. This Earth experience is rough, but it's not our final destination. Earth is the bus stop. Heaven is our home.

Knowing Christ in a relationship means we understand there is a God who loves us no matter what or who we are. He may be heartbroken over some of our choices, but nothing we do or don't do will cause Him to stop loving us.

God became flesh in Jesus for one reason—to restore a broken relationship. We were always created to have a relationship with our Creator. Our sin severed that relationship because God is not only love, He is also holy. His holiness and justness will not allow sin to exist in His presence. His holiness destroys it and anyone it is attached to. That is why God prepared another pathway. *He* would pay the cost for our sin so our sin no longer blocked a relationship with Him. "The wages of sin is death, but the gift of God is eternal life through Jesus Christ our Lord." Romans 6:23 tells us that Jesus paid the price of our rebellion: "He bore our sins in His own body, on the Tree" (1 Peter 2:24-NIV). Really, people! He was fully God and fully man, experiencing everything we've ever had to go through, but He gives us this ultimate gift of restoration. Our sin separates us from Him. His blood pays the ransom demanded for our sin if we accept it. No more separation from God. Jesus proved He is *the* Way by coming back to life and appearing before many witnesses (1 Corinthians 15:1–11).

He come back to life so we may choose life, too . . . Freedom, Baby. I may drive like hell, but I'm taking the highway to heaven.

There's the hope of heaven in my heart where real freedom and living begins. We don't become angels and sit on clouds playing harps. That would be hell.

Christianity is the only religion where God loves us even with all our junk and mistakes. He loves the liars, cheaters, addicted, and immoral. He loves you and me (Romans 8:1–2). But because God is holy, He must punish sin. Yet because God is loving, He didn't want to punish us. On the cross He satisfied both the holiness and the lovingness of God. He offered a gift that we shouldn't refuse. Mark Twain had it right: "Heaven goes by favor. If it went by merit, you would stay out and your dog would go in." That doesn't mean we can ignore what God asks. He gives us the Ten Commandments, not the ten suggestions.

Jesus says, "Come to Me, all of you who are weary and carry heavy burdens, and I will give you rest" (Matthew 11:28, NLT). Just as I was thinking on this, one of my best friends from junior high called. I hadn't spoken to her in years, but we picked up where we left off, talking and laughing like we just spoke yesterday.

Nora is the only one who calls me Doobie and the one who can sing perfect harmony with me on "Going to the Chapel." I started talking to her about love and other stuff, and we got to the part of the conversation where I asked her if she was in a relationship. "No, I'm single again," she said. It was another "Relation-s@#$," she said.

"What kind of name or title do you prefer for being homosexual?" I asked.

She said, "Nora," and we both laughed. Then she said, "I just might say, 'I play for the other team,' or 'I'm Lesbianese.'"

I love Nora. I do. I called her again the next day, and we couldn't stop talking and laughing. It's refreshing to hear someone in their early fifties, like me, talk about love, life, freedom, and being *real*.

Nora and I don't have to believe in the same things, but we believe in each other and we really do love one another. Right before Jesus went back to heaven, He said, "I give you a new commandment. Love each other. Just as I have loved you, you should love each other" (John 13:34).

As I sat on the floor (and focused), while in Target, talking to her on my cell phone, I said, "Nora, you're not going to change something in your life because I say you should and I won't either." Nora and I can both be free and authentic with one another. I want, and you want, we all want to know real love and real freedom, which comes from having a relationship of real love and not religion. My mantra is "Be ye fishers of men. You catch 'em, He'll clean 'em." You catch people with love and accepting them right where they're at and let God take them after that. I am not their judge. I am a fellow traveler.

Love God, love others, and let God do what He does best—

meeting everyone in love no matter who they are or what they choose. Real love never fails. Christians without love are just annoying, a clanging gong or symbol.

Nora said to me, "I know there is a God because when I was at the very bottom, He was there to lift me up." Not far away there's someone who is afraid and needs our encouragement and our time. They need to hear they're loveable. While they might not see the light at the end of the tunnel, we can tell them a time when we're at the bottom and yet the light did eventually shine through. We can tell them how to crawl out of the pit because we've been there and we know there's a way out. This old adage is so true: "People don't care how much you know until they know how much you care."

When we bring a smile to the face of someone in pain and hope to someone's heart, we have brought Christ to them. We define ourselves by our response to human need. The question is not how we feel about our neighbor, but what we have done for him or her. We reveal our heart in the way we listen, speak, and show kindness.

One of the most important principles of having a relationship with Jesus (Christianity) is knowing that it's not the rules of religion that change you or your performance in being a "good person." "Real change doesn't happen as a result of being told you need to change. Real change happens as a result of being loved." These are words from Tullian Tchividjian, author and pastor, who knows the story of the prodigal son because he is one. And so are the rest of us. When we follow the desires of the flesh, we think we can be kings and queens of our own lives. Following the flesh can be thrilling, but there is always a payback. An illicit affair can be thrilling and the devil will help you do it, but he always exacts his payback. And if he can, he will try to keep you down with guilt or shame and of course, the consequences. Not because he wants you to learn. He just wants you to believe "It's too late" or "God has given up on you."

We fail and we fall, but by God's grace we get back up again because Jesus did not come to be our condemner. He came to be our Redeemer. "For there is therefore now no condemnation to them which are in Christ Jesus, who walk not after the flesh, but after the Spirit" (Romans 8:1). I have fallen, too, (many times), and this gives me a much softer understanding and compassion toward others who are falling or falling, too.

We all want to know who we really are and some of our desires are so strong that we think they must be from God. "Who am I?" you ask. "Where do I find my identity?" God tells you. As a theatre person, I have a variety of friends who identity as homosexual or transgender, and they are some of the most fun, compassionate, and talented people I know. God loves us all and as I've heard Tim Keller say, "Homosexuality doesn't send you to hell any more than heterosexuality sends you to heaven." Sin separates you from God. God will reveal your sin when you ask Him to, and He'll provide forgiveness and strength to keep on keeping on. He knows you. He created you and He can tell you if you're going the wrong direction. When you refuse to believe who God is and who you are in Him, it becomes easier to push Him out so you can be more comfortable with your sin. My advice is to pray for the person to surrender to God and not try to "be God" in their lives.

Below are the stories of two different men who identify as Christian, but each reached a different conclusion about his struggle with homosexual desires. It's so important to listen to one another's hearts, to love and not judge. I've heard stories or testimonies like the ones below and it's helpful to understand different journeys, so I share two men's stories with you.

David, from Australia, left his role as a gay activist and part of his story is what you read below, from an article entitled "A Gay-Rights Activist Leaves His Life Old Life Behind":

> I decided that after dating so many people, I would stay single for a year, and after my best friend's boyfriend fell in love with me and I reciprocated, I felt dead inside. I felt like David in his situation with

Bathsheba—the fatal repercussion being the death of a close friendship. I had become the clichéd secular hypocrite. My broken morality and evil heart trumped my "rational" ethics every time. At Christmastime, I had a debate with my Christian uncle. "There is no absolute truth!" I proclaimed over the family Christmas table. "To say there is no absolute truth is an absolute truth," my uncle retorted softly. "The truth is a person I know, not a static concept in my head." My postmodern worldview was disarmed. I stormed out.

Three months later, I found myself in the Dolphin Hotel in Surry Hills, and had spotted a young filmmaker from my university who was a finalist in Tropfest Short Film Festival. I wanted her for an interview in the student magazine—definitely the best local story we would have all year. As she revealed her faith to me, I pushed back against her talk about God until she asked me one piercing question. *"Have you experienced the love of God?"* I didn't know you could experience God. I didn't know about the Holy Spirit. She offered me prayer and suddenly I just said yes. As she prayed fervently, I felt an incredible sensation on the top of my head, a soft tingling that intensified. It felt as if someone was pouring a vial of oil over my head. The powerful sensation ran all over my body and then surged in power. In retrospect, I believe God was anointing me like Jesus in Isaiah 61 and baptizing me in his Holy Spirit. At this stage I started to weep and felt a voice say to me "Do you want me?" three times. This came as exactly the question I needed to hear at this time—a mutual desire. The third time I said yes. I still didn't know which god this was. Then, like a breath entering me, I could feel this new life in my soul. I was born again. I heard the Father's voice ask me: "Will you accept My son Jesus as your Lord and Savior?" I said yes. God poured out His love in my heart and I was overcome with arbitrary tears. This time I felt his power like a heat in my body. I had become a Christian.

When people ask me whether homosexuality is a sin, I point them to a greater sin—refusing to share or receive the love of God. Like that girl in the pub, I am praying for more Christians to step out in this love and refrain from hanging the morality of law over people's heads. Gay rights activist or not, when agape love wins the war, we find the permission to repent from death and live—the very good news of Jesus Christ. Nothing is more transcendent or ultimate than the God who is agape love and for whom it is worth giving everything up.[27]

The other story I share is from a man who shares how he's at peace with his homosexuality. The organization "Room For All" is where this man shares his heart. "Letter from a Gay Christian":

> I am a Christian. I was raised in a Christian home; my father was a pastor. I was taught to love the Lord and to serve Him. This I have done all my life. My relationship with God has never been stronger, and I am more thankful than ever for the redemption that I have through Jesus Christ and His work of redemption on my behalf on the cross. I know what repentance is, and I know what forgiveness is. I am also a homosexual. My journey has been difficult. I have tried time and time again to deny my own acceptance of my sexual orientation. Many nights have ended with tear-stained pillows as I have pleaded with God to release me from the pain I have experienced through this. God has remained faithful through all of it and continues to let me know each and every day how He loves me.
>
> I also believe that it is God's plan for all of us to know love and be loved. I know that this is His plan for me as well. To believe otherwise would be for me to understand that God is vengeful and has played a very cruel trick on me. Homosexuality is not a choice. It is an orientation. It is no different than eye color, or being right-handed or left-handed. My sexuality is a gift from God, and I believe that He intends for me to rejoice in that by knowing the love of another in a lifetime, monogamous relationship.
>
> The Bible needs to be read in the context in which it was written. For us to read it literally makes a mockery of Christianity, as the

---

[27] David Bennett, "A Gay-Rights Activist Leaves His Old Life Behind," October 9, 2015, [Web log post], https://www.eternitynews.com.au/good-news/a-gay-rights-activist-leaves-his-old-life-behind/, viewed May 14, 2021.

Bible certainly says things that modern-day Christians no longer adhere to.

We cannot use the Bible as a weapon to propagate our own political or social views. And while we accept the Bible as God's written word for us, we also accept Jesus as God's incarnate Word for us. Jesus never said anything about homosexuality. He did however admonish us to love one another. Adherence to that admonition is absent in your attitude toward the LGBT community. We have to be listening for yet another word from God being spoken to us from the Holy Spirit. The Holy Spirit may be telling us something new in this. God is still speaking. The church and Christians are seen as being judgmental and intolerant of others. This is not the message Jesus came to bring. His message of love, forgiveness, acceptance, and grace is what we should be demonstrating to the world. As I stated earlier, my journey has been difficult. I am just trying to do my best with the gifts God has given me. I don't need my fellow Christians tripping me up by condemning me and marginalizing me for something that is natural—for me.

Your Brother in Christ.[28]

Rev. Jacob Smith is the Rector of Calvary-St. George's in New York City, a man of God, a man of the Word and a man under whom our son Marco interned for one entire summer as an upcoming pastor himself. I've learned much from Rev. Jacob on the grace of God. He was interviewed by the podcast duo of "Crackers and Grape Juice," Episode 288, and said this on this subject: "The most powerful thing about "the church" (Christians) is it should be the one place, as an embassy of a new creation, where we leave our identity politics right at the door and we, as pastors, give out the goods of the forgiveness

---

[28] Identity not given other than "Brother in Christ," " Letter from a Gay Christian," August 3, 2012, Web log post, https://roomforall.com/dt_testimonials/letter-from-a-gay-christian/, viewed May 14, 2021.

of sins to absolutely everyone. We have this great pastoral insight from Paul in Galatians 3:28, 'There is neither Jew nor Gentile, neither slave nor free, nor is there male and female, for you are all one in Christ Jesus.'" Reverend Jacob continues, "The one big gift the church has to offer is simply this: 'Your sins are forgiven.'" *Bam!* He nailed it or rather Jesus did (no pun intended). Dr. Billy Graham, in an interview with Hugh Downs on ABC's *20/20* program is 1997, gave this reply when Downs asked Mr. Graham the question, "If you had a homosexual child, would you love him?" Graham's immediate reply: "Why, I would love that one even more."

The subject of our sexuality is a strong discussion no matter what background or perspective you come from, and whether you claim Christianity or not. How you grew up as a child, and what you experienced as a child, all play into who you are now. I hesitated to even write about this topic, but so many I love are homosexual, and I thought it would be helpful to hear two heartfelt testimonies. We all need to be heard. When I asked, "God, who do You say I am?" And firmly He told me, "You are My child whom I dearly love and I will never fail you." I believe we should focus less on telling others how they should live and more on who God says they are. Listen to people; hear their hearts and stories. We are all sinners, all in need of a Savior.

All the stories I share in this book are about real people with real struggles whom I know or read about and listen to. The Apostle Paul reminds us in 1 Timothy 1:15: "Here is a trustworthy saying that deserves full acceptance: Christ Jesus came into the world to save sinners—of whom I am the worst." I think about that Scripture all the time. I picture myself waving my hand wildly in the air shouting, "*I am the worst* of all sinners!"

No matter where (or when) you fail or fall, there is a God who never fails in fully knowing you and fully loving you. Love and truth *never* fail. You don't have to agree with me or like the stories and testimonies I share. You don't have to like what you read in the Bible, either. However, I do believe when you truly want to know of God's love and grace, you also want to truly know what He has to say about your life, your choices, and who He says you are. Choose to trust Him over your self-ruling and self-righteousness. God loves you. No one will ever love you more; when you really believe this, you walk in love and are able to give grace to others—to all the Noras, the Debbies, the Ricks, the Susans, the Bills, and the Bob People who struggle with mistakes, have dreams, losses, and an ache in their hearts for complete peace. Yep, God loves you and when we love ourselves, then we can follow the commandment to "love our neighbors as ourselves" better too. (Mark 12:31). That puts you right in sync with the wise words from Dr. Seuss, "Today you are You, that is truer than true. There is no one alive who is Youer than You." This Earth experience is short compared to eternity. It is the bus stop. Heaven is our eternal home, welcoming all of us.

16
HOPE IN THE WILDERNESS OF ANXIETY

"In my distress [when seemingly closed in] I called upon the Lord and cried to my God; He heard my voice out of His temple (heavenly dwelling place), and my cry came before Him, into His [very] ears."
— **Psalm 18:6 (AMPC)**

EVERY YEAR OUR FAMILY would travel to Minneapolis to visit dear friends. They have five children and, along with our four boys, we had a great time going to the zoo, laughing, talking, swimming, eating out . . . the list goes on.

But in 2009 I was wandering in the wilderness, wondering if I was going to make it out of the pit I was in. I was having anxiety attacks and, out of the blue, fear would grip my body to the point where I wanted to flee, feeling like a caged bird with nowhere to go (except maybe to the toilet to throw up). It's been years since I was in that season, but to this day I will never forget the horridness of it all but do appreciate how such hope came out of it. I recall the hope of that time because I still have anxiety attacks; sometimes, I think the feelings will kill me. Of course, it's not true. Our feelings can't kill us, but they can sure wreak havoc on our emotional, physical, and spiritual self. "Yet this I call to mind and therefore I have hope: Because of the

Lord's great love we are not consumed, for His compassions never fail" (Lamentations 3:21–22, NIV). Yet, in those times of severe anxiety I sometimes have thought, *If God is so compassionate and understanding, why doesn't He just take away my anxiety?*

This Earth is not our home. In it there will always be sickness, diseases, horrors, and tragedies. God may provide healing here on Earth and it might be that it's not seen until we're home in Heaven, but if not for God's compassion to carry us through a trial, a lot of us wouldn't make it. Sometimes, in moments of intense pain, all we can think about is the quickest exit out to numb the pain or, in severe cases, some choose to exit out of life. *But God* is faithful and He will always provide a way out to stand up under the trial even though what we want and pray for is immediate removal of the pain. "No test or temptation that comes your way is beyond the course of what others have had to face. All you need to remember is that God will never let you down; He'll never let you be pushed past your limit; He'll always be there to help you come through it" (Corinthians 10:13, MSG).

So, the morning of zoo day found me roaming the hotel hallway, nauseated and panicked, hoping someone would answer my cell phone calls for help.

I needed my good mentor friends to speak truth, so the running obsessive, crazy tape in my mind would stop telling me that I had a terminal illness, that I was going crazy, and that I would never be well again. I needed hope to carry on. But none of my friends was available, so I walked into the hotel's public restroom, locked the door, opened my cell phone, held it to my ear, and began talking to the One who I knew was available—Jesus.

First, I shared my thoughts out loud, telling Him how afraid I was.

"Is my constant nausea due to stomach cancer? Why am I losing weight? Why is my parents' divorce so hard? Oh, God, it's all crashing in on me! I'm a mess! Take it all away!"

And then I put my head between my knees and moaned. But as

I became still and stopped moaning, I heard Him speak the verse I had memorized the week before, Micah 7:7.

I repeated it out loud and it was hope to hold onto:. "But as for me, I will look to the Lord and confident in Him I will keep watch; I will wait with hope and expectancy for the God of my salvation; my God will hear me." I said aloud again what I heard God speaking to me in my weakness and frailty, "Debbie, I am right here. I see you. I know you. Wait. You are feeling afraid but know and be confident that I am keeping watch and you will come through. Wait in hope and expectancy. I see you. I hear you. When you are weak, my strength is perfected." I didn't feel different but I knew differently. I knew there was hope. I knew God hadn't abandoned me, and I could come out of the bathroom.

It's important to always remember that God is not surprised by what we are experiencing; our trials first have to pass through Him before they come to us. We need to live in the present, not the "what-ifs" of tomorrow. Of course, that can be extremely difficult because living in the present is sometimes living in the pit. But if we're there, God is also there; present, faithful, strong, loving, true, and resurrected.

In a weakened emotional state, it's hard to hear the truth and think clearly. So first I think, *I'm gonna choose, in my troubles, to focus on the possibilities and not on my problems.* Then I say aloud, "God, I feel so afraid. I feel like I can't make it. Help."

I know this might sound a little corny, but I actually say, "God I choose your peace rather than the fear I feel."

God tells us in John 14:27 that He gives peace, so I've stopped asking for it and now just say, "I will take some. Amen."

It's weird, but I do receive peace. I don't necessarily feel different, but I know differently. I know that my feelings won't last forever. I know God is bigger than my feelings. I say aloud what I hear God speak because He does answer.

I hear God speak from what I've read and memorized from the

Bible. I still hear Zephaniah 3:17: "Debbie, I am a living God, a mighty Savior. I take delight in you with gladness. And with My love I will calm all your fears."

Over and over I've often asked, "Why? Why is life so difficult?" But God says, "I won't always give you the answers to all your 'whys,' but I am the Way, and I will show you the way to walk and give you the strength to face difficult people and difficult places. And one thing you can be confident of is that I will never leave or forsake you."

I realize, too, that I might not know the mind of God, but I can know His heart by the promises He keeps. Tullian Tchividjian wrote a brilliant piece entitled, "'Get Better' Doesn't Work." The excerpt I share below is really encouraging, so look it up on his website and read it in its entirety:[29]

> People who are hurting would, overwhelmingly, rather not be hurting. If they could simply choose to be happy, they would. If the depressed could simply choose not to be depressed, they would. If those with panic disorders could simply choose to be relaxed, they would. That they can't simply "snap out of it" implies a deeper problem.
>
> We need an intervention, and I don't just mean in a "We're all here because we care about you" sense. We need someone to come into our pain, into our depression, and into our panic. Christianity, alone amongst the world's religions, philosophies, and systems of thought, posits a God who doesn't wait (or ask) for the hurt to heal, for the depressed to cheer up, or for the panicked to chill out. Our God crosses the chasm to us, rather than waiting for us to build a bridge out of our pain and into his glory.
>
> Everyone knows that telling someone in a bad mood to cheer up is a losing proposition . . . but we can't stop ourselves. We don't know any other way to be. It doesn't stop us from offering platitudes to our friends or "Five Steps to a Better Blank" sermon

---

[29] https://www.tullian.net/articles/get-better-doesnt-work, viewed January 14, 2022.

series to our congregations. We figure that if people just have the right road map, they can get to a better place, despite the fact that that has never worked in our own lives!

Painful and uncomfortable as it may be at first, being upfront about our problems is the better route. Churches, especially, ought to be places where brutal honesty is possible. Too often, though, they are places where the truth is hidden: we want people to think that we're on the spiritual path to glory, not hurting, depressed, angry, and panicked.

God's first word—the Law—comes into our lives, not to give us the road map out of our struggles, but to magnify them to the point where they become impossible to handle on our own. Casual Friday and a company paintball trip only mask the issues; they don't solve them. In fact, as Burkeman argues, they only serve to make us feel worse. We need God's second word—the Gospel, the Good News about Jesus Christ—to break through the impossibility of our human problem. We don't need to be encouraged to get out of our depression, we need to be given joy. We don't need to be cajoled out of our anxieties; we need to be given peace.

The Good News of the Gospel is that, in Christ, we have been.[30]

It's the absolute Truth which Tullian shares, and I'm so thankful for what he's doing in ministry and the transparency of who he is and where he's been. He's someone who was busted and broken but now lives in restoration and redemption.

Ministry is hard. I know God made me the way He did with my unique personality and passion to share the Living Word, God Himself, with others. If I thought it was about my having "it all together," I would have stopped talking long ago. When I first wandered into the wilderness of anxiety and depression, I thought I had ruined God's plan for me in sharing the Gospel as a Speaker Girl. I mean, I

---

[30] Tullian Tchividjian, "'Get Better'" Doesn't Work," Web log post, January 15, 2021, https://www.tullian.net/articles/get-better-doesnt-work, viewed January 14, 2022.

was having trouble functioning as a human with simply eating and sleeping, and here I was a wife and mom of four sons, ages fifteen, twelve, ten, and eight years.

Now, here we were a family going on a weekend getaway of three hundred miles to Minneapolis to spend time with our dear friends, and I didn't know if I would be able to leave the bathroom stall when we stopped to get gas an hour into our trip. I remember going into the bathroom stall and having an anxiety attack that was intense enough that I thought I might not make it out. I leaned against the cold tile wall and cried out to God, whispering Psalm 91:1 (later calling it my 911 verse). "God, I am going to the Secret Place of where You are, the Creator of me and the whole universe. I am protected by You. Oh Lord, I need stability to walk out of this bathroom and get back in the van. I know it's not a magic incantation and You're not a Genie in a Bible but You say in Psalm 91:1, 'He (She) who dwells in the secret place of the Most High Shall *remain stable* and fixed under The shadow of the Almighty Whose power no foe can withstand.' (AMPC). I took a deep breath and exhaled slowly. I walked back into the van and rode the rest of the trip like a Zombie Mom. But, I was stable enough through God's Word and He enabled my legs to work.

The most frequently asked question, after I speak at a conference or retreat, is "How do you know so many Scriptures; how do you memorize it all?"

I suppose being a theatre major and having had to memorize numerous lines for plays has helped. But I'm intentional, too. I have to take the time and work at it. I write out a verse and put each sentence of a verse on a different recipe card. I think of it as cake layers, like a wedding cake. I *really* think on the one sentence and what it means and how to apply it to life and I memorize it. I don't move on to the next card (or layer) until I really have the one sentence memorized and it's in my heart and head. I might put the card on the refrigerator or bathroom mirror, the vehicle dashboard, or wherever I can see it, learn it and let it sink in. Eventually all the layers are added and I have the one notecard with the verse and I "get it." I apply and trust the Word God's given me because He *is* the Word and it is Him speaking by His Holy Spirit. He then helps me to recall Scripture as needed. It's the sweetest, most delicious thing I can put inside my body for sustenance and stability.

So, it's been since 1995 that I've been consistently reading the Bible, writing down words of encouragement in a little spiral notebook, which came to be known as my "manna" book. God gave the Israelites manna as they journeyed toward the Promised Land, giving them precisely what they needed each day, and if they stored more than they needed, it was stinky and maggot-infested the next day.

I learned that the same is true for me. I can't harvest and store all of God's Word I need on Sunday mornings at church, or even at a really good Bible study on Thursday nights. I need to feed on the truth of God and His promises every day.

Without Him life stinks, and with Him it still stinks but it stinks less. The Earth experience is hard and it's not our home, it's not our final destination. Jesus died on the cross for our sins, our troubles, our weaknesses.

Jesus didn't die on the cross so I could have a religion, but He died and rose again so I could have a real and personal relationship with Him. You cannot have a relationship with someone who is still dead.

There are so many life challenges with marriage, parenting, family relationships, the basement flooding, health problems, financial concerns, busyness, and the burden of "self" that gets in the way. It helps to know God who is alive and well, and we can talk to Him at any time.

Being in the pit sucks. Yet, those dark months of anxiety and depression, which lasted eight months and required me going on meds, are a time I can now say I'm glad I was allowed to walk through. I know someone needs to hear this: You're not a failure in your faith because you went on meds.

Derek Sweatman is a church pastor at Atlanta Christian Church and writes a blog as a resource site for pastors that I find extremely relatable and helpful. In a piece titled, "The Anxiety and Depression Cocktail," he gives some good advice to mull over:

> In 1 Timothy 4:12, Paul writes: "Let no one look down on you for your youth but set an example for believers in speech, in conduct, in love, in faith, in purity." The word for *example* here is *typos* (τύπος), a word that describes the aftermath of opposition. It means the "mark" of a hit or cut. Ministry will always leave a mark. It's not possible to go through this unscathed. Scars, and the stories behind them, are to be expected. Even embraced. But it seems that we have the choice in the kind of mark ministry leaves on us. Look at that list again: the mark of speech, of conduct, of love, of faith, of purity. (And can we just agree on the genius of the sequence of this list? Isn't it always the case that when we're under a lot of negative pressure that the first thing to go is our speech? Which can open the door to destructive conduct. Which can erode our love. Which can bring conflict into our faith. Which can erase our calling to be set apart.)
>
> We have the choice of the kind of mark ministry will leave on us.
>
> Ministry is a sobering vocation and must be embraced as such. Its leader is to stand on his own two feet, tall in the midst of whatever comes his way, unwilling to bury and hide the troubles underneath escapist behaviors. Ministry must be allowed to hit and to hit hard. The velocity of suffering and pain and anger and doubt and confusion and insecurity is enough to leave one in the valley of the shadow of death, stunned and uncertain. But do not run.
>
> Stand still.
>
> Encircled.
>
> Afraid.
>
> Desperate.

Inadequate.

It is here reliance emerges. The Lord again becomes the guide, the way through, and the way out. Resurrection begins with death, not life.[31]

Death to self, to thinking my strong will with my own ability to simply "pull up my bootstraps" is not the solution. Only Jesus is the way to get to the other side. As my friend Josh Retterer so succinctly put it in a tweet he shared, "Just because Jesus is in the boat with you doesn't mean there won't be occasional throwing up over the side."

I understand what being in the boat is like when there's a storm of hurricane proportions going on inside of me. I know the anxiety of nausea and throwing up on the side of the road or in the toilet. I understand others in a way I could not without first walking that road. I understand grace on a whole new level. I need it so desperately, how can I afford not to give it as well?

As I left the hotel bathroom that spring day in 2009, I didn't have a happy-go-lucky-it's-going-to-be-a-great-day-at-the-zoo kind of day, but I did have hope. I was able to leave the hotel and take the next step to the family van.

As I walked to the parking lot, I will *always* remember the end of my phone call with God saying aloud the words from Micah 7:8: "Rejoice not against me, O my enemy! When I fall, I shall arise; when I sit in darkness, the Lord shall be a light to me."

And that truth, along with the sunny day walking outside at the Minnesota Zoo, was all the faith I needed.

Fortunately, faith isn't a feeling. Faith does not always keep me from having trouble; it most often carries me through trouble. If I never had trouble, I would never need faith. I also needed faith to trust Him

---

[31] Derek Sweatman, "Unforeseen Lessons, Part 2: The Anxiety and Depression Cocktail," April 14, 2021, Atlanta Christian Church, https://forthepastor.org/2021/04/14/unforeseen-lessons-part-2-the-anxiety-and-depression-cocktail/, viewed May 26, 2021.

to work through medication which (as I said) I did go on for stability. My pride almost prevented me because, while I thought it was okay for others to go on meds for mental issues, I wanted to say, "Yep, my stellar faith pulled me through." But we limit God when we think there's only one way; He's gonna work in our lives or we try to direct Him in how He should work in our lives. *But He's God. I'm not.* He knows best how we work and how to help us "keep on keeping on."

It's also very crucial that you let someone know the pain you're experiencing. Transparency is crucial, and if you're able to find someone who's older and has traveled the road of anxiety and depression that you might be on is extremely helpful. My Aunt Ginger was that support person for me. She continues to help me to be honest and aware of triggers and circumstances where I need to "come clean" and be honest on how I'm coping with my pain. She was especially helpful when the first medication didn't work *at all* (Lexapro for me did all the crazy things the paper insert from the pharmacy warns about) but sure enough the medication Auntie Ginger recommends (Paxil) was the one that worked for me.

God also says, "Don't worry about tomorrow, for each day has enough trouble of its own!" And to that I say, "Amen!" Moment by moment is how you're going to have to go through a lot of days even without the anxiety/depression medication cocktail.

There is always hope no matter how horrid your feelings or circumstances might be. "It" (whatever the "it" is) will get better. You are not alone *and* God knows every hair on top of your head and every hurt stored up and every dread. He has promises to make all things new. I promise you, there's hope, but more importantly Jesus makes that promise. He makes a way.

"See, I am doing a new thing! Now it springs up; do you not perceive it? I am making a way in the wilderness and streams in the wasteland" (Isaiah 43:19 NIV).

17
DO YOU KNOW WHERE YOU'RE GOING?

"The Lord is not slow in keeping His promise, as some understand slowness. Instead, He is patient with you, not wanting anyone to perish, but everyone to come to repentance."
— **2 Peter 3:9 (NIV)**

"THIS OLD MAN IS GOING TO HEAVEN SOON." So said my dear friend Willis, who had been sharing this news with others for the last few years of his life.

Willis was ninety-eight years old when he and I had our last good long talk. He lived alone in a one-bedroom apartment in California, and he was retired—but not really. Every day he got up and went about his day with purpose. Each day he had a plan of things he wanted to accomplish and people he hoped to connect with. He knew Proverbs 16:9: "We can make our plans, but the Lord determines our steps."

Our phone conversation reminded me again how God gives each of us enough grace for one day at a time. He gives us opportunities to see Him work in us and touch the lives of others so that we might fulfill God's purpose—to make Him real to everyone we meet. We all can discover what Willis knows; each day our purpose is right in front of us by knowing the answer to one question.

It is through my Uncle Dewey that I came to know Willis. Uncle Dewey and Willis met at North Central Bible College in Minneapolis and it was recently at my Uncle Dewey's funeral that I heard one of the questions that Willis lives by: "Are you ready to go to heaven?" Uncle Dewey was ready, at the young age of seven, to go to heaven. He understood that nothing he could do would ever be good enough for him to earn "rights" to heaven, but by accepting what Jesus had done for him, he had the hope of eternity and at age 93 Uncle Dewey went "home" to be with Jesus.

When you grow up with a religious background, it's hard to really grasp what this means because religion is so works-oriented. But by the right actions of a Holy God in Christ, He paid the penalty of death for our sins and then He came back to life and lives so we might live. Leonard Ravenhill was an English Christian evangelist and author who sums up precisely why God came down to earth in the image of man "Jesus did not come into the world to make bad men good. He came into the world to make dead men live."[32]

I did not grow up in a religious home, nor was I given the "Good Christian Girl's List" of "dos and don'ts." I was taught the grace of God, a God who loved me so much He took my place, and my only "job" was to receive what He offered. My Aunt Ginger delivered His Good News when I was seven and continues this day to mentor and encourage me in God's graciousness. It was also different churches I attended and individuals I met that helped me see clearly, too, that God doesn't love me because I am good. He loves me because He is good. Whew.

We all have this offer, this hope available. It's a good place—this heaven place—because it's where real life perfectly begins with no more tears and pain. I'm not sure exactly what we do in heaven, but I do know we continue on as purposeful beings where there will be eating, laughing, and dancing.

---

[32] Leonard Ravenhill quote, https://www.azquotes.com/quote/668234, viewed February 5, 2022.

Yet while here on Earth we can live well. Uncle Dewey did a whole lot of living as a husband, father, and friend, and he served for twenty-five years as president of Northwest University in Kirkland, Washington, as well as holding many notable positions, traveling the globe, and spreading the gospel of grace.

Uncle Dewey's favorite pastime was fishing in Alaska. It's where he developed a long-term friendship with an ol' fishing guide who eventually prayed with Dewey to receive Jesus into this life. After years of seeing Dewey live out his relationship with Christ rather than preaching religion, the fishing guide wanted to catch what Dewey had caught. It's like one of my favorite mantras I shared earlier: "Be ye fishers of men. You catch 'em, He'll clean 'em." You catch people with love and accepting them right where they're at and let God take them after that. We are most changed by having relationships with others (namely Christ) and not by receiving a bunch of information and rules but by receiving love and understanding.

We are all given gifts to "catch" others with God's love. Ministry is simply ministering to whom God puts in front of you each day whether it's a clerk in the supermarket, a parent, pastor, teacher, mill worker, doctor, or a prisoner as the Apostle Paul was in Rome. God's still working on us, and we're still working on sharing His love unconditionally and freely just as we are.

I love the story in chapter nine of the Gospel of John. Jesus meets a man who's been blind since birth. I don't know how brief their encounter was, but in that time Jesus bent down, took some mud, and rubbed the man's eyes with it, and when he opened them, this man could see. Immediately the Pharisees—the religious leaders—questioned the man and wanted him to proclaim Jesus a sinner. . . . *What?* But the blind man's response is brilliant in John 9:25: "Whether He is a sinner or not, I don't know. One thing I do know, I was blind but now I see!" He didn't know how or why he had been healed, but he knew a miracle had taken place and he wasn't afraid to tell the truth.

We don't have to have all the answers in order to share Christ with others. What's important is that we tell people the truth of how God's love and forgiveness has changed our lives.

I have spoken at a woman's shelter on getting a DUI and about the pain of shooting spears on my spine after my scoliosis back surgery and then sleeping on the bathroom floor with nausea and dry heaving little sips of water I was trying to keep down. I share how God met me on the bathroom floor and gave me His hope and peace as I started to panic because in that moment, I thought I might never get better. Yet, God heard my cry, and His presence filled the room in such a way I knew I'd get off the bathroom floor even though I felt wretched. The girls at the shelter were silent as I shared my testimony. Prior to that, I was trying to give a Bible lesson with a verse (a verse that had helped me), but they were restless and not paying attention. Our shared experiences and humanity connect us all. The best way to minister is to help others see God as real and His deep compassion for us during our bathroom floor miseries.

After many years serving in revival ministry in small towns and with everyday people in the Midwest, as pastors and professors, both Willis and Dewey found themselves on the West Coast, and Willis eventually ended his latter career asnd became a Cadillac salesman in Beverly Hills. He sold cars to Doris Day, Bing Crosby, and even Elvis. But I digress. When Willis and I spoke on the phone, I needed reminding on why I was "still here." On that particular day, when having our phone conversation, I was feeling sorry for myself. The calendar had flipped into February, but I felt I was stuck in one long month of January with International Falls weather being twenty-five below zero with a "real feel" of minus thirty-six. I couldn't fit into my favorite jeans; finances were tough, and I was angry with my husband Dan, and I was pretty sure I had a sinus infection. Blech.

Willis told me how and what he was doing, and that it had occurred to him that in the last five years he had shared the message of

God's grace and the hope of heaven more than any other time in his life. Because, one morning at age ninety-three, he asked God, "What can you do with an old man like me? What difference can I make?" And God answered.

That very afternoon in the grocery store, the checkout girl asked him how he was and, without missing a beat, Willis replied, "Well, this old man is going to heaven soon." What followed was a series of questions from Susan, the checkout girl, asking how he knew that was true. She told Willis how she had read the Bible many times, but wasn't sure if she was going. Fortunately, there wasn't a line at the checkout, so Willis had all the time in the world to answer her questions, and what followed was her reaching out to hold his hand and pray.

With tears running down her cheeks, she asked Jesus into her heart, and now has the hope and assurance Willis was talking about. She's ready to go to heaven, but when she's ready to leave this Earth, only God knows. Every day since Willis has been given countless opportunities to share God's love with others. Willis reminds us how our purpose is right in front of us.

"Well, I guess it wasn't enough just to want to see Uncle Henry and Auntie Em and it's that if I ever go looking for my heart's desire, I'll look no further than my own backyard because if it isn't there, I never really lost it to begin with," said Dorothy Gale, of Kansas.

That's right, Dorothy and Elton John share the same truth, in John's case via "Goodbye Yellow Brick Road." It's *all* in front of us. The lost and alone, the person in front of or behind us. Some days are harder than others, but there's always this efficient grace that comes one day at a time to help us avoid fatigue and burnout, weariness, and "mind crazies." We must learn to live one day at a time. That's why Jesus teaches us in Matthew 6:34 to meet each day's challenges as they come and not to borrow trouble from tomorrow. If we do that, then at the appointed time God's grace will be available to us in sufficient supply to help us face and overcome whatever might occur in our lives.

I've found that my purpose is to serve others with the love and grace God has served me. You start with those you have in front of you each day. When Mother Teresa was asked how she was able to meet the needs of so many, she replied, "I simply serve the person God sets before me each day." I suspect she was ready to go to heaven at a very young age, but she didn't leave Earth until age eighty-seven.

I've found that the part of you you're most afraid to share is the part others are waiting with bated breath to see so they can be vulnerable, too. It's a risk, but it's one worth taking, to fully love with our whole hearts. To be grateful for what's in front of us and to know that what we experience—the good, the bad, and the ugly—isn't wasted, but provides a way in which we can connect and make a difference in someone else's life.

But we must believe in this important truth: "You are enough in Christ." Because when we work from a place that says, "I know my identity in Christ," then we stop trying to be someone we're not, or someone whom others believe we should be. There is freedom that comes with knowing who we are and knowing who we're not, and the reward is that we begin to feel alive and begin to really live.

I am at this stage in my life that I know and recognize that so many circumstances and people are frustrating, so I try to find "the funny" in all of it to let off steam, and it's the way that I am more of my true self, too, just because I'm being me. When I would drop off brownies at my swimmer son's spaghetti feed and announce that I haven't brushed my teeth and my pajamas are on under my puffer jacket and wind pants, I get smiles and nods of "I get you" because there's this connection—there's honesty. Other times, at a parent/teen social event, I've just sat next to someone, looked them in the eye, and said, "I don't have the answer, but I know it's hard and I'm sorry. Let me sit with you. Talk if you want . . . or not."

It's a big life question: "Are you ready to go to heaven?" which you can know for certain. But while you're still here, you can live and be truly filled with hope and life. Once you have the vulnerability to live authentically and with Christ within you, then you have this desire and purpose to share what you know is true.

That's what Willis did every day when he walksed in the mall or went to the grocery store. He connected with those in front of him with his one statement: "This old man is going to heaven soon."

Maybe you're in a season like he was, when it seems like you're living every month like you're stuck in January and you want heaven to come sooner than later. It's okay. I get you. But I also get God and His love for you and me, and as long as I'm here I will be sharing as honestly as I can the truth that in this hard life there's no condemnation. You're enough because He's enough and you matter to more people than you could ever imagine. Share your stories honestly and sincerely and listen to those who need to be heard, too. *That's* how we change the world. We serve the one in front of us with hope and unconditional love.

NOTE: Willis passed away peacefully on March 27, 2020. He had a long and good life of 101 years.

18
PARENTING ISN'T FOR WIMPS

*"Train up a child in the way he should go;
even when he is old, he will not depart from it."*
— **Proverbs 22:6 (ESV)**

WE DIDN'T LET OUR OLDEST OF FOUR SONS watch *Power Rangers* when he was young, even though he desperately wanted to. And the reason was, I dunno, maybe the magic and power of the Rangers might confuse him with the power of Christ or something like that, or maybe they're bad role models? Yeah, well good for us, because in 2008, when our youngest son was six years old, all he could talk about was his love for the Red Power Ranger. We had caved. It was also the summer of 2008 when our third son, Joey, was eight and came home from "Explore the World" Day Camp very excited with exciting news: "Mom, there's this place with books you can get for free with really cool information and stories about the world *and* we even have one in our town! "Really, I said. "What's it called, Joe?" It's called the library."

"Good to know Joe. This place sounds really great."
I didn't get "Mom of the Year" in 2008.

The first two boys of the four not only had the most photos taken but also the most library visits. Joey arrived eighteen months after Peter and so, apparently, the knowledge of a large building with books you could borrow for free was never introduced to the younger two sons. Now I think of the access to all sorts of news, information, and "stories" via the phone they hold in their hands. The internet has been a godsend as well as one of the most harmful places for our children (and ourselves) to fall prey to. We start to wonder and compare. "Who does the world say we are? Are we good-looking, successful, and "doing it right," and how many "likes" is good enough?" Sadly, we compare ourselves to others in the world trying to find our identity.

Our Creator doesn't make mistakes and it's only because of sin and evil in this world that we're not perfectly perfect and life is not perfectly perfect as it will be one day in heaven. You are not a mistake even though you make mistakes. You're not a failure because you failed at something. Plus, keep this next truth continually rolling around in your head (which is the point of all the stories in this book): "God can redeem all things. Nothing is wasted with Him."

Zero judgment from me if you've used media on any device as a pacifier for your children to be occupied and calmed down. You are not a bad parent. You're a parent. It's trying, tiring, and frustrating at times. The television, the internet, and the Xbox can be of help and "save you" at times. It's helped me, too. My young sons grew up in the era of *Blues Clues* and *Dora the Explorer* television. There was this show called *Dragon Tales* that came on around 5:00 P.M. that I let the boys watch sometimes because it gave a measure of calmness when preparing dinner before the storm of us all gathering round the table. Yet, there was always a tinge of guilt that came with letting them watch *Dragon Tales* because a well-meaning Grandma-Person from church said it was a bad show for kids with the emphasis of magic powers that allowed the two siblings to travel to Dragon Land. "Oh, Lord have mercy," and I know He did. We just have to establish healthy boundaries for our children *and* ourselves and not worry about what the church folk might think.

Over the years our sons have listened to some great programs on the Gospel and the power of Christ that would put any Power Ranger to shame, through YouTube and podcasts and other internet media outlets. I know, too, from having a shared Netflix account that some shows have not been (at all) "Christ Centered" but they could say the same for me, too. Then again, when Netflix really became an outlet for our family, David, the youngest, was already ten years old. We needed to have discussions about what they were watching and we prayed because Jesus needed to be a part of those conversations too.

As Christians, we are supposed to be telling people the Gospel, which is the Good News about who God is. We should proclaim what He has done to bring us into a right relationship with Him despite our lack of curiosity about Him, and our focus on ourselves instead of Him. The precondition to loving God and sharing the Gospel is to know Him. Most people are born into a certain religion or learn it from their parents or their culture and they either adopt it without thinking, or they reject it without thinking. They are not interested in using reason and evidence, including scientific and historical evidence, to investigate who God is. That does not mean the evidence isn't there. A good start would be reading either Josh McDowell's book *Evidence That Demands a Verdict,* Lee Strobel's *The Case for Christ*, or C. S. Lewis's *Surprised by Joy* and *Mere Christianity*.

It also helps to realize that in order for our children's behavior to change, there needs to be a heart change. Oh yeah, I'd said to the boys, "I'm not asking what you want. I am asking you to obey." There are stages in parenting. First, we train when they are little. Second, we coach our kids by directing and holding them accountable. Third, we cheer on good choices and discourage bad ones. Lastly, we are our children's fans when they leave home and try and give advice only when asked (I am not so good at unsolicited advice).

Try to speak to your child's heart and not just their head. To tell a teenager to stop hanging out with a group they like, could get the response; "Let me live my own life." But if you appeal to their heart and maybe share your past mistakes, well, you might actually see some change. Many parents I've talked to feel they can't tell their kids that going to an underage bonfire drinking party isn't a good idea because they did that as a teenager. They don't want to share that sex before marriage isn't God's best for them because they had sex before marriage.

You are not the spokesperson for God, and while they're young you can encourage them with the promises of God, but He's your parent, too. His love is beyond a love we can understand for ourselves or give to our children. The best investment of your time is to trust God with your prayers to let your children find their path to Christ and develop a relationship with Him. Encourage them to investigate if God is real. If He isn't, who cares what He says? If He is, we should all care what He says. It's wrong to say that investigating doesn't matter or that all religions are the same. God has left clues of who He is in the natural world and in history—He expects us to be looking for Him. He is as real as any other person you know, and His character is as defined as any other person you know. He says, "He who seeks Me diligently will find Me." He doesn't say you will find Him if you seek Him flippantly. "You will seek Me and find Me when you seek Me with all your heart" (Jeremiah 29:13). We can't expect our kids to know and accept God without searching and asking questions, too. When they ask me, as their mom, I can share my personal relationship with God along with sharing my mistakes and how God never left me even though there were times I left Him. God will never disown us and nor would I or my husband disown the boys no matter how many mistakes they make or heartbreaks they give us.

I recently connected with this statement while reading a book or an article—I can't remember the title—but I wrote the truth in my journal: "We have made a very fatal error in our search for meaning and significance. In our frenzy to reach the 'top,' whatever or wherever that is, we mistake prominence with significance." Humanity has deluded itself into thinking that if I am well-known, well-liked, in great demand, and prominent, then I will find true meaning. The brokenness and heartache of places such as Hollywood would beg to differ. Mistaking prominence with significance and meaning is a very deadly error. It results in a mad rat race as people, desperate to fill the emptiness, scurry to the "top." No thought is given to whether they will actually find what they're looking for. No consideration is given to the thousands of people who made it to the world's idea of top and then were bitterly disappointed. The top just doesn't cut it. Position and prominence will never fill the eternity God has put in our hearts.

As with so many things in regard to the Kingdom of God, the road to significance and meaning is the direct opposite of the world's path. Jesus said that if you want to be great, if you want to know that you're making a positive contribution, if you really want to find meaning, then stop trying to be important. Jesus's answer to a world frantically searching for meaning is *learn to serve*! In being a servant—someone who seeks to lighten the load of others—we find fulfillment and freedom. Serving and loving others, especially the "others" who completely annoy me, is a lesson I'm always going to be learning and applying, and it's a lesson I hope that our four sons have caught on to as well.

Find the freedom. Find the identity in who God says you are. Let your children find Him, and along the way you might be surprised at what else they find.

I believe through all the trenches of parenting, social media, and *Power Rangers* that our four sons have all found Jesus. They know Him personally. The pull of media can be bad, but there are also a million ways to find the blessings within good boundaries.

My husband and I are now "empty nesters" and, honestly, I love it. God continually reminds me, too, that despite my "bad mom" moments, and meltdowns, He was there all along seeing my struggles and loving in the mess of me. Not that long ago I received some satisfaction, that despite some missteps in parenting and my negligent library days, God had been mindful. Our youngest, David, was visiting home for a few days and *"this"* happened:

"Dave, why are you going to the library? Are you going to meet up with someone?"

"Ah, no, Mom. I'm going to check out a book. I can return it when I'm home next time."

"Really?"

Really. And he did and he does (and reads them). Joey, too, was apparently reading and checking out books all along—riding his bike and getting his own library card without me even knowing. Who knew? God does. He knows us. He knows His kids and all the crazy things of this world. Now when I think about the boys watching *Power Rangers* shows, it doesn't seem crazy at all. Whatever way you parented, (library visits or not), the library may be of use to you now with expanded resources and Bible commentaries for the deeper questions on spirituality and religion. "Why would God send anyone to hell?" or "Is hell real?" are the poignant conversations that we now have with our youngest son and other "sons" we've "adopted" along the way. "Aren't we all born good?" is another one, too, that so many people now ask in deconstructing their faith. Yet, for the question, "Does God love you?" the answer is always, "Yes." We are all created by God in His image, He loves us *all*, but not all of us are children of God. Scripture teaches in John 1:12, "But to all who did receive Him, who believed in His name, He gave the right to become children of God," God only dwells in those who have put their faith in Christ. All others, while God's offspring by creation, are separated from Him because of sin. God makes a distinction between those who know Him and those who do not.

My husband and I love all of our children, and we're thankful they're also God's children. They trust our love. They trust God's love. They can ask questions of doubt and we can listen with ears of love. Love and listening are always going to be the best way to help our children navigate life because every single one of us have questions of doubt. Love does have the victory, despite our unanswered questions, and one day with Jesus, everything we questioned will be clear. Right now, we can have enough of our questions answered to have the assurance and hope on where we spend eternity. We also have the assurance that He's a loving father who will never leave us or forsake us. God's never failing love is written in many books at the library too. Oh, thank You, Lord.

Galatians 4:6–7: *"Since you are God's children, God sent the spirit of his Son into your hearts, and the spirit cries out, 'Father.' So now you are not a slave; you are God's child, and God will give you the blessing He promised, because you are His child."* (NCV)

PRESCRIBED PATIENCE

19
WHERE'S THE VERSE OF THE DAY?

"It is clear that you are a letter from Christ, the result of our ministry, written not with ink but with the Spirit of the living God, not on tablets of stone but on tablets of human hearts."
— **2 Corinthians 3:3 (ESV)**

NO MATTER YOUR GENDER, OCCUPATION, culture, the color of your skin, or circumstances, you most likely want to know what your purpose is. You might not even have a belief in God, but somehow you want a "higher power" to speak up so you can live a life that's meaningful.

Peter, our second son of four, is in the US Navy. A couple of years ago he was wondering what specific job he should commit to and be trained for. After being a seaman for almost a year, and with a good experience, it was soon time for him to make a decision.

The journey hasn't been without some waves of frustration and anxiety. Peter, like so many of us, might not know what tomorrow holds, but he knows who holds tomorrow. When your higher power is Christ the Lord, you eventually realize that life is more about serving others than serving yourself.

Peter has a relationship with God, not a religion of dos and don'ts. God knows us strong-willed types don't do well with "you should" or "you'd better." He's found a church, has a mentor, *and* is in a men's Bible study. It's not an easy route when the world entices you with what gives the most pleasure, especially for a young man in the military. But prayer works. We prayed Peter would "enter through the narrow gate, for wide is the gate and broad is the road that leads to destruction, and many enter through it" (Matthew 7:13, NIV).

Peter and I rarely get to talk on the phone, but when we do, I ask him what he needs as prayer for specifically. He always asks me to pray for his division on the ship. I remember one time we talked he lamented, "Mom, I'm struggling. I just don't know what I'm supposed to do with my life." I reminded him of James 1:5: "If you need wisdom, ask our generous God, and He will give it to you. He will not rebuke you for asking."

Peter and I both understand that having a belief in God is not the difficult part. The difficult part is trusting in God alone when your feelings and circumstances are all over the place and you're tempted to go to others for comfort or by comparison of what you think your life should look like. God also admonishes with the following verse, James 1:6, "But when you ask Him, be sure that your faith is in God alone. Do not waver, for a person with divided loyalty is as unsettled as a wave of the sea that is blown and tossed by the wind" (NIV). Appropriate for a sailor.

We so often have FOPO (Fear of People's Opinions) exacerbated by social media. Peter has been an inspiration to me in that regard. On occasion he decides to take month-long breaks from Instagram because of its plague of FOMO (Fear of Missing Out) on something you must have in order for your life to be more complete. I'm still on Instagram, but I get its dark side.

"It's a dark place," says former National Basketball Association guard JJ Redick. "It's just this cycle of anger and validation and tribalism. It's scary, man."³³ The 76ers are one of several teams in the NBA that have tried to implement "phone buckets" or "phone bags" on occasion during team meals. Put the phone in the bag and, you know, have real conversations. "I've been on teams where you literally don't talk to each other at dinner," Redick says. "Just six guys on their phones."³⁴ Reddick eventually quit social media. Social media propagate the lie that we are what we do, that our worth comes from what we produce, not from whose we are.

A lot of us suffer from anxiety. We worry about the things we can control and even more about the things we can't. Only by completely surrendering your future to God will you have a peace that passes understanding. God loves you like crazy and He has a road for you to follow, but be ready to trust Him.

In my own journey I've met a lot of people who may follow other religions or gods, and I believe God might allow other religions to exist as part of His providential plan, but there is no eternal peace with God outside of faith in Jesus. Of course, just because you have freedom in Jesus doesn't mean you'll have freedom from problems, but you can have peace. Sometimes a tragedy is where we meet God for the first time. We must lose religion, where it's all about rules and proving ourselves, and instead rest in a personal relationship with God who knows exactly what we're going through and how to take care us. Jesus working through us and not focusing on our own works or man's laws is what's important. God always loves us. He will not fail us. Peace really sets in when your relationship with God deepens

---

[33] https://sports.yahoo.com/nba-players-teams-tackle-dark-place-social-media-addiction-phone-buckets-blackout-periods-233802489.html, viewed February 24, 2022.

[34] Jason Owens, "NBA Players, Teams Tackle 'Dark Place' of Social Media Addiction with Phone Buckets, Blackout Periods," October 1, 2018, https://sports.yahoo.com/nba-players-teams-tackle-dark-place-social-media-addiction-phone-buckets-blackout-periods-233802489.html, viewed February 7, 2022.

and the best way for that relationship to deepen and develop is by reading the Bible and then committing His Word (Scripture) to your head and heart.

When I shared the Scripture from James 1:5–6 with Peter he said, "Mom, I recognize what you're saying is from the Bible. It's amazing how you can just give me verses whenever I have a question about something. It used to really bug me when you did that, but now I've actually bragged about this skill of yours to others, because it makes a difference to really know and apply it."

God's Word is something that I committed to learn, know, and memorize while abroad in Japan on a three-month summer mission trip in 1989. Although I had a roommate, we each had our own room with the host family we lived with. Each night I read the Bible and wrote down a Scripture in my journal to memorize. I then got these little note cards, which looked like mini recipe cards, and wrote down any verse that jumped out at me. As I committed each verse to memory, I taped it to the wall of the bedroom.

By the end of summer, I had about forty verses taped to the wall. After all these years, I still have the recipe cards, and more importantly, the verses in my heart. I continue to journal and listen to what God is saying and memorize what I believe He's asking me to. Yes, I hear from God. You can, too. He will speak clearly and simply, and He'll never contradict His Word. He doesn't tell me that others need to give me money, but He might ask me to give to someone else.

So, all these years later, Peter is the age I was when I began to memorize God's Word. Peter has taken up a different mantle by reading the verse of the day on his phone. He started to share this with some of the sailors, but then stopped because he did not want to offend anyone. Three days went by and on the third day with no verse from Peter, three different guys at three different times came up to him and said,

"What the hell, Griffith? Where's the verse of the day?"

"You guys want me to keep reading the verse of day?" Peter said.

"Hell, yeah, it's part of the routine now."

"What was cool, Mom," Peter said, "was that right before bed that night this one guy came to me and said, 'I'm not a Christian and I don't even know if I believe in God, but I gotta tell ya there's something about hearing that verse of the day that makes a difference. Keep it up.'" And so, he has.

There you have it. The Spirit of God is working in Peter and Christ is there on that ship with those sailors. He's a living God and so is His Word living and active because the Word became flesh and dwelt among us. In Isaiah 55:11 we see that God's Word (the verse of the day) won't return to Him empty but will accomplish everything He purposes it to do.

Amazing.

We're all broken, but He makes us whole. Like in Japan the ancient art of Kintsugi (or Kintsukuroi, which means "golden repair") is the art of fixing broken pottery with a special lacquer dusted with powdered gold, silver, or platinum. Beautiful seams of gold glint in the cracks of ceramic ware, giving a unique appearance to the piece. That's what God does with our brokenness. But it's not my job or anyone else's to tell you what sin separates you from God. He's a great God and He will tell you and because He's not a killjoy but a "givejoy." He wants you to live in freedom.

There's nothing we could do to earn His love and nothing we could do that would cause Him to stop loving us. A good performance brings momentary happiness, but not everlasting joy. His love never fails, even though we might.

Another time when Peter called, he said he had an idea of what job he might pursue. "It's called an RP, Mom, and it's a person who helps a Navy chaplain." I looked up the definition and it reads, "Religious Program Specialists (RPs) serve God and country. They prepare devotional materials, organize faith-based events, maintain religious records, and serve as a source of personal security for Navy chaplains."

Snap. Who knew? God knew and knows because He created Peter and you and me. God doesn't want to hit you over the head with His law but wants to embrace you with His grace. It might work for Pete to become an RP or it might not, but deep in his heart I know that Peter knows he's called to serve others in love with the gifts he's been given.

We are here for the purpose to worship God, and He came for the purposes of redeeming, forgiving, and saving us. God doesn't call the qualified. He qualifies the called for the purpose for which He knows best where you and I fit. Reading or citing a verse for the day isn't going to change you; what changes you is the belief and trust in what God says in those words because He is the Word. There is an end to this Earth experience, but with Christ there is truly a new beginning eternally where everything is perfectly real and forever wonderful. God Bless America, God bless our World, God bless you.

Verse of the Day for Chapter 19
"It isn't that we ourselves are qualified to claim that anything came from us. No, our qualification is from God."
— **2 Corinthians 3:5 (CEB)**

20
PARENTING A PETE

> *"Jesus replied, 'If anyone loves me, they will obey my teaching. My Father will love them and We will come to them and make Our home with them.'"*
> — **John 14:23 (NIV)**

"**B**OY, IS HE ANGRY."

Those are the first words I heard from Dr. Knaak as I delivered our second of four sons. I did not hear "You did it," "Congratulations," or "It's a boy." Instead, I heard what pretty much described our son Peter when he was in his teens.

"Boy, is he angry."

After our first son, Marco, was born, my husband Dan and I were ready to go on a parenting tour because we thought we had it down. At three months of age, Marco was sleeping through the night, taking regular naps, and eating his vegetables. But three years later Peter arrived and we canceled the tour.

Each of our sons in his own way has taught me more about who I am and what it means to live for someone other than myself. But Peter gets the award for reminding me each day that without God, I'd be toast.

I can think of nothing else that has brought me more tears or more joy than parenting a Pete. He is passionate, sincere, engaging, self-focused, a communicator, mouthy, handsome, fun, endearing, and aggravating. He is me.

My understanding of God's grace and love for me has deepened because of Peter. Yet, certainly there were the days and weeks where we'd fight. He'd yell, and I yelled louder. If I wasn't too upset or irrational, I'd bring up the problem to God and He'd show a direction to take.

The way to peace begins with accepting the truth of myself, which means I get a grip on God's Word and examine my own selfishness, and irritable and defensive attitude. My struggle to deal with Peter many times has a simple explanation: He represents precisely those things that I have refused to acknowledge and accept in myself. Real and lasting change comes from a heart change and only God can change a heart. When the heart changes, so will the behavior. By the power of the Holy Spirit this can be achieved. Otherwise, I get stuck trying to perform as a mom, or worse, I want my children to perform, which is just speaking to their heads and not their hearts. It seems like such a simple thing to "let go and let God," but it's actually hard because it's about trusting God's way when I can't "see" the results I want, which of course all boils down to having faith in Jesus:

"Help.

"Thanks.

"Amen."

That's a prayer for me personally and one I need in being a mom. It's a way to have peace even if I don't feel at peace.

Philippians 4:7 tells us Jesus gives peace when we shouldn't feel at peace, and it doesn't depend on our shifting feelings and moods. The peace that comes through accepting the whole truth about myself is rooted in Christ "who has reconciled all things to Himself, making peace through the blood of His cross" (Colossians 1:20).

I am at peace knowing that Peter has a personal relationship with Christ. We did not raise him or any of our boys to be religious. Yes, as a family we went to church (pretty consistently), and the boys went to Sunday School and youth group. But a person doesn't become a Christian by osmosis of being raised by Christian parents or by what church they attended or if they were baptized or not. A person is a Christian because they know the realness and love of Christ in a relationship and have accepted His forgiveness for their sins. "For it is by grace you have been saved, through faith—and this is not from yourselves, it is the gift of God—not by works, so that no one can boast" (Ephesians 2:8–9, NIV).

Peter was twelve when I knew that he knew God is real. Peter not only can pray and talk to God, but God answers Him back. That's relationship.

When there was an emergency in our family in August 2010, my brother's wife, Jonell, offered to pick up Peter and David at home in International Falls and take them to the family resort, Maplelag, while I sorted things out. Marco was at running camp, and Joey was with my husband and friend, Tim, campaigning in Southern Minnesota. However, when this crisis hit, Dan was in the ER trying to pass a kidney stone. Meanwhile "back at the ranch," Auntie Sharon was life-lifted to Duluth for her emergency situation. After leaving the hospital with Peter and David, I thought, maybe we just said our last goodbye to Auntie Sharon, and my mind was swirling with a million other concerns. It was then I informed Peter that Karen (aka Mrs. Layman) would be bringing him and David to Bemidji, Minnesota, where Auntie Jonell would pick them up while I dealt with either going to Duluth or Hutchinson, Minnesota. I added an instruction to Peter before Mrs. Layman would be coming by to pick them up.

"Oh, and before you leave," I said, "mow the lawn."

Had I asked Peter to cut off his arm so I could mail it to an armless child in another country? No, I had not.

"What? Who's Karen? No way. I'm not going anywhere. And I'm not mowing the lawn!"

It's exhausting to tell you how I tried to reason with Peter, but rather than our usual warfare of yelling, I was numb. So, I only repeated myself quietly, with zero expression. I then decided to leave the house and go sit in the van parked in the driveway to get away from Pete.

He followed me to the door and screamed, "I'm not going with Karen, and I'm not mowing the lawn!"

I replied, "Well, then you just talk to God about your answer," and I left the house.

I sat in the driver's seat and my immediate reaction was to call Dan and have him talk to Peter, but Dan was on morphine in the ER. So, I did the next clearly brilliant thing and looked up toward heaven and said, "God, will you talk to Pete?"

Time went on as different people stopped by the house to see about Auntie Sharon (who ended up having a full recovery), and I answered their questions and thanked them for their prayers. About fifteen minutes later I saw an incoming call from home.

I answered.

"Hey, Mom, it's Peter. I talked to God and I'm going with Karen."

"Good," I said. "What about mowing the lawn?"

"I haven't asked Him about that yet."

Two more people came by and then a second call from home.

"Mom, it's Peter again. Yeah, I talked to God and now I'm mowing the lawn, too."

"Thanks, Peter. I love you."

I wish I could tell you I've continued to follow that pattern, but I didn't. There was the time when I was cleaning the big work sink in the basement, Peter's sleeping quarters at the time, and we starting a screaming match because he was using the sink as a toilet. Never mind that it was only ten extra steps to the basement bathroom. It was ugly yelling.

I left and he slammed the door. I knew he was waiting for me to go upstairs, but instead I just sat on the steps, angry and spittin' mad. When Peter opened the door to "check on me," I did the very mature thing of spraying him with the bottle I had in my hand. It had bleach in it. I know, not smart, not kind. Liquid bleach cleaner went everywhere because the bottle splattered open when Peter hit it out of my hand. It ruined the rug at the end of the stairs and Peter's sweat pants he was wearing. He still has those pants (as if we need that memory reminder) but again, with God, "nothing is wasted." It was a lesson for us both; as the years went by I saw the blessing, too. God showed me my weaknesses and only in Him was I strong to face the many challenges as a parent.

I share this for those of you who need to know you're not alone. This, too, will pass. There is a God and He's parenting all of us. You're a good mom despite your bad missteps into the yelling zone or even caving in and not keeping a boundary you set.

Jesus makes a home for all of His children, and He says simply, "Make your home in Me, as I make Mine in you" (John 15:4). Home is not a heavenly mansion in the afterlife, but a safe place in the midst of our anxious world. Home is that sacred space—external or internal—where we don't have to be afraid, where we are confident in love. In our world, we have a lot of lost people who never come home to themselves. They seek a safe place through alcohol, drugs or security in success, other people, or even a little religion. They have become strangers to themselves, people who have an address but still have not found home. No matter what Peter did or didn't do or how crazy he made me (or I him) I wanted him to know there was always love from me, his mom, the woman who has known and loved him the longest.

When I asked Dan, "Doesn't Peter frustrate you like crazy, because I think I'm going nuts here?"

Dan's steady answer remains, "I'm not giving up on him. I want Peter to know that no matter what, he is always loved and he always has a home."

That's it. Truth. Love. It's Jesus love. It's real. In religion it's about what you do; with Jesus it's about who you are. It's not about how good you are but about how good He is to us as our heavenly Father. There is nothing we can do to cause God to love us any more than He already does, and there is nothing that will cause God to love us any less.

I know Peter loves me, too, and he's a clever one in connecting with me and others with his contagious congeniality. He would ask thoughtful questions while I was making dinner or working at the computer. I remember him asking me in a calm moment but shortly after he'd been disciplined with the question, "Mom, what do you love most besides God, family, and friends?"

"That's a good question, Peter. I love people. I do. And I love to laugh. I love to make people laugh by finding the humor in everyday life and telling stories."

"OK, good. Can I have my phone back?"

"No. But I love you. I'll never stop."

I wouldn't trade parenting a Peter for anything . . . most days. God gave me a Peter because He loves me, and He made Peter the way he did for a purpose, which couldn't be fulfilled had He made Peter any other way. Part of that purpose was in training and teaching me the ways of God for my own journey as a wife and mom, and working in ministry with the variety of positions God's given me. It's true that Peter is the center of most of my parenting stories over Marco, Joey, and David, but it's also true where I was most humbled and had to lean on the strength of God.

The kids you raised (or are raising) are not mistakes, and their personalities are what they are for a purpose. God is for you and not against you, just like He's for your child and not against them. Keep on keeping on with the grace God gives you and extend that same grace to the Peter people in your life.

I parented a Pete. You can, too. God never gives up on His kids.

21
ATTENTION! HE'S NOT FINISHED WITH YOU YET

> *"Being confident of this, that He who began a good work in you will carry it on to completion until the day of Christ Jesus."*
> — **Philippians 1:6 (NIV)**

It's hard to believe you're not a stupid failure when someone's yelling at you every single day.

"Why are you so stupid?!"

"How can someone who's such an idiot be here?!"

"What's it like riding the short bus?!"

For two months drill instructors hurled such insults at our son Peter while he was in navy boot camp. He did graduate, but whoa . . . the words to knock him down were harsh.

While in boot camp, recruits don't have their phones or rights. So as parents we had to wait to hear the extent of his experiences after boot camp.

After three weeks at boot camp, Peter called and told us it was the hardest thing he has ever done. Most of us have heard that boot camp is no carnival cake walk, but when it's personal to one of your children, you have to suppress the desire to return some pain to the drill instructor who is trashing your son.

"Why are you so (effing) retarded, Griffith?"

"How are you even able to be here you, mother (effing) dumbass?"

Somedays the drill instructor would order other recruits to clap for Griffith being a dumbass and they would obey.

Peter did struggle in school academically. He had special assistance up until seventh grade because of a learning disability. If you were to tell him, "Go straight and take a left," he could follow, but if you extended the direction with, "Go straight, take a left, turn the corner, and on the left-hand side you'll find the store," well, he'd probably get lost.

What Peter does possess, though, is *grit*. He does not quit. He told me he sang the song, "Wait and See" by Brandon Heath every day to keep his spirits up. The basic message of the lyrics:

"There is hope for me yet
Because God won't forget
All the plans He's made for me
I'll have to wait and see
He's not finished with me yet."[35]

Right out of the womb, Peter was strong willed. I never really remember a baby cry coming out of his mouth because it was more like a screech. When Peter was three, we were having one of our mother/son battles of the will when my friend, Diane, called to tell me that while she was sitting in her rocking chair sewing, God very specifically told her to share with me that Peter's strong will was God-given and God created him that way for a purpose. You can't imagine how this helped me. Some days I thought we'd never make it, musing either that he or I would inevitably be placed in special care.

Peter told me he'd get so discouraged sometimes and pray, "God,

---

[35] Brandon Heath, "Wait and See," August 19, 2008, on What If We [CD] (Nashville: Provident Label Group).

why did you make me this way? Why aren't I smart?" God did not make a mistake. He just made him different. "What sorrow awaits those who argue with their Creator. Does a clay pot argue with its maker? Does the clay dispute with the one who shapes it, saying, 'Stop, you're doing it wrong!' Does the pot exclaim, 'How clumsy can you be?'"(Isaiah 45:9, NLT).

Peter excelled in physical fitness. The challenge for him was all the scholastic tests. Every night he would stay up and study with another recruit, the smartest recruit in the bunch. He told me that was as hard as he ever studied in his life. He returned the favor by helping others with their fitness challenges in form and timing.

He also became known as the guy who prayed. Everyone heard, all day, too, how he was yelled at for being stupid. His prayers and those of others must be working. He was still there.

"Hey, Griffith, you're religious, aren't you? Will you pray for me?"

"Sure, I'll pray for you, but I'm not religious. I have a relationship with God. He's real, and *that* makes *all* the difference."

There are a lot of tests to take before you can graduate. One friend of Pete's was on his last chance to pass a written test. As he was saying his goodbyes, Peter said, "I can't face the fact that I might not see your smiling face every day, so I'm gonna be praying for you."

After the test Peter told him, "I was praying for you all day. How did you do?"

His friend grinned wide and said, "I *knew* something different was happening while I took the test."

Yep, God is real.

Up to the very last week Peter didn't think he was going to make it. One afternoon he was ordered to eat breakfast early and grab his backpack. He thought he was being "ASMOed" which is the term used when someone has to be "sent back" and cannot graduate with their class. Peter told me it was tough holding back tears, thinking he was being sent back three weeks because he had failed. The thought of calling us to share this news was devastating to him. He reported to the chief, who growled:

"Griffith, you know why you're here?"

"Because I'm being ASMO'ed and sent back?"

"No, Griffith. You are graduating in the top 3 percent."

"But that doesn't make sense. How is that possible?"

"Believe me, Griffith. I'm surprised, too, but I've checked twice. Now get ready, because you're meeting with three other chiefs to determine what happens next."

Peter walked into the next room completely stunned.

On graduation day, Peter was dressed in his sailor whites (the cutest sailor on base), pinned with a special ribbon indicating he was a top 3 percent grad who had also moved up in rank. He, with the other 3 percent honor grads (out of about a thousand sailors), was standing at attention before all the other divisions came into the area for the ceremony.

Who knew? God knew.

And so, I will continue to remind our boys and all of God's kids that until we are finally "home," God's not finished with us yet. He began a good work in you, and He'll carry it to completion until the day He returns (Philippians 1:6).

Remember, too, that fear is a liar, and it takes courage to go forward when your feelings, circumstances, and others are telling you you're not good enough. But the deal is we don't have to be good enough because God *always is*. He's never surprised by what happens to us and He's always on the move to work all things for the good. He's real. Prayer works *really* well, too.

Let the words of Brandon Heath's words song continue in your heart and mind always:

"Still wondering why I'm here
Still wrestling with my fear
But I've seen enough to know that I'm not here for nothing
He's up to something
He's not finished with me yet."[36]

---

[36] Heath, "Wait and See."

22
THE QUARANTINE CHRONICLES OF COVID

"For the Lord your God is living among you. He is a mighty Savior. He takes delight in you with gladness. With His love, He will calm all your fears. He will rejoice over you with joyful songs."
— **Zephaniah 3:17 (NLT)**

YOU FELT ALONE.

You felt crazy.

I understand you.

And I want to assure you, you were not alone. you were not crazy in the crazy time of the COVID pandemic when so many of us were alone and isolated with so many questions and thoughts.

We continue to deal with crazy times, but "all the feels" were working overtime during an intense season of COVID-19. Who knew that wearing a mask or not wearing a mask would cause so much division and tension? Kindness may have meant wearing a mask because you believe it helped others remain safe from being exposed to the virus; you researched and believed the science supported your belief, or kindness might have meant not wearing a mask because you believed exposure to the virus would help build your immune system and the science supported your belief. No matter what you chose, you did out of kindness and thoughtfulness. Kindness needs to rule because everyone you meet is struggling on some level with something difficult. The last thing I needed during the pandemic was to get into "Mask Wars." Only by the grace of God did I keep my opinions off social media, (thank You, Lord). Ask Him about anything and everything, and then go in peace with your decision while respecting others in theirs.

The "to wear a mask or not wear one" debate is one dilemma, but there are a million other emotions that come in large waves that can be overwhelming. My advice will always be to try and talk through your anxieties to another person who's willing to listen—someone you can connect to who provides empathy and not another graph or chart to look at. And in turn, ask the other person for their thoughts and feelings, and be a good listener. Talking to God aloud helps, too (it's called "prayer"). I also suggest reading the Psalms aloud. King David of Israel wrote most of the Psalms when he was under stress, and he knew how to lament. He also knew the source of strength and comfort, the Lord God Almighty.

Lastly, I recommend reading books that reveal the heartfelt testimonies of others. Specifically, during the season we were in but it also applies to most every other season we're in. Three individuals whose writing inspired and gave me perspective during the COVID Chronicles were Francis Chan, Nadia Bolz-Weber, and Brennan Manning. All three are unique individuals who have faced unique challenges, but their similarities are in knowing of God's great love, His grace, and His forgiveness.

Francis Chan's passion, his zeal for God and others, inspires me. He grew up in Chinatown in San Francisco, where his parents had immigrated to from Hong Kong in the 1960s. Sadly, his mother died in childbirth giving birth to Francis. His stepmother would later die in a car accident when Francis was eight, followed by the loss of his father to cancer when Francis was twelve. Hard stuff, and yet when God pursued Francis, he not only accepted God's unconditional "crazy love" for him, but also the call to serve as a pastor wherever God called him. Francis attended seminary, wrote books, and planted a church. Then in January 2020 he moved his family to Hong Kong, where he now works in Sham Shui Po, the poorest area in Hong Kong and the neighborhood where his mother used to do ministries in the 1950s.

Francis's book, *Crazy Love*, impacted me when I read it years ago. Recently, I wanted to read a section in the book on "safety." Chan is not playing life safely but is secure in where God leads him. He writes, "We are consumed by safety. Obsessed with it, actually. Now, I'm not saying it is wrong to pray for God's protection, but I am questioning how we've made safety our highest priority. We've elevated safety to the neglect of whatever God's best is."[37] It certainly is thought provoking and especially during the season of "Rona." God is always more concerned with our character over our comfort.

Like so many of you I tried to "keep calm and carry on" with the wisdom and grace God gave me, but it's not like I wouldn't get into a discussion on "Safety vs. Freedom." For the most part I don't post my opinions on social media. My immediate family is different, though. We have discussions, or, as our pastor son Marco would say, "Mom, it's arguing and not a discussion with you." (Some truth to that.) When I tried to use Mr. Chan's quote on safety to argue a point, Marco replied, "Francis isn't talking about being reckless for selfish reasons. He's saying don't let safety interfere with a far greater calling." Good point. Good Truth. When I'm scared or anxious, whether the threat is real or imagined, I'm often praying to have God remove the awful circumstances, rather than praying for His peace, strength, and courage to walk through the difficult circumstances. I need the Holy

---

[37] F. Chan, *Crazy Love* (Colorado Springs: David Cook, 2006), chapter 7.

Spirit to guide me rather than my fear. Fear comes from a lack of trust and confidence in God's way and provision. I mean it always comes back to me asking myself, "Where or who do you put your hope and trust in, Debbie?"

Another honest and fresh perspective on living the Gospel authentically comes from author, speaker, and pastor Nadia Bolz-Weber. Her book, *Accidental Saints: Finding God in All the Wrong People*, is worth the read. Nadia grew up in Colorado Springs with a fundamentalist Christian family. In 1986, at age seventeen, she started getting tattoos, and the ones on her arms mark the liturgical year and the story of the Gospel. She briefly attended Pepperdine University before dropping out and moving to Denver, where, she says, she became an alcoholic and drug abuser and often felt like one of "society's outsiders."

In 1991 Nadia sobered up; as of 2020 she has remained so for twenty-eight years. In 2008 Nadia became an ordained Lutheran pastor and started her own church, named The House for All Sinners and Saints, (which is often shortened to just "House"). Her church is open and welcoming to all who enter. One-third of her church is part of the LBGT community and comforting to people with drug addiction, depression, and even those who are not believers of her faith. I don't agree with everything Nadia shares, and I'm sure she would say the same of me. I like her. I've learned from her. Her words below have helped me in "Times of Cray."

- To everyone who has watched the date of their wedding or graduation or their birthday, or their dissertation defense, or their long-hoped-for vacation, or their family reunion, or the "nonessential" medical procedure they hoped would change their life, come and go, I ask God that Your presence and Your peace be felt. And if that's not possible, could you just nudge the right person to reach out and call them? Just that, Lord. Just that?

- Grace is the cargo train that distributes into my life all the good and beautiful things that are un-earn-able: forgiveness, mercy, endless second chances, the good will of those who write me off, the sun rising each day, a perfect peach in summer and love.

- Never once did Jesus scan the room for the best example of holy living and send that person out to tell others about Him. He always sent stumblers and sinners. I find that comforting."[38]

I think we've all probably felt, like Nadia, that we're outsiders looking in at others who appear to have it all together. But the truth is we're all messed up on some level and in need of God's grace every single second.

Lastly, but certainly not least, is the man Brennan Manning, who's since passed on from this life into eternity. Brennan was born and raised in depression-era New York City, and after finishing high school, enlisted in the US Marine Corps and fought in the Korean War. After returning to the United States, he enrolled at Saint Francis University in Loretto, Pennsylvania. Upon his graduation from the seminary in 1963, Manning was ordained a Franciscan priest.

In the late 1960s, Manning joined the Little Brothers of Jesus of Charles de Foucauld, a religious institute committed to an uncloistered, contemplative life among the poor. Manning transported water via donkey, worked as a mason's assistant and a dishwasher in France, was imprisoned (by choice) in Switzerland, and spent six months in a remote cave somewhere in the Zaragoza Desert. In the 1970s, Manning returned to the United States and began writing after confronting his alcoholism. There is so much wisdom and love in his writing. It's where I first heard the truth of God's love so succinctly put: "God loves you right where you are at and not where you should be because you'll never be where you should be."

The Ragamuffin Gospel, a book he wrote, is oozing with wisdom.

---

[38] Nadia Bolz-Weber, *Pastrix: The Cranky, Beautiful Faith of a Sinner & Saint* (New York: Jericho Books, 2014).

I even have the devotional of the same name with excerpts of his writing. I share with you what I read on May 4, 2020, during the pandemic from that beloved, worn-out book:

> In the winter of 1968–69, I lived in a cave in the mountains of the Zaragosa Desert in Spain . . . On the night of December 13, during what began as a long and lonely hour of prayer, I heard in faith Jesus Christ say, 'For love of you I left my Father's side. I came to you, who ran from Me, fled Me, who did not want to hear My name. For love of you, I was covered with spit, punched, beaten, and affixed to the wood of the cross.' These words are burned on my life. Whether I am in a state of grace or disgrace, elation or depression, that night of fire quietly burns on. I looked at the crucifix for a long time, figuratively saw the blood streaming from every pore of His body, and heard the cry of His wounds. "This isn't a joke. It is not a laughing matter to Me that I have loved you." The longer I looked, the more I realized that no man has ever loved me and no one ever could love me as He did. I went out of the cave, stood on the precipice, and shouted into the darkness, "Jesus, are You crazy? Are You out of Your mind to have loved me so much?" I learned that night what a wise old man had told me years earlier: "Only the one who has experienced it can know what the love of Jesus Christ is. Once you have experienced it, nothing else in the world will seem more beautiful or desirable.[39]

Brennan is right. There is no match in Christ's love for you. He fully knows you and He fully loves you.

Yes, there are the good book writers and the good speaker people, but nothing is more comforting than knowing the Good God and Lord of the universe. His perfect self accepts, loves, and forgives our imperfect selves. He forgives our sins. I can barely wrap my head around the fact that He loves us for who we are and not for what we

---

[39] Brennan Manning and A. Weinheimer, *Reflections for Ragamuffins: Daily Devotions from the Writings of Brennan Manning*, May 4 Entry (London: SPCK, 2003).

do. Our righteousness comes from what He did "right" by going to the cross, by His death and resurrection.

There are days I ache with self-pity or regret; sometimes I'm just really angry, too, but when I cry out to God, I can hear Him speak. "My sheep hear My voice. I know them and they follow Me" (John 10:27). I don't read the Bible because I have to, but because I get to. I memorize Scripture that I write in my journal because I know there will be times of such angst that I can't open a book or call someone, and I'll need to hear His voice alone.

There is another voice that will try and speak to us, too, and it's the enemy of our souls, Satan. He's a liar who wants to destroy us, our hope, and our lives. We can get really frustrated with people and circumstances in thinking *they're* the enemy but they're not. Remember: just as God works through others to meet us in need, so too will the enemy use others for his sick plans. But wait, here's literally "good news," the Bible, the "Sword of the Spirit," which is a weapon we have available to us at all times. It's not only defensive but offensive, too. We also have the Holy Spirit when we've welcomed Jesus into our lives and the fruit of the Spirit is not what you need to do to get God to smile over your life. The fruit of the Spirit is the effect that the Holy Spirit has on people as He dwells in us.

God is not a genie in a Bible, yet I know His Word is life-changing. The whole book is not about you, but about Him as a God who restores and redeems. I always marvel that Job, after such loss of material items, family, and his health, was still able to say, "My Redeemer lives" and not "My Disciplinarian lives." Read the Bible. Read of His crazy love for you, His grace and His mercy that are new every morning, and you'll know you're not crazy and you're not alone whether you're a masked or unmasked warrior in this world.

23
'HOPE' SPREADS EASILY, TOO (LIKE COVID-19)

"For I fully expect and hope that I will never be ashamed, but that I will continue to be bold for Christ, as I have been in the past. And I trust that my life will bring honor to Christ, whether I live or die."
— **Philippians 1:20 (NLT)**

I WAS WAITING.

I had words.

"David! If you're going to come home past 11 p.m., you have to call or text and let me know what's going on! We live in the Icebox of the Nation, and the Community Center is at least a mile away. I don't care if you ride your bike, but it's the month of March, eighteen degrees outside, and we still have at least a foot of snow. Your bike doesn't have snow tires. I worry. You're all alone in the theatre, and I don't know what's going on unless you tell me."

David had words, too.

He stood in the entryway of the house hanging up his coat while I sat on the couch.

"Mom! I'm stressed. A lot is going on. I don't even know if the show is going to happen because of this virus. I've been painting and working on the set for hours, figuring out the music, props, costumes, and all other elements, but I'm worried that in the six days remaining, it's not going to happen. I have homework, the speech meet was cancelled and probably the whole season will be, too, and this is the year I could have made it to the state competition. I'm processing a whole lot of drama in my life. I have a lot of people counting on me, including me, and your yelling is stressing me out even more. I'm sorry I didn't call, it's just that . . . "

David's voice broke. He didn't want to cry. He wanted to be brave, yet it takes bravery to be vulnerable, too, to be honest with who you are and where you're at.

Fortunately, my "Mama Bear Love" kicked in and I told him to come and sit on the couch with me. I put a pillow on my lap and my lanky six-foot teenager put his head down as I combed through his hair with my fingers. "Go ahead and cry, David. Let it out, crying is cleansing and cathartic." He did, a little softly at first, but as I encouraged, he sobbed out all the frustration, anger, and disappointment. He was grieving, but in between sobs he would say, "I think you're really going to like the show. The set is coming together nicely and my actors seem ready. I'm getting kinda excited."

We talked about a few other things such as school, speech, and his friends. Then he got up off the couch, blew his nose, and went to take a shower. He asked if I'd make something to eat. Never mind that it was now 12:30 A.M. We were the only two beings at home, and a hamburger and fried potatoes sounded just about right. My husband was out of town and the other three boys no longer lived in the house. (Marco was a pastor near Minneapolis, Peter was in the navy at sea, and Joey was away at college.) Dan and I had the "baby" at home.

In the next few days, things progressed rather quickly with the alarm of the COVID-19 virus. David's directing debut of *Pinocchio* was canceled. The speech season was canceled, prom was canceled, and his post-secondary education (as a senior in high school) was moved online (gathering at the college for classes was canceled). However, the threat of the virus brought Joey and Marco home, and I actually welcomed their laundry. Social distancing is one thing but isolation is another. We need one another. The more family the merrier, but this still left Peter overseas, across the Atlantic. But we heard from him and he was in good spirits, connecting with others where he was and thankful to serve. Truly.

I declared the season of the COVID-19 pandemic one of grief and disappointment, too. There was so much to let go of, so much "wait and see." It was difficult. And I'm sorry for the disappointment and grief you, too, experienced. Weddings had to be postponed; funerals didn't happen where a group could gather; and family vacations, graduations, and conferences all had to be postponed or canceled. *This* was a process of grieving, letting go, and accepting.

It's interesting that David (he actually pointed this out) was born October 4, 2001, and three weeks previously 9/11 happened. That, too, was a season of grief and tremendous loss, but somehow it didn't seem to halt the world as COVID-19 had done. I'm the first to admit that I'm the person who's more apt to say, "Don't worry so much. It's fine. Everyone just settle down. Do we really have to close the doors of most every establishment and no longer gather as humans in our own flesh and blood? Because, while physically I may be protecting myself and others, I thought that mentally I might have a breakdown." But the answer was, "Yes. Yes, we do, Debbie. Keep calm and carry on."

So, like most of you, I used my common sense. We all needed to wash our hands faithfully and continually, BUT honestly, my complaining got in the way of my using my hands (or heart) to pray and praise in the midst of the pandemic of grief and disappointment. Moan, groan, and grieve what you've lost and mourn your disappointments as David did, but thank God He is sovereign and has a plan in place to redeem *all* of this.

Having suffered a horrendous season of anxiety attacks in 2009, I know how wretched *feelings* can be. The thing about an anxiety attack is that even if you've been there a million times over *and* you know your body is having a physical reaction to an unknown fear, you still *feel* like *this* time it's gonna kill you. Yet it won't. You need to remember that anxiety is not a feeling itself, *but* the result of trying not to feel. Ask yourself, "What needs to be felt?" With David it was sadness. So, cry if you need to cry, scream if you need to scream, and punch a pillow a thousand times over if you need to punch. Sometimes I have to find a movie to watch or a song to listen to, which I play over and over, so I can release the swirling panicked emotions and emote.

But wait . . . this coronavirus is *real* and the "what could happen" is scary and possible. So now what should you do? Do this: Take a deep breath, release . . . slowly . . . and then know that the answer you are looking for . . . His name is *Jesus*.

Truth is the antidote for fear, and Jesus is The Way, *The Truth*, and *The Life*. I'm not simply trying to give you a "patty-cake," "here's a verse," "feel-better" sticker to put on your fridge. I'm telling you, from experience, that it works to trust God and believe He's on the move. God reminded me of the Book of Lamentations and the Prophet Jeremiah *lamenting*. And I'll say, "I *so get* this guy."

In Lamentations 3:19–20, we read how Jeremiah's mind is a whirlwind of emotions with all the problems he sees and is facing, and his "soul is bowed down within him with sorrow." However, he declares in Lamentations 3:21, "But this I recall and therefore I have hope with expectation." Now he makes a turn. He says, "Okay, I'm going to get something else in my mind that gives me hope with the expectation of good." His hope is in God. He fixes his mind on the positive, which begins to pull him out of the pit he's in. In Lamentations 3:22–24,

Jeremiah talks about the Lord's mercy, His compassion, and His faithfulness. Jeremiah's positive thoughts about God bring him out of the depressed, miserable state he was in. When we think about our problems, we sink lower and lower, but thoughts about the goodness, mercy kindness, and faithfulness of God give us hope. God's mercy is new every single morning; great is His faithfulness. I'm glad. I use my allotted portion every day.

When we feel the load is particularly heavy and *so* hard that we can't handle it, I think it's because we carry more than He's asked us to. We're trying to carry what He's already taken care of or He's in the process of taking care of and redeeming. This silly phrase, "God doesn't give you more than you can handle," is not a verse in the Bible.

Read a chapter such as Romans 8 and you're filled with so many great promises. Romans 8:28 is one: "*For we know* that *all* things work together for good because we love God, He loves us and He has a purpose, for us, in this season." *All* things are not good. Yet "the good" and blessings that can come out of difficult places can be amazing. I have many stories of blessings received from challenging times, both big and small: my recovery from scoliosis back surgery, getting a DUI, missing an airline flight, and having the flu, losing a contest and not being cast in a role I desperately longed for—in all these scenarios God gave me a way to know He was with me. He showed up in ways I never would have expected, and He blessed me.

Christ encourages us in 2 Corinthians, saying that His grace *is* sufficient. The present verb *is* means "right now"—whatever is going on, *God is* at work. Boy, do I need everyday grace when it comes to judging others. Judging is a recreational activity that's so easy to do. When you're quarantined and watching another season of *The Office*, you can easily feed your fleshly desires to judge at the same time. But judging is not a Holy Spirit-led activity. We scroll through social media and look at people's responses, their comments, and their posts, and we judge. There are graphs, articles, a link to an article, and a "share" from someone else's page, and we judge. I was getting very judgmental. The more judgmental I got, the more irritated I became. So I stopped, deleted the graph I had posted on a thread, and I prayed.

It was so clear, it was almost audible, as I heard His voice speak directly to my heart: "Debbie, have you prayed about 'it' as much as you've talked about 'it'?" My answer was no. I had talked more about the problems with humanity and the virus more than I had prayed. I had complained and lamented for days. I was also jealously judging everyone else's beautiful, quarantined life on Instagram. Scrolling through Insta, my thoughts were, *Wow, their house is so nice* (as a girlfriend took us on a tour of her home and laundry). *Sure, they have laundry like I do, but look at that vintage tile in their bathroom. Or, oh my goodness, how many 'beyond cute' outfits does she have? Do her children always look so adorable? Clearly everyone is better looking and having more fun than I am. But seriously, how does she get her hair to wave so perfectly to the side? I wonder where I can buy that hair clip.* This was my *day* three, in the same pajamas with no shower. I needed to stop.

I took a shower and lamented, but I also prayed. By allowing God's Holy Spirit to move in and through me, *everything* changed. It was late evening, after I had been "pissy" and complaining *all* day long, that David actually said, "Mom, you seem different. You don't seem angry now. What happened?"

"David," I said, "I stopped talking and I listened. I let Jesus take over." I am strong willed, and a get-'er-done type of gal. But to be clear, this change did not come about because of my will or greater effort. It was *all* Jesus' power.

The Lord parted the Red Sea. He healed the little girl who was sick and about to die. Lazarus was dead, and He touched him and

Lazarus rose up. The woman with the bleeding issue was healed once she touched the cloak of Jesus. All of these miracles happened because people had faith and because Jesus is God. And so, I ask myself, *In this pandemic, am I an example of someone who only believes in God, or am I an example of someone who trusts God?* He is the same God, "yesterday, today, and forever" (Hebrews 13:8).

Like the rest of the world, I'm very mindful of what not to expose myself to, *but* I also wonder, *Am I mindful enough to not expose myself to all the 'talk' on the news and social media posts? Do I tune into Him every day first or the "news" on my phone? Go to the throne before you go to the phone—how's that workin' for you, Debbie?*

Maybe now is the time to go to that address book you have with all the names and places of people you've written down and not yet documented onto a computer file. Sit down and write a note of encouragement to those people. Bring out the markers and the stickers (stickers make me happy) and have a craft party with others with whom you're quarantined. David thought to write a card of encouragement to each of his cast members. Genius. Think about all that you can do, instead of all that you can't do. Yes, it takes discipline to exercise, create a care package, and to choose what you think on. In reaching out to others, I found that "day-drinking" really was "a thing" to numb a little of the pain just like food or online shopping (how many leggings does a girl need?). But you can make good choices because there is a good God with His grace. There are also good people who are hurting, and connecting with another in whatever you can is quite vital to our mental health.

Hope got me through this pandemic. "Hope," I've always defined, "is the belief that 'it' will get better." It bears repeating: "Truth is the anecdote for fear." How timely (and so like God) that Proverbs 29:25 popped up on my computer screen the day I thought it was okay to rant about being quarantined: "The fear of man will prove to be a snare, but whoever trusts in the Lord is kept safe." Christ is here with us now and He's not leaving. He's not surprised by what's happening, and His plan is in place for redemption. Hope can spread rapidly, too.

24
'THERE'LL BE DAYS LIKE THIS,' MAMA SAID

"So do not fear, for I am with you; Do not be dismayed, for I am your God. I will strengthen you and help you; I will uphold you with my righteous right hand."
— **Isaiah 41:10 (NIV)**

"Mama said there'll be days like this
There'll be days like this, Mama said
(Mama said, Mama said)." [40]

THE 1960s MOTOWN GIRL GROUP, The Shirelles, give us the facts on life in their song, "Mama Said." There are gonna be hard days, there just are. Now, as a mama of four adult sons, I can tell you that some days were so challenging I didn't feel as if I was gonna make it through. I'd scream in my head or aloud, "This is so nuts! You've got to be kidding me!"

I still remember one particularly nutty day seventeen years ago,

---

[40] Jane Minogue, The Shirelles, "Mama Said," (1961 by Luther Dixon), March 5, 2018, https://www.dailydoowop.com/the-shirelles-mama-said/, viewed September 7, 2021.

because it was a day that defines "crazy mom" and also the four personalities I worked with on a daily basis. Peter was nine and a half years old and (no surprise) we were having a yelling match. Of course, I don't remember what the war was about, but I remember we both wanted to win.

Usually, I would have the last word, but on this particular day Peter wanted it. I was shouting and reminding him that, "I am the mom," as he turned his back on me and walked to his room. He shut the door, and held it tight to prevent me from entering. I used all the strength and yelling I could muster for him to open the door. Eventually, I managed to get a crack of the door opened, so I began pushing with my right foot to get a big enough space to squirrel through. It didn't work. Instead, my barefoot middle toe got stuck and it lodged itself underneath the door so the skin pulled away from the toenail. I screamed in pain. It was loud and long.

Joey, age eight, immediately appeared in the hallway and, holding the cordless phone, he asked in his monotone voice, "Should I call Dad or 911?" I told him to call Dad and then go downstairs to get his brother Marco, age twelve. Marco bounded up the stairs and demanded that Peter open the door. Peter obliged and then Marco pinned Peter to the bed and said, "You don't talk to our mother like that." Peter began to talk back, so Marco gave him a slap to the face and repeated, "You do not talk to our mother like that."

Peter was quiet and stunned. Marco left the room and went back downstairs. Joey, sitting quietly in the living room, was waiting for possibly more instructions. But where was David, age six? Down the hall he was in another room kneeling on the bottom bunk bed with his hands folded and crying, "Dear Jesus, help our family. Protect my mom and Peter from each other." My toe healed fine but it hurt like heck, and hours later, after my husband Dan came home, we all had a story to tell. Yep, Mama said there'd be days like that and there were many more just like it that followed.

I came through those early years of parenting more empathetic to other people, and not just moms. Because of those hard days, I am better and not bitter. No one, *honestly*, has a story on being a "perfect mom." The "perfect mom" ideal is left to Instagram with edited and staged photos and, yeah, sometimes my mom world looks that way, too, on my Instagram. Of course, there are perfectly wonderful moments that are captured in photos that are honest and true, and I thank God for them. I am fiercely proud I had all boys. I love to tell someone, "I'm a mom of four sons." I believe I'll get the girls later and at an age that's more agreeable (for me) through daughters-in-law and granddaughters. Lord knows there were enough hair products and hormones with me being the only female in the mix. God knows me and didn't make a mistake in making me a "boy mom." But He knows I've made plenty of mistakes in being a mom because I'm human but He also gave me His strength and a confidence to persevere. He literally upheld me with His righteous right hand when my hands were wiping away tears of frustration

There are so many stories in parenting that are hard, funny, or endearing. Sometimes those sentiments are all mixed together but the most important factor in raising the boys is the peace that comes in knowing that your child has an understanding of God's unconditional love and a personal relationship with Him and not a religion with a "good behavior" checklist. Our sons Marco, Peter, Joey, and David, on some level, know of God's grace. Only God knows our hearts, so that's why I say, "On some level." Do any one of us *really* get it? Can we really fathom God's sacrifice in paying for our debt of sin—a payment we could never cover or earn? He offers this gift to us with no conditions. He promises redemption and to work all things for the good—now and for eternity. Seriously, that is such *good news* that if we really pause, take a breath, and think, it can make all the bad days doable.

I do think that a lot of how we see God is how we're raised. I was raised without religion; because of my Aunt Ginger, I was given a clear understanding of who Jesus is and how to connect with Him personally. My husband, Dan, didn't grow up going to church and didn't care to know God. Then after serving as a senate page and having his idealistic view of government shattered, he decided he wanted to know if God was real. Dan will tell you he spent a year and a half looking for evidence of a God and eventually prayed, "God, if you are there, I want to know." Proverbs 8:17: "Those who seek Me diligently find Me."

Dan and I know Christ in a personal relationship, and it definitely helped us in guiding our sons to know Him, too, even though they went to public school—*ha!* I have to mention that because in the 1990s it seemed if you had four or more children, it was assumed you were a Christian home-schooling mom. I can say yes to Jesus reigning in my life, but a hard no to homeschooling. My "one-liner" at the time was, "I don't home-school and my kids eat white bread," (*but* it was from the grocery store bakery, if that gives me points). I have many mom friends who home-schooled and they "rocked" at it. I'm just thankful that I didn't get that call. Now, two generations later, I might have done a little of both in home-schooling and public school. Only God knows.

We are gonna often find ourselves on the "Struggle Bus" at one time or another. There will be messes and mistakes and Jesus is our only real hope in life. The Bible is not a book of "Rules on Good Behavior," but is a "Love Story" of Redemption. The book of Romans, specifically, is a great read for understanding Christianity. The Apostle Paul, as the author, understood that the things we *do* are separate from *who* we are. He teaches that once we know who we are in Christ, our behavior (our "do") will change, but trying to simply change behavior will never work. Transformation comes to our "do" as we understand our "who" from God's perspective. We cannot earn God's love, it's a gift He give us with forgiveness for all the mistakes, lies, judgment, coveting, and hatred we have as sinners. Our choice is to accept or reject what He offers and then we are made righteous in Him; we do not have to live under guilt and condemnation. "Jesus, You knew I was like this and You still love me?" His answer will always be, "Yes" and nothing can separate us from His love. Nothing. Nothing.

Legalism will torch and burn up your kids so that they want to run for refreshment elsewhere and follow the opposite direction Jesus is leading (even though legalism is what they're rejecting). Sin is fun—that's why we all do it, but it isn't fun forever and the end result, without repentance, is death and God's wrath. I'm not making this up to scare anyone. Read the Bible, ask God, and discover what He has to say and love them as God loves you. It doesn't mean you "cancel" your kids from attending church, Sunday school, and the Wednesday night kid's group or youth group. Instead, encourage them to attend, but don't "guilt" or manipulate them to get them there. Setting up a rule list that makes them feel that their good works are worth more than receiving God's grace is not what Jesus had in mind. Good works are good but they aren't your salvation. Remember, too, that "more is caught than taught." Prayers for your children, to let God move in and guide them, really work.

Our son Peter shared his testimony at our home church when he was on his first leave from the navy. He said to the congregation on that Sunday morning, "I have memories of my mom's Bible being messy with her underlining verses and lots of notes and dates in the margins. . . . My dad showed what it is to have wisdom," Peter said. "Not only is my dad smart but it's also something deeper, something you can only get when you seek God with all your heart." Peter also shared how his older brother, Marco, (the one that pinned him down during the "911 Mom episode") had helped him see Jesus as real, too.

People need to see us live our lives in such a way that they know we believe and trust in Jesus despite our feelings and difficult circumstances. They need to see our missteps and struggles and how only the grace and strength of God, with lots of prayer, change everything. Our sons saw a lot of the way we handled hurt and hard places; a lot of times they saw how we fell and failed BUT they saw us get back up again with hope.

When I needed counseling over past hurtful relationships, I went and got it. When I needed medication for my anxiety, I got some. You can't limit the way God wants to work. It's not this formula of "If I do 'such and such' along with reciting this Bible verse, then *this* all will work out." To this very day I read my Bible almost *every day with* a journal by my side to write down how I can apply *God's Word* to *my life*. Of course, I've missed days or even weeks of reading the Bible and writing in my journal but it's a pattern and plan which is a life changer, and I will continue to have it until I leave this Earth.

On most nights when all or any of the boys lived at home, Dan would announce, "It's time for five-minute Bible study." He sometimes does this as a conference call and puts whatever sons can gather on speakerphone. It's fun to listen in; as that's the time I am folding laundry and putting it away. Afterward Dan *always* prays for them specifically. All of this, "Parenting with Jesus as Leader," is not a special formula or from a devotion book. The boys and Dan simply read a few Scriptures and then discuss. I prayed with them all the time, too.

We can be in a conversation and something's happened that's either difficult or it could be news, and I'll just pray for God's direction and peace or thank Him for His goodness toward us. We pray through our anger and frustrations, too. It seems when I talk to Joe, most often we're praying to find something he's lost or misplaced. It has always been found. Serious. And Joe calls me back and we thank God together (we actually have this "thing" that Jesus has teleported our lost items to the very place we looked for them a million times over). Being honest with your own struggles when you were a kid or even now as their parent helps them, it helps when we share in each other's humanity.

But what if you do all the "good and godly things" and your child still rejects God? It happens to many people I know and love. Remember, your child has a free will and can still make good or bad choices. God has no grandchildren, only children because each person has to make their own choice. If you are struggling with a child walking away, hold on to this promise from Joel 2:25 (NLT) where God reassures, "I will give you back what you lost to the swarming locusts, the hopping locusts, the stripping locusts, and the cutting locusts."

My radio friend at a conference said, "It's not like I didn't know the Proverb 22:6, 'Train up a child in the way they should go. When they're old they'll not depart from it.' But our oldest daughter is determined to do everything the hard way no matter what advice and direction we give. Why didn't this verse apply to our family? We felt as if we failed God, failed our daughter, but God's grace showed us that despite our best efforts and prayers our daughter had a free will to choose her own way. It's not that she departed from the way she was trained, she just never arrived there in the first place. We did our best with our own imperfections."

This friend and her husband will never give up on their daughter; God certainly won't either. God cares and loves our children more than we do. My biggest achievement in parenting was not anything I did but what Jesus did in me and having the humility to know what both my strengths and weaknesses were. It was His Word changing me and prayer and not expressing every feeling aloud and trying to control everything and everyone. The boys and Dan saw a change in me, in that I was slower to speak and quicker to listen when I was listening to God. I let go having certain expectations I had on how the boys and Dan should behave. Yep, sometimes you have to let go of the picture of what you thought parenting would be like and learn to find peace in the story you're actually living. I asked God to help me become more "chill" and less critical or demanding. I gave more grace to Dan, the boys, and myself. I let God in and He let out a better mom.

It's funny because as an adult, to my adult sons, I think I've apologized more *now* than when they were little. I apologize most often for overstepping and offering unsolicited advice. Unconditional love, I know, means I love them no matter what they do or don't do. Real love means I let them make choices, with their free will, to live a life of love based on knowing who they are in Christ. If they *don't* follow Him, I love them unconditionally, too. Bottom line: We all have hard seasons, and, as Mama said, "There will be 'days' like this," but there are great days here now, too. There is so much to look forward to in our final Home of perfect peace. This isn't it. You "got this" Mama because God's got you and He always has the final Word.

DEPENDENT ON KINDNESS

25
LOVE SERVES: MUCHO GRACIAS

"Work willingly at whatever you do, as though you were working for the Lord rather than for people."
— **Colossians 3:23 (NLT)**

AT FIFTY-ONE YEARS OLD I worked a couple days a week at Barajas Mexican Bar and Grill for a total of three years before they went out of business. It served the most authentic homemade food and was owned by a couple who easily could be my children. Both are from Mexico and lived in the Icebox of the Nation, the most-northern town in Minnesota and the coldest spot in the US.

The restaurant was bright, with artfully carved booths, with orange as the dominant color (my color). The location is next to one of two grocery stores in our small town and the one movie theatre. How convenient, no? If you want to have a few margaritas and not get into your car afterward, you just walk a few feet to the theatre and catch the latest shows available.

My gig and role as server girl began summer 2017. This was after I was no longer working as a managing artistic director for a summer children's theatre company (Gooseberry Park Players) where I lived in Fargo, North Dakota, for two and a half months, 250 miles from my home. I began serving Burrito Locos at the Mexican Bar and Grill only three months after being charged with a DUI. By the fall of 2017, I thought about leaving my new role as Server Girl and going back on the list as Substitute Teacher Girl. But was that really the best move for me and the students? I was the substitute teacher running down the hallway a minute past the first hour bell rang, yelling out to the students, "I'm here, Mrs. G. is here! Can someone hold my bags while I unlock the door?" I'm not a morning person. I know, 8 A.M. is not early for most, but it sure is when you're a night owl and turn off the bedroom lamp most nights at 2:30 A.M.

So, the substitute teacher form did not get mailed and I stayed at the restaurant. Truth be told, this was one of the more challenging roles I've had, because of the variety of characters hired that would come and go with cooks, chips and salsa carriers, bussers, and servers, and we were an eclectic bunch. I learned *a lot*. I was frustrated a lot but I grew to love a lot, too, and I was loved in return. In the restaurant business, one needs to understand that there is a certain level of crazy, with conflicts in personalities and the ways of operation. It was only after watching *Narcos* on Netflix that I realized what I was getting into; I was working at a cartel-type operation. Now, take a deep breath. I do not mean a drug cartel, so let me explain my definition of a cartel-run establishment. It is an arrangement and understanding of how we will all work in business with one another, but also as a family. We will be loyal, serve others, and work hard. We will fight. We will reconcile on some level of understanding. I saw that there were expectations and policies that were different than other typical American restaurants. In some way, we all were adopted into the Mexican culture. When conflicts arose, we'd work through them. If not, we'd be out, *but* when the cartel has your back, "you're in" and they're there for you. If you don't accept working in this style or system, then "you're out." It's that simple.

It took some explaining to the owners, Ruben and Gabriella, on what I meant when I referred to work as a cartel (and to others in our small town) but when they understood, they hopped on board with me and now are forever known as my "Cartel Family." Ruben was referred to as Don Ruben and later just Mijo Don Ruben (my son Don Ruben). My attorney husband was referred to as "Saul" from the series *Breaking Bad* (and then the spinoff series *Better Call Saul*) and he was able to come alongside many of the gang to help in legal matters and give advice. I was Mama Whiskey and need I even explain why?

Maybe a month after this declaration that I worked at a cartel, I got frustrated with a party I was serving seated at C7. I was venting to Ruben while refilling their sodas. Ruben looked me in the eye and said with his beautiful Spanish accent, "Don't worry Hun-ney, the cartel has your back." I smile every time I think of that because I know it's true.

No matter where we work or what we do, we need to know we belong and have a purpose. One evening when Server Girl Ramsey and I were closing the cartel, we first shared a plate of grilled chicken nachos, with guacamole and sour cream. We had previously had some "Jesus loves you" talks, and Ramsey knew where I was coming from with my faith as did the other employees. She prefaced the news she wanted to share with me by first saying, "I know you probably don't believe in palm reading, but I had a palm reader tell me that my purpose in life is to help and take care of others." I love Ramsey. I smiled and looked into her deep brown eyes and said, "Ramsey, you don't need a palm reader to tell you that because we actually all have the same purpose. We're here to serve others."

Life is not about us. First, of course, we need to know how loved and treasured we are. We need to receive and experience God's gift of grace, otherwise everything we do will be selfish, and all the good deeds we do will actually begin to drain us as we try to prove to ourselves and others that "we're okay" and "we're good enough." Freedom comes not from us performing, pretending, and showing OUR strengths but rather from God's strength and His open arms welcoming and accepting us as we are. When we accept Christ's strength in us, we can be honest about our weaknesses. We don't need the approval of others because we're fully approved in Him and that's all that really matters. The good deeds we do are out of love for Him and not because we must show God or others how important we are. You and I are unique and beautiful creations; God has our dreams in His hands with the different gifts He's given us. While it might seem like He's denying us our dreams, He might, in fact, only be redirecting them. God might be wrecking our plans when He sees that our plans are about to wreck us. He has the whole world in His hands (as the song goes), and He's very mindful of us specifically and personally. So, with me, it meant working in a restaurant serving quesadilla rancheras (chicken or beef), folding silverware, and cleaning a toilet as needed. There are many seasons of life and a variety of jobs or roles that we all have. It's important to know that no one is more significant or important because they hold a degree, come from a wealthy family, or may have incredible opportunities presented to them. Ralph Waldo Emerson nails it: "The purpose of life is not to be happy. It is to be useful, to be honorable, to be compassionate, and to have it make some difference that you have lived and lived well."[41]

I traveled as a Speaker Girl maybe once a month with this basic message, "Jesus loves you no matter your age, race, gender, or occupation, where you're from or what family you're born into. Because, believe me, when I was cleaning a toilet, mopping and scrubbing the kitchen, or running back to blend a mango/banana daiquiri and then

---

[41] R. W. Emerson, (n.d.). A quote by Ralph Waldo Emerson, https://www.goodreads.com/quotes/64541-the-purpose-of-life-is-not-to-be-happy-it, viewed February 9, 2022.

back to the bar area to squeeze lime juice for an organic margarita, all the while hoping the quesadilla ranchera wasn't getting cold in the kitchen because the kitchen bell ran (signaling the food was up), I was not feeling so "high class." Yet mistaking prominence with significance and meaning is a deadly error. Position, power, money, and prominence will never fill the eternity that God has put in our hearts. I never thought I'd be using my feet as a Server Girl to share the Gospel whether I used words or not. "Oh, how beautiful are the feet of messengers who bring Good News!" (Romans 10:15, NLT).

God wants to fill the emptiness we feel and experience. He sees our struggles and He doesn't condemn us for them, in fact, He wants us to see them, too. One of the worst things is to actually think that it's on our own strengths and strong will that we can overcame obstacles. Stinky pride will set in when we become "The Fixer," rather than admitting our brokenness and realizing that God alone is the only One who can mend and make amends.

When I first began the speaking ministry, in 2007, I had some fun merchandise to sell such as Everyday Manna Pajamas and some coffee mugs. I had a friend create a cartoon logo of me holding an oval circle sign that read, "Everyday Matters." I could hardly wait for the mugs to arrive, but when they did, I was devastated! *What!* How in the world did the company, producing the mug, not realize that the cartoon logo of me should be *so* much larger? The mug was a size bigger than most and perfect for a great cup of coffee or tea. I was very upset. This was a big purchase for me and now I had boxes of mugs sitting in my garage that looked stupid. I wanted to return them all but still, I waved a prayer of Romans 8:28 over them saying, "God I know You promise to work *all* things for the good, and that certainly includes large coffee mugs with a logo that's too small, so *help!*" That evening I then shared the devastating news with my husband. Succinctly and lovingly Dan said to me, "Debbie, it's not about you," and what followed was a lesson of love and grace from Jesus in John 3:30,

"You must decrease so I can increase." The ministry of Everyday Matters wasn't about me; it will never be about me. The message of the ministry is Jesus loves you in every way and every day no matter what happens or how you feel. So, to God be the glory! The "Little Debbie" size logo on the mug is perfect with the added verse of John 3:30. I call it the "Shrink & Drink" mug. We need to shrink, to drink in all God has for us.

Still, it doesn't mean that I don't struggle with self-importance in my insecurities. I still check my Instagram too often, and during my restaurant days I wondered why I couldn't just be a Speaker Girl full time. Yet, I knew that season wouldn't be forever. God knows my heart, and He put me at the restaurant for a specific time and purpose. I am called to serve. Period. And for three years I worked at a genuine and real Mexican restaurant, where I connected with so many people whom I love and call family. I saw brokenness just like I knew the broken parts in me, and so I knew how to pray. I also knew joy wasn't about my circumstances but in having hope that God promises to fill our emptiness and restore and redeem our broken parts. The Israelite people are those we can relate to because they made broken choices, but they also experienced God's hope of restoration. It serves to remind us, too, that we are free to choose, but we are not free from the consequences of our choices.

Though chosen, rescued, and promised, God's people suffered through severe consequences for their continual rejection of Him and His covenant. Ezra was a religious leader of the Jews who returned from exile in Babylon. He read from God's Word and recited His Law to the people (recorded in Nehemiah 8), and they were shattered by their vast disobedience and rebellion. "Their exile was severe, both in its brutality and how it burned into the minds and identity of the people."

When Ezra said, "The joy of the Lord is your strength" (Nehemiah 8:10) he was speaking to the remnant of Israel who had returned to

Judah to rebuild the city and its temple. It was a time of restoration, not only of the ruined city, but also of obedience to the law of God. Yet, because of God's unfailing love for His people their relationship with Him was not lost. "He was willing to rebuild and restore His people," Meg Bucher writes in her blog, What Does 'the Joy of the Lord Is My Strength' Mean? "The day God reaffirmed to them that they were still his chosen people, and he was still their God. That is a joy that could impart strength. His love leveled them then as it humbles us now, to consider the New Testament sacrifice of God's only Son for our own personal restoration through salvation."[42]

Happiness is based on circumstances that happen and not all are "happy" ones. Joy is more powerful. Ezra instructed the people to find their strength in God's joy. He also told the people to eat, drink, and send food to those who had nothing. They understood his instruction and got busy being a blessing. The Bible says clearly, too, in Acts 20:35 that it is more blessed to give than to receive. Honestly, nothing releases supernatural joy in our lives more than being a blessing to other people. God has chosen you and me to love, to bless us, to serve us with undeserved grace and forgiveness. We can choose to reject or accept Him, but nothing will cause Him to stop loving and pursuing us. When we choose to imitate Christ in being a "server" to others we receive a joy that brings peace no matter how hectic or maddening one of your "restaurant days" can be.

Despite the conflicts with others, the long hours on my feet, the times of aggravating customers and the stress of restaurant life, I was able to experience the joy of the Lord as my strength. Funny enough, too, but there was something calming about scraping rice and beans off a plate in the back garbage while watching Chris the dishwasher

---

[42] Meg Bucher, "What Does 'The Joy of the Lord Is My Strength' Mean in the Bible?" September 4, 2019, https://www.biblestudytools.com/bible-study/topical-studies/what-does-the-joy-of-the-lord-is-my-strength-mean.html, viewed July 10, 2021.

"crush it like a boss," wearing a garbage bag. It's kind of like the calm I get sorting laundry or organizing the refrigerator. Every Monday and Tuesday when I would work, I'd come in and first greet Chris with a hug. At least once in my shift I'll yell out, "Hey, Chris?" (and I knew each time he thought I was asking him for more clean silverware to roll) and each time I would say, "I appreciate you, Chris." He always answered with, "Ah, thanks, Debbie. I appreciate you, too." A person who feels appreciated will always do more than is expected and this was true for all of us.

We shared birthdays, weddings, and other social gatherings in my own family's personal home (I officiated a union between a cook and a server girl). We offered hope and encouragement to each other in walks, workouts, prayers, laughter, and tears. There were many times I thought about leaving because it was hard in ways spiritually, emotionally, and physically and, I guess I just didn't expect that. Sometimes I felt so foolish or even dumb and insignificant but, in my spirit, I knew God had placed me in this job to be a blessing and to receive many as well. I would continually tell Gabby, "God will make it clear when I am to leave and move on from this place." In Spring 2021, when the restaurant could no longer survive due to the effects of the pandemic, I made my exit from the Cartel Restaurant (with a few other loyal members). Dan is still the Grandpa-Man to the three small children of Ruben and Gabby who stop by as often as they can at Dan's office for treats and hugs. Another other dear server girl's children adore him too and call him, "Danny Boy."

Yes, my "cartel family" deeply impacted me and will forever be a part of my life as will the many blessings and lessons I received. A really good life is about real and sincere love, and real love serves. It's where happiness and joy are found and to that I say, "*Muchas gracias, God, muchas gracias.*"

26
SERVER GIRL BLUES AND ORANGE

*"God keeps an eye on His friends,
His ears pick up every moan and groan."*
— **Psalm 34:15 (MSG)**

STANDING BEHIND THE COUNTER of the Mexican restaurant where I worked as Server Girl, I felt insignificant, stuck, and stupid. I was alone, save for the cooks in the back and the one couple seated at a booth eating Nachos Locos and Two for One Monday Margaritas.

My orange T-shirt had the name of the restaurant printed on it, but I felt it also made the statement that I had hit rock bottom. Honestly, my gig at the restaurant over the summer had been a great choice, and so I decided not to go back to substitute teaching in fall. Sure, I was still writing, the radio feature was broadcasting, and speaking engagements were happening, but my pride thought that by now I'd be on bigger stages sharing my theatrics, while presenting the Gospel full-time.

Yet, there I was at the Mexican Bar and Grill standing at the counter feeling sorry for myself. I looked out through the big glass doors onto the cold Minnesota parking lot and caught the sun reflecting bright off the hood of a car and in that moment, I heard God speak, "I see you." His voice was so clear that I started to cry. What I heard at that moment was Jesus reminding me that no matter where I am, or what I'm doing, He sees me. He loves me. And He's always on the move; whether I feel or think it, He is working. He is an active God.

He reminded me again that I wouldn't be forever stuck where I was and that the snow would melt and the dreams He'd given me (His purpose for me) were presently in motion according to His way, will, and timing. In fact, He was blessing me right where I was in my role as Server Girl. I was significant like everyone else with whom I worked, based on my being God's child and not my titles, education, or financial status. Shortly after this revelation, a couple came in to eat, and I was off grabbing chips and salsa and back into the routine of my everyday serving job.

We get messed up when we believe blessings are about being rewarded materially, along with expectations of Disney magic, pixie dust, rainbows with pots of gold, and a parade with everyone cheering our name. But, "What if your blessings come through raindrops, or your healing comes through tears?" (from "Blessings," by Laura Story.) Yeah, what if, like the song lyrics, we discover that the difficult seasons in our lives aren't about breaking us, but instead about bringing the breakthrough we've been waiting for? That's my story over and over again. The biggest blessings come in the hardest of places, and most often we only "see" the blessed result after the trial and not in it.

"Orange is the New Blessing," is the title of my story of being charged with a DUI, which landed me in jail, covered from head to toe in bright matte orange. Four hours spent in "The Cop Shop" was a shock and a blur. The full blessing of the trial came in the eight-month season in which I challenged the charges. That experience was a "game-changer," a grace-filled time where I learned and grew in ways I never would have imagined (growth in muscle tone included, as I biked and hiked most places after losing my driving privileges).

The year was 2017 and I had just recently turned fifty. While there are better ways to "come of age," I was in a solid place of knowing my identity in Christ and being able to say, "I am the righteousness of God." Righteousness in Him means that I receive all the goodness, love, and acceptance that I could possibly need without doing anything to earn or deserve it from God. His amazing grace and forgiveness for our confessed sins (which we all wretchedly have) is what He needs from us because it's all about Him working in us and not our self-planned and self-righteous performances. You, too, can say, "I am the righteousness of God," when you know that you are in right standing with Him by what He did "right" on the cross. It's not your good works but His blood payment for your sins.

But yet we pray, "God bless me with this plan I've come up with to honor and give You glory." Really? How about this instead, "Thank You God for who You are. Holy is Your name, and I thank You for Your grace and strength for this day, knowing that tomorrow I'll receive new mercy for that day. How can I honor and make this day all about You and not all about me? Amen."

It's so opposite of worldly thinking, which says that the amount and measure of love we hand to our neighbor sets in motion the kind of love we receive from God. But Christianity should teach that our righteousness displayed and acted on comes from what God did right for us on the cross. He didn't come to bring punishment, but to bear ours, and all we have to do is receive His act of sacrificial love and forgiveness first.

My failing did not make me a failure, and I was even able to write the words, "Nothing is wasted" in jail before I was discharged. I know that with God all things are redeemable for the good.

Perseverance. That's the ticket. Waiting on God to show us His way, that He is God and we're not.

Are you wondering how my husband and four sons responded? Yes, they were shocked, disappointed, and embarrassed by my title of "DUI Debbie," but not devastated. It didn't define who I was. Weeks later in a conversation with my eldest son (now a pastor), I heard Marco share, "Oh, that with Mom? Her DUI is not an issue, but what does bug me is how she . . . ."

We must choose to own our story so our stories don't end up owning us. But our part in receiving God's grace is just as crucial. We so desperately need to accept God's grace instead of trying to "prove ourselves" or make excuses. Not only do we hurt ourselves by refusing grace, but we then can't turn around and offer that same grace and kindness to others. No one needs judgment; they need grace, which you don't know how to give unless you've received it. How we respond to someone else's trial either in kindness or condemnation makes all the difference in being a blessing or a biatch.

Truth.

I mean, how much of our time is spent trying to show God and others how good we are? "Hey! Look at me over here! Aren't I a good girl, doing everything right? I'm certainly doing a bit better over here than Loser Linda over there." Blech. It's not helpful. What makes the Gospel such Good News is that we are righteous because God, on account of Christ, has decided to call us so, not because we've earned favor or salvation by our works as Super Susie Christian or Doug Do-Gooder. Let the thought of what Jesus did for you melt your heart into friendship, one that is personal and intimate. See God working everywhere in the everyday trenches with everyday people. Listen sincerely and share your heart honestly.

When I share that I've been stuck in hard places and how God brought me through, I'm able to bring comfort to another who is weary, sad, and scared. You're not alone in going through deep waters where it feels like God is shaking you. Jesus is the one who is really shaken so you could stand. Hear Christ speak. He has a blessing for you no matter where you are or who you are. Nothing will change your life like hearing the voice of God through Scripture, the Word of God, His word of grace.

The life we live, here on Earth, is no picnic yet we can have peace in the midst of it. What we all desire in this life is to be understood or heard and to be loved for who we are and where we are. Jesus knows everything. He fully knows and sees you better than anyone and still loves you. He knows me, my dramatic self, my ache from relationships that are broken and have never been reconciled, the "poo" in parenting, the messy in my marriage, and the illnesses that came into the lives of family and friends. He knows my past and present issues with anxiety attacks and depression and the unfairness of circumstances and every single mistake I've made. *But* . . . my Redeemer lives and not my Punisher. He will find a way to work all things for the good and for the glory of His name. My responsibility is to step back and let Him be God. This unconditional love He has for us is hard to fathom because there is no one else who is like Him and loves so completely. He's God of the hills and the valleys, and He offers Himself at our every turn.

Christ's power gives me purpose in everything I do, whether performing on stage or serving someone a Burrito Loco. Serve the person He puts in front of you each day and in whatever role you have. Giving and serving others, not self, is what makes us "feel" good and live purposefully.

When we understand we're fully accepted by the Father, in Christ, we don't have anything to prove because He proves faithful. We can walk humbly in grace. Humble people are happy people and fun to be around.

Without the trials of scoliosis pain and surgery (especially recovery), rejection, anxiety, and loneliness (even when there were lots of family and friends), I wouldn't be the person I am today. If I hadn't gone forward when I was scared or feeling stuck and stupid, I wouldn't have received certain and specific blessings that have changed who I am, nor would I be the blessing I can be. "Don't give up," is the best advice I can give you, especially when your feelings are telling you otherwise.

The blasts in life make us better; don't let them make you bitter, because in a strong relationship with Jesus you can endure anything *and* be blessed. You and I are of such great significance no matter what color the season is. Hold on in faith with what you know is true. Faith is not a feeling. "Now faith is confidence in what we hope for and assurance about what we do not see" (Hebrews 11:1 NIV). Wait and see how God will follow through with His promises, turning the bad into the good, with beautiful blessings. Your "blue" days can become hopeful orange days bursting with colorful hope.

Be still. Listen. He speaks. He sees you, in whatever "counter" you're standing at.

27
PRIDE GOES BEFORE THE FALL

"Humble yourselves before the Lord, and He will lift you up."
— **James 4:10 (NIV)**

"I'M JUST FINE. LEAVE ME ALONE AND LET ME DO IT MY WAY. And I'm gonna do all the talking and none of the listening. I know the answer, just ask me. I don't need help. I've got this."

Pride stinks.

King Solomon shared such wisdom in the book of Proverbs with verse 16:18: "Pride goes before destruction, and a haughty spirit before a fall."

My attitude of pride literally caused me to fall. Only by God's grace was I scooped up and rescued.

It was 2012 and I was flying into Nashville to shoot some short teaching videos for the Everyday Matters Ministry. I use props and not PowerPoint, so I had the mothership of theatrical items all stuffed inside a gigantic rolling suitcase. I had another suitcase, not quite as huge, which held my outfits (aka costumes). My shoulders managed a cross-body purse and computer bag, along with a large tote to hold my books. I know, right? I was "all that and a bag of chips."

I was so proud I was able to get *all* my luggage and me brilliantly down the escalator on my own. I even checked my phone to read a text from my friend, Mack, who was praying for my trip. It was a verse from Exodus. "I am sending an angel ahead of you to guard you along the way and to bring you to the place I have prepared" Exodus 23:20 (NIV).

Perfect.

When I got off the escalator, I found the counter to sign papers and get directions to pick up my rental car. It was hot. I was hot and the trek to Rental Car Land was a good hike, but whatever. I adjusted my luggage ensemble and thought, *I can and will do this*, and set off.

Kenny, the airport guy, saw me and my hot mess. I saw him as he drove over to offer help. I'm not saying that the extended golf cart vehicle he was driving wasn't tempting, but I was out to prove that I could manage just fine on my own.

I told Kenny that I was fine, but thanks for asking. Kenny wasn't convinced because three minutes later he circled in a little closer and asked again. "Are you sure, ma'am? It looks like you could use some help."

"Oh, Kenny, I'm fine. I know I look crazy, but I'm not. I made it down the escalator all by myself. I'm good." I said this with that strong, Midwestern Scandinavian hoo-haw that all independent northern girls carry with them (even when we're not Scandinavian). Kenny still wasn't convinced. He followed and watched.

When I got to the escalator to ascend to the rental car floor, Kenny tried a third time. "Ma'am, I would not advise going up that escalator. Let me take you where you need to go *or* you could just take that elevator to your right."

"Kenny, I appreciate your concern, but I'm fine, just watch."

Remember that Proverb?

I started to fall about four steps in and my luggage went everywhere. I don't really remember much of it, but for Kenny pushing all bags and suitcases aside and scooping me up in his arms. To get a visual on Kenny, picture Mammy and her demeanor with Scarlett from *Gone with the Wind* and you have her kin, Kenny. Kenny sat me gently on the cart, retrieved my luggage, wiped his brow, while breathing heavily and shaking his head. "Oh, gurl. You 'bout just done give me a heart attack."

"I'm sorry, Kenny. You're right. I should've accepted your help. I'm sorry."

Kenny followed with this: "Don't you know I was that angel God sent to protect you?"

I was speechless. "*What* did you say, Kenny?"

He repeated. "I'm your angel, darling. I'm here to help you."

Wow!

So yeah, "Me, myself, and I" are the greatest problems I have. I've spent time and energy admiring myself and simply being full of myself, when in reality, I'm supposed to be full of God and empty of self—totally empty. I know that God resists the proud, but gives grace to the humble.

God's called us to *love* one another, and pride and love do not mix. Love is not rude and haughty. It's not boastful or conceited. It is not puffed up. Love does not look down on others and it doesn't see others as little and insignificant. Because love values every individual; everyone who comes in contact with a person who is full of love will be made to feel special and encouraged.

It is in love that we receive as well as give help. I am encouraged when someone receives what I have to offer. Well, guess what? Someone is encouraged when I receive their help, too.

Kenny now had my attention, and I'm guessing he took the extended route to get to the next floor because he had things to say.

"I'm gonna tell you a story and I want you to listen, Miss Debbie, ma'am. There was a terrible storm that came into a town and all local officials sent out an emergency warning that the riverbanks would soon overflow and flood the nearby homes. They ordered everyone in town to evacuate immediately. A godly man of faith heard the warning and decided to stay, saying to himself, 'God's gonna save me, God's gonna save me. I put my trust in Him.' The neighbors came by his house and said to him, 'We're leaving and there is room for you in our car, please come with us!' But the man continued. 'No thanks, God's gonna save me. God's gonna save me.'"

Kenny continued. "The floodwaters rose higher, pouring water into his living room, and the man had to climb to the top floor. A police motorboat came by and saw him at the window. 'We will come up and rescue you!' they shouted. But the man refused, waving them off saying, 'Save someone else. God's gonna save me.' The flood waters rose higher and higher and the man had to climb up to his rooftop.

"Finally, a helicopter spotted him and dropped a rope ladder. A rescue officer came down the ladder and pleaded with the man, 'Grab my hand and I will pull you up!' But the man *still* refused, folding his arms tightly to his body. 'No, thank you! God's gonna save me.' Shortly after, the house broke up and the floodwaters swept the man away and he drowned. When in Heaven, the man stood before God and asked, 'I put all of my faith in You. Why didn't You come and save me?' And God said, 'Son, I sent you a car. I sent you a motorboat. I sent you a helicopter. What more were you looking for?'"

Point taken.

We arrived at the rental car location and hugged. I thanked and apologized to Kenny and he smiled and said it was nothin.' Kenny put my luggage in the car and made sure I had my seatbelt on and I was off on the freeways of Nashville.

What the world longs for in the Christian is our sincerity. Brennan Manning gave good advice, "Be daring enough to be different, humble enough to make mistakes, wild enough to be burnt in the fire of love, real enough to make others see how phony you are."[43]

---

[43] Brennan Manning quote, November 21, 2021, https://minimalistquotes.com/brennan-manning-quote-159832/, viewed February 12, 2022.

This is authentic Christianity.

When we experience this real and authentic love, then we're set free to give and receive love and we're also much more fun to be around.

Pride stinks and it's not fun to be around stinky people.

When I shared my story with Mack, who gave me the verse about an angel sent to protect and prepare the way ahead, he said, "I won't be surprised if back at the airport you won't be able to find a guy named Kenny."

He was right. God was there with what I needed—and when I needed it—despite myself. And the lesson and blessing I received are something I'll always carry.

28
YOUR PARENT CHANGES BUT LOVE DOESN'T

"Jesus Christ is the same yesterday and today and forever."
— **Hebrews 13:8 (NIV)**

THERE IS STRENGTH IN MUSIC and often when I'm feeling weak, anger, or anxious, and I need strength, I go to the music of Broadway that I love and sing out loud. When the boys were little and off to school, I didn't wait to get into the shower to belt out a song, but I'd stand on the hardwood hallway floors, like a stage, and let it rip. Often, when I'm driving, I'll go to a Broadway ballad and sing it at the top of my lungs. The song I most often choose for this surge of strength is, "Don't Cry for Me, Argentina," from the musical *Evita*. I used this song as an audition piece back in the day when I was auditioning for shows in Minneapolis before my wedding, babies, and a move to the Icebox of the Nation.

In the months of my mom transitioning to an assisted living apartment due to her dementia, I've found that going to Broadway in my car is again helpful. I've needed strength driving to and from my growing-up home at the family ski resort, where I stay when visiting my mom's new place of living. Her new digs allow for some basic assisted services needed because of her memory, health, and for safety. The move, for me, was harder emotionally than I thought. Of course, it was an adjustment for my mom, but she's also an entertainer and storyteller, so its occupants provide her with a new audience and purpose with her extrovert personality.

The decision by the entire family is wise and practical, but that doesn't mean it's practically free of tears and frustrations for all of us. Call me "dramatic." I don't mind. On one such trek from her home to her new apartment, I knew I needed Broadway, but because it was Christmastime, I didn't feel like going to "Argentina," so instead I went to Bethlehem. I chose the song "In the First Light" by the a cappella group GLAD. It sounds like a Broadway power ballad, especially at the end when I'm gripping the steering wheel and singing boldly and dramatically envisioning myself on a perfectly lit stage. After repeatedly belting the song out for twenty miles the message begins to sink in:

> "In the first light of a new day
> No one knew He had arrived
> Things continued as they had been
> While a new born softly cried.
> But the heavens wrapped in wonder
> Knew the meaning of His birth
> In the weakness of a baby
> They knew God had come to Earth!"[44]

My mom's new circumstances moved me physically and mentally. The message of the song began to hit my head and then my heart. God left His throne to come to us as a baby and grew into a man—Jesus. He came so He could redeem us; not because we deserved redemption as sinners, but because He loved us so fiercely. I

---

[44] B. Kauflin, lyricist (2008, December 9). *In the First Light* · GLAD A Capella Group Christmas-Benson Records. Retrieved March 3, 2022, from https://www.youtube.com/watch?v=IOob4CRW8m0

think of the text my sister-in-law, saint Jonell, sent: "All that we're doing isn't for Mother Mary anymore. She has no recollection. We do this for each other, God, and for her, with no points."

Jonell's words put everything in context for me. It's brilliant. It's a mind shift. Instead of thinking, *I'm doing acts of kindness for Jesus, I think, I am kind because of Jesus. He loves us and gives us grace so we in turn by His love and grace can give to others.* It's not that I don't want "points" at times because of all the *work* of it, but I know God has changed my heart toward my mom in the last month. Prior to that, I was getting so frustrated I would insensibly get angry with her as her dementia progressed. If I was angry with God, I would tell you. I think it's okay to get angry with God. I mean, He's God. He can take it. My mother needed my patience and kindness. What I was giving her was frustration and correction. I needed a change of heart.

That is what God does for us. He changes our heart. It's the enemy, the devil, who hands out despair and wants us to doubt the reason we celebrate Christmas. Jesus is the Word who became flesh and lived among us, He has the final say, and death and sickness have no permanent power over us if we have a relationship with Him. And it's not God's fault that people get sick and change. It's the sickness of sin in this world. If "this" was all there was, then I'd be upping my medication and probably finding other ways to ease the pain of life.

Of course, there's the sadness that my mom will not return to live in her home on the lake. Sadder still is that she's not the same mom I grew up with. She was a pioneer, a hardworking mom who worked alongside my dad tapping maple trees for our maple syrup business. She would let me cut out early to make lunch for the crew because I wasn't an outside girl. My mom was always supportive of my dreams. I still have significant theatre memories from my mom. She gave me brown paper packages tied up with string after each performance when I was in *The Sound of Music*. She also made the ruby slippers for *The Wizard of Oz* and gave me little notes of encouragement stuffed in the toes after the show ran. Those memories both increase and abate the sadness now.

I think there is nothing sadder than if at the end of one's life all you have are the memories but no hope of seeing someone again after their earthly death. That is what God changed for us. When our loved ones pass through the stages of life to that end, it is not the *final* end. God made a way for those we love not to be left to our past, but to be in our future.

God still is speaking with the same message the angels proclaimed: He is Lord, He is King, and He is good because He is Savior. That is what Christmas is all about.

We might never understand "why," but we can trust there is a *way* that God will redeem and work *all* things for the good, even when all is not good. It's a promise found in Romans 8:28. When I returned to my mom's house to pack up some more kitchen items, I again saw the little flea market wooden plaque that sits by the sink. It's painted with a little girl in a pink polka dot dress, and she is standing by the words that read, "Life with God is good." *Every time* I read it, I disagree. Life is messy and life is hard and isn't always good, *but God is* in the messy and hard. The more I look to God, the more I see the blessings in the mess, but it's critical I look to Him and not myself or others for redemption.

Our time on Earth is such a puff of time, a wisp. "You are just a vapor that appears for a little while and then vanishes away" (James 4:14). I spent days and hours with my mom in the beginning of the transition and we watched Hallmark Christmas movies, which I've always considered beyond hokey. At the end of one long day that went into the night, my mom said, "Thank you for spending all that time with me." It made me think of the adage, "People will forget what you say and forget what you do, but they'll never forget how you made them feel." Of course, a few days later she didn't remember me being there at all.

I have been the bossy, impatient, and exasperating daughter and, unfortunately, my four boys took note at Thanksgiving of my less-than-stellar behavior toward Grandma Mary. Thankfully, there's forgiveness given by her, my kids, and our very gracious God. He never gives up on us. He might be heartbroken over our choices sometimes, but He never lets go or fails us. God is ever ready to renew and restore us.

"My life isn't one that looks like Jesus's. It's a life that looks like I need Jesus," (my favorite Tullian Tchividjian quote). Our legacy is not what we leave behind, but how we treated the people we leave behind. I treasure singing in the car on long drives, annual trips to the Minneapolis Children's Theatre, and, of course, shopping. After the theatre production, I would convince Mom to go down to a little riverbed by the church in which I was baptized. We'd sing a song and then sprinkle snow on top of our heads like we'd seen fall to the stage. Magic. The first Christmas for Mom living in her new home, the First Lutheran Church sent carolers to her apartment building. Mom said she joined them. She followed them throughout the three housing units singing along. When the group of carolers left, Mom went back to her room.

New traditions, but the same songs. My mom has changed but my love for her never will never change. God's love for us will never change, no matter what season we're in, especially the difficult ones.

29
'I GUESS I CAN JUST PRAY"

"Then you will call on Me and come and pray to Me, and I will listen to you."
— **Jeremiah 29:12 (NIV)**

SOMETIMES WHEN I WAKE UP ... wait, who am I kidding? Most times when I wake up, I think only about myself and my problems. So, I found rather than begin the day with a "Self-Pity Party," I ask God, "Who do You want me to pray for? Who needs it?" And *every* single time I ask, a name comes to mind.

Recently a friend I see maybe once a year shared on Facebook about a health concern she had. It's funny because the spelling of her name, spelled J-a-n-e-l-l-e, came to my mind rather than just the name. Normally, I think of Jonell, my sister-in-law, if I hear that name mentioned. I believe God had the spelling of the name come to my mind so I could specifically pray for the correct Janelle. So, I simply prayed for her health, hope, and restoration. Then I moved on to the next person.

Later that day I decided to send a message to Janelle to tell her I was praying for her. Her response was, "What a pick-me-up to hear from you. I need prayer and I know yours are making a difference. I needed the encouragement right now." And you know what? Her response picked me up and really encouraged me, too. It also reminded me how uniquely personal God is in our lives.

Life seems like it's getting harder for me, maybe because I'm trying to sort and settle all that happened during the pandemic or maybe it's because I'm getting older and more of my friends are assisting their aging parents (like me), and death and sickness have hit us more personally. Plus, the fact that I'm writing and reflecting more on the significance of our present life and what happens after we die. I find in myself an urgency to proclaim the hope of Christ like never before. Life is short and eternity is well . . . forever. And yet, my selfishness, in only thinking of my own problems and concerns on how life affects me personally, astounds me. It is hard to think of anything but only about our own problems and fears. Perhaps a lot of you, like me, want to stay in bed and numb the pain and try and sleep until the pain lessens or isn't so overwhelming.

You wonder, *What can I do, when I can do nothing?* It feels like we're only really productive when what we've done is seen and acknowledged. Yet prayer is done in quiet moments and without any fanfare. Prayer shouldn't be a last-ditch effort to being productive but rather a first response to doing something that's wonderful and completely effective. There's a prayer group at my church that's offered on Monday evenings and most times I don't feel like attending but every single time I do, even though there's only a handful of people, I think how meaningful and productive it really is, and I'm always changed from being there.

I often cry and end up sitting on the floor in surrender even though everyone else is sitting. Yet, I'm united with others, and we sense the wonder of being heard by a Holy and Loving God. "The prayer of a person living right with God (because they've humbly submitted to His righteousness) is something powerful and effective, to be reckoned with" (James 5:16b, MSG). Prayer changes things. It might not be an immediate change you and I will see or an answer we want, but one thing for sure is that change will happen. Whether or not your circumstances change, God will be at work changing you, if you allow Him to. He will show us His way and His will on how to approach any situation we're in. The Lord is always present whether or not we feel His "presence."

Prayer isn't just about talking to God but it's listening to Him as well. In 2010, our local newspaper, *The Daily Journal*, interviewed our son, Marco, who was fifteen years old at the time, about his trip to the Philippines. Marco said, "So, I've got a relationship with God and it's great because when I was younger it was the religion stuff—go to church, memorize verses . . . but when I really started talking to God, He started talking to me, I got along a lot better. I want to get that through to people in the Philippines. God is a person that you talk to. Not a person really, but God, and you can talk to Him and He'll talk to you. And it's not a one-way conversation." Exactly, just as we can read in Jeremiah 33:3 (NIV): "Call to Me and I will answer you and tell you great and unsearchable things you do not know."

We also have the instructions from Philippians 4:6:7 telling us to not to be anxious about anything but in everything, pray. Pray, with thanksgiving (not complaining). Thank God for what you do have and not all you don't and then bring before Him all that you need (set your petition before Him), and the peace that is beyond what you could ever understand will guard your heart and mind in Christ. I'm "in!" How 'bout you?

I break down Philippians 4:6–7 all the time and pray through it very specifically. I also pray anywhere and everywhere, in my mind, out loud, in the kitchen, in the bathroom, in my vehicle, and in my journal or in a message by sending a text to God, which means I send it to my own cell number. Still you might wonder, as I often have, does prayer really work or when people say they're gonna pray for me, do they mean it? I know I've said I would pray for someone and then completely forgot to do so. Now, I try and make a habit of praying "on-the-spot" as soon as the request is made. This means I reply with a prayer in a message or a comment thread, or I pray out loud but quietly. This "on-the-spot" habit almost always ensures that God will bring the person to mind again. This is what God's done for me when I wake up in the mornings with my own problems and anxieties. A frequent and simple prayer of mine goes like this, "Lord, thank You that You know and care. This is hard. I pray Your healing touch and hope. Protect us from evil. Thanks, Jesus. Amen." A prayer doesn't have to be any sort of lengthy dissertation to be effective. God is always listening. Anne Lamott's book, *Help, Thanks, Wow: The Three Essential Survival Prayers,* encourages this kind of praying. The book was insightful and funny just like Anne is. She wrote the book several years ago and gave an interview on National Public Radio's *Morning Edition* in 2012. I have to share the interview highlights because it's so helpful:

> **Anne Lamott**: "Well, I've heard people say that God is the gift of desperation, and there's a lot to be said for having really reached a bottom where you've run out of anymore good ideas, or plans for everybody else's behavior; or how to save and fix and rescue; or just get out of a huge mess, possibly of your own creation. And when you're done, you may take a long, quavering breath and say, 'Help.' People say 'help' without actually believing anyone hears that. But it is the great prayer, and it is the hardest prayer, because you have to admit defeat—you have to surrender, which is the hardest thing any of us do, ever."
>
> **Staff Interviewer**: "Many pray only when they need something."
>
> **Anne Lamott**: "A lot of the time we don't know when we're surrendering that we're actually, at the same time, maybe establishing connection... to a power greater than ourselves—or something in the next concentric circle out whose name is not me. So, that

to me is where help begins. You know, we're often ashamed of asking for so much help because it seems selfish or petty or narcissistic, but I think, if there's a God—and I believe there is—that God is there to help. That's what God's job is."

Staff Interviewer: "The second prayer, 'Thanks.'"

Anne Lamott: "Thanks is the prayer of relief that help was on the way. . . . It can be [the] pettiest, dumbest thing, but it could also be that you get the phone call that the diagnosis was much, much, much better than you had been fearing. . . . The full prayer, and its entirety, is: *Thank you thank you thank you thank you thank you*. But for reasons of brevity, I just refer to it as *thanks*.

"It's amazement and relief that you caught a break; that your family caught a break; that you didn't have any reason to believe that things were really going to be okay, and then they were and you just can't help but say thank you."

Staff Interviewer: "On the third prayer, 'Wow.'"

Anne Lamott: "Wow is the praise prayer. The prayer where we're finally speechless—which in my case is saying something. . . . When I don't know what else to do I go outside, and I see the sky and the trees and a bird flies by, and my mouth drops open again with wonder at the just sheer beauty of creation. And I say, 'Wow.' . . . You say it when you see the fjords for the first time at dawn, or you say it when you first see the new baby, and you say, 'Wow. This is great.' Wow is the prayer of wonder."[45]

I didn't always think this but now I believe prayer to be one of the most effective ways we can absolutely help another in need. Yet, "back in the day," I admit I was a person who might try to fix, help, and encourage a person by saying, "Here's a Scripture, now feel better." The hope we have (the belief something will get better) is trusting

---

[45] "Anne Lamott Distills Prayer Into 'Help, Thanks, Wow,'" National Public Radio, November 19, 2012, https://www.npr.org/2012/11/19/164814269/anne-lamott-distills-prayer-into-help-thanks-wow, viewed July 10, 2021.

God's promises and prayer for Him to fix, help, and encourage. I also know I feel better when someone can empathize with my issue in some way and responds with, "I understand. I'm so sorry it's hard right now. Here's a hug and I'll pray for you." Often, on social media, when someone says they need prayer I leave a comment of prayer with, "Jesus, help. Thanks. Amen," rather than a comment saying I'll pray. Like I said before, if I don't pray right then I'll forget. I have sensed many times a person must be praying for me, when I'm anxious and distraught, because all of a sudden my anxiety will seem to dissipate. It might be a day or even a week later, but I'll usually hear from someone later who says, "Oh, you came to mind that you needed prayer, and so I prayed for you."

My dear friend Kim and her husband were really struggling; their teenage daughter was making a lot of poor choices with drugs, alcohol, skipping school, and then running away. They loved her fiercely and set rules, boundaries, consequences, and told her they wanted to help her because of their commitment and love for her life. They found programs and counselors to help, and yet the poor choices continued. Kim called me for prayer. Of course, I was already praying for the situation with their daughter, Brittany, but I wasn't praying consistently. So, I told Kim that I would make a commitment, for one month, to pray every single day and I'd send a prayer text that Kim could simply respond to by saying, "Amen" or not.

The first four days of sending a prayer it seemed that the situation with Brittany was getting worse. I thought for a minute, *It's not working. I shouldn't bother.* Of course, that was a dumb thought, but I thought it. I thought about me exercising for three days and then deciding it wasn't working because I didn't have a toned and flat stomach. I know. So, I continued praying and after a week there was a positive change in the choices Brittany was making and there was a better connection between mom and daughter. But then, two days after that, there was another setback; Brittany had again run away and the police were called. Yet, I continued praying. Most days Kim would simply respond with an "Amen" to the text message or I'd hear from her two days later. But at the end of the month circumstances had changed for the better and, more importantly, Brittany was beginning to have a change in heart and what followed then was a change in behavior. Everyone was encouraged. Instead of offering my friend another Scripture verse, or another program she could enroll her daughter in, I offered the most powerful way I could help. I prayed.

It's the perseverance of committing to an act of doing something without giving up, whether it's a diet, an exercise program, or a treatment program. Persevere in prayer, knowing that when you remain "under God," He is actively listening and He is on the move.

Prayer isn't really that popular, even in the Christian community, because it doesn't "feel" strong and active enough. We can't see movement right away and it's usually quiet, sometimes with words and sometimes without. Just think about how many books, programs, and podcasts there are dealing with having a healthy relationship with another person and how prayer isn't offered as a way to make things better. Still, I've gained some good insight from listening or reading some of these podcasts, yet nothing has improved my relationships more than when I've consistently prayed. I remember receiving an email newsletter from a popular influencer about "self-care," which could be beneficial to our relationships with other humans (and I agree), but I had to reread one of the topic points, more than a few times, to make sure I was understanding her correctly. The first few suggestions to be talked about were good. 1) Take care of your inner self and don't just concern yourself with outward health, and 2) Create a life that you don't want to escape from. *Great*, I thought. But then I read the third suggestion, "Refuse to be selfless. This is the best way to care for others and the world." Okay, what? I looked up the definition of "selfless" and put the definition in the sentence and it read, "Refuse to be more concerned with the needs and wishes of others than with your own. This is the best way to care for others and the world."

I am not trying to be a meanie toward this other thoughtful Speaker Girl, but from experience, when I focus more on myself than others, I fall into selfishness and that isn't the best route for me or others in the world. Spending too much time with "inner searching" I only get stuck with more pity problems, thinking everyone else needs to change but me. If I recognize that I might be falling into this pit, I literally have cried out Psalm 139:23 in prayer: "Search me, O God, and know my heart; test me and know my anxious thoughts." Then I'm usually reminded of Philippians 2:1–4, which is a Basic Course in imitating Christ's humility and putting others before myself. The Message Bible Translation says it this way:

> If you've gotten anything at all out of following Christ, if His love has made any difference in your life, if being in a community of the Spirit means anything to you, if you have a heart, if you care—then do me a favor: Agree with each other, love each other, be deep-spirited friends. Don't push your way to the front; don't sweet-talk your way to the top. Put yourself aside, and help others get ahead. Don't be obsessed with getting your own advantage. Forget yourselves long enough to lend a helping hand. (Philippians 2:1–4, MSG).

Of course, it's all about balance, so let me explain what I believe is a healthy approach to self-care. Interestingly enough, my definition was solidified by eighteen-year-old Ella, who was working at the library the day I was working on this story. Ella told me, "As a more introverted person, I have recognized that in order to really care and help fill another's 'cup,' I must first fill my own. I do this through internal and external self-care." I asked Ella what that looked like. She responded, "On Wednesdays, my self-care is focused more on outward care. I'll do a face mask, give myself a manicure/pedicure, or do hair care, etc. On Sundays, I focus solely on internal self-care, through silence and solitude, prayer/guided meditation, and developing and connecting with others in meaningful relationships. When I'm able to fill my 'cup' well, I'm much better at serving and helping others fill theirs."

What Ella shared filled me up with some great insight. It caused me to pause and be less judgmental of the other Speaker Girl, which then led me to pray for her rather than preach against her. Praying for those that I disagree with, or those whom I am bugged by, is one of the best ways to be less bugged. Like I said, prayer changes you. Anyway, like Ella, I, too, am an introvert. This confuses people because they assume theatre people and communicators are extroverts. However, extroverts get their energy from being around others, and introverts get their energy from time alone. Another way to explain, is that introverts like to talk "to people" rather than "with people." Attending a casual social party is perfect for my extrovert husband Dan, but for me, no *bueno*. In order to survive a Super Bowl party, I need to find one person who, first, also isn't interested in football and then engage with them in a meaningful conversation. Usually because I like to "go deep" with a lot of questions, I discover an issue with which the person might be struggling. So, guess what? We pray together or I later send a text message of prayer.

Not being able to work at the restaurant as Server Girl during the pandemic really messed me up. I didn't have a schedule, and so I could easily justify putting off writing projects or making dinner or taking a shower. I felt like nothing really mattered, and so I would continue to look at all that was wrong and difficult and all that was not right and not good. Sometimes, I thought it would have been easier to still have all four boys living at home and at the ages they were in grade school. I would be serving people who needed me and there would be a schedule of purpose, but then when talking to moms who had "this gift," they all expressed they wanted what I had. If we operate from the point of view that life is "all about me," we're doomed. If our only concern is ourselves, then our focus is on our pleasures of what we eat, how we're entertained, what material items we have (or someone else has that we want), and what position we hold. We'll always be searching and craving more. It's a miserable existence to live only for self.

When I focus on what I can do and disregard what I can't do, I always find peace. Here are some activities I often do that help me mentally, and it especially helped during the pandemic:

- I make gift packages for people in my small hometown with puzzles, books, and word games along with fun treats.
- I make a lot of homemade cards with my collection of stickers and colored markers and send a personal and encouraging message.
- I bring meals in tinfoil containers to families and set them on their doorsteps.
- I also take walks with my husband, a son who was home, and with a friend who was "starving" for fellowship, too. We needed to know we weren't alone with our feelings and thoughts and that we weren't going crazy but rather "dealing"with crazy."

Easter, during the pandemic 2020, was on April 12. It was weird and sad not to attend church in a building and instead be in my pajamas all day (I know, I could've and probably should've gotten dressed). It was a loss of celebration in a way that we were accustomed to. I read a post on someone's Facebook page that said, "I'm gonna be honest. There's nothing 'happy' about Easter this year," and then they proceeded to list and lament all the things they weren't able to do. Okay, fair enough, I thought, but it's not about being happy. Happiness is based on what happens to me, which means all circumstances in my life need to be good for me to have my joy ("be happy"). I can choose to have *joy* no matter what's happening. I have a free will to "think on purpose" on how I'll respond to any given situation. Self-centeredness turns my focus in on self and blocks my joy, but giving does just the opposite. We're "happy" when we're reaching out to others because we're then functioning in the will of God. God has not called us to "in-reach," He has called us to out-reach.

So, on Easter Day 2020, Dan and I decided to take a walk with a basket of Easter candy and two poster signs I had made. (I put on wind pants over my pajama pants as well as a puffer coat, along with a hat and mittens because it was "that" cold.) One sign read, "He Is Risen" and the other sign read, "Indeed" and "Happy Easter!" We went to about eight homes of families from our church, in the trailer park, and in our neighborhood. We'd knock on the door and then hold our signs up in the window. Some people would come to the door to receive the candies and others would have us leave them on their steps. It was around thirty degrees in International Falls that day with a biting wind, but my attitude was so sunny, and I could not have been happier. I will smile every time I think of Easter 2020.

We all need joy when there's no "happy" to be felt, but when we can bring joy in the form of a happy, thoughtful, or fun gesture, we are all better for it. We need hope that we'll make it to "the other side" from the hard places we're in.

I'm often reminded of the story in the Bible where Jesus calmed the ferocious storm while He and His disciples were on the lake (Mark 4). The lesson of Jesus telling the storm to "be still" is powerful, both physically and emotionally. Physically, Jesus completely restored the environment to complete stillness; emotionally, He calmed the storm *within* His disciples. But what strikes me most in this passage (verse 35) is when Jesus said to His disciples, "Let's cross to the other side of the lake." And I realized, that's it! I will get to the other side of "this!" God will use all our troubles, in stormy times, to bring a lesson and a blessing to us when we look to Him because, once again, nothing is wasted with Him. Yet, even if we miss any lesson or blessing,

His grace and love will still bring us to the other side. So, the question I ask myself *daily* is, And, *Have you prayed about "it" as much as you've talked about "it"?* God and the power of prayer is everything.

The following true story was reported by a medical missionary at his home church in Michigan and the importance and power of prayer:

> While serving at a small field hospital in Africa, I traveled every two weeks by bicycle through the jungle to a nearby city for supplies. This required camping overnight halfway. On one of these trips, I saw two men fighting in the city. One was seriously injured, so I treated him and witnessed to him of the Lord Jesus Christ. I then returned home without incident.
>
> Upon arriving in the city several weeks later, I was approached by the man I had treated earlier. He told me he had known that I carried money and medicine. He said, "Some friends and I followed you into the jungle knowing you would camp overnight. We waited for you to go to sleep and planned to kill you and take your money and drugs. Just as we were about to move into your campsite, we saw that you were surrounded by twenty-six armed guards."
>
> I laughed at this and said I was certainly all alone out in that jungle campsite. The young man pressed the point, "No, sir, I was not the only one to see the guards. My five friends also saw them and we all counted them. It was because of those guards that we were afraid and left you alone."
>
> At this point in the church presentation in Michigan, one of the men in the church jumped up and interrupted the missionary, and asked, "Can you tell me the exact date when this happened"? The missionary thought for a while and recalled the date. The man in the congregation told this side of the story:
>
> On that night in Africa it was morning here. I was preparing to play golf. As I put my bag in the car, I felt the Lord leading me to pray for you. In fact, the urging was so strong that I called the

men of this church together to pray for you. Will all of those men who met with me that day please stand?

The men who had met that day to pray together stood—there were twenty-six of them![46]

Reading such a testimony of God moving on the hearts of others to pray is powerful; it's inspiring. But do you think that kind of prayer-power is only for the people in ministry, serving abroad or in churches? Prayer works for everyone. God moves and cares about every single human He created in His image. I have known of miraculous healings when cancer or a mass of disease was on an x-ray one day and on the next day the doctor's visit showed a clear picture and report. Sometimes, healing doesn't happen but eventually it will. Healing might not happen while you're here on Earth, but the hope of heaven promises we'll all be healed and perfected there. Oh, how the Lord wants a relationship with every one of us, to hear us, and to speak to us. This communication is all through prayer, and praying is probably the most productive and valuable act of service you can do for another. You might never know how much until you reach heaven. Keep on keeping on. Cry out to God. Call on Him and pray to Him, and He will listen to you (Jeremiah 29:12, NIV). Don't let prayer be the last-ditch effort to change or improve a situation, but be a Prayer Warrior, be a "First-Responder," and just pray.

---

[46] Grace Bible Baptist Church, Leesburg, Florida, https://www.gbbconline.com/twenty-six-men/, viewed July 17, 2021.

30
RELEASE & REPLACE: THE THREE C'S TO PEACE
PART 1, PART 2, AND PART 3

> *"Obviously, I'm not trying to win the approval of people but of God. If pleasing people were my goal, I would not be Christ's servant."*
> — **Galatians 1:10 (NLT)**

"BECCA HAS EVERYTHING. Great hair, fast metabolism, and she can sew. Did you know she sewed all the outfits for the von Trapp kids in our community production of *The Sound of Music*?"

Yeah, I found that out at the cast picnic when I showed up with brownies that I bought from the grocery store. Becca presented her homemade apple strudel. Sheesh. Or perhaps you've had thoughts that go like this: *I'm depressed. I am. I'm pretending like everything is okay when it isn't. Some days I literally can't get out of bed. I didn't think the rejection of my last writing project would hit so hard and then with the "no invitation" to the girl's trip that Susan planned, that just set me in a downward spiral. I feel like an absolute loser. No one understands me, my emotional pain from past family drama and how there's my back pain from the stupid scoliosis rods pinching nerves on my left side. Nobody cares. I'm so alone. Screw it. I'm making myself a screwdriver cocktail and going to bed.*

But wait, you can't sleep! The thoughts that swirl in your mind won't shut down. Maybe it's something like this: *It's so stupid how unfair life is because of Marilyn and her high-end fashion statements. of course, she can dress like a fashion model with all the money she has. Did you see the new purse she bought? It's not a knock-off but a flippin' Louis Vuitton Alma bag. Plus, the attitude she has, in thinking she's better than everyone else, is wrong, Especially when she calls herself a Christian. How can she act that way after all those problems she's had with her addictions? Whatever. I might not have the purse, but at least I'm not as bad as her. Sure, I'm a sinner but she's worse.*

When I'm speaking at an event, I'll often come down the aisle as "Super Susie Christian" wearing a hard hat with a plank of wood attached. As Susie, I'll talk about people who have issues. "Oh, I know I have issues, too," Susie will admit, "but they're nothing compared to Nancy." The hardhat that Susie is wearing illustrates Matthew 7:5: "You hypocrite, first take the plank out of your own eye, and then you will see clearly to remove the speck from your [sister's] eye." Yet how can we expect to perform surgery on our sister's eye when we have a whole plank of issues jutting out of our own eye? We can't. Any time I've tried to pass off gossip talk as simply prayer concern for another, the Holy Spirit convicts me, and I literally feel like my plank begins to grow longer like Pinocchio's nose.

But I know I'm not alone in having those mad and crazy thoughts of jealousy, comparison, and pride. We covet what others have, we compare their lovely lives with our unlucky ones, and in our pride we become self-righteous and judgmental. And even though everything in our lives is really not okay, by golly, we're gonna work really hard to show our lives as all sunshine, butterflies, and bunnies.

Do you strive to have an Instagram or Facebook page that looks like you live a magical life? How much of your time is spent wishing you had hair like Robin, metabolism like Ashley, a body like Cindy, money like Marilyn, a spouse who cared like Sue's, children who are smart, athletic, and attractive like Nancy's, and then there's Karen's job you wish was yours. The words from Joyce Meyer ring true so true when our minds take flight like this: Plenty of people have wishbone (in wishing they were somebody else), but there are too few with enough backbone (people who stand up and understand who they are in Christ). When we're "rooted and established in God's love, seeking His approval, we have confidence to be who He created us to be. Ephesians 3:12 says that through faith in God we can approach Him with freedom and confidence and ask Him for the "backbone" to stand up and do what He's called us to do. If we experience a setback or failure, we don't have to fall apart but rather believe God will use the experience to train us for the next steps. Isn't that helpful and encouraging?

I'm a wretch without Jesus. I want to be honest about my "beautiful" life by sharing the good and the bad. I have pictures and words that are "sunny," but I know the "cloudy" and "gray" photos speak many more words of comfort.

I understand and I hear you. I've fallen into the "I wish" trap more than I care to admit. My mind fills with negativity and comparison. I wanted to *stop*, so I came up with a plan that I know was a "God plan" because it works. I share it with others because we all need help, here on Earth. I call this exercise plan "Release and Replace." I teach and apply the principles over and over to myself, and then share this plan at speaking events, using different characters and props to communicate the message. It's a process of release and "letting go" of unhealthy thoughts and "letting God" replace them with healthy ones. It's absolutely freeing. I can be "me" and know that's more than okay because God didn't make me to be a "Karen" or a "Nancy" or a "Becca." I had to come up with something because I want to be a blessing of encouragement to others rather than an insecure drama queen whom no one wants to be around.

You and I choose what we think on. We can take captive to negative thoughts (2 Corinthians 10:5) and replace them with thoughts of hope and kindness, no matter who or what is bugging us. "Breathe on me Holy Spirit" (John 20:22) is my prayer because I don't have the strength to carry out "this plan" without His presence in me. So, I came up with the Release and Replace Plan and, let me tell ya, it's a game changer. When you go from negative to positive thoughts you live life differently. You live with hope and don't think (as much) how life isn't fair.

Here's the Release and Replace Plan—The Three C's to Peace:
Release Coveting—Replace with Celebrating
Release Comparison—Replace with Compassion
Release Competing—Replace with Confession

We often know what we "shouldn't do" (we shouldn't think negatively about ourselves and others), *but* if we only release the negative thoughts and don't replace with positive thoughts, we'll find ourselves in bigger messes of confusion, frustration, and depression than we ever could've imagined. *I know, but I just couldn't help myself*: those repetitive negative thoughts happen when there's no replacement plan.

Let's go. Let's break it down.

PART 1: Release Coveting—Replace with Celebrating

First, release the *coveting* or jealousy of others and replace with *celebrating* who that person is and the gifts they have. But then, just as importantly, you must celebrate the gifts God's given you to bless others. For example, I celebrate Terri, who likes to bake. I applaud her and the other women who bake homemade frosted sugar cookies, muffins, cakes, and pies, and then share them with our family. "Hey! Don't all 'good' moms bake (as well as sew, craft, and garden)?" Well, God tells me I am a good mom and I don't do any of those things, so there's that. When our four boys were younger, I asked them one year what they wanted for Christmas cookies. They thought for a moment and then replied, "Fig Newtons and Chips Ahoy." Bam. Done. I am a good mom.

The next year, the church family ladies discovered my lack of baking talent *and* my disinterest in it (you have to follow rules in baking; you can't just creatively sprinkle in all the baking powder that you feel you need). Each year we now receive several plates of cookies, all brilliantly displayed with variety and creativity by some of the best Midwest bakers *ever*. Now remember, while I'm celebrating those "Baker Girls" and their gifts, I must also find something to celebrate in myself.

When I'm speaking at an event, I use an oven mitt (prop) to illustrate the point that I don't bake, but then I take off the mitt and "release it" and "replace" it with a prop, which is a disposable tin-roaster pan. I celebrate the fact I like to cook and bring meals to other families. It's fun. As I mentioned, I don't like baking because you have to follow directions, plus I'm "saltier" more than "sweet," but you can be very creative with spices when cooking. There are many times God puts on my heart to make a meal for a family that is stressed or maybe they just need a break in the kitchen. I can prepare a mean cranberry chicken dish and cheesy potatoes (I now call them "Trinity Chicken" and "Trinity Potatoes" because each have three ingredients). These dishes are greatly celebrated by the recipients. Each of our four sons has been a delivery partner with me on such errands.

The short conversations, laughter, and thankfulness found in a home's entryway, by a mom and her children, is meaningful and lasting. I believe that the thirty minutes of conversation in the entryway, letting someone share their heart through tears and/or anger, means more than the cheesy potatoes. It's called, "empathy." I might not have experienced everything this woman is going through, but I can certainly find a way to relate to a time when my own heart was shattered, and the hole I was in seemed so deep and dark. Sometimes when *I'm* in the dark, I don't want to do anything but sit and eat a pint of "poor me" while thinking about life's unfairness. *But* when I choose to *get up* and give, with a simple act of kindness, by sharing a meal, I *know* it is helping me, perhaps more than the one I'm giving it to.

We all need to know, so desperately, that we're not alone and we are loved right where we life has us. We all need hope and understanding. Having a party with "Pity" is never a good idea, and *any* coveting I had in thinking how this mom I'm now serving might have a better life than I do has completely disappeared. I *really* had no idea how hard her struggles were until I showed up with my Cranberry Chicken and Trinity Potatoes (Recipes are included at the end).

Here's the scoop: God doesn't need me to be heard on the radio, write books, or be a speaker-girl. He loves me for who I am and not for what I do. He gives us all purpose with the gifts He's given us, simply because He loves us. "For we are God's workmanship, created in Christ Jesus to do good works, which God prepared in advance for us to do" (Ephesians 2:10). The good works we do will come as a result because of our love for God and not because we have to earn His love from good works. You'll find that serving and celebrating someone else will bring you more joy than receiving praise yourself. Freedom comes by knowing who God says we are and finding our identity in Him. We have to look at who we are and how God uniquely made us. There's this "safe place" where we can be completely transparent and authentic with God and ask Him, "What is it that makes me unique so I don't fall into coveting what others have?" You, too, have something unique that can bless others. I don't covet what you have; I celebrate you right now. I'm cheering for you to discover your gifts and share them with others.

PART 2: Release Comparison—Replace with Compassion
Let's move forward with the plan:

Secondly, release *comparing* and replace with *compassion*. Don't get stuck into thinking that you're all alone and no one understands your hard places. Look up from the downward spiral you're falling into and find the hurting person who needs your compassion and empathy. The prop I use for the illustration of "Comparing to Compassion" is a scarf with which I cover over my whole head. As I speak through it, I lament how alone, afraid, and sad I feel with a season I was in. "No one cares. I'm all alone. I can't go through another day." And as I'm doing this skit, I'm softly speaking, even though the words are raging loud in my mind. There are so many hurting hearts that need to hear, "There's hope. You're not alone."

I continue speaking with the scarf covering me, but I then slowly take it off and put it around the speaker's stand to show how covering someone with compassion will not only bring them hope but change you, too. Being transparent with our lives to God, ourselves, and others brings freedom to live compassionately, giving us the peace and joy that we all long for. Doing one simple act of kindness, such as writing a personal note of encouragement and putting it in the mail for someone, has literally changed a whole day for me, when all I really had planned was to lament with angry tears, a cocktail (or two), and frustration due to crazy/difficult circumstances. I make homemade cards out of construction paper with a million stickers on them and add words of encouragement with colorful markers in fun shapes. It's another unique and "signature" thing about me (our son Joey tells me I have a "magical gift" in card making).

I am able to express compassion on a whole new level now. That's because in 2009 I had that very scary and difficult season of anxiety attacks and depression I mentioned earlier. The hole was dark and deep. I came through by the love of God and support of others who reached out to offer me hope when simply getting out of bed was difficult. I came through by the power of medication, too. This also was a season where I realized I wasn't a failure with my faith in Christ. I went on medication to stabilize and God said, "It is good." If I would have needed blood pressure meds, God would have also said, "It is good." AND, I wouldn't have thought, for a second, that my faith was lacking. Yet I might begin to think, *If I'm on "mental meds," shouldn't my strong faith be the antidote?*

Comedian and speaker Chonda Pierce was helpful when I needed to take some medication and swallow the pill. I remember watching a clip of her being interviewed on *The 700 Club* (no laughing matter) and how openly she shared her need to take prescription medication for severe depression. She said, "We limit God when we decide there's only one way. He can work good in our lives to bring stability or restoration. After much wrestling in my mind with taking medication for my depression, I took my prescription bottle and taped a piece of paper on it that read, 'God loves you, Chonda. Take your medicine.'"

Chonda's sharing her struggle helped me in mine. I am better. My faith is stronger from my experience with anxiety attacks and depression. I can reach into the lives of others and help them because God allowed that difficult season in my life. Yet, it still surprises me how many others are still so afraid of the stigma that comes with a Christian believer taking prescription medication for their mental or emotional issues. Again, the point being, no one judges a diabetic for needing insulin.

God used the time of panic attacks and depression to teach *and* bless me on many different levels because He's good and He loves me. It makes Romans 5:3–4 in the Bible somewhat comprehensible: "Not only so, but we also glory in our sufferings, because we know that suffering produces perseverance; perseverance, character; and character, hope." Going through suffering while persevering means we are learning to remain under God, His love, and His power and direction to see us through. It also means we have hope that either our circumstances will get better or our attitude about them will get better, or both. The work of perseverance in our lives helps us to come alongside others who are in these kinds of trials with love and allows us to offer hope. Simply sit with someone and just "be" by giving them grace and not giving them another Bible verse (that a million other people have already tried to do).

"Here's a verse. Feel better?"

"Nope."

Sitting alongside someone and letting them cry while you comfort them will mean more than anything else you can do. "I'm sorry it's hard," I've said to a suffering soul. "Let me sit with you and you can talk if you need to, or not, but I'm here with you no matter what." It's the person who's been in and out of the hole who knows what is most helpful and needed—"You will pass through this season; God's not surprised you're in it and you're not alone." When you're hurting, you don't need a person delivering, "You should do this." What you need is the person who can say, "I've been there and I understand. 2 Corinthians 1:4 is truth: "There is God who comforts us in all our troubles, so that we can comfort those in any trouble with the same comfort we received." As far as being a "Christian" goes, those who are matured and have depth are the ones who have failed and have learned to live with their failures and walk with hope. I'll always be a work in progress but I try to release comparing my pain against another's and instead offer a heart of compassion to the someone who needs to hear, "You are deeply loved right where you're at. There is always hope."

PART 3: Release Competing—Replace with Confession

Lastly, there's the trap of *competing* with others, which is nasty dangerous: this "C" needs to be replaced with *confession*. When I say "competing," I mean it in the way where we try to "one up" a person and prove we're better by our more stellar performances. But that's exhausting and such a waste of energy. The prop I use for this part of the message, is a pair of sunglasses. I put them on and talk aloud, with my nose in the air, proclaiming, "I don't waste money like Nancy, but instead I use my money to support missionaries abroad. My children are better behaved than Rhonda's. I don't drink any diet pop, unlike Jenny who drinks six cans of Diet Coke a day. I know I'm not perfect but I'm actually better than most."

So Yucky. We must release this competitive pride mindset, thinking we're better than others, because we haven't "fallen" as they have or perhaps as far. But then I take off my sunglasses and put on another pair, where I've taken the lens out completely. This is so I can look into my own life and confess my sins to God. Let's clearly look into our own lives to see what areas and issues we need to work on. To judge another person shows pride. Only God knows what is in a person's heart and the effort it takes to function where they are. We might assume Nancy has the perfect life by the way she dresses and what she posts. But it may be all a cover of photos because it's easier for her to pretend than it is for her to honestly share her struggles with addiction and depression.

Paul wrote, "You, then, why do you judge your brother or sister? Or why do you treat them with contempt? For we will all stand before God's judgment seat . . . So then, each of us will give an account of ourselves to God. Therefore, let us stop passing judgment on one another. Instead, make up your mind not to put any stumbling block or obstacle in the way of a brother or sister" (Romans 14:10, 12, 13). When we stand before God, He won't ask us why our friend or family member did what they did. He will ask us to give an account of ourselves. To manage ourselves is a full-time job. The Holy Spirit doesn't need us to do His job.

No one is interested in the performance of "I have my life and ('poo)' all worked out, and I've documented my almost perfect life on all my social media accounts." Instead, we must confess our sins, our "poo" specifically, and ask for God's grace in every area of our lives. Every. Single. Day. Again, when I say, "Competing is nasty dangerous," I don't mean competing in a game of tennis. I'm talking about the attitude of the heart that tries to "show up" others by performing good works lest we stop and get real enough to discover that without God's grace and intervention we're all toast. We make mistakes and we're all sinners. People who walk around in the arrogant role of "I'm better than you because I behave better" are hurting and have insecurities like the rest of us.

Bringing homemade baked goods to picnics and parties, having teeth that are straighter and whiter than most, along with kids on the "A" honor roll plus the fact you've *never* had a DUI, can lead a person into believing they're in a special camp of "I'm Pretty-Much-Perfect." But, excuse you. Who welcomes that attitude? People with this kind of pride and arrogance are difficult to be around because they're not genuine. Can you say this from 1 Corinthians 4:3–5, "I care very little if I am judged by you or by any human court; indeed, I do not even judge myself. My conscience is clear, but that does not make me innocent. It is the Lord who judges me. Therefore, judge nothing before the appointed time; wait until the Lord comes. He will bring to light what is hidden in darkness and will expose the motives of the heart. At that time each will receive their praise from God." Oh, I strive for those words to ring true in my life. Yet, let's face it, we all fall into this judgmental pit of condemning others no matter how much we "know better." If what you call discernment is your ability to see sin in others but not also the ability to see the spiritual gifts and spiritual growth in others, then you're not discerning, you're just critical.

Recently on a road trip I was listening to a virtual sermon podcast, and the pastor asked us to collectively repeat the words of confession shown on the screen. I did my best to follow along as I was driving. But then Pastor Steve said, "Now take a moment to silently confess your sins to God. I did so aloud because I was alone in my car. I confessed my judgmental thoughts and attitude toward others and asked forgiveness as I listed each one specifically by name. When Pastor Steve was ready to begin the lesson, I was only halfway through my list of people who I had judged because they had hurt or offended me. Is there hope for a wretch like me? Yes, and for you, too.

I love James 5:16 for the power of hope it brings. Many of us are familiar with the latter half of the Scripture that reads, "The effective prayer of a righteous man availeth much." BUT the first part of the verse is the true release to freedom comes. It urges us to confess our sins to one another, and pray for each other so we may be healed. *Wow*. Rather than hiding your sins, confess them. I love how the Amplified Classic Translation of James 5:16 is so clear about the power of confessing your sins. With confession there comes healing, and then tremendous power is available when we do pray.

James 5:16, AMPC: "Confess to one another therefore your faults, your slips, your false steps, your offenses, your sins and pray for one another, that you may be healed and restored. (The earnest, heartfelt, and continued) prayer of a righteous person makes tremendous power available and dynamic in its working."

I read that verse and I want to stand up with my hand raised shouting, "Sign me up! I confess, confess, confess!"

In her book *Liturgy of the Ordinary*, Tish Harrison Warren offers wisdom that is so on point. "Confession reminds us that none of us gather for worship because we are 'pretty good people.' But we are new people, people marked by grace in spite of ourselves because of the work of Christ. Our communal practice of confession reminds us that failure in the Christian life is the norm. We—each and all—take part in gathered worship as unworthy people who, left on our own, deserve God's condemnation. But we are not left on our own. Our failures or successes in the Christian life are not what define us or determine our worth before God or God's people. Instead, we are defined by Christ's life and work on our behalf. We kneel. We humble ourselves together. We admit the truth. We confess and repent. Together, we practice the posture that we embrace each day—that of a broken and needy people who receive abundant mercy."[47]

That's so good. Thanks, Tish. Competing to be the "best" in the

---

[47] Tish Harrison Warren, *Of the Ordinary: Sacred Practices in Everyday Life* (Downers Grove, IL: IVP, 2019).

group with good behavior is exhausting. Covering our sins, being selfish, and prideful are all dark and sad because greater self-effort will never bring lasting results. Only by letting all our deeds, thoughts, and actions come into the light by confessing our sins and then receiving God's grace will bring us the freedom and healing for which we all long. We need His grace so desperately; without it, we can't really give grace to others who need it from us.

It's amazing that God forgives ALL our sins. Not only that but He chooses to never recall our past sins again. "I will remember them no more," He says in Isaiah 43:25. Hebrew 8:12 and Jeremiah 31:34 state the same truth. You are made new in Him. Oh, the freedom to walk forward in this truth of grace and forgiveness. Of course, because God *is* God, He could retrieve our sins or ask someone to go get them and present our sins before Him. But *again*, "He has removed our sins as far from us as the east is from the west," reads Psalm 103:12. He chooses *not* to remember our sins for His own sake because if He did it would stand in the way from us having a relationship with Him.

When we covet, compare, and compete rather than celebrate, show compassion, and confess our sins, we fence in what God can do in and through us. Oh, how I try and follow Galatians 6:4: "Pay careful attention to your own work, for then you will get the satisfaction of a job well done, and you won't need to compare yourself to anyone else." Exactly. It's being mindful of the gifts and work God has called each of us for and not what we or anyone else thinks we should do. He's the brilliant one. He created us and knows best how our gifts and talents work to serve.

I didn't feel or think I was pretty growing up. I was different, not like other girls. I didn't fit in. But I know other girls likely looked at me thinking I didn't have concerns because I didn't struggle being overweight. We compare our "insides" to other people's "outsides" and only God really knows how we struggle with self-acceptance and self-worth.

I also think of the time I judged another on the outside and it made me jealous. I was able to mentor a young woman named Megan whom I had met in Minneapolis during the theatre days. We were in a musical together (she's a generation younger than me) and eventually Megan left for Hollywood, where she had great success. She made a music video singing a song written for her. It was really good. But instead of feeling happy for her, I was jealous. I called my husband right away and said, "Megan made a video and it's good and I'm jealous. And, Dan, it doesn't feel fair. She seems to have 'everything' with her looks and talent, and success comes so easily for her." Yet something beautiful happened as a result of my telling Dan. As soon as I confessed my jealousy, it left me. It no longer had power over me.

Later that evening when my husband saw the video he said, "*That is really good.*"

"I know," I said, "and I am *really* happy for her." Months later, when we were doing a mentoring session over the phone, Megan shared some of the challenges and struggles of basic life she was working through. I remember thinking to myself, *But your life is perfect. When you have the looks, talent, and opportunities of success, how could anything ever be wrong?* Megan is human and she's not perfect. Having this simple revelation has helped me ever since when jealous thoughts try and mess me up.

"Jealousy is cruel as the grave: the coals thereof are coals of fire, which hath a most vehement flame" (Song of Solomon 8:6). Jealousy is a poisonous fruit of the flesh (not a fruit of the Spirit); it has a way of eating us up without our knowing. Jealousy brings harm to the jealous person more than it does the other person. It makes us bitter and it's impossible to be satisfied with the good things happening around us because we're so caught up in what we don't have and the other person does (and it's not fair). If you *feel* jealous *at all*, try and confess it aloud immediately before the enemy can get a foothold, 'cuz once he gets a foothold, he can get a stronghold and it's all downhill from there.

Try to stay mindful that, "Someone is always in need of someone else's transparency." No one is in need of someone who thinks their arguments are the winning ones and they have enough links with comments to prove it. Self-righteous people are pretty intolerable. Hurting people hurt people, and broken people help people. When I speak of brokenness, I speak of our pride being broken and removing our masks to become honest and vulnerable and better able to empathize with others. What I believe we all have in common is that place in our lives where we've felt and believed we weren't enough and it was all up to us to "be enough" by our good behavior. We've had fears of being unlovable because of the shame of our past or present failures, and so we listen to the enemy of our souls that we're nothing. Oh, but we are *something* to God, and nothing we've done would cause Him to stop loving us. He sees and knows us fully and loves us fully despite ourselves. We can be completely vulnerable because of His unfailing love. He is enough, and we are enough in Him.

Before I end this story, I have to share how knowing God's love has helped me to never garden again. Oh, I like the decorative part of flowers and some landscaping that makes the outside of a home more attractive. When it comes down to it, however, I'd rather spend money on a new pair of shoes. It's been years now since my front window box has had flowers in it or the front step and old wagon (sitting on mulch at the end of the house) had a pot of flowers on display. When I share this story at an event, I use the "Release and Replace" Plan. I put on a garden glove and say, "I don't covet my friend Mary and her gardening abilities, but instead I celebrate them." Then I take off the garden glove and replace it with a hand-held microphone prop and say, "I celebrate my abilities as a storyteller who likes to make people laugh aloud." One afternoon, and this was at a time I had decided gardening wasn't "my game" anymore, I was outside getting the mail when my friend Mary and her husband Dale drove by our home. Mary rolled down her window and asked me, "Why haven't you planted any flowers?"

"I don't care anymore," I said. "I'd rather have a new pair of shoes."

"Oh, but Debbie," Mary continued, "it always looked so nice. You know what, Kmart has all flowers and plants at 50 percent off because we're at the end of July. Tomorrow we'll go and take care of your gardening situation."

I kinda shrugged my shoulders like, "whatever." I really like shoes. About ninety minutes later Mary came back with Dale carrying a large pot of geraniums with green sprig-things sprouting out with other "things" added for detail. They set it on the front step. They also put a pot of flowers in our rusted red wagon *and* a humus plant in an old tin boiler that just had dirt in it. Mary explained that this plant was a perennial; so each Icebox winter I could store it in the garage, and then I could bring it out in the spring and it would be the same pretty green plant with white streaks on the leaves. I clapped, hugged her, and celebrated this gift. Sometime later I went to Mary's house to tell her about one of my latest adventures at a speaking event, and she laughed aloud.

Yes, I'm quite sure it was a humus plant. But when I told this story for the first time at a speaking event and was explaining the wonders of a humus plant, most of the faces in the audience had real quizzical looks. "Maybe I have the name wrong," I said. As I tried to describe my humus that was able to come alive each spring with zero maintenance, a "girlfriend" in the front row waved her hand at me and shouted, "It's not a humus plant you're talking about; it's a hosta plant." Oh, my bad. But to this day, when I ask one of the boys to haul out the tin boiler in the spring. I make sure to say, "Go grab the humus and put it by the red wagon." And then I go online to decide what kind of new shoes I'm going to own.

My advice is to begin to compliment the very ones you're coveting, the ones you're comparing yourself to and the ones you're competing with. It's the road to freedom in your spirit and will help get you out of the "It's not fair" and "I wish I had what they had" mind games. Initially, you might not feel any different when passing around praise, whether the person is difficult or not, but the more you celebrate another, show compassion, and confess your need for God's grace, you'll begin to experience that "peace that passes all understanding" vibe. Try it out right now for fun: "What great hair you have, Helen." "I'm so happy you could go on vacation, Veronica." "I celebrate your brownies, Brenda." "The way you stay organized and on task is stellar, Susan." Next time you see Linda, compliment her on her toned arms. But ya better start celebrating who you are, too, and do it aloud.

Take the steps you need to implement the Release and Replace Plan. Oh, to release your Coveting, Comparison, and Competition and replace them with Celebration, Compassion and Confession will bring healing to your heart and peace into your life. The first three Cs are the thief of joy but the replacement three Cs are the way of peace. I'm cheering and celebrating you as I imagine your finishing this chapter. Get up and go be the person God uniquely and purposefully created you to be.

Trinity Chicken

(6 to 8 boneless, skinless chicken breasts)

2 cans of whole berry cranberry sauce

1 salad dressing bottle (15 oz.) French, Russian, or Catalina salad dressing

1 package dried onion soup mix

Get a casserole dish or Dutch oven with a cover. Put the dressing, cranberry sauce, and onion soup together and stir, and then add the chicken breasts. Cover and put in the oven at the same time you might be putting in the Trinity Potatoes. Bake at 350 degrees for one hour but uncover for the last 15 minutes.

Magic.

Trinity Potatoes

1 package shredded hash brown potatoes, frozen

1 8 oz. package of shredded Colby/Jack Cheese

1 pint/carton of whipping cream

Get a casserole dish and use a paper towel to butter it down really well. Then begin to layer the thawed, shredded hash browns, shredded cheese, and any seasonings you desire such as salt and pepper. I like to use garlic powder and then cayenne pepper for kick. The *magic* is pouring the whipping cream on top of your layers. Then, I scoop some butter in a cup and melt it in the microwave while finding whatever crackers to crumble in a plastic baggie. I put the crumbs and butter mixture I have and kinda sprinkle it on top of the Trinity Potatoes. Bake uncovered for about 1 hour in a 350-degree oven.

Magic.

BUZZING WITH GOODNESS

31
THE MATTER OF LOVING ALL

"And so, we know and rely on the love God has for us. God is love. Whoever lives in love lives in God, and God in them."
— 1 John 4:16 (NIV)

It STARTED WITH A REFRIGERATOR.

Four days and nights was the amount of time my two youngest sons (David and Joe) and I had booked for a hotel stay in Fargo, North Dakota, while we attended musical theatre productions and connected with friends in the summer of 2016. We could not afford to dine out the entire time, so a quick call down to the front desk brought us a refrigerator free of charge.

Isaac was on maintenance, so he made the delivery. Per usual, I began my interview as I welcomed Isaac into our room. As Isaac maneuvered the fridge into a far corner of the room, I was able to gather that he had been in the United States for less than a year. He loved being in the USA and said he hoped he could bring his son to live with him soon.

Isaac is from Liberia. It was a country I knew hardly anything about, but I would soon know more in the days that followed. What connected Isaac, Joe, David, and me was that we all knew Jesus personally. That information came out toward the end of questioning as Isaac shared that his name meant "laughter" in accordance to the story in Genesis about Abraham and Sarah finally being able to have a child. They named him Isaac because it was laughable that they would be holding a newborn of their own when they both were past the age of having children.

When Isaac found out all our names had biblical origins, he asked if we knew the love of Jesus, too. We did. We took a selfie and all was good, and we figured we'd not meet again. But when the boys and I returned to the hotel from buying groceries the next day at 10:30 P.M., we ran into Isaac. I asked if he could score us a microwave. He smiled from ear to ear and nodded. When he arrived with our newest appliance, we now had cream soda and Funyuns to share, so we asked Isaac to join us for a late-night snack as he indulged in his first experience with perfect American junk food.

Not once did it strike me as odd that Isaac was sitting in the desk chair with the three of us on the double beds asking questions and listening to his story. Isaac's parents had been killed in the civil war during the early 1990s, and so he was left to care for his father's other two wives and siblings. He was the eldest, and so it was his job to carry fresh water atop his head to and from the village each day, walking many miles each way. I could understand Isaac quite easily as his English was good despite his heavy accent, but because he spoke so fast, I still felt the need to translate some of what he was saying to my sons. We got into serious topics, too, such as the tribal practice of female circumcision. We also talked about witch doctors, other traditions, and ways of life that we all had only really read about, but we certainly didn't have this kind of personal connection.

Because we had exchanged phone numbers, Isaac texted me the next day and wrote, "I sure am going to miss you people when you leave." So, of course, we had him over the next night for the renowned Duane's House of Pizza of Moorhead, Minnesota.

Isaac was so eager to connect with us and thankful that we were interested in what he had to share. The next day I couldn't help but think of his text saying, "you people" in relation to myself as the crazy white girl and her kids who invite strangers into their hotel room to hunker down and share life stories. But I am quite certain Isaac thought more about my eccentric personality than he did about my skin color.

It is now only because of the state our country is in, that I paused to think more about our different skin colors. I do know that on some level my naïve northern white girl attitude thinks there aren't color issues and surely more people think like I do as a Christian Caucasian female. Surely, no one is really racist or *that* self-righteous, but just because I feel this doesn't mean it's not happening out there.

The summer of 1979 when I was twelve, I spent two months attending the Minneapolis Children's Theatre Company where, in my jazz and improvisational class, I was the minority white girl. I remember being a little weirded out. True to my character, I said aloud what I was thinking and complimented a few girls with, "Your eyes are pretty, like big Oreo cookies." Thankfully, they took it as the compliment I intended and teased and loved me back.

I guess because Isaac is black, there's this part of me that says I am such a good Christian because I am talking to a black person with no fear, which sounds totally self-righteous and kind of racist because it kind of is. I have *always* been like this in that I love to engage people and drill them with question after question. Just as much as I *love* to share and tell my stories, I love to listen, too. The act of listening is where love is. I mean, really listening to the heart and asking questions. We need to be better listeners. Actually, there is no black or white, just different shades of brown. Acts 17:26 says, "And He has made from *one* blood *every* nation of men to dwell on all the face of the Earth." In other words, we did not evolve at different rates like the Nazis claimed so that one race is superior to another. We all came from one blood.

When I stumbled across a post on Instagram from author, speaker, and podcast-queen Allie Beth Stuckey, I read something that really resonated with truth in my spirit. She was able to articulate what I couldn't seem to put into words: "When a country forgoes—and even demonizes—its shared values and instead categorizes people as oppressed or oppressors based on their race, religion, gender, class, etc., you don't get equity, equality, or empathy. You get resentment, bitterness, strife, and violence." Allie also continued with a comment next to her post, "The Christian worldview frees us from this kind of narcissistic, unjust, and divisive thinking. When we realize that 1) we are all image bearers of God and are therefore endowed by Him with equal dignity and certain inherent rights, 2) that the only two ultimate categories that exist are those who are dead in sin and those who are alive in Christ (Ephesians Two), and that 3) we do not necessarily carry the burdens of culpability or victimization carried by our ancestors or by people who happen to look like us, we can give up our addiction to grievance and pursue goodness, unity, and justice as God—not the world—defines them. Until then, we can expect more confusion and chaos."[48]

When I enter into any community, I know I can find at least one person who just needs to be heard and who needs to know that Jesus is personal and always hears us. I don't want to add more confusion and drama into their lives but love and understanding. When others leave or fail me, Jesus doesn't. Because I have met Jesus personally, I can meet others personally. I am secure because I know Him and He knows *all* of me and loves me no matter what. I don't need to perform or hide.

Sometimes when I attend church, I feel like I have to perform with, "I'm good. How are you?" because it's harder and sometimes takes longer to share the truth or really listen to another. But I'm getting better with just being me. Church can be in a hotel room, too, where we can meet people such as Isaac.

---

[48] Allie Beth Stuckey-Instagram Christian World View. https://www.instagram.com/p/CPGg5ORL-PR/, viewed August 23, 2021.

My story has parallels and connections to the stories of Isaac because we both have felt alone, lost, scared, in pain from the loss of love from another, and in physical pain, too. And *that* is how we connected, in person, honestly sharing our hearts. Jesus is personal. Pain is personal. And when you know Christ, He finds a way into the conversation. It's where love takes you.

Joey and David were wide-eyed and listening the whole time and asking questions, too. Multiculturalism is not a hot topic in northern Minnesota. In general, as Christians, we try to "love others" as Jesus loves us. It makes me smile every time I think of the Scripture Joey chose as his confirmation verse, which was from Acts 17:26. He went to the microphone, stated the reference, and then said, "And He has made from one blood every nation of men." I had no idea why he had chosen the verse, but later, when asked, he was quite emphatic of the importance to understand that we were all created as one race and therefore we are called and able to love everyone. "There's no need to be a racist, Mom."

"Okay, Joe."

I am a fan of what author and Pastor Timothy Keller has to say from a biblical perspective. Most recently, after the atrocities of events in Charlottesville, Virginia, he wrote:

> This is a time to present the Bible's strong and clear teachings about the sin of racism and of the idolatry of blood and country—again, full stop. In Acts 17:26, in the midst of an evangelistic lecture to secular, pagan philosophers, Paul makes the case that God created all the races "from one man." Paul's Greek listeners saw other races as barbarian, but against such views of racial superiority Paul makes the case that all races have the same Creator and are of one stock. Since all are made in God's image, every human life is of infinite and equal value. When Jonah puts the national interests of Israel ahead of the spiritual good of the racially "other" pagan city of Nineveh, he is roundly condemned by God. One main effect of the Gospel is to shatter the racial barriers that separate people, so

it is an egregious sin to do anything to support those barriers. When Peter sought to do so, Paul reprimanded him for losing his grasp on the Gospel.[49]

Every one of us who claims to be a follower of Christ cannot ignore the fact that God loves all people of all shapes, sizes, and colors, just like the nursery song, "Red and Yellow, Black and White, They Are Precious in His Sight." God just loves us as we are and not as we should be, because we'll never be where we should be and He *knows* this . . . He *knows us*.

We all have ways to show and give love. I have a mouth and personality that makes connecting with people fun. I love to have in-depth conversations. We don't all have to engage in hotel room ministry, but we are called to love and minister to others in some way with the gifts God has given us. He tells us in plain simple language, "Others will know you are Mine by the way you love one another" (John 13:35).

You matter. I matter. We all matter to God and when God matters to us, then we actually desire to share His love and grace with others no matter who they are. This is what makes the world go round and round.

---

[49] Timothy Keller, "Race, the Gospel, and the Moment," *Current Affairs*, August 15, 2017, https://www.thegospelcoalition.org/article/race-the-gospel-and-the-moment/

32
IT'S NOT EASY BEING GREEN

*"So, whether you eat or drink or whatever
you do, do it all for the glory of God."*
— **1 Corinthians 10:31 (NIV)**

My EATING AND DRINKING HABITS have certainly not been all about the glory of the Lord. When I was around forty-two years of age, I never really ate breakfast, unless you counted the Diet Coke and plain Lay's Potato Chips. I ate what I wanted when I wanted. At age forty-one, standing in my kitchen one morning eating and drinking what I pleased, I remember thinking: *I feel so great! I wonder how long I will be able to keep this diet going.*

I thought because I was healthy in my relationship with God, reading the Bible, and doing Pilates occasionally, that I'd be just fine. Who needs green, leafy vegetables? But five months after having these thoughts, I started getting sick with a lot of different infections and then came emotional anxiety, and, well, I kinda crashed.

Oh, my goodness. It's all about balance, right? We need to take care of ourselves, both physically and emotionally. It's what we put into our bodies, like food, drink, and the thoughts on which we choose to think. Plus, there is the issue of getting enough sleep and exercise. We have to be intentional.

I can read the Bible's promises and instructions, but I have to choose to believe, trust, and apply what I read if I want it to do any good. Jesus says: "Think on what is good, Debbie" (Philippians 4:8). "Keep on keeping on, and don't give up, Debbie" (Galatians 6:9). "Don't worry about tomorrow, Debbie. Right now, there's just what you need" (Matthew 6:34).

Life is tough. There are everyday irritants that seem to almost wreck us. Then there are the bigger blows, such as broken relationships, cancer, the loss of a job, bills we can't pay, the addiction we just can't kick, people talking ugly about us behind our backs. *It's hard!* It ain't nice. *Arghhhhhhh* . . . .

So, because it's rough we sometimes try and put forth the perfect image. Focusing on the outside, to look and appear amazing. Attention feels like love.

Look at the photos that are posted on social media, namely Instagram. It's mostly photos of toned and fit bodies and scrumptious-looking food. It's kind of an oxymoron, isn't it? Granted, some of the food pages and posts are healthy, but I tend to like the average Joe and Jill holding a plate of donuts. I don't even like donuts, but they're so pretty in photos.

We project the successful image. Who wants to project their failures and fatness? Jesus is about humility and the need for forgiveness. I guess projecting success is our defense against our own faults.

Oh, but the problems with projecting the perfect image. It's simply not true. We are not always happy, optimistic, and in command. Projecting the successful image keeps us from reaching people who feel we just wouldn't understand them. Even if we could live a life with no conflict, suffering, or mistakes, it would be a shallow existence. The successful Christian has failed and learned that their failure does not define them.

Don't give up. It's hard, but worth it. You have to be intentional. You cannot expect to get fit by watching motivational videos of other people working out. You have to get in the game. We're all in this together. There's gain in the pain.

I would have preferred to hear in my teenage years and early twenties, "You're cute and thin," because I was not a fan of hearing, "You're so skinny; you need to eat more." I tried, but that crazy metabolism thing. I mean, what's the likelihood of hearing someone say, "You're so fat; you need to eat less." I know. I'll shut up.

Now I'm fifty-five, and for the last few years now I've been trying to get a handle on the shift in body parts and the slower metabolism. It's not so much about losing weight as much as it is learning to accept things as they *are*, not as I want them to be. I like being a certain size because I feel good about the way my clothes fit and it brings me a certain confidence, which I know can quickly turn to pride if I'm not careful. Pride stinks.

I can say I want to be a good example of healthy living, but that's not the real reason. Who am I kidding? Not God, that's for sure! Our hearts need to change if we want behavioral change, and only God can change a heart. It's all from the inside out that lasting change happens. So, ask God for help and He'll give it to you. "Jesus, I need help. Thanks. Amen."

We can see and we can have vision—they are not the same. Seeing depends on our eyes. Our eyes can reveal if we are spacious or cramped, welcoming or critical, compassionate or judgmental. The way we see other people is usually the way we see ourselves. If we've made peace with our flawed humanity and have embraced our wandering identity, we're able to tolerate in others what was previously unacceptable in ourselves. The eyes are the windows of the soul.

Sadly, many of us have ripped on others and their looks to feel better about ourselves. Maybe not always audibly, but we've all had the voice in our head comparing ourselves to someone else. Perhaps our identity is too wrapped up in how we look because it affects our feelings so much. Nobody studies and scrutinizes us like we do ourselves. *Blech.*

I know God's vision of me is not what I see. He looks at my character and potential. I look too much at my body and success. *Oh, Lord, I know I should be reflecting Your image.* And the more we look to Him, the more the glory of His image gets imprinted on us. Yep, that works. When our self-image gets completely wrapped up in God, we stop with the self-focus and critique, and in this process we're set free. I want to be free.

"Now the Lord is the Spirit, and where the Spirit of the Lord is, there is freedom" (2 Corinthians 3:17).

You know, there were other factors that played into my physical and emotional "crash" in 2009, but I heard God clearly speak to me. He had great plans for me, but I needed to take care of my diet. To this day, I need to put less time into social media and more time with Him and my family. 1 Corinthians 16:20 was a strong instruction in that season, saying to me, "I don't just belong to myself; I'm God's girl and I honor Him by the way I live my life and take care of myself." Jesus validates us for who we are in Him. Let's care enough about who we are in Him by taking care of both our inside and outside appearances and health.

Yes, it's easier to chase happiness on the outside than the inside because of the immediate gratification and "likes." There was a time I believed my outer appearance, relationships, and success would bring me happiness on the inside. It is actually the reverse. Peace that surpasses understanding refers to peace despite the outside, not because of it.

Jesus is The Way, Truth, and Life, and no one comes to the Father but through *Him*. There is no real hope or contentment until we care enough about what He says, which is that He loves us as we are. Yet He is always cheering us to run the race with all that we are and, of course, the best of who we are is accepting what we can't change on our own strength. The goal is to be healthier both physically and mentally to keep running well.

Food is fun. It's one of the best sources of pleasant entertainment. We entertain our palates with the taste of food, the atmosphere, and people with whom we eat it, and for the strength and nourishment of our bodies. I'm not saying that donuts and Coke are the best ways to nourish the body, but you can look at it as a choice you make to eat and drink for fun and not as a "cheat" when you remember it's all about balance. I made a new friend on Instagram lately, and she's great with fitness and food. Sara Stuebs coaches women to, "release guilt, remove obstacles, and curate optimal health," so says her Instagram bio. I trust her. When I first discovered her, she had just written a post that read: "Nutrition isn't a Prison." And suggested "Swap This for That" as part of her BlueRose Wellness Program. This is what she shared:

- It isn't a list of "cans and cannots."
- You are free to eat and drink whatever you like. However, consequences from what we do are always there and those either will be favorable or unfavorable, depending on your choice.
- Always stick to the 80/20 rule with best intention:
  o 80% nutritious, whole foods, in caloric/macro amounts that sufficiently give your body what it needs.
  o 20% sail away, Baby! Pizza, drinks with friends, ice cream etc. (moderation in portions because, we still do love our bodies.)
- Consider these swaps below:
  o Swap honey for sugar
  o Mixed greens for iceberg lettuce
  o Duck eggs for chicken eggs (great option to try for those allergic to chicken eggs)
  o Coconut milk for cow's milk
  o Avocado oil for canola oil[50]

There are *so* many diet programs out there to choose from, but

---

[50] Sara Stuebs, "Swap This for That—Nutrition Isn't a Prison," BlueRose Wellness, https://www.instagram.com/p/CR386q3tSyc/, viewed July 28, 2021.

quite often, once you're off the program, you'll slide back into cookies and chips at 11 P.M. each evening, so it's better to find a wellness program that fits realistically with who you are and what you can seriously commit to. Drinking lots of water and eating green leafy vegetables, along with a basic and consistent exercise program, will always be a game changer for your health and well-being. Finding someone to come alongside you in an "Eating Well" journey will help, too. Celebrities are not the greatest motivators because they have personal chefs and trainers, and *time* to look the way they do.

But, let me digress for a moment (again) and talk about being content with the way God designed you and your physical appearance. So let's talk about me. Of course, you like my nose. You see nothing wrong with it. Okay, good for you, but I'm not a fan of it. When my dad was traveling in Thailand, he had a few paintings done by an artist who would use a photograph given to him and then replicate it. The two paintings I received, one with my husband Dan and one with my sailor son Peter, my nose looked like that of a wicked witch. The only thing that was missing was a wart. Trust me. Not one family member or friend who saw the paintings disagreed. However, the paintings weren't telling the truth about my nose. If I thought the look of my nose was really problematic (meaning it was really wrecking my self-confidence), I would have probably changed it. But it's better to accept that my nose works and it's the one God gave me, making me who I am.

Look at the actress Jennifer Grey who played "Baby" in the movie *Dirty Dancing*. She was pretty with a pretty unique nose. Sometime later, after the movie, she got a nose job and it really changed her entire appearance. Every interview, I've even seen of her, the topic of her nose job comes up. (I've seen the interviews from watching *Dirty Dancing* clips on YouTube obsessively). She said, too, that when her children saw the movie, years later, they remarked how they liked her face better in the movie. "You shouldn't have changed your nose,

Mom," she relayed. However, I see nothing wrong with the fact that some people get plastic surgery to change something that troubles them. It's all about balance, Baby. We all can name celebrities who've taken it too far.

The reality is this—it takes discipline to eat well and exercise. There will be times you just cave into your flesh and do what feels good. When your emotions are screaming for a pint of Haagen-Dazs, you give into them. It's okay. For me, it's only by the grace of God, that I can get back up on the horse to be healthy and move forward. And most often, for real success, I need to ask for help and find a program, a person, or people for accountability. Reaching out for help is extremely advantageous for your emotional health, too. You need to be intentional and stay grounded; by that, I don't mean grounded to the couch.

I also found that when I share my progress with someone, it helps to keep me going in the right direction, "I did the Ten-Minute Core Crunch four times this week," Girlfriend. My declaration is always met with, "Good job," "Good for you," or, "Tell me what program you're doing, Debbie." I've had girlfriends do the Nike Core Crunch with me when I've been at their home or on a girlfriends' getaway. I plead, "C'mon it's only ten minutes! The app is right on my phone." Even at the Mexican restaurant where I worked, Alyssa, Gabby and I, in our server-girl clothes, would get down on the carpeted floor and get 'er done after the close of the day. It was always so fun because pretty much the entire time Alyssa was yelling at the gal leading us in our "core battle."

It might be only ten minutes, but it's intense and laughing through it all made it all the more doable. You can always find someone who's able to understand you in your health journey to encourage and laugh with you and you can do the same for them. It's a win-win for everyone involved. Of course, it very easy to fall into comparing yourself to another. Then what often follows is jealousy of someone else's success, but praising them rather than picking them apart is always the healthiest path.

I've mostly done simple exercise programs in my home, and each of them has helped when I committed to them and I found "the funny" in them, too. Jane Fonda's cassette tape workout followed me to college, and I knew how to mimic her perfectly while envisioning her with her awesome leg warmers which were featured on the cover of the tape, After college and before motherhood I went on short runs five days a week and that was a plus for my mental health, too.

When I entered into motherhood, I remember the first workout programs I bought were on VHS tape. It was in the 1990s and the program was called *Body Flex*. Greer Childers, the founder and leader with very long platinum and blond hair, was in her sixties and wore a Barbie pink leotard. I actually think it worked and I actually got friends and family to do the exercises, too. It was uproariously funny because it involved this weird breathing system. Ms. Childers inhaled deeply and then exhaled deeply and, in that process, it was as if she was sucking in the last bit of oxygen on Earth. You follow right along with her because it's not that difficult and you think it actually works. (It worked.)

I then moved to Tony Little with his flowing blond locks and followed his Total Body Target Workouts. Tony always gave a pep talk before the workout began and asked, "Do you feel pretty? You should. Do you feel positive about life? You better." "Okay, Tony. I'm in." The great thing about all the workouts I chose to do was that none of them lasted longer than thirty minutes. I also did Winsor Pilates twenty-minute workout, Turbo Jam, and the Beach Body workout for thirty days (I never used the weights). Now I'm in in the Nike Training Zone routine, but I only do the exercises that are ten minutes or less.

All of these programs had something humorous about them and *that* is so important (find the funny). My husband Dan has joined me in each workout system and that makes it more fun and funnier, even though he's inconsistent. I believe the Group Glass Exercise Programs could work for me, too (I've tried some) but I've found that the In Home Workout with Pajamas Programs work best. Consistency, humor, and accountability will always be a key for success. Here are five favorite memes I cycle into my workouts every now and then that might help you too:

- "I lifted up my shirt to check out my abs and a Cheeto fell out, so there's that."
- "How many boxes of thin mints do I have to eat before I start seeing results?"
- "I choked on a carrot this afternoon and all I could think was, 'I bet a donut wouldn't have done this to me.'"
- "My yoga pants have never been to the yoga, but they have most certainly been to the liquor store and Target."
- "Don't let anyone tell you that your leggings aren't pants. You don't need that kind of negativity in your life."
- "Forgot to do yoga yesterday. That makes it six years in a row now."

Humor helps in pretty much all areas of life and especially in the way we view our bodies. When we're a healthy weight, we have a healthy mind and that's so important for the simple reason of being in a good place to thrive in life and not just survive. It's also helpful to be realistic. What screws us up most is the picture in our head of how it is supposed to be or how we're supposed to look. Right now, God says you're a beauty of His, and His grace ensures that we don't have to be or do more. Like the late author Brennan Manning stated, "Only when God's love for us goes from information in our head to a deep understanding in our heart, does lasting transformation come about." Knowing God's unfailing love and kindness, knowing His strength works best in your weakness, and knowing He's there to help you transform your mind and body, is the absolute truth to being the best you.

I am created in His image and it's His image I want to reflect, and that is being the best me. It means being honest with others without trying to portray "pretty-much-perfect" when I'm in the flesh or on social media. It also means I do what I can to show an appealing and genuine image of myself, but I don't stress out on what I can't do or change. Yes, there are days I am too focused on the outward—my hair, the wrinkles, the zit—I try to stick my tongue out in the mirror when I get hypercritical, and it always helps. But please don't think I'm lacking face creams and serums that target every feature I have. I also take vitamins daily (in a package for gals that the General Nutrition Centers (GNC) put together). I color my hair and I'll be chemical dependent to the grave. I exercise sporadically despite the programs I listed, and I try to take three walks a week for at least a mile.

A heathy human is a happy human and, of course, there's always hope for your health. Ask for help. "God, help. Thanks. Amen." Find a gang of gals or one individual for accountability or ones (or one) who want to join you on a journey to health. *Always* remember to find the humor in the journey, too. Most importantly, discover the truth that you're on this Earth for a reason no matter what you look like and God's loving you so much for who you are. He sees the heart.

Here's what you need to know, for sure, from 1 John 3:19–20 (NIV), "This is how we know that we belong to the truth and how we set our hearts at rest in His presence: If our hearts condemn us, we know that God is greater than our hearts, and He knows everything."

God knows you inside and out. He loves you inside and out. He's not condemning you (don't you do it either) for your missteps or lack of discipline, but instead He's cheering you in "your race" to remain fit to "fight the good fight" (1 Timothy 6:12). There's kindness from Him every step of the way. It's not easy being green but it's simple to accept that God is always for you and not against you (Romans 8:31). Keep on keeping on. Don't give up. Green is good. God is good.

33
GREEN BEANS FOR BREAKFAST

"And you shall teach God's commands diligently to your children and speak of them when you sit at home and when you walk along the road, when you lie down and when you get up."
— **Deuteronomy 6:7 (BSB)**

YOU FEED THEM GREEN BEANS for breakfast because once you start spooning in the apricots and pears, it's unlikely their little tongues are going to receive the green stuff. Even introducing sweet potatoes, the babes may suspect you're holding out on them.

At six months of age for each of them, for an entire two weeks, I started my sons on vegetables for breakfast, lunch, and dinner. No fruit allowed. It worked. I felt I was winning as a mom. However, you're kidding me if they were gonna be fooled to somehow swallow that pretend turkey dinner in a jar. I gagged just opening the little Gerber's container.

Yeah, well, whatever. The only boy who will eat green beans now is my eldest at twenty-three, and the rest don't really eat vegetables (isn't that what vitamins are for?)? Fruit is not a big favorite for anyone either. It's pretzels rods for the win, along with "Top the Tater

Chive/Onion" sour cream dip, which can now be found in a family size container.

Before I delivered our first son, I read the mommy books, the "Jesus Help Me" mommy books, the "I Don't Have a Clue" mommy books, and I asked for advice from other mommies who'd been there, done that. Yet, no matter, I was determined to follow Proverbs 22:6: "Train a child in the way they should go, and when they're old they'll not turn from it," which is why the green beans for breakfast seemed brilliant. Never mind I was eating Lays' Potato Chips and drinking a Diet Coke for *my* breakfast, but that would change. Because the best training for my sons was to first train myself in making healthy choices.

Eventually, my breakfast was an egg and toast, along with a cup of tea. (I hate coffee.) When sparkling water became readily available, that was "a must" as I love carbonation. I also began to read the Bible consistently (every day) even if it was only one Proverb. The Bible was the best place to spiritually get fed. I then slowly and steadily began to trust God in faith and not by my feelings. I needed Him to get through it all, from folding laundry to falling apart as a mom.

"It" really hit in June 2003 during my recovery from scoliosis back surgery. "It" was so hard I wanted to go Home to Jesus. Why would God allow such pain in my life?" Our sons were ages seven, four, three, and one and a half. "It" was hard. When I arrived home after two weeks in the hospital, not one of them really understood why Mommy couldn't hold them. She always seemed to sleep on the bathroom floor due to vomiting and zero ability to tolerate any pain meds.

But it was in this place I learned that blessings can come in trials and what it meant to receive peace from God and not from my circumstances. On the bathroom floor I said to God, "I don't think I'm gonna make it here. This is too much." But then I remembered John 14:27, where God says, "Peace I leave with you. Peace I *give* you."

I had recently memorized this verse a month previous. Saying the verse aloud does not bring magic healing, but applying it brings hope. So, I said aloud, "Jesus, I choose to receive the peace You give and not the fear I feel." And . . . it worked. I didn't feel different, but I knew something was different. What came over me was peace and hope. I knew I would someday get off the bathroom floor. And I did. I recovered.

Up off the bathroom floor I came away with an understanding that the best way to train my children was to lead by example. "More is taught then caught." How I respond to pain, whether difficult people, circumstances, or disappointment, shows them where my hope comes from. Is it Jesus? Is it the world's ways? Is it my strong will and good works? Maybe a combination of it all? The question is asked and answered in Psalm 121:1–2, "From where does my help come? My help comes from the Lord." Seeing His grace work in my life is more effective than any preaching I can shout.

One rule or habit I did implement with our school-aged sons was praying over their little heads as they stood in the entryway before heading to the school bus. This tradition began when the youngest was around second grade and the oldest in ninth. I'm not a morning person, so this was a mom decision I made one weekday night as my husband was praying for the team at bedtime. Most mornings my prayer was done on automatic pilot. With my hand on each of their heads, one at a time, I prayed, "Jesus bless _____. Cover them with Your love and protect them throughout their day. I pray You bless and protect their future wife, too. Thanks. Amen."

Done. Out the door.

About a year after this routine began, I also began traveling and speaking. I was often gone on Friday mornings, leaving my husband, Dan, in charge. I'll never forget the Sunday afternoon I called from the airport in Rapid City, South Dakota, to ask how everyone was and specifically how "Friday send-off" had gone. Dan said he had gotten up as they were headed out and, quietly from the entryway, he saw our oldest putting a hand on top of each of his brother's heads. Marco prayed what he had heard a thousand other mornings from me: a blessing, protection for each brother, and their future wives.

Now, I love having an empty nest. I'm thankful. Yep, I said it. Amen and out the door. I'll always be a mom, but now more of a cheerleader than a coach. I'm still learning. For example, don't just give advice without asking permission first. You might have the wisest counsel on the planet with the best of intentions, but your adult children need to be asked, "Do you want my opinion or advice or do you want me to just listen?" Most times their response is, "Just listen." One thing remains constant; the more control I give God, the less control I feel I need to have in my sons' lives *and* the more they actually come to me and ask what I think.

I always want to strive to find the core of what matters most and laugh at the rest of it. Funny stories to tell later on seemed to help make the yucky parts doable. Dirty diapers, potty training, and drama in the bathroom are all part of being a mom. Those days are long, but the years are short. And all moms learn, "This poo will pass."

Looking back, I figure we had just enough religion to get them to church, but not enough religion to keep them from Jesus. It's true: "Rules without relationship lead to rebellion." Religion is about rules, but a relationship with Christ brings freedom and leads to life. We can all try and perform and look good on the outside, but our goodness doesn't bring His favor, His peace, or our salvation.

The clearest training as parents we tried to follow and teach is that by Christ's death and resurrection, we are made right; it's by His grace we live. It's not a spiritual checklist even though, at times, that might have been easier.

The biggest investment into our children's lives was helping them to know and trust Jesus Christ. When our children know that no matter what they do you'll always love them, then they are shown real love. It's what God says to us. He's saddened by our sin but He loves us. We can be disappointed in our child's choices or attitude but we don't withdraw our love (we maybe yell more than needed, but we try).

Ask questions and then listen. I've asked everything, "Tell me about your friends. Tell me what you're hopeful about, and what are you struggling with? Are you vaping or drinking? Have you tried pot? Do you think you're going to? Are you attracted to boys or girls? Is there anything making you anxious? How's your relationship with God? Do you have a real friend you can share with or a group that you feel like you can be yourself? How can I pray for you?"

A harder question, but one of the best ones, is to ask, "Is there anything I've done I need to apologize for?" I sometimes was surprised at the boys' responses, but an apology and the forgiveness that came with it was also so full of restoration. Another good piece of advice to keep in mind is this: Be the person you needed when you were younger.

The late priest and author, Father Robert Farrar Capon, has a great statement in his book, *Between Noon & Three*, and it really is a summary of what I hope our boys learned about Jesus:

> Trust Him. And when you have done that, you are living the life of grace. No matter what happens to you in the course of that trusting—no matter how many waverings you may have, no matter how many suspicions that you have bought a poke with no pig in it, no matter how much heaviness and sadness your lapses, vices, indispositions, and bratty whining may cause you—you believe simply that Somebody Else, by His death and resurrection, has made it all right, and you just say thank you and shut up. The whole slop-closet full of mildewed performances (which is all you have to offer) is simply your death; it is Jesus who is your life. If He refused to condemn you because your works were rotten, He certainly isn't going to flunk you because your faith isn't so hot. You can fail utterly, therefore, and still live the life of grace. You can fold up spiritually, morally, or intellectually and

still be safe. Because at the very worst, all you can be is dead—and for Him who is the Resurrection and the Life, that just makes you His cup of tea.[51]

Jesus is my life and He's a part of my husband's life and our four sons' lives. *That* is what I am most thankful for. I am certainly proud of their accomplishments, but the character of love and kindness by the love of Christ is what makes me most proud And, honestly, a lot of what my boys have learned from me is what *not* to do (DUI Debbie), but they know too that I can muster the faith of a mustard seed to "keep on keeping on" with hope, humor, and the grace of God with difficult relationships and difficult circumstances. My sons know they are loved unconditionally and that prayer works. My hope is that they, too, will train their own children in the way they should go, which of course is to know that Jesus is The Way, the Truth, and the Life, and, of course, I hope they begin feeding their own children green beans for breakfast some day.

---

[51] Robert Farrar Capon, *Between Noon and Three: A Parable of Romance, Law, and the Outrage of Grace* (San Francisco: Harper & Row, 1982).

34
GROWING UP WITH JESUS

"For God so loved the world that He gave His one and only son, that whoever believes in Him shall not perish but have eternal life."
— **John 3:16 (NIV)**

I'VE BEEN CUTTING AGAIN. I hate this about myself. It's my hair. I keep cutting it.

Honestly, I can say that in our wee small town of seven thousand, I know every hair stylist in every salon and they know me. Jessica cuts hair and when she just moved into town, I made an appointment immediately. She and I then became fast friends. I obsess. I want change and so I obsess on something I can control on the outside and ignore the inside turmoil, which is exactly the place I need to look at for change and any real healing or peace.

I knew I was spiraling and needed intervention, but I wanted my way. As I traveled to speaking events, I used my free time to sit in various chairs while a stylist textured, layered, point cut, and trimmed my hair to the point where I was looking at the pixie I had been trying to grow out for more than a year. I hated to text my Aunt Ginger, who was always encouraging me to grow out my hair because she thinks (and I agree) that it looks better longer and makes me look younger. I needed to let her know where I was at. I hated to not only disappoint her, but reveal my total lack of self-control and obsession with my outside self. She texted back:

Ginger: "What's going on inside that you're hurting yourself?"

Me: "It's my drug. It's the battle of the flesh."

Ginger: "I get that, but to numb what? What's the temptation? We act out of something we aren't dealing with so we don't have to focus on the real pain or truth."

I read her texts and didn't want to think about them. I wanted to go and trim my bangs.

Me: "It's just that I'm writing and sharing a lot more of me—the real stuff—and I feel scared. Plus, there seems to be more expectations and responsibilities that go with that."

Ginger: "And you feel inadequate and insecure and think people are going to find out you're an imposter. It's an emotional roller coaster you're riding."

Me: "Yep, pretty much. But I think it's spiritual, too."

Ginger: "I am praying. I have things I do to avoid my real pain, too, things that are self-destructive. I squeeze and make zits out of nothing, for one example."

Me: "I know you get it, and I do that, too. I hate to disappoint you."

Ginger: "I *love* you even with too-short hair. It would be good to make a list of all that's hurting you right now."

Me: "Oh, I have the list."

Ginger: "We can talk when you come to visit. We need Sabbaths and margins."

Me: "I've tried to not step into other people's messes to add drama to my own. But it's challenging."

Ginger: "Yep. The Earth experience is wicked hard."

Ginger was the one who shared with me what having a relationship with Christ was and not a religion of "dos" and "don'ts." I was seven years old and at my grandparents' home in Moorhead, Minnesota, when she put a plastic Good News Glove on my hand, with different-colored fingers, to explain the Gospel. I remember that the middle finger was black and I said, "I have sinned," which gives new meaning to giving someone the finger. I don't really remember why I agreed that I was a sinner, but because I loved and trusted Ginger so much, I agreed that I was one. If I had to explain it to a child now, I would say, "Sin is when you think you are the master of your own universe and you don't need God at all for help or direction."

Dr. Timothy Keller, pastor and author, also helped me in understanding the simplicity of the Gospel. His teaching makes sense, "What sends you to heaven or to hell really has to do with your faith in the Gospel, which is that you can't be your own Savior through your performance and good works. What sends you to heaven is getting a connection to Christ because you realize you're a sinner and you need intervention from outside. What sends you to hell is self-righteousness, thinking you can be your own Savior and Lord."[52]

Yep, I'm a sinner, but the red ring finger said, "Jesus Christ died and came alive for me." I simply had to receive this gift from Him because I could never earn my own salvation, and that's what the white pinky finger signified. Jesus cleansed the stain of sin in my life. The yellow index finger reassured that "God loves me and is the light of the world." I prayed and asked Jesus to be the Ruler of my universe. I meant it. I just didn't realize how hard it would be to give up control as I grow older.

When I talk about "surrendering all to God" I can always hear that praise and worship song, "Jesus, Lover of My Soul," by Paul Oakley, play in my head:

---

[52] Timothy Keller, "The Importance of Hell," https://timothykeller.com/blog/2008/8/1/the-importance-of-hell, viewed July 29, 2021.

> "It's all about You, Jesus
> And all this is for You
> For Your glory and your fame
> It's not about me
> As if You should do things my way"[53]

And still, I can't honestly sing it the way it's intended because, *really,* what's in my mind is the way I rewrite the words:

> "It's all about me, Jesus
> And all this is for me
> For my glory and my fame
> It's all about me
> And You should do things my way."

When I get to where it says, "my way/ways," I sing it out real loud to hear how ridiculous it all is and then I'm reminded of the joke that asks, "What's the difference between you and God? God never thinks He's you."

Finally, there's the green thumb, which represents growth in my relationship with God and sharing the "Good News" with others.

Me: "Can I go next door and share with the twins what you just told me?"

Ginger: "Sure."

And off I went to make disciples of the neighborhood.

God is nice to me and gives me an opportunity to be heard on the radio with a short feature of encouragement called *Everyday Matters.* I get to skip around the country sharing the hope I have in Christ and asking, "Can you see the real me?" When we are willing to look at our bad selves, we can deal with our real selves. It's the bad sin of self that needs God's redemption and grace. While grace is often

---

[53] Paul Oakley, "Jesus, Lover of My Soul (It's All About You)," https://us.napster.com/artist/paul-oakley/album/the-best-of-paul-oakley, viewed February 24, 2022.

tough to comprehend, it seems easier to understand when I need it from someone.

Years ago, I took some money out of my son Peter's savings account for some money he owed, but I didn't tell him I had done it. I was traveling at the time and when I looked at my phone and saw eighteen missed calls from him, I knew he was on to me. I asked him to please forgive me.

Me: "Peter, I need grace."

Peter: "But you don't deserve it, Mom."

Me: "Exactly. Grace is giving me what I don't deserve."

What makes the good news so good is that there is always hope, and God is always on the move to redeem our messes into something good.

I believe part of what has helped me as a Christian Speaker Girl is that I didn't grow up in a religious or politically charged household. I was the Laura Ingalls of the 1980s, who lived in the woods, hauled sap with her family to produce pure maple syrup, and my Mom cooked our meals on a blue enamel cook stove. We heated our basement home with a double-barrel wood stove welded together, and for three of those eight years we didn't have hot water unless heated on the stove. We bathed as a family in a sauna down by the lake. Eventually, a lodge and buildings were constructed and the home in the woods became a family cross country ski resort, which still operates today.

My family was stable with parents and brother, whom I love and they love me, but of course we were far from any perfect Norman Rockwell setting. The escape and rescue into the world of theatre helped me to fit in and to feel I had an identity, other than being the weird, skinny girl who wasn't interested in boys at all and whose favorite musical artists were Billy Joel and Judy Garland. My dad helped me carry my dream of Broadway and didn't balk when I declared myself a theatre major in college. In high school I never missed a play rehearsal even though it was a twenty-mile trek each way to the theatre.

My mom was a champion, too, when it came to giving me freedom. When I came home at fall break my freshman year, I told her I was gonna smoke pot (because, duh, all theatre people experiment with pot and other shenanigans) and she said, "I don't think it's a good choice, but it's your choice to make."

Back at college after fall break, I remember a joint being passed round the room. When it came to me, I nonchalantly said, "No, I'm good." To this day I've never smoked weed. Had I been told, "No, it's stupid, it's a gateway drug," I think I would've jumped back into college ready and happy to inhale.

I always keep this in mind when I tell people about Jesus. A rule sharing a "you should" list never works. My Aunt Ginger continues to speak God's grace into my life because life is hard and we need encouragement to carry on.

Without our understanding and need for grace, we wouldn't be able to extend grace to others. I like how Mockingbird Ministry founder and author David Zahl puts it: "The cross of Christ both exposes the futility of our efforts at establishing ourselves and answers them. It ushers in the real freedom that we are loved and valued, not according to what we do, but what Jesus has done. That is, we are good because God is good, not because we are good. The shackles are off, once and for all!"[54]

It would be easier and more comfortable to stick to the message of, "Love God, love others, and do stuff," but don't offend people by bringing up sin and our need to change direction from what feels good. Sin can be really fun. No one wants to be challenged with what the "pleasure center" in our brains tells us will make us happy. Don't I have a right to be happy and fulfilled? God made me this way. Leave me alone. But we're all sinners, and God's directions are

---

[54] Charlotte Donlon and David Zahl, "The Mockingbird Devotional: Finding Grace and Being Found," May 23, 2017, https://mbird.com/2017/05/the-mockingbird-devotional-finding-grace-and-being-found/, viewed Spring 2021.

perfect because he knows and loves us best.

I do think we withhold love when we don't acknowledge that some of our behavior *needs* redeeming. Once we confess, God forgives, cleans us up, and by His grace we can stop living for self, pick up our stuff (cross), and follow Him. Sin might be in, fun, and popular, but it always comes with a payback. Forgiveness from sin is thrilling and freeing. Pastor and author Paul David Tripp says, "Denial is rooted in fear and confession is rooted in hope."

Here's the deal. When I share my mess, my pain, my sins, and my mistakes, and the stories where I've fallen and struggled, but I've gotten back up and "repented" (or in nonreligious lingo, changed direction), I'm sharing God's light and way in dark places. 1 John 1:9 is a golden promise from Jesus, "If we confess our sins to God, He can always be trusted to forgive us and take our sins away." (The blood red of the glove finger symbolizes what Christ did on the cross for us.)

I thank God that I have healthy relationships with most people in my life, but I also have broken relationships with some who hurt my heart deeply, and it's only by His perfect grace that I have the hope they'll be mended.

There comes a point for everyone where we have to surrender our sin, if we want to be free. I love people. God loves people. I want to sing, shout, speak and proclaim the Good News with the plastic glove or any other fun prop I can use. I will always be growing up in Jesus, but oh how I look forward to the day of heaven when it's all perfectly purposeful.

I hope to see you there.

35
'LOOK UP, CHILD, THERE'S HOPE'

> *"Now faith is confidence in what we hope for and assurance about what we do not see."*
> — **Hebrews 11:1 (NIV)**

I SAT ON THE FRONT STEPS, next to Joey, on a hot and sweaty Saturday, May 31, 2020, before he headed down to Minneapolis to serve with the National Guard concerning the demonstrations surrounding the George Floyd incident. I looked down at our broken & messy sidewalk and felt the same way that the cement looked. My heart was heavy and I was down. I prayed aloud with Joe and then waited until Dan came home to say goodbye. There were so many emotions swirling around in my head, my heart, & my spirit. It was almost overwhelming.

Joe left, then Dan did, too.

I sat alone still looking down.

But then I distinctively heard God say, "Look up, look up, Child."

I head God's voice. I know Him. John 10:27 says, "My sheep hear My voice. I know them and they follow Me." Memorizing Scripture has been a gift to me. I know hundreds of verses not because a church or group study told me I should, but because as I read the Bible and wrote in my journal, I would hear God say, "You're gonna want to write this down and then memorize it."

There are so many times when I'm hurting and I can't open a book, can't pick up the phone, but I'll hear God's voice through Scriptures. I looked up and suddenly I seemed to recall all of Romans Chapter 12, which I had read the day previous. I've specifically memorized verses 17–21:

"Do not repay anyone evil for evil. Be careful to do what is right in the eyes of everyone. If it is possible, as far as it depends on you, live at peace with everyone. Do not take revenge, my dear friends, but leave room for God's wrath, for it is written: 'It is Mine to avenge; I will repay,' says the Lord. On the contrary: 'If your *enemy* is hungry, feed him; if he is thirsty, give him something to drink. In doing this, you will heap burning coals on his head. Do not be overcome by evil, but overcome evil with good.'" (NIV)

"Burning coals" is *fiery* love. It is "loving your enemies" just as God does, too. He loves us all.

Then I heard God say, "Share thirty days of, 'Look Up, Child.'" I thought, *Even though I heard from God, I don't have to do 'this'*. He will love me regardless. I did not *feel* like sharing *anything*, but the blessing of obedience is always a freedom in my spirit *and* life is not all about "me." I began sharing on social media June 1, 2020, via Instagram and Facebook.

The Lord cares. He cares about every single person no matter their shape, size, color, age, faith, or gender. He fully knows us and fully loves us. He *is* "here" ready and on the move to redeem *all* things. Nothing is wasted with Him.

On that same Saturday I went to Mass, by myself, because the church was open, it's quiet, with a presence of holiness. I also like not having to talk to anyone. I know it might be odd because I'm not Catholic (Who goes to church on a Saturday evening?) and I can't take communion, but I find my time at our small town's only Catholic church extremely comforting. It was Pentecost "Sunday." John 20:22 was read where Jesus breathed on the disciples and they received the Holy Spirit.

"Breathe on me, Holy Spirit," is often my prayer.

The Holy Spirit strength is the power we all need to forgive others. Sometimes it means forgiving ourselves by first repenting and changing the direction we've been heading. Although we have the power to forgive sins, it is not always easy to forgive sins.

Whenever someone does something to me where I need to forgive, I must pray, "Holy Spirit, breathe on me and give me the strength to forgive this person." I do that because my emotions are screaming inside of me, "You have hurt me—and it's not fair!"

At that point I have to remember to let go and allow the God of justice to work out everything. I have to remind myself that my job is to pray; His job is to be my Vindicator.

When we trust God, He always makes wrong things right in due time. I understand it's hard when someone does something hurtful to you. So, go to the Lord and receive from Him the strength to place your will on the altar and say, "Lord I forgive this person. I release them; I let them go." OR, sometimes the biggest struggle is not forgiving others, but to forgive yourself. Christ died for that sin, too. You do not need to keep recrucifying yourself for some terrible thing you did or a good thing you failed to do. Late author and philosopher Aldous Huxley addresses the power of repenting in his book *Brave New World*. "Chronic remorse, as all the moralists are agreed, is a most undesirable sentiment. If you have behaved badly, repent, make what amends you can, and address yourself to the task of behaving better next time. On no account brood over your wrongdoing. Rolling in the muck is not the best way of getting clean."[55]

I know it might be hard to forgive someone or yourself, so ask for help. Just like the father who pleaded to Jesus to heal his child (Mark 9:34), "Lord I believe; help my unbelief." Sometimes we need the supernatural to get us to the point of even wanting to forgive. God

---

[55] Aldous Huxley, *Brave New World,* https://www.goodreads.com/quotes/9406-chronic-remorse-as-all-the-moralists-are-agreed-is-a, viewed July 29, 2021.

knows this. Ask Him for His help. He wants to give it. The real challenge is if we are willing to accept it. I've been to a counselor more than once with the pain of addressing the hurt and then the process of forgiving and letting go.

Once you have gone through the process of forgiveness then let it drop. Don't think or talk about it anymore. Do not keep replaying the hurt or failure in your mind. If God says He will remember it no more, we need to follow His example. However, that does not mean we keep our struggles and hurts to ourselves. First, we must be honest with God (who knows us perfectly anyway) about our sins and pain. Confess to Him your heart hurts and then share your pain with a trusted friend or mentor, one who will keep in confidence what you disclose because even after numerous counseling sessions you need "a person." It's helpful and hopeful to bring your hurts and struggles to the light where healing can begin. Secrets you keep in the dark have power over you and in the darkness the pain will grow, bind, and suffocate. God wants to set you free to walk in the Light and Freedom of His love and grace.

"If you think that God's primary goal for you is that you be an example of moral goodness rather than a trophy of His grace, you'll never be honest about your deepest sins, struggles, and secrets. Ever. You'll always feel the pressure to pretend you're better than you truly are," writes pastor and author Tullian Tchividjian. He continues, "Someone once said, 'We glorify a water fountain by coming thirsty and drinking deeply.' This means that when we are real—by confessing our sins, demonstrating our desperation, acknowledging our neediness, telling the truth about our fears and insecurities and struggles and secrets, admitting that we are selfish and arrogant and controlling and self-righteous and faithless and unforgiving—that is when we bear witness to the world about a Savior who came, not for the righteous, but for sinners. That's how we glorify the God who graciously rescues bad and weak people who fail because there aren't any other kinds of people."[56]

I love the Word of God in 2 Corinthians 2:14 from the AMPC translation: "But thanks be to God, Who in Christ always leads us in triumph as trophies of Christ's victory and through us spreads and makes evident the fragrance of the knowledge of God everywhere." We are trophies of Him, by His grace and as His children. We can walk in victory and freedom and be a sweet presence (fragrance) to those around us.

The Holy Spirit makes His home in us once we've received the gift of the Savior. Then we need to follow 2 Timothy 1:14 (AMPC) and guard the truth we're given by Him. "Carefully guard the precious truth that has been entrusted to you by the power of the Holy Spirit who makes His home in you." Friend, author, and pastor David Housholder wrote the book *Light Your Church on Fire without Burning It Down*, and I like how he explains the Holy Spirit in us. "All believers have a pilot light of the Holy Spirit, but not all of us keep it turned on full flame. We go through empty periods when God seems distant."[57]

When we receive Jesus, we also receive the Holy Spirit, although having the Holy Spirit burning in our hearts requires more than just "I believe in God." We must read His Word and do what it says. In the Bible, in the book of James we read, "Don't just listen to the Word and so deceive yourselves, *do* what it says." The Holy Spirit is meant to be more than a pilot light. It should be a vibrant flame which is on fire to do what God gives us with passion, love, and humility. When we have this fiery love inside of us, it makes the task of looking up

---

[56] Tullian Tchividjian, Facebook post, November 19, 2020, https://www.facebook.com/245226152254546/posts/weve-been-told-that-in-order-to-be-an-effective-witness-for-jesus-we-need-to-be-/3310241922419605/, viewed April 21, 2021.
[57] David Housholder, *Light Your Church on Fire without Burning It Down* (Huntington Beach, CA: David Housholder, 2009).

with hope much, much easier because you feel free.

The logo of the Everyday Matters Ministry is an orange slice because it symbolizes the fruits of the Spirit listed in Galatians 5:22–23 (NLT). "But the Holy Spirit produces this kind of fruit in our lives: love, joy, peace, patience, kindness, goodness, faithfulness, gentleness, and self-control." I want all the fruits to be evident in my life for myself and others, but of course that means I stay connected to the Vine of Life—Jesus and allow His pruning and the cutting away of things that limit my growth. John 15:1–5 (NIV) offers such good growth advice: "I am the True Vine, and my Father is the Gardener. He cuts off every branch in Me that bears no fruit, while every branch that does bear fruit, He prunes so that it will be even more fruitful. You are already clean because of the word I have spoken to you. Remain in me, as I also remain in you. No branch can bear fruit by itself; it must remain in the Vine. Neither can you bear fruit unless you remain in Me."

Tchich Nhat Hanh, a ninety-four-year-old Buddhist monk, has a quote on growth and understanding in chapter five of his book *At Home in the World*. He uses a vegetable analogy rather than fruit, but the insight is just as good:

> If you plant lettuce and it does not grow well, you don't blame the lettuce. You look for reasons it is not doing well. It may need fertilizer, or more water or, less sun. You never blame the lettuce. Yet, if we have problems with our friends or family, we blame the other person. But if we know how to take care of them, they will grow well, like the lettuce. Blaming has no positive effect at all, nor does trying to persuade using reason and argument. That is my experience. No blame, no reasoning, no argument, just understanding. If you understand, and you show that you understand, you can love, and the situation will change.[58]

---

[58] Tchich Nhat Hanh, "Empathy Quotes, Thich Nhat Hanh Quotes," *At Home in the World: Stories and Essential Teachings from a Monk's Life* (Berkeley, CA: Parallax, 2016), https://www.pinterest.com/pin/203928689361375754, viewed

I believe absolute love and understanding come from knowing Jesus. When you understand His love personally, you can give, receive, and show love supernaturally, and this kind of love is a game-changer.

Christ is the source by which you are made new. When you allow the Holy Spirit to lead you, He becomes involved in every decision you make—both major and minor. He leads you by peace and by wisdom, by what God says in the Bible. He speaks to your heart and He is the only One who can change your heart. Having a heart change leads to behavioral change and that, in fact, changes how we respond to our circumstances and others around us and, most importantly a healthy heart helps us grow into a healthy human. "Oh, Dear Child of God," I hear Him say, "I Am the answer to all of your questions in life and the One who longs to care for you and show you compassion. I want the best for you. I give you the strength so you can 'Look-Up,' and carry on."

Singer and songwriter Lauren Daigle has many songs that I played a lot during the year of 2020-21. The few lyrics below from her song "Look Up Child" are an encouragement that in the dark days there is always hope because the Son is always shining down on you.

> You're not threatened by the war
> You're not shaken by the storm
> I know You're in control
> Even in our suffering
> Even when it can't be seen
> I know You're in control
> I hear You, I hear You calling my name
> I hear You say
> Look up child[59]

April 21, 2021.
[59] L. Daigle, J. Ingram, J., and P. Mabury, "Look Up Child. On Look Up Child-Lauren Daigle." United States: Centricity, August 28, 2018.

36
WHAT MATTERS MOST AS A CHRISTIAN?

> *"Jesus declared, 'Love the Lord your God with all your heart and with all your soul and with all your mind.' This is the first and greatest commandment."*
> — Matthew 22:37–38 (BSB)

WHAT MATTERS MOST?

And it's actually pretty simple. Relationships and to know where you're going after you die are the most important thing.s My unbreakable love and unshakeable confidence in the Lord is a megaphone to the world that announces, "He's alive. He's actively working in my life." First and foremost, my relationship with Jesus is everything. When we boil it all down, our lives are really most meaningful by the relationships we have with others—with our kids, our parents, our close friends. That's the Gospel in a nutshell. What does God treasure? Why did Jesus come down to Earth, then suffer and die on a cross? He did it to restore a broken relationship. Sin separates. It separates us from each other, and it separates us from God. "For God so loved the world that He gave His one and only Son, that whoever believes in Him shall not perish but have eternal life" (John 3:16). The treasure is people.

There are so many important issues and there are so many people, yet God cares about every issue and loves each individual personally. Life can be messy rather than meaningful, and because of that we miss sharing the simple truth of the Gospel. Sometimes, Christians come across as self-righteous in their beliefs and argue over issues regarding God's impact in our lives.

Religion makes you self-righteous; a relationship does not. Religion is you "earning" your way to heaven, so why wouldn't you compare how others measure against you? The thief who asked Jesus to remember him wasn't seeking a religion.

In his book *What's So Amazing about Grace?*, author Philip Yancey writes:

> In one of his last acts before death, Jesus forgave a thief dangling on a cross, knowing full well the thief had converted out of plain fear. That thief would never study the Bible, never attend synagogue or church, and never make amends to all those he had wronged. He simply said "Jesus, remember me,"and Jesus promised, "Today you will be with me in paradise." It was another shocking reminder that grace does not depend on what we have done for God but rather what God has done for us. Ask people what they must do to get to heaven and most reply, "Be good." Jesus' stories contradict that answer. All we must do is cry "*Help!*"God welcomes home anyone who will have Him and, in fact, has made the first move already.[60]

Tullian Tchividjian makes it clear: "Jesus got angry. But what's interesting about His anger was that it was almost never directed at the "bad" people. It was, instead, almost always directed at the "good" people, the religious people, the rule keepers, and those who believed they were morally superior." Okay, so let's say that before someone becomes a Christian, he or she is always eating but never really filling up—they're always hungry. But one day they taste and see that the

---

[60] Philip Yancey, *What's So Amazing about Grace?* (Grand Rapids, MI: Zondervan, 2011), Chapter 4.

Lord is good and they realize they were actually starving (Psalm 34:8). But once Jesus is in their lives, they're completely filled up.

So, I'd ask the unbeliever, "If you saw someone who was starving and you had at one time been hungry and starving yourself, would you be superior to that person because you're not starving anymore?"

A big problem lies in the fact that a lot of people think that Christianity is just another religion of judgment. But Jesus didn't die on the cross so we could have a religion. He died and rose again so we could be saved and have a real and intimate relationship with Him, one that leaves us filled and satisfied.

I think it's safe to say that most sin stems from pride. It's an independent spirit that wants to do its own thing without any authority or direction from anyone else.

The truth is, as stated in Proverbs 6:16–19, God lists seven things He hates—and one of those things is pride. The only way to uproot pride is humility—freedom from pride and arrogance, a modest estimation of your own worth. It doesn't mean you think lowly of yourself, but it means you are very careful not to think more highly of yourself than you ought to. It's easy for me to think I don't have pride when it comes to certain features I possess, like my feet for example; they're not attractive. I don't get pedicures for the simple fact that I don't want to draw attention to my toes (my big toes look like someone smashed them with a hammer).

Yet, I have certainly struggled with pride in thinking that I know better or more than another. There's been my unwillingness to really listen and my tendency to harbor resentment while not leaving it to God to avenge me. All of this is pride, and pride stinks.

"True humility is not thinking less of yourself; it is thinking of yourself less," C. S. Lewis wrote.[61] In Matthew 11:29, Jesus says,

---

[61] S. Arnold and C. S. Lewis, March 4, 2020, "5 Quotes from C. S. Lewis to Make You a Better Person," https://medium.com/interfaith-now/5-quotes-from-c-s-lewis-to-make-you-a-better-person-7055045adbb4, viewed February 18, 2022.

"Learn of Me for I am humble." He then goes on to describe Himself as gentle, meek, and lowly. Those character traits are beautiful and so are the "feet of those who bring the Good News" (no matter what their big toes look like).

On the other hand, a spirit of pride is often harsh, hard, sharp, and pressing. People like that are difficult to be around. You seem never able to please them, and enough is never enough.

I have fallen in the pride pit. Here's how to stay out and walk in humility:

1. Be quick to forgive.
2. Don't brag.
3. Wait patiently for God to avenge and promote you.

"It is yet to be seen what God could do through a person who would give Him all the glory," is a quote attributed to D. L. Moody, evangelist and founder of Moody Bible Institute. When you recognize that your gifts and abilities come from God, you'll begin to live a confident and humble life. The older I get, the more I understand how much grace I need from God. I see that there's nothing of greatness in me, but it's all Him at work, giving me opportunities and the words I share with others.

Sometimes, when someone compliments me on something I share on social media, I have a hard time receiving their encouragement because I have only to think about my judgmental thoughts from the last thirty minutes to realize the wretch I really am. That's why I need to look up and give God all the glory for the goodness of who I am and what I'm able to do. I can also enjoy the uniqueness of my appearance and you can, too. It's okay to enjoy the way you present yourself with a fun "costume" (some refer to it as an outfit), a hairstyle, highlights, and "putting on your face." It was a difficult season when acne entered into my life as a young adult, and I became obsessed with my skin. It'd rock my world if I had a zit or zits, so I'd squeeze and do surgery on them until my face was a scabby mess.

It recently happened again. I was alone in a hotel room with a sterilized needle, and I dug a white bead zit out of the middle of my forehead until it bled. Two days later when I arrived home, I had a large scab.

The second thing after, "Hi, Mom," and "Hi, Pretty Debbie," when I got home was, "What's on your forehead?" I explained the situation of how I had done a procedure to produce a crater on my forehead. The third sentence which *both* Dan and Joey stated was the same, "It actually looks like you're of Indian royalty." I took a photo and posted it on Instagram. I have no pride but my sense of humor is intact.

It's embarrassing to admit how much time I think about my outer appearance more than the condition of my heart, but on the drive home I also thought about many of the big issues our country is dealing with and I asked myself, *What really is most important right now?* I answered aloud, "To know that God came down as Jesus to reconcile Himself to us." Ironically, my Monday *Everyday Matters* airing on stations that very week was called, "Justice Delayed."

"Everyday Justice Delayed"
Friday Matters

Life is promised to be wonderfully perfect *and* with purpose in heaven. This Earth is not our home. There's something more! Psalm 145:8 is good: "The Lord is kind and merciful, slow to get angry, full of unfailing love." His love for us waits, waits for us to know and accept Him and what He did on the cross for us and our sins.

Dr. Joad was a broadcasting personality of the BBC and the head of the philosophy department at the University of London. He was known for undermining Christianity in the college world. He believed that God was an impersonal part of the cosmos and that there was no such thing as sin.

But before he died, Dr. Joad came to the understanding that there was sin as the Bible describes and the only solution for sin was the cross of Jesus Christ. He became passionate about following Jesus. God's love delayed justice, giving this man time to recognize his own sin and receive life in Christ. In this instance, justice delayed is condemnation denied. God and His love are real . . . every day.

There are *so* many issues that need our attention (unlike forehead zits), but let's not become lost in them and forget what's most important, "For God so loved the world that He gave His one and only Son, that whoever believes in Him shall not perish but have eternal life." (John 3:16). The reason that "God so loved the world" is the most important thing to know. He's the only one who can save us and give us the hope of perfection and purpose in eternity with Him, Yet, so many Christians are divided over issues and ideas. Speaker and author Francis Chan, from Crazy Love Ministries, spoke at the International House of Prayer (IHOP) in Kansas City in August 2021. He engaged with a panel of pastors, on stage, on the subject of "Choosing Unity or Division." Chan said, "It's easy to find reasons to divide with other believers, but Christ's call to love changes our desires and leads us toward unity."[62] Exactly.

One of the comments on Chan's Instagram posts from Lilie Juarez @lilieofthevalley, (which showed a clip from the event) read,

"It's not a salvific issue," and that right there is what has caused the body to be so divided. We're so focused on things that are *not* a heaven-and-hell issue based on salvation, but we focus more on opinion and that has divided us. We can't argue about what God has called sin. We cannot be divided by our personal choices and opinions. So,

---

[62] Francis Chan, Crazy Love Ministries, https://www.instagram.com/p/CSH3nyVJDLN/, viewed August 4, 2021.

I love how Francis has shared in past conferences. He's been so open about how God has been working in his personal life; touching the sensitive places of his own theology and reconstructing his mindset. It has truly been a blessing to me in my own personal season right now."[63] I completely agree with Lilie and say, "Amen."

God created and loves *all* people, and we all matter dearly to Him. While it's true that, "All Lives Matter," I tried to explain to my mother why that phrase on her door in her assisted living apartment might trigger some staff members. "But why?" Mom wanted to know. "You're right, Mom, but some people take offense because they believe it minimizes the need for empathy and the need for action specifically for the black community." She didn't understand, but wanted to be sensitive so she removed the poster from her door. Regardless of whether we completely understand all that matters to others, we can understand that to God we are all loved by Him no matter what we do or don't do. We can choose to Live Well.

Living well is knowing and *receiving* God's grace (which we all so desperately need) and then giving that same grace to others. *Living well* is walking in love. It's holding a biblical worldview which gives us all truth to know mercy, love justice, and walk humbly with the Lord our God. We don't need to borrow from secular theology to be more understanding or empathetic because the Bible is the source of God's love for all whom He created.

Evolution teaches that different races evolved differently so that some races are superior to others. The Bible instructs in Acts 17:26 that God has created all people of one blood.

God also decreed that we are created in His image—therefore we are *all* created equally and endowed by our Creator with certain inalienable rights. The Lord God went to the cross for us and paid our debt. He rose again and lives so that we might live, too. Oh, this is

---

[63] Chan.

God's amazing grace. His grace doesn't depend on what we have done for God, but rather what God has done for us.

"Oh, Lord, thank You, and Amen."

Carry on dear heart and live well with what matters most—a relationship with God, others, and the hope of eternity.

HIGH ON FAITHFULNESS

37
SKIPPING TO CHURCH OR CHURCH SKIPPING?

*"And let us not neglect our meeting together,
as some people do, but encourage one another,
especially now that the day of His return is drawing near."*
— **Hebrews 10:25 (NLT)**

Yep, I'm a church skipper. And I'm a Christian, follower of Christ, lover of people. I believe in the importance of church and community, yet I skip.

I'm not a morning person, so there's that, and there are people. While I dearly love people, they also can be truly annoying. And like family, we don't pick who slips into the fold.

There are so many people who define church differently and there are forms, blogs, and discussions about the importance of church. Ol' Webster tells us that church is, "a body or organization of religious believers: such as the whole body of Christians." But just because someone calls themselves a Christian does not mean they follow, obey, or understand the grace of Christ. Plus, there are all these different denominations and who's the judge on who's right, wrong, or "on point"? Could it be that each type of church that calls on Jesus as Lord is in good stead with their various traditions and liturgy, but they're just "different"? And, of course, church can be held anywhere and at any time, but I am referring to the traditional morning hour, on a Sunday, that most Christians would call "church-going." And did I mention I am not a morning person?

First up, no matter when you go, if you go, or how often you go, and what denomination you're a part of, "A church is a hospital for sinners, not a museum for saints."[64] This is a proclamation I've read on Pinterest and other social media posts and blogs. Yet, we seem to be in an age when simply *being* in church is one of the most countercultural moves we can make. Author and friend Sarah Condon, who's a wife, mom, and priest says, "People tell me regularly that they do not want to go to church because they have been burned by it, that it is full of hypocrites, and that people only attend church as a status symbol. I don't care where you are on your spiritual journey with the Lord: pharisee, apathy, or agnostic. Maybe you're mad at Him? Maybe you're acting like you're not? Maybe you need a place to fall apart. Or maybe your ten-year-old daughter does. Just find a back pew at a church and take a seat. You are not there just for the sermon. Like I said, human beings can be hit-or-miss. You're there for Jesus. Or rather, He is there for you. Listen to Him. He will wash your feet. He will tell you to love one another."[65]

Yes, preach, Girlfriend. Let's run to Him and fall at His feet and He will wash them and every part of us clean.

When our four boys were young and challenging, and with Minnesota winters being cold and testing, church was not on my list of

---

[64] Pauline Phillips, P. (n.d.). Pauline Phillips quotes, https://www.brainyquote.com/quotes/pauline_phillips_381033, viewed February 18, 2022.
[65] Sarah Condon, "When Jesus Gets Crucified and Churches Get Bombed: Take a Seat This Holy Week," April 24, 2017, Mockingbird, https://mbird.com/religion/when-jesus-gets-crucified-and-churches-get-bombed-take-a-seat-this-holy-week/, viewed August 16, 2021.

favorite activities. Yet, I wanted my boys to go to church because I thought it was good for them, and it turned out it was . . . for all of us. As the yelling to "Hurry up!" and "Stop complaining!" would leave my mouth, I'd sometimes hear, "Why do we have to go to church anyway? I don't want to go." My answer was for them just as much as it was for me: "Because it's not about you. Love God. Love others. Get in the van."

Our spirit is willing, but our flesh is weak. On a lot of Sunday mornings, the down comforter was comforting, along with the realization that I probably shouldn't have had that second glass of wine, and of course there's that writing assignment I knew was due on Monday so I could pretty easily justify staying in bed and skipping. However, when I do go to church, God always seems to put someone in front of me to love and someone there who loves me right where I'm at. Church is community and that's something we all need.

Several years ago, when my eighteen-year-old son, Joey, and I were on a retreat, we got to stay in a very 1980s-style cabin, which had an old tank TV, VHS player, and four VHS movie choices. We chose *Bruce Almighty*. It was better than we expected and a lot of it due to the storyline. Jim Carrey's character, Bruce, is given one day to "be God" (Morgan Freeman portrays the actual God), but before Bruce has the power for the day God lays out the ground rules.

God: "There are only two rules. You can't tell anybody you're God; believe me, you don't want that kind of attention, and you can't mess with free will."

Bruce: "How do you make so many people love you without affecting free will?"

God: [snorts] "Heh, welcome to my world, son. If you come up with an answer to that one, let me know."

The scene that struck Joey and me as most powerful (no pun intended) was when Bruce tries to get his girlfriend, Grace (Jennifer Aniston), to love him. Bruce can command some pretty spectacular events, such as decorating the sky at night with moon and stars in specific formations, and directing the weather, but when he stands on a ledge with arms reaching out to Grace to receive his love, he's powerless. Grace is at work, as a teacher on the playground, ready to go back inside with the kids, but for the moment they have together, Bruce uses his hand and arms in super-power gestures to try and move her to love him. He's behaving so weirdly she asks annoyingly, "Are you drunk?" Finally, with all the passion he can muster he shouts, "*Love me!*" Her response is simple: "I did love you," and she walks away.

Love cannot be forced. It is a free will choice. While we can have feelings that go with our love, it is a commitment and choice to love. We choose to love God or reject Him. We choose to let Him have the power, or not, but no matter what we do or don't do, He'll always love us. He also gives us a choice to go to church. And I know as you read this, that either you or someone you know has felt that their faith and love of God, with their identity as a Christian, is measured by how often they attend church. But I've yet to meet anyone who knew God through rules and religion.

Not that long ago, Joey told me that when I'd drop off him and his older brother, Peter, at youth group, it was the perfect distance of two miles to walk from the church to our home to complete the time of being at youth group. It made me smile. I said, "Joe, I love that you and Peter felt you had the freedom to ditch youth group." Yes, maybe "back then" I would have felt differently about not following "the rules" but *now*, I love that they felt that they had a choice and would not be punished for it.

Joey spent the summer after college (2021) at home. He loves children. He wants to be a dad and that's his dream, so it was wonderful that he was able to help our son, Marco, in Children's Church, where the kids go to learn and play while the sermon is taking place.

Joey had an encounter with Caleb, who was five years old, and Caleb was not interested in sitting in circle time for the group lesson.

Caleb drifted off to the side of the room to examine the toy options on the shelf. Joey followed him and his first question to Caleb was, "What's your favorite color?"

"Blue," Gabe said.

Joey asked, "Light blue or dark blue?"

Caleb replied, "Both."

Caleb then proceeded to tell Joey that his favorite food was a tomato and mayonnaise sandwich and that he wished that light abers from *Star Wars* were real. Joey asked a few more questions and then Gabe leaned into Joey and said, "I don't like Children's Church."

"It's fine," Joey said, "I didn't like it either when I was your age."

Joey became project manager for activities for Children's Church. He bought (with his own money) three hundred dollars worth of good lightsabers from a site that specializes in authenticity. "I need to do it for the children, Mom."

Okay, Joe, God bless.

Then there's church Facebook. You can "zoom in" and watch/enter into worship and hear a message being delivered, which is great, but not. It's not so great because we aren't gathering in fellowship. Through the Facebook feed, we can't see body language, facial expressions, or hear the tone of voice of another who we really *need* to see and they need to see us, if only for a connection and a hug.

So, getting into a discussion about church on a Facebook thread is not something I recommend; however, it might help the one commenting to understand why they have the reaction they do. In my case, it helped me to articulate why I think people leave church and why I would. A young woman posted a comment that she didn't think religion should dictate government policy and that the reason so many young people were leaving the church was because of religious hypocrisy. My response was this: "I don't think religion should dictate government policy, either. I believe it's only by the prompting of the Holy Spirit that we enter into a personal relationship with the living

God. The Holy Spirit can direct our lives and guide us in our choices. Church is where people can gather for encouragement and accountability, but just because "the Church" says "you should" do something, or says "you should not" do something, does not necessarily determine what God is saying."

Yes, I would agree that religious hypocrisy and legalism with expectations of how you should perform as a Christian would have people completely looking for the "Exit" signs. People leave religion and the church because they don't understand or have a personal relationship with Christ, nor do they understand His mercy and grace. If they did, they'd realize how desperately they need it and therefore can't afford to shame or condemn another or withhold His grace from another. There's no perfect church, only a perfect, Holy, and Loving God "There is, therefore, now no condemnation for those in Christ Jesus" (Romans 8:1 NIV) and "'Not by might nor by power, but by my Spirit,' says the LORD Almighty" (Zechariah 4:6 NIV). That's my response still. Nevertheless, the gal deleted my Facebook comment. I probably came across as "preachy" rather than empathetic to what she was trying to communicate. Oh, well, I had also prayed, and I know His Word does not return to Him void (again, nothing is wasted). "Oh, Lord, we receive Your love and grace to love others as You do. Protect us from evil. Help us. Thanks. Amen."

Of course, people come to church and get to know Jesus personally because of *His work* on the cross. His death and resurrection are powerful. There's power, too, in sharing with others, honestly and sincerely, our personal struggles, missteps, and hopes. "Oh, you, too. I'm not alone?" can be the most refreshing words we hear all week. What if church was more like an AA meeting? "Thanks for sharing. Who would like to share next?"

Facebook discussions are rarely beneficial because you can't read the face or hear the tone. Yet there I was again responding to a post that came into my feed on a Sunday morning from a gal named, Amy.

I chose to get into the discussion because I wanted to affirm the awesomeness of God. Amy had written: "Church is not God. God is not religion. On this Sunday morning, I want to remind you that God is love and that if your religion is telling you anything else, including to judge or turn away people for how they live their lives—that is not God. My God loves you for you—my God doesn't require me to live a certain way or behave a certain way. My God doesn't require me to show my faith in a church where people have been cast aside for generations and where the religion has encouraged discrimination and unjust systems. My God is pure and loving. What/who is God to you??"

Of course, there were mostly affirmations for Amy on what she shared and about her beauty both inside and out as a fitness/health coach. I added my thoughts and said: "God loves all whom He created. His love will never leave or forsake us. He will never stop loving us regardless of what we do or don't do. Church is people. Religion is rules. The question is who is Jesus to you (us)? He is God, my Lord and Savior. I have a personal relationship with Him and have accepted His forgiveness. He loves me. He hates sin, but He's got me covered. I could never earn His love. He loves me right where I am at and not where I, or others, think I should be because I will never be where I should be. His grace is sufficient for each day despite my feelings screaming differently, on some days, yelling, 'It's too much, God!' I shared Romans 8:38-39 (ESV) too. "For I am convinced that neither death nor life, neither angels nor demons, neither the present nor the future, nor any powers, neither height nor depth, nor anything else in all creation, will be able to separate us from the love of God that is in Christ Jesus our Lord." I concluded my comment with, "Amy, you are dearly loved and wonderfully made."

Four days later, on Thursday, I was still pondering her Facebook post, so I found the thread and chose to add another comment:

Amy, I've been thinking about this post all week and so, too, I've been praying for you. I see, in you, a woman of strength and courage, a woman who is a blessing to many and who wants to help and encourage others. God has given me a speaking and radio ministry to share the love, hope, and forgiveness of God. My job is to love and not judge. We are all sinners and fall short of the glory of God (Romans 3:23). I used to think that my strong will and greater self-effort could bring lasting change, but nope. I must surrender everything to Christ, receive His grace, and be led by the Holy Spirit. When I give everything to God, real and lasting change happens. It really comes down to these two questions He asks me, "Debbie do you trust Me? Do you believe I'm good even when circumstances and others are not?" I added another comment after hitting 'enter' (Jesus is so patient with me and my hope is that others are blessed by my sharing and not "oppressed").

I wanted to share my simple testimony with you, Amy, because you matter to me, and I also want to apologize if anything I've ever posted or shown in my behavior has hurt you. I am part of a church and if the church has hurt you, I am sorry and ask your forgiveness. Truly. You are always welcome to talk with me about faith, and I would love to connect with you to hear more of your heart. How can we learn to really love one another if all we do is preach, rather than listen and talk to one another? Lord, have mercy. I know I'm not where I should be, but thank God I'm not where I used to be.

That comment post was one of my better moments on Facebook. I try to be an encouragement by what I post and the way I interact but believe me, I have been in a battle or two (or three) in comment threads and it hasn't always gone well. At all.

Facebook truly is a land of judgment (even when you're using good judgment). There's not a day that goes by that I don't check it. I hate to even admit that because it sucks up way too much of my time. And by God's grace I'm getting better. Like I said to Amy, "I know

I'm not where I should be, but thank God I'm not where I used to be." I try to keep Luke 6:37 (NIV) in mind too: "Do not judge, and you will not be judged. Do not condemn, and you will not be condemned. Forgive, and you will be forgiven."

Our identity needs to be from God who says we are not what others say or think. It's hard if you tend to be an approval addict. So, it's with super thankfulness that I am certain each of our four sons know who they are in Christ. We all have insecurities on some level. So it would be understandable if our youngest, David, as a young teen, who looked lean and athletic, would feel he needed to follow in his older brother footsteps as an athlete, but he was the theatre geek and he "owned it" and we are all proud of him. We have a passion for Christ because of His passion for us and we might do churchy things, but we don't want to be religious. Our identity is in Him, not what church we go to or how often.

My specific pet peeve is when someone says they want to represent Jesus well. I don't represent Jesus well, but He represents me well by the work He did on the cross. I mean, I could never do enough good things and perform Christianity well enough. I need Him. It's too much pressure on *me*, not Christ. But I know that people who say that mean well. I need community and church for accountability and confession just as much as I need to be encouraged to do good things for Christ because (as all Christians know) "faith without works is dead." A gem from Robert Capon's book, *Between Noon and Three: Romance, Law, and the Outrage of Grace*, reads, "If we are ever to enter fully into the glorious liberty of the children of God, we are going to have to spend more time thinking about freedom than we do. The church, by and large, has had a poor record of encouraging freedom. It has spent so much time inculcating in us the fear of making mistakes that it has made us like ill-taught piano students: we play our pieces, but we never really hear them because our main concern is not to make music but to avoid some flub that will get us in trouble. The church, having put itself in *loco parentis* (in the place of a parent), has been so afraid we will lose sight of the need to do it right that it has made us care more about how we look than about who Jesus is."[66]

Our oldest son has a master's degree in pastoral ministry from Moody Bible Institute in Chicago. I love that He knows the power of God's grace but has a firm grasp of the Gospel, tradition, and history of the church and God's Word. Now, he is a twenty-seven-year-old youth and associate pastor, married and serving in the church he grew up in. (Do I have to go to church now because our son serves as a pastor where we attend and it will "look bad" if I don't attend?) Ha! Marco is "in the world but not of the world" and hasn't fallen into a theology that interprets Scripture based on what's happening in the world to fit the world's ideologies and how one feels. Marco keeps me grounded, too. "Well, Mom, of course you are to do good works to represent Jesus well," he tells me. And I'm like, "Duh, I know, but sometimes we think God loves us more if we do good works and 'Christianesy' activities, and I'm just at the point of sharing the bottom-line truth: Jesus loves us no matter what we do, and He gives us 'works' to do out of His love for us." Serving others gives us meaning in our lives. God knows this. He gives us talents to serve others so we have purpose. Out of our "who" comes our "do."

Oh, if we could really grasp this crazy wonderful love, Christ has for us. All of my sons have taught me and shown me God's love with their unique personalities and David is no exception. One of the radio features I wrote years ago shares the confidence our David had, knowing He was loved.

---

[66] Robert Capon, *Between Noon and Three: Romance, Law, and the Outrage of Grace* (Grand Rapids, MI: W. B. Eerdmans Pub, 1997).

"Everyday Confident Love"
Friday Matters

Our family was stunned, when years ago, our seven-year-old David, the fourth son, decided to walk down the aisle at church. The pastor invited a child to come forward to read a Proverb. As David left the pew he said, *"I'm a really good reader."* The truth is most of first grade he had a tutor for reading but progressed so much that by the end of the year the tutor had been dropped. Plus David read a lot to us as a family aloud, and each time he'd read we'd say, *"David, you're a really good reader,"* and then we'd hug him. David was confident when he read his verse (never mind that he pronounced a few words wrong).

And I thought, *Think of all the things we could do if we believed what God said to us.* I mean like… how much He loves us, He's cheering for us, He sees our hearts and knows and cries with us when we're hurting. Go forward in that confidence, fully known and fully loved . . . every day.

David is now twenty years old and while he was home visiting the summer of 2021, we had a mother and son dinner and movie date. The most significant part was the heart-to-heart talk David and I had. We have a wonderful relationship of transparency and trust but "above all love" (2 Peter 4:8). We talked about ideas, God, culture, and ideologies. Dan and I always told David, growing up, that he had such a good heart. He did and he does. He told me that one thing he really appreciated about our parenting was the focus on having a heart toward others, no matter who the person was or their lifestyle or what background they came from. "I never felt that you and Dad directed me to be a certain 'type' of person, other than one who had a sincere heart to care about others, Mom." That means a lot to my heart. It makes me think of the Scripture Matthew 6:20 and the real treasures in this life, being people. "Store your treasures in heaven, where moths and rust cannot destroy, and thieves do not break in and steal."

No matter who you are or what you do, I am sure, like me and David, you struggle with your identity as different seasons come and go. We all want to be seen, to be heard, to be loved as we are. It can be a real struggle.

David and I didn't agree about everything we talked about. I interrupted him too much and tried to share my great points, but I think the very root of our conversation was about loving people who are different than us. It can be difficult to understand why God might not like all that we do, yet He loves all of who we are. It all comes down to a real and unconditional love which only God can give. Our part is to trust Him with our friends and family, whom He loves even more than we do. Christ gives no conditions for us to accept His love. He gives us grace and forgiveness simply out of His love for us and not by our good works, good intentions, or right attitudes. David needed to be heard. I listened because I love him no matter what and after our discussion I prayed and then we hugged, my long and lean baby, at six feet, one inch, cried while I held him in my arms. "I love you so much, Mom," David said. "This talk really helped me to just share everything I am thinking and believe right now without being judged. Thank you for being my mom." God is the same with us. We might not understand all His ways and the "whys," but He accepts us where we're at and nothing can separate us from His love. I don't care about our differences in ideas, but I care that David knows the love of God, His family, and that there is life after death and our free will lets us choose where we spend it.

You'll have people say, "Hey, I'm a Christian. I believe Jesus died for me. I've given my life to Him and I've accepted Him." But if you don't see any change in that person's life, with identity-shifting behavior, or any sort of transformation, you're thinking, *Where's the joy, the peace in their life? What's the problem?* Maybe it's because they have no real grasp on how desperately God's grace is needed and therefore there's this stingy attitude toward life and others.

I would also add that the hypocrisy of "Christian' sinners is more difficult than sinners who deny Him. Maybe the people who reject Christianity only understand it as a religion, a church, or denomination but never knew God's real love? Because once you truly know Christ, you receive a love like no other; gracious, unconditional, and fogiving, a perfect love. How could someone reject *that* or rather Him?

If we're looking at people and their good works and judging like, "Oh, Lord. Wow. This person is a mess and they are *not* doing well. They don't deserve grace." 'But it's not our job or problem to determine who's worthy or not because God deems us all worthy. None of us deserve anything. We all have a mothership of debt, and therefore the size of the payment is beyond comprehension.

To really understand grace, and for grace to be transforming, first we have to understand the debt. The second thing we have to understand, besides the size of the debt, is the magnitude of the provision. There are people who do understand that they are pretty bad and flawed, but they aren't convinced of the magnitude and sufficiency of the provision. The gospel of salvation by grace through faith and the work of Jesus Christ alone, and substitutionary atonement . . . we just don't get it. But when we begin to get it . . . *Wow* . . . we're alive, the church is *alive*.

Our second-oldest son, Peter, was in West Palm Beach, Florida, for a year at a big megacampus church. You know, the ones with the coffee latte bars and bookstores. It was quite different than the two-hundred-member church in which he grew up. Yet, Jesus was there to meet him. Peter found community and is still in touch with a couple young men who mentor and keep him accountable. Who knew? God knew because Peter's relationship with God is personal and not religious.

As Christians we want this for our kids and so does God . . . for all of us because we're all His. At the end of the day (or week) isn't it about having a heart to serve and worship God? Let's go to church because we get to and not because we have to. And when we don't go, it's okay because God goes on loving us.

The Earth experience is hard, but it's not our home. We are all on a journey and will complete that journey either in a relationship with Jesus or without it. "All the nations will be gathered before Him, and He will separate the people one from another as a shepherd separates the sheep from the goats" (Matthew 25:32). Admittedly, Instagram has been "church" for me at times, and by that I mean a collection of pictures and posts shared by sinners and saints who recognize their need for Jesus.

Author and priest Kenneth Tanner's had a post on Instagram with a shepherd and his sheep that caught my attention in a very good way, and I've kept it filed away with other thoughtful points on the Gospel: "The radical message of the cross is that the oppressed and the oppressors alike are the objects of God's love and redemption. In the end, the Gospel is not about justice in human terms—none of us gets the justice we deserve or demand. What if we did? Thank God especially that humans don't get the justice they demand. There is never an "us" (the good folks) over against "them" (the bad people) because of the Gospel. For every hand reached out to the oppressed to rescue and protect, there is a hand reached out to the oppressor, to reconcile and invite into a new way of life. The Gospel compels us to pursue truth and accountability alongside reconciliation and mercy. I know this is offensive but it's important: Christ is not on a "side" here. He wants us all."[67]

Ain't that the truth? He wants us all, the weak and the strong, the ones with titles and success financially and the ones without, the "woke" and the "un-woke," the liberal, the progressive, the conservative. He loves all of us. God is on our side against evil but to

---

[67] K. Tanner, November 13, 2020, www.instagram.com, https://www.instagram.com/p/CHIuKn_pfPw/, viewed February 18, 2022.

simply say, "God's on my side because I am doing everything pretty well according to what He tells me in the Bible" is simply arrogance and self-righteousness." The question should really be, "Are you on God's side?" Do you trust in Him more than your circumstances and feelings?

You might miss out on attending church, but don't miss out on the truth and grace of the Gospel of Jesus Christ. Gather with others in a way where you can collectively, praise God, confess your stuff, and share your needs. Skip church but don't skip-out on God's love for you. My motto still works for me personally. "Love God. Love others. Get in the van."

38
UNCLE PETER, GOD IS GREATER IN OUR WEAKNESSES

"Be strong and courageous. do not be afraid; do not be discouraged, for the Lord your God will be with you wherever you go."
— **Joshua 1:9 (NIV)**

I'M NOT BRAVE.
And then I was.
I was so weak.
But there was God's grace.
It was a fight.
Tears, yelling, running, stillness, laughing, vomit, fear, waiting, hoping...
All of it was a part of the fight.
It was messy. I don't like messy and then I was weak and I don't like being weak. But the part in being brave, the part of you that steps forward in courage when everything in you screams, "Hold on! I did not sign up for this," that brave part of me went forward despite my feelings because of the grace of God and the people who fought with me as prayer warriors.
God knows.

Those were all the thoughts racing through my mind the day I left to help my Uncle Peter with my son Peter.

God knew there would be a day when little niece Debbie would be there for Uncle Peter just as he was there for her. When I visited Grandpa and Grandma as a little three-year-old girl I'd yell, "Pete!" from the top of the stairs down into his basement bedroom. He cheerily came upstairs through the hanging hippie beads to come and play. Uncle Peter was my playmate. He would build hundreds of card houses just to let me smash them all over the living room floor of Grandpa and Grandma's home. I'd scream, "Twist me" in the spinning chair by the front windows and Uncle Peter dutifully obliged. He fed me strawberries, took me to church, and let me sit on his lap for cuddles because I wanted to be with him at all times. When I was eight years old and visiting, he took me to a Pentecostal church, and I was introduced to the Holy Spirit and people speaking in tongues. It was both "wow" and weird.

Uncle Peter was only fourteen when I was born, being ten years younger than my mother and five years younger than my aunt, his only siblings. He was an accomplished man with a master's in divinity, a master's in counseling, and a bachelor of arts degree. He went on to have a full ministry serving varied populations including pastor at the First Presbyterian Church in Holton, Kansas, and director of chaplaincy at Topeka State Hospital and Menninger Clinic. His chaplaincy work extended to providing services to first responders in NYC following the September 11, 2001, terrorist attacks as well as providing clinical pastoral education training to military service members.

Uncle Peter was always curious and passionate about learning more and broadening his understanding. He went on to receive his licensed specialist clinical social worker certification from the University of Kansas; an undergraduate degree with an individualized major in aesthetic communication, combining art and journalism;

and was pursuing a PhD in transpersonal psychology from Sofia University in Palo Alto, California. Uncle Peter was also an accomplished athlete having participated in more than one hundred triathlons, twenty marathons, and a dozen or more ultra-distance events, such as the Ironman Triathlon. And . . . Uncle Peter was an alcoholic.

He embraced life and had many successes, but he also embraced addiction. Addiction is no respecter of persons. Sadly, all those accomplishments did not help with the disease of alcoholism and two divorces, estrangement from two ex-wives and three daughters, and his two sisters; all were affected by the "darkness of the drink." One very sad aspect of being an addict is that it affects so many others around them. To be sure, we're all sinners in need of a Savior and by His grace there is always hope and healing. But we all make choices.

In the last fifteen years of Uncle Peter's life, I was the last person on the family list he was still able to reach out to. His behavior led to everyone else having a strong and strict boundary of basically no contact. In 2016 I drove to Kansas with my son, Peter, to move Uncle Peter out of Crack Alley. I felt like I was trying to drive through a force field that was set up by Satan, and I actually sensed a presence of evil that made driving forward difficult. I cried for most of the trip. Previously, I had traveled to Topeka in 2007 for a "fun" visit with my son Peter. I met Uncle Peter's daughter, Grace, for the first time. Uncle Peter was stable, and his job was picking up scrap metal off the streets and bringing it to a recycling center for cash. He had an old truck, which had a breathalyzer device that he had to blow into before it started, as there had been one too many DUIs. We had fun activities with kid museums, movies, and anything indoors because of the *heat*. We had some hard discussions, too, that involved family and a relationship with God. At one point Uncle Peter got angry with me and called me "a whitewashed tomb" because I challenged him on choices he was making and asked about his views and relationship with God. After the exchange I went outside to get something from my vehicle. When I came back, I said,

"Uncle Peter, I came here to love you and to connect with you. I don't want the memory to be on apologetics or doctrine but on love and grace extended no matter what's going on with you now."

It was the breath of the Holy Spirit wafting into the hot and sticky apartment and we moved forward. The next nine years there were conversations every few months. Then in February 2016 Uncle Peter took a brave step and called me for help to go to rehab. He was intoxicated and speaking in a way that I knew it might be his last cry for help. Because of Uncle Peter's crap choices (which we all can make), I was literally the only person on his list of remaining family or friends for him to reach out to. I thought *now* was the time, and Uncle Peter was ready to go forward. Jesus and I together could save him.

It took months to arrange all the legalities with insurance, lodging, and treatment centers, but the day in August came to travel to Topeka, Kansas, from International Falls, Minnesota. No offense to Kansas, but leaving the Icebox of the Nation to head to the heat of Kansas in August was like entering the land of Hades. Nevertheless, I knew I had to go and that my uncle was at a breaking point. I took our son, Peter, his namesake, with me on this journey in 2016.

Uncle Peter was showing courage by accepting his dependence. I was scared, too. Scared for my uncle, scared to go through his yuck, and scared it wasn't happening fast enough. I am used to being strong, having a plan, and following it. My Aunt Ginger says I am a "getter doner." But I was struggling. My feelings were raw.

One sob session was driving late at night on the freeway as we traveled through South Dakota or Iowa or Nebraska or maybe almost Kansas . . . wherever. It was raining pitchforks, and I had to pull over to wait for it to clear. I discussed the forecast with former cop guy, Nick, in a gas station as we watched the rain pour down. He gave me a shot of hope, saying, "If you can make it twenty more minutes, the downpour will let up and then you'll be fine." He added, "I talked to my wife and she says it's not raining where we live and that is thirty minutes from here."

Unfortunately, Nick was wrong because, yes, for twenty minutes of driving it was better, but then came an additional forty minutes of driving during which I saw signs telling me to get off the freeway, and so I did—barely. I was about to hydroplane. I was terrified.

Now, remember my son, Peter, was with me. The more scared I was driving, the goofier he got. That was not helping to balance out my hysteria. He also screeched he had to "go pee" and being a boy, he could either get drenched on the side of the road, or use an empty Mountain Dew bottle if necessary. Peter stayed in the vehicle.

We saw the gas station light in the distance, but we couldn't find the road to get to it so I stopped our little vehicle and just cried and then yelled while Peter called my husband. The gas station was closed, but there was a motel. It looked sketchy, with its bulletproof glass and a slit for me to slide my card through but at least we were not on the main road anymore where the world was spinning so fast and I could no longer remain sane. We slept with our clothes on and on top of the "bedspread" because it was that "sketch."

The next day was *the day*. We arrived at Uncle Peter's Crack Alley apartment which was the name it was known by. I could hardly take it in. The smells, the garbage, the mass of disorganized stuff, and brokenness was almost too much to bear . . . along with the heat. I decided we were going to pack up as if it were on fire, taking only my Uncle, his dog, the family heirloom chair, photos, and books.

I wanted to strip off my clothes, and our son took off what he could and wrapped his head in a turban with his t-shirt. We had to prioritize, too, as that evening Uncle Peter would be going to a thirty-day treatment center before moving in with us in Minnesota with the plan to attend a long-term program called Teen Challenge. Needless to say, we left his apartment with much still in it and nothing cleaned—it was that kind of situation. We left the door unlocked. Are you kidding me? It was not worth any $500.00 deposit money for cleaning that dumping ground which we walked away from.

I can't tell you how thankful I am for the dairy farm family God provided to take Uncle Pete's dog, Karma. A year earlier I had met four of the eleven-member farm family at a retreat. They were and still are the most down-to-earth and kind family, right out of the Anne of Green Gables motif. I mean, heck, they named a cow after me, "Debbie," and I get to continually name all the babies she delivers (she has twins a lot), so taking Karma was, well, good karma.

After leaving the apartment, my son and I went back to the hotel and waited for Uncle Peter to finish up at the post office and other errands. He met us at the hotel, where we now had the dog, to say goodbye and I remember thinking this was the last time to really talk. So, I said, "Remember how Jesus simply wanted the Apostle Peter to allow His love to touch Him in his weakness. The apostle told and re-told the story of his own unfaithfulness and how Jesus touched him. When he proclaimed the gospel of grace, he preached from his weakness the power of God. That is what will convert us, and the people around us, if they see that the love of Christ has touched us."

I continued: "Uncle Peter, the best thing you can do right now is this: Rather than rely on your brilliance with your talents and education, rely on your brokenness, because that's where the light of God's love can get in. Go into treatment with what you can give and not what you can get. It's not keeping rules with clenched fists, but receiving a gift with open hands."

Uncle Peter listened and dropped his head and nodded.

We walked into the center and saw a lot of beautiful characters with colored hair, stocking caps, and wonderful tattoos. Counselor Amanda handed me a lot of forms and had a lot of questions. For some reason I began to have a panic attack, the kind where that scary fluid runs down your arms and makes its way to your stomach so you think you're gonna be sick.

I said aloud, "Ah, is everyone okay here because I feel like everyone is performing and carrying on like everything is 'normal' and I don't think this is 'normal.'"

Amanda said, "This is a big thing, Debbie. You're right. This is a really big deal."

And then I started to cry and so did Uncle Peter. Between sobs I said, "We want you back, Uncle Peter. We love and pray for you. We want you back. Your daughters want you back. They need you. Your sisters want you back, I want you back, and we all love you."

I pulled back and looked him in the face and with all the drama and courage I could muster I yelled, "*You don't give up now! This is it, and you are not going to give up! There is too much love here! Don't give up!*"

Then I sat down. It was quiet. I thought, We will go forward. That's what God's grace is all about. I didn't feel it, but I knew it. What had just happened would not have happened without Him. Wow. There is a God, and He does not limit His view to our present state.

Later in the car, my son Peter said, "Mom, you're amazing; everyone knows it." Nice, especially since we fought much of the time on our road trip. And, of course, I am not amazing. God is.

August 24, 2016: My journal entry reads:

Only His grace . . . only through Him and His provision could I walk forward in courage. I am not taking any credit for this. It was not me because "me" would not have done this. I would have opted out of this drama and not taken the part. And you better believe I sense the strong resistance of the enemy in the journey even weeks before the actual trip with headaches and random crying episodes. It was with faith and the hope to believe that things would get better, that I was able to move forward.

Of course, my son Peter and I made it home, but that's not to say we had a perfect road trip. *Why* is there a battle about where we eat every time? Can't we *both* go to McDonald's just like I went to Subway when it was his turn to pick? And how hard can it be to take the cap off in the engine to fill it with oil? It's not embarrassing to have your mom make a gas station production out of asking for help.: Is it? Yet, there was *zero* discussion on me hitting "repeat" over and over on the MercyMe"CD called *Welcome to the New*. Maybe because I cried most of the time while it played for 167 miles?

> "Cause I hear a voice and He calls me redeemed
> When others say I'll never be enough
> And greater is the One living inside of me
> Than he who is living in the world . . . "[68]

The power of God's Word is the Sword of the Spirit, and this was a battle. The truth is that I couldn't have done it without my son Peter to help me. This sort of trip is one you can't fully explain with words or pictures. I know God will use this in our son's life in years to come. He witnessed all the prayer, grace, and help God gave us through others such as my Aunt Ginger, who named our mission rescue project "Little Miss Sunshine." Ginger kept me grounded with her wisdom, compassion, and humor as I processed all that was happening and experiencing. She wrote to friends to pray and said, "We laughed, cried, gagged, and hoped against hope all day. Sadly, Uncle Peter did not take to sobriety. He did not complete the thirty-day treatment and never made it to the long-term treatment in Minnesota. It's hard to comprehend this, but I have never stopped praying and loving him."

I read Psalm 37:39. God is a stronghold in times of trouble. The battle is not over.

I'm not sure how Uncle Peter's final battle on this Earth ended, but I do believe that heaven's doors welcomed him home into that perfect and final place of purpose and rest. After I left Uncle Peter at the treatment center in Kansas, it was only ten days later when he left

---

[68] Bart Millard, MercyMe, "Greater" (official Lyric Video), July 11, 2014, https://www.youtube.com/watch?v=GXI0B4iMLuU, viewed August 23, 2021.

the premises and was looking for somewhere to live and "do sobriety" on his own. Somehow, due to my own ignorance and misunderstanding of the insurance, I was also left with the $3,000 ten-day treatment bill. I don't share this for you to think, *poor Debbie* (okay maybe a little), but more so that you know you're not the only one who's gotten stuck financially trying to help an addict. Uncle Peter wanted to come and live in our home after leaving treatment, but I knew that was not a solution and a boundary that I needed to make.

When I received the call from my cousin, Cicelia, that Uncle Peter had died from a heart attack on Friday November 20, 2020, I wailed. It was a shock along with deep grief. I felt sick. *This* was not the way I wanted to finish my story on Uncle Peter. After I refused Uncle Peter's request to live with me and my family in September 2016, he changed into a person I didn't recognize. I received ugly and nasty voice messages, text, and crazy posts on social media. I even called the Topeka Police Department to check on his new place of residence to see if he was really driving to International Falls, Minnesota, to set our house on fire.

The last time I mailed some of his items along with some "I love you" gifts was January 2020 not long after our last conversation. Sadly, his three daughters and two sisters never saw him free from his addictions or healthy enough to have had contact with him before he died.

Later I found out that Uncle Peter had been sober for five months before he died of a heart attack. This came from an old friend of the family with whom he had reconnected. She said, "There were regrets he had, but there was hope." There is always hope. *But still*, I wanted to scream, "*Why, God?* Why weren't any of us able to reconcile here on Earth? It seems like such a waste of life."

Uncle Peter's daughter, Cicelia, is an amazing artist. She revealed some of her struggle with her dad in her exhibit, "I Love You Are You Okay, 2017." It is a tangible art experience in which the viewer is directed to walk into a large room with waiting room chairs and artificial plants. It was and is a unique display of art and emotion. Each participant in the viewing would be instructed to form two lines at each plant and read the text messages embroidered on the plants in a dialogue format. The messages were texts sent between Cicelia and her father Peter in heartfelt hard times and hurt. It's a beautifully sincere display of real life, love, and art.

There's a beauty of God's work in each of our lives, however it was lived. Uncle Peter created beautiful pieces of jewelry art, wrote poetry, and was hospital chaplain and a Presbyterian minister who definitely made a difference in other peoples' lives. I believe I'll see Uncle Peter again. God promises in 2 Peter 3:9: "The Lord isn't really being slow about His promise, as some people think. No, He is being patient for your sake. He does not want anyone to be destroyed, but wants everyone to repent." I looked up the definition of *repent* and it reads, "Repentance is the activity of reviewing one's actions and feeling contrition or regret for past wrongs, which is accompanied by commitment to and actual actions that show and prove a change for the better." Uncle Peter was so often trying to change—falling, getting back up, and then getting stuck (mental health issues got in the way, too) but he'd get back up with determination and by God's strength he would "beat this demon."

Uncle Peter knew Jesus and had accepted Him as his Savior despite all the demons that would continue to pop back into his life. This excerpt from the Wintery Knight blog with the shared insights by a friend who wrote to a family member (who rejected historic Christianity for progressive Christianity) and was asked to give the basics of salvation, and his attempt to explain the Gospel to them is below:

> So, you've asked the 10,000-talent question (alluding to Matthew 18:23–35). You are basically asking me what I think the Gospel is. I'll try to answer that in a minimalistic way, using my own

characterization of it rather than just making doctrinal statements.

One must accept that there is a God, who is a higher authority than themselves. How much one must first believe about that God is debatable, but candidate beliefs would be that He is personal (having a mind like, but greater than, ours), powerful, and the creator of this cosmos and everything in it—He owns it all.

This commitment to the Lordship of Christ naturally leads to the acceptance of subsequent beliefs. If Jesus is indeed Lord, then He holds all authority, and what He said and taught to His followers is our guide—the New Testament. And if this is the divine story, as intended by God for men, then we have reason to believe that it is comprehensible to us, and He will insure (despite the fallibility of men and demonic plots) that its essential message will not be lost or corrupted until all things are completed. Given that Jesus affirmed every categorical section of the Old Testament, and claimed to be its promised Messiah, then that, too, is a source of truth and understanding.

Those doctrines that are sometimes characterized as "essential" for salvation, are merely the highlights of this redemption narrative, which are those things being clear and consistent, and which indicate that someone has yielded themselves to the authority of Christ and the Scriptures and understands these things. It is not that believing them is what saves, but they are what the 'saved' naturally come to believe. Confessing them is the tangible, verbal act of affirming the Gospel, but is not necessarily identical to a life committed to putting it into practice, which is saving faith.[69]

Only God knows, but it would seem that Uncle Peter's last few months on Earth were about moving forward in grace and hope of reconciliation. And even though it seems he wasted the last generation

---

[69] Wintery Knight, "How to Explain the Gospel in Less than 1000 Words," August 23, 2021, https://winteryknight.com/2021/08/23/how-to-explain-the-gospel-in-less-than-1000-words/, viewed August 24, 2021.

of his life, he nevertheless had an impact on many individuals and families before his addiction took control of him. And you know what else? This life on Earth is a whiff and a puff of time compared to eternity, where we are perfectly whole, with no more tears or pain but still with purpose, a challenge (in the very best meaning of that word) to continue moving forward and doing something that's beautiful and meaningful. I can't wait to see what that is for Uncle Peter now and for me—I wonder, too, what I'll be doing?

Theologian Francis Schaeffer said, "True spirituality consists in living moment to moment by the grace of Jesus Christ."[70] I couldn't agree more. We are all broken in need of God's great merciful healing and forgiveness. Receive the grace and peace God gives despite the circumstances. Give grace to others. Wait. Pray. Grieve. Pray some more and then keep on keeping on with a song of hope in your heart:

> "There'll be days I lose the battle
> Grace says that it doesn't matter
> 'Cause the cross already won the war
> He's greater." [71]

---

[70] Francis Schaeffer quote, https://quotefancy.com/quote/1402268/Francis-Schaeffer-True-spirituality-consists-in-living-moment-to-moment-by-the-grace-of, viewed February 18, 2022.
[71] Bart Millard, MercyMe, "Greater" (official Lyric Video), July 11, 2014, https://www.youtube.com/watch?v=GXI0B4iMLuU, viewed August 23, 2021.

39
MAKING BEST FRIENDS WHEREVER YOU GO

"God has given each of you a gift from His great variety of spiritual gifts. Use them well to serve one another."
— 1 Peter 4:10 (NLT)

"WE'RE BEST FRIENDS NOW!" is something I seem to be saying a lot lately.

Everyone has a story. I find myself taking the time to listen to people's stories, such as my taxi driver from Thailand, who I met in November 2016 and drove me two hours to the Bangkok Airport; or Roger, a gas station owner from smalltown USA, who I met one weekend after speaking at a Christmas brunch. I always take a selfie afterward to capture the memory and then add, "Well, now that we're best friends, we'll always be in touch."

Another new best friend I met one fall at a retreat is Gigi, who is originally from Brazil. She loved this whole concept of "best friends in thirty minutes or less" because when you ask questions and listen to the heart, there's this wonderful joy that turns to love as you begin to fully know a real person and not a "fluffy-fluff" performer or poser kind of friend.

With that wonderful accent of hers, Gigi shared her wild-child past living in Brazil. She let me practice her accent as I love to "speak ethnic" to express the fun and diversity of so many wonderful humans. As I listened to Gigi, it was fascinating to hear about her life in Brazil. For many seasons she lived in darkness, making harmful choices, and yet, because of her relationship with God, she has not let her past define her future. She is fully known by God, loved and redeemed, which enables her to be a huge blessing as a friend, wife, and mom.

In the fall of 2016, I visited my dad in Thailand, where he was vacationing with his new wife. On my flight from Chicago to Abu Dhabi, I met two new best friends. I happened to be sitting in between Seerat and Prakash. They had no idea who I was nor did they know each other. It was a sixteen-hour trek in the air, and I slept through a lot of it. When I awoke, I had the best conversation with my new seatmate friends. Seerat is originally from Bangladesh and was going there to visit family. She lives in Oklahoma and works in the Oklahoma Department of Mental Health and Substance Abuse Services, as well as being a director for Distressed Children and Infants International. She is Muslim. Prakash was going abroad to visit family in India. He and his immediate family own and operate a Super 8 Hotel in Missouri. He is Hindu.

I asked as many questions as I could while they shared their stories of family, travel, politics, religion, and all the things you usually try to avoid talking about when making new best friends. I shared my story, too, and they listened. We all became best friends.

The best part of my travels abroad was not the sites, food, or scenery (although that was significant), but it was meeting new people and listening to their stories. I gained new insights and saw different perspectives. Connecting with people from different backgrounds and hearing from their hearts is not something I could gather through the media. I believe God is living, and He will make

Himself known to all, and He gives us all opportunities without cutting or bashing someone's culture and traditions. Jesus is alive! Jesus charged us to go out to the entire world and preach the Good News that He is alive (Mark 16:15).

It's taken me years to really grasp that God fully knows me and yet He fully loves me, completely, just as am. I can live authentically, free, and unashamed, and I can share this love with others so they, too, can be set free. What God doesn't love is sin because it's a barrier to our having a relationship with Him. Sin wins unless pardoned.

God is absolutely holy. In His holiness He must punish sin. We are all sinners. Yet because He is love, He didn't want to punish us. He offered Himself as a sacrifice on the cross to pay the full price for our sin. His resurrection proves He succeeded.

We celebrate Christ Mass (Christmas) to commemorate that Christ came down from heaven, lived as a man to fully understand and love us, and then sacrificed Himself so that we might be set free by accepting His gift of atonement for what separates us from Him.

I am thankful for God's call on my life to love others. He hasn't called me to hand out a rulebook or a list of "you should" and "you should nots," which means He hasn't called on me to point out the sins of others. He knows I have enough of my own stuff to clean up, and with His grace, how can I afford not to extend this gift to others?

I love people. I want to have fun, be real, love God, and love others. But it's also important to note that God *never* stops being holy. Out of His great holiness, power, might, and mercy do we then deny our own sinful desires and bow to Him. Our flesh wants what it wants and more of it. So, it's only by God's Holy Spirit, in us, that we can deny the flesh. I know the message of "sin is not in" and love always wins, but true love involves compassion with truth. If you remove one or the other, you no longer have love.

Don't fret about your sin issues because God first pours out His love to you and then He gently exposes your sin, offering a way for you to change direction and to receive full pardon and freedom.

This is what He did with the Samaritan woman at the well. He didn't meet her with condemnation. He first met her thirst. He offered her Living Water (eternity with God), but also let her know He knew all about her. She ran back to town to tell others about Him, not because she felt condemned, but because she had been offered hope and a way out.

People are not drawn to judgment. They are drawn to true friendship, and that is what Jesus is—a real best friend. No greater love can a man have than to give His life for His friends (John 15:13).

I did make one best friend in Abu Dhabi and it was Ihtazaz, my taxi driver from the airport to the hotel. We are still in contact, as we share pictures and stories about our culture. My dad had booked my flight to Thailand to include a one-day layover by myself in Abu Dhabi (which I seriously had to Google to find out that it was the capital of United Arab Emirates on the Persian Gulf).

But I did get confused by my second taxi driver, who I guess was more like a chauffeur. His name was Khaliq, and after I took a two-hour nap, he picked me up at the hotel and brought me to a museum, a shopping place, the Grand Mosque (and please visit my Instagram to see me fully covered with head scarf perfectly in place), and then to a place to eat authentic Arabic food. My thoughts at the time were, *Khaliq just sits in his car and brings me around to all these different locations and waits so patiently. And when I got lost in the mosque parking lot, he found me. Why then don't I invite him to get a bite?* Khaliq accepted. I admit I found it odd that I never had to pay him a taxi fee, but he explained it was part of the hotel setup. Ah. Okay. *But when Khaliq drove me to the hotel and said,* "So I bring you to airport tomorrow then, okay?"

"Okay, sounds good."

"So, then no problem I stay with you tonight?"

"Ah, yes. That's a problem."

"Yes. No problem."

We weren't right by the hotel entrance, but near enough for me to exit the vehicle as I made things very clear.

"There is no staying with me at the hotel or anytime ever. The answer is *no* because this is a very big problem. Goodbye."

I think Khaliq wanted to be best friends on another level that wasn't in my best friend package. Upon reflection of this great cultural experience, I, Abu Debbie, recognize that there needs to be sensitivity to other's traditions and way of living (but with the Dramamine and complimentary wine on the flight over, one can become a little foggy in their thinking). I also recognize that I was *covered* in prayer and prayer works. God's *love* covered and protected me despite my free-spirited personality. My husband no longer reminds me to "be safe" when traveling, but instead tells me, "Debbie, don't be crazy."

The rest of the trip was "no problem" and I met many best friends from all over the world. There are Martin and Clark from England; Neung from Thailand; Jose and Caterina from Spain; Jay and Lauren from Chicago; and Mohammed from Pakistan and his wife and five small children. I received an apple from the little girl as we played on the floor in Abu Dhabi. They were moving to begin a new life in Oklahoma. The apple placed on my dresser is still the home screen photo on my cell phone six years later. I have photos and memories, but most of all God's love, which will keep them in my heart and prayers always.

What makes us family and friends? In God's family, the Holy Spirit makes us one. 1 Corinthians 12:13: "We have all been baptized into one body by one Spirit, and we all share the same Spirit." The Spirit is not only God's presence and power in us, but the Spirit is also God's spiritual DNA that connects us to each other and to our Father. This spiritual bond transcends human family, race, nationality, gender, and any other human barrier. The Spirit's presence ensures that we are God's creation here on Earth.

I am so thankful for the opportunity I had to travel and meet new best friends. I love people and I want everyone to feel welcomed. God wants us all to know we are loved and we're not a mistake, even if we've made mistakes. He has a place for us all but not our sins, so of course He made a way for us to be clean.

We are all sinners, which is why our first step toward reconciliation is to confess our sins, receive His pardon, and walk forward in a restored relationship with our Creator. We cannot do anything to merit grace, and yet we look at someone like Mother Teresa and think, surely, she entered into heaven because of what she did. If we emulate her sacrificial love in some small fashion, we are lulled into a false sense of security that persuades us that we have no need of repentance today. When the little saint humbly confessed her brokenness and her desperate need for God, either we were uncomprehending or we secretly suspected her of false modesty. Yet she got it, and by the love she received, she gave in great amounts to others.

Once we have His love unwrapped in our hearts, we can help others by listening, showing compassion, and taking care of any needs we can. Living abroad a year in Sweden, my three-month mission's trip in Japan and my travels to Mexico and other places, here and abroad, have given me a gift of perspective into someone else's culture and heart. My commitment to really listen to others, and not just do all the talking, has led me to many new "best friends." It has also exposed me to many other religions, cultural traditions, and ways of living that are outside of my box.

God is a friend to us all. Receive His love and friendship, and you'll find ways you never expected to tell others about Him. Jesus can become their best friends forever, too.

40
MY TESTIMONY: 'I'M STILL HERE'

"So, let's not get tired of doing what is good. At just the right time, we will reap a harvest of blessing if we don't give up."
— **Galatians 6:9 (NLT)**

I LIKE PINK. I DIDN'T KNOW I did until recently. And, I mean the musical artist and not the color. A friend of my family was selling her concert tickets in a nearby city along with her latest CD as part of a package. He gave me an extra CD, which was super cool; otherwise, I might have never known how much I like Pink.

I played the CD loud and long in my vehicle on a two-hundred-mile solo road trip. I can't say that I like everything, but yup, on pretty much every song, and especially, "I am here," I was able to make a connection. That song got my immediate attention and by the third time of hitting "repeat" I was yelling out the chorus with Pink:

"*I AM HERE, I AM HERE*
I've already seen the bottom, so there's nothing to fear
I know that I'll be ready when the devil is near
I am here, I am here
All of this wrong, but I'm still right here."[72]

---

[72] Pink, "I Am Here," October 18, 2017, https://www.youtube.com/watch?v=Dz6mL1eyK4Q, viewed August 25, 2021.

You are too. *You are here.* And for today and every day that is enough. Life is hard. "Why is the Earth experience so difficult?" you might ask. Because it's not our permanent home; while we are still here on Earth there's a lot that's wrong and challenging and painful. Yet, we're here. I am. You are. That's my testimony. It's your testimony as you read this. Remember you're not a failure, even though you might fail in certain areas. Never stop trying. Never give up hope. If you have no other testimony, you have this one: "I'm still here."

It's a big deal to be here, to be present. Now, don't get me wrong, I love to be alone, all introverts do (which might surprise some people because I speak and perform), but on stage I am focused on connecting to an audience as individuals. One-on-one connections energize me. At gatherings or parties, I prefer to seek out one person to connect with. So yeah, don't expect me at a Fourth of July downtown parade with the activities that follow and people just mingling around socializing. Not a fan.

I did the group activities when our four sons were young because I felt it was on the list of "good mom" responsibilities. Now that they're all grown, they go to the Fourth of July and other group holiday events while I *stay* home, sit alone in the quiet, which is good for my soul. The need for alone time is also the reason I often book an extra day at a hotel when I travel to speak. I will say aloud (while taking the longest shower possible), "I'm so thankful, so thankful," on that extra day retreat. I am alone without expectations or responsibilities after a wondrous conference/retreat of people, with their laughter, tears, and talk.

But there have been lonely times in a hotel room when I didn't want to be alone, and I was feeling insecure and afraid and thought, *What if people knew the real me, the all of me that doesn't have it all together and never will. I'm not always confident, at peace and fun just because I appear so on stage?* Yet, that is what I try most to share with others, the vulnerable me along with the silly me. I *know* there are others who need to hear that they're not alone. I'm "here" with them. I get it.

In the fall of 1989, I wanted to end my own life at age twenty-two. I doubt anyone really knew the dark hole I was in while student teaching at a high school in the Minneapolis area. My Auntie Ginger knew about anxiety and depression, and she was instrumental in helping me climb out of the darkness. It's why we need to remember to *be kind* to everyone we meet. We're all fighting a hard battle and, quite honestly, the strongest people are not those who show strength in front of us, but those who win battles we know nothing about.

But sometimes an individual loses their battle with loneliness, insecurity, and fear; they cannot stand another minute of being "here," the pain is that intense. They literally end up taking their lives into their own hands and end their existence here on Earth. Suicide is such a sad and tragic death. I remember driving away from my growing-up home back to Minneapolis, where I was living and student teaching at the time. It was the fall of 1989, and I was on Highway 10 and twenty-two years old. One hour into my trip, I decided the pain was too great and I must end my life by driving fast and furious into a tree or over a cliff. Instead, I stopped at a gas station in Wadena, Minnesota, and called Auntie Ginger from a pay phone outside, and for an hour she talked me down.

Isn't it heart-wrenching? I believe we *all* know someone, either personal or distant, who's taken their life. It's hard. It's so, so hard. One of the reasons I'm so passionate about sharing the *hope* of Christ is because I want every single, beautiful person created by God to hear His still small voice in the darkest of times when they feel like nothing will ever change, and forever they are doomed. "Hear Him speak," I'd say. "Listen. You are loved. You are strong even if you don't feel it. You are being held. This too will pass." It's the truth. Jesus is all the things we aren't because He's the great I *Am* and all that we need. And know this, He sends others to let you know who He is, too. Need a hug? I'm hugging you. I understand. I love you.

Sigh. (I literally took a deep breath after I wrote the above paragraph knowing that you needed that hug I just gave you.)

But when someone doesn't get that hug or hope in time, along with the belief that real love is available, then they're left with such darkness and despair that the only way out is to put an end to it all. In the wake of a suicide, we naturally try to answer the questions everyone wants answers to: Why did this happen? I didn't know it was that bad. What can we do to prevent this from happening to more people?

That's the question writer Charlotte Donlon shares in her piece written for Mockingbird Ministries titled "Suicide, Our Darker Emotions, and the Goodness of God." Charlotte writes:

> I don't think we have to stop asking these questions, but there's room for more. There's room to explore our own personal fears and anxieties that crop up in response to tragedies. When we name our emotions after high-profile suicides, this might be some of what we come up with:
>
> 'I am angry God let this happen.'
>
> 'Whenever there's a celebrity suicide, any suicide, I grieve a loved one who took his life.'
>
> 'I'm terrified of losing someone I love.'
>
> 'I'm uncomfortable with the fact that God doesn't always save us from ourselves on this side of eternity.'
>
> Navigating our own emotions instead of focusing our energy on trying to figure out why something happened will make us more vulnerable with each other, encourage helpful conversations, and will limit unnecessary speculation.[73]

Donlon's therapist, Dr. Gordon Bals adds: 'The times of mystery and anguish are helping us to name things we don't want to feel. Yet as we name them and feel them, they open us up to parts of the Lord we are not encountering when we hide from the fallenness of this world.

---

[73] Charlotte Donlon, "Suicide, Our Darker Emotions, and the Goodness of God," July 10, 2018, https://mbird.com/suffering/suicide-our-darker-emotions-and-the-goodness-of-god/, viewed August 25, 2021.

"The darker emotions propel us toward mystery and searching out God, and tend to war against certainty and the more comfortable emotions. Phillip Yancey says we go to God looking for answers when He wants to give us more of Himself. In the darker emotions lie deeper questions and opportunities to get to know the Lord more intimately."[74]

In the days following the deaths of fashion designer Kate Spade and celebrity chef Anthony Bourdain, I thought of them each sitting alone on a hotel room bed just like me. I wondered how it was that they had reached such desperation that they chose not to call out to someone to try and rescue and help them in a most dark and desperate moment.

Charlotte Donlon says too, "I watched as several media outlets, including a number of Christian ones, turned to the whys. When I asked Dr. Bals about this observation, he responded, 'It seems like faith (the willingness to walk in mystery, i.e. not having answers but trusting God's goodness) gets marginalized and instead leaders may too often want to provide certainty instead of inviting their followers into more meaningfully engaging God and the mystery of how He works.'"[75]

I've heard people say, "You've only one life to live so make the most of it." Surely, if this were true, many people would have given up and ended their earthly lives just as I've written about. The grief and pain experienced (even when comparatively it isn't anything like those in a third world country war zone) can cause someone to do something/anything to end the deep angst they're experiencing. When you live in a dark place, no matter who or where you are, with dark thoughts getting darker and pain getting greater, it's hard to think it will end unless you "end it."

In the book of Hebrews, Chapter 11, we can read a list of faithful sojourners who, despite their hardships, doubts, and mistakes, had

---

[74] Donlon.
[75] Donlon.

hope. Abraham and Sarah are on the list of the faithful who did not receive all the things they were promised. However, they "saw them" and welcomed them from afar. They acknowledged that they were strangers and exiles on the Earth" (Hebrews 11:13).

Oh, what a day that will be when Jesus returns, and the fullness of the Kingdom will be ushered in. There will be purpose, people, eating, laughing, and dancing. We are fully resurrected as Jesus was and is. There is no more pain or tears in this Heavenly Country. Look at the promise we have from Hebrews 11:14–16 (BSB):

> Now those who say such things (like Abraham and Sarah) show that they are seeking a country of their own. If they had been thinking of the country they had left, they would have had opportunity to return. Instead, they were longing for a better country, a heavenly one. Therefore, God is not ashamed to be called their God, for He has prepared a city for them.

I'm so thankful for that promise. Nicole Conner is an author and speaker from City Life Church in Australia, and I am thankful for her, too. In her book *Journey To Freedom,* I have almost every page underlined as it talks about walking in freedom and not in fear and bondage of the enemy. Nicole gave a "Soldier's Message" on the goodness of God in the midst of life's contradictions at the 2006 Northwest Baptist Convention in Washington. I have listened to the CD message often because it talks hope and gives perspective during our times of suffering, loss, and disappointment. The "fire" and focus, in the message, is to keep on keeping on, despite our trials and our confusion of why God heals some but not others or allows some tragedies but not others. So, can we truly say, "I will trust God and I serve Him." Do we honestly believe God is truly good when everything around us isn't?

Nicole shares that the Hebrew Word for *good* is *towb*, which means "better."[76] That's insightful. We can choose to trust in God's

---

[76] Old Testament Hebrew Lexicon, King James Version. https://www.biblestudytools.com/lexicons/hebrew/kjv/towb-2.html, viewed August 25, 2021.

goodness despite our wretchedness or the wretchedness of this world because there is something better ahead, and He promises redemption in all things. Nicole talked about speaking in third world countries and sharing the hope of a Heavenly City that God promises us. She said, "You know when I read the Scriptures from Hebrews 11 and talk about heaven to third world nations, faces light up. One time I was talking to this big hostel of blind women in India. Their families had forsaken them, and they were basically waiting to die. When you start talking about heaven to them something wonderful happens. They have that pilgrim theology which is an understanding that life can dish me "this" or "that" and it can be really difficult but there's hope, an eternity for those who love Him."[77]

That is why we can still be "here." We have the hope of something better, a place of perfection with purpose. We're not going to have all the answers in this life, but we can have assurance of life after death with Christ with absolute freedom and joy. You're a sinner. I'm a sinner but *oh, joy*—when we receive the gift of His payment for our sins by His death and resurrection we are saved from all worst of the worse and we begin to really *live* as He intended from the very beginning of creation. He wants us all to live here now with hope and to know Him as the Redeemer, not the Disciplinarian. Remember, the "whys" of this life never really bring relief, but knowing He has *a way* of redemption, to work *all* things for the good, does bring hope and relief. He is right be your side as one of my favorite Psalms reassures, "I know the Lord is always with me. I will not be shaken for He is right beside me" (Psalm 16:8 NLT). When we can't walk or stand, He will hold us and one day He will set all things right where are joy will be complete and never ending.

God is still speaking and He wants us to know Him all the time, especially in the dark, but in the light, too. There is joy and love to

---

[77] Nicole Conner, *A Soldier's Message* (CD), Northwest Baptist Convention: Northwest Baptist Convention Tech, 2006.

experience here on Earth; it mostly comes by shared experiences with others with eating, laughing, and singing (no matter what your voice sounds like).

Back to liking Pink. Her song continues with these lyrics and you can sing alone and aloud while making up your own melody:

"I don't have the answers, but the questions are clear. Where does everybody go when they go?"[78] *And* that's where I want to jump into the song and sing, "I have the answer for that question: They go on living" (either with God or without Him).

Pink shares that she has a hope or feels in her bones that she is enough.

And, again, I, Debbie, want to jump back into the song and loudly sing, "You're enough. You're always enough in Jesus. He is the Light of the World. He is love. And He is enough."

We will never have all the answers we want, but we have God who is good even when we or others are not. In fact, He is better than anyone or anything we can have in the hardest places of this life. But don't be fooled, there is also an enemy who is the evil in this world. He tries to get us to doubt that God is not good with the horrors of this life. So, we must hold onto the strength, by the power of the Holy Spirit God gives us to overcome. The lies of the enemy from the very beginning of time whispered to Eve were, "You can overcome, heal, and fix the world on your own strength. You can be God, too." All of our good intentions and efforts are hogwash. Only God is good.

You are here. I am here. We can make it, but let's stick together, be vulnerable and honest, love and embrace one another, rely completely on the grace of God and by that we have the hope of something better today, *here* and now and into eternity.

---

[78] Pink, "I Am Here."

41
CHOOSE WHAT YOU THINK ON

"Fix your thoughts on what is true, and honorable, and right, and pure, and lovely, and admirable. Think about things that are excellent and worthy of praise."
— **Philippians 4:8 (NLT)**

WHY DIDN'T RHONDA RETURN my phone call or even text? Is she mad at me? Would I look better if I got bangs at my next haircut? I feel frumpy, chunky, and old. My metabolism has changed, and getting on a healthy eating plan is hard. Is our son, Joey, safe being in the National Guard right now? Should he have made that long-term commitment to the army? What about our other son, Peter, who is deployed in the navy? What if something happens to him **and** I can't see and hug him again? Is David going to be okay in the Minneapolis area taking his "gap-year" after high school? What about Marco and his new wife Rachel; are they safe where they live outside the Twin Cities, and will his position as a pastor ever resume to what we know as "normal?"

I hate wearing a mask, but are people judging me, thinking me selfish if I don't? I think God made our immune systems to handle viruses of all kinds, so maybe I should post and share a link to prove my point?

I'm gonna respect the rules, I just don't like them. But then, I haven't made a statement about racial injustices in our country. Does that mean I'm not sensitive enough or "checking my white privilege?" Should I post and share a link on how much I care and love all people to prove my point? Lately, I feel wonky with headaches, a queasy stomach, and diarrhea. Am I sick? Maybe I need to increase my anxiety meds or maybe I'm depressed because some weeks all I want to do is sleep and avoid people. I hate wearing a mask. Maybe I shouldn't have alcohol in my life at all and practice abstinence? Sometimes, I think it has more control over me that I have on it. What about our finances? Are we going to be okay with Dan's business and my speaking less because of COVID-19? I love being able to serve at the Mexican restaurant again, but I hate wearing a mask. Why is finishing this book I'm writing so difficult? I feel like a loser. And on it goes with my mind whirling and spinning . . .

It's so great being back in the studio to record my Everyday Matters *feature, but as I began pursuing radio stations again, I feel discouraged in trying to connect with program directors. Last week I had a rejection email. I feel like a Loser. My dad and mom are like "old" now. Who knew there'd be so many adjustments that are challenging with her living in an apartment for the elderly and him stuck abroad in Thailand with his new wife? Between my mom's memory and health, along with my dad's and his crazy adventures, I feel like I'm their parent now. It's all good but it's all weird. My prayer list is long, too, with extended family and friends who have their own family issues, finance woes, and health concerns. Should I be doing more to help them and give less time "helping" others by commenting and sharing my opinions in Social Media Land? Did I hurt someone's feelings? Should I apologize even if they don't? Maybe I need to reach out and be in community with others more? But church is hard now and because it's all so different. I hate wearing a mask. Isn't eating Lay's Potato Chips in the morning like hash browns for breakfast? I wonder why Rhonda's mad at me and hasn't gotten back in touch with me. I hate wearing a mask.*

What you just read is a barrel of my thoughts that swirl rapidly in my mind's orbit for ten minutes or so and then the thoughts go back on rewind, and repeat. Man, our minds have so much power, yet we choose what we think on. When I choose to be led by my feelings, life is very hard for me. *Right now*, life is crazy for our entire world, no matter who we are or where we live. Do you need a "mind change" just like your vehicle needs an oil change now and again? I sure do.

Sigh.

I have to remember I am God's kid. I belong to Him and my identity comes from Him. Therefore, I can choose to think on the truth of what He says and have hope in the craziness.

None of us was born into a perfected world or made perfectly. We all enter into a fallen and sinful world, and we're all sinners. The good news, in a bad world, is that God loves us so much that He came down and paid for our debt of sins. He didn't come to condemn us but to save us. He gave His life on the cross and then His resurrection meant that we, too, might live forever. "Thank You, Jesus."

Of course, God didn't make a mistake in creating us, but because of sin there are genetic diseases, earthly problems, and evil doings all because of Satan, but yet so many of us blame God. In Ephesians 2, Paul described those outside of Christ who were unbelievers, following the prince of the power of the air, who is Satan. "They follow the way their master leads." In verse 1, Paul pointed out that all were once dead through their sins, but believers are now *alive* in Jesus Christ. He tells us we're not governed or led by our lower nature—the impulses of the flesh. Many Christians (I'm raising my hand) have trouble in this area because they haven't learned to control their thoughts by the power of the Holy Spirit. Feeding the flesh feels good, especially when we have immediate gratification and at that moment we simply don't care about any consequences. To be sure, all of our feelings are valid but they might not all be true. Our pain from an experience long gone, can resurrect after seeing someone's post/video on Instagram. There are many hurts which we haven't dealt with. Because of that we haven't taken the steps and acted on the responsibility to heal. It gets messy when we project our past hurts on the person who has posted something that triggers a past pain. Oh, my goodness, we need to be mindful to heal in the places of our past hurts. We need to become self-aware of what triggers our hurts *because* when we're self-aware, we can begin to heal. We can begin to hear what's being said without the filter of our wounds. What's hard, too, is that childhood messages don't go away just because you grow up and become an adult.

I talk to people all the time who believe in God and call themselves a follower of Christ even though they haven't taken their thoughts captive. *Part of my responsibility as a child of God is to keep my thoughts healthy and strong.* You might know a lot of Scripture, and volunteer in church and also help with other needful organizations working on social justice issues, showing mercy and loving others—and *that* is wonderful. Yet, with all the good works, your thought life and mind can be a mess. Good works can't bring lasting peace of mind.

When I read the Bible, listen to a sermon, or even sing a song, I need to be mindful in asking myself, *Am I allowing the Holy Spirit to change me and my thought life, or am I thinking about whether I should have bangs cut at my next haircut or why Rhonda hasn't contacted me back? Perhaps I am faithful in good causes but lacking in the Word of God?* The devil can sneak in so quietly and unassuming. He doesn't care how long it takes for a sin to wreak you as long as "it takes." The renowned English Baptist preacher, Charles Spurgeon, who died in 1892, was quite wise. I think the following quote is an example of his insightfulness. "When Satan cannot get a great sin in, he will let a little one in, like the thief who goes and finds shutters all coated with iron and bolted inside. At last, he sees a little window in a chamber. He cannot get in, so he puts a little boy in, that he may go round and open the back door. So, the devil has always his little sins to carry about with him to go and open back doors for him, and we let one in and say, 'O, it is only a little one.' Yes, but how that little one becomes the ruin of the entire man!"[79]

We might be doing the right things outwardly, but not really thinking on the right things. God is clear from Philippians 4:8: "Think on whatever is true, whatever is noble, whatever is right, whatever is pure, whatever is lovely, whatever is admirable—if anything is excellent or praiseworthy—think about such things." But how often do we do the opposite and think on what is negative, awful, challenging, difficult, and worthy of complaint? For me, I need to spend less time on social media and listening to worldly news, thoughts, and opinions and instead think on "the Good News" while applying the promises of God to my everyday life.

If your mind is messy, it might be time to make some lifestyle changes because, know this, the devil would love to camp out in your mind every second of every day to bring you into despair and doubt God's goodness. I often read the Psalms aloud and it really helps. Ephesians 6 includes the "Six Piece Armor Set." I clearly remember a day doing laundry in the basement while Joey was playing a video game. I sat on the steps before coming up and said to Joey, "I feel anxious again today."

"I can tell, Mom," he said.

Instead of talking about the latest worldly concern or the podcasts he was listening to, I said, "Let's pray." I prayed the armor of God over us and then went back upstairs. It made such a difference. I try and pray that way *every day*. It's a battle out there, and it's a spiritual one.

God tells us to *put on* the armor of God because it isn't gonna

---

[79] Charles Spurgeon, *Spurgeon's Sermons*, Vol. 6: 1860 (Ingersoll, Ontario, Canada: Devoted Publishing, 2017), 260.

just jump on us by itself and we need to be putting in on every day. When it's cold outside, you put on a coat and you do that every single day it's cold because it's not a just a one-time thing to protect yourself from the cold weather. Below is the way I easily remember to "suit up" and on YouTube I have a video with the props explaining what this looks like in case you're interested to have a visual:

1. Helmet of Salvation (comb in hair or product)
2. Breastplate of Righteousness (bra or t-shirt)
3. Belt of Truth (underwear)
4. Feet of Peace (socks or shoes)
5. Shield of Faith; extinguishing the enemy's darts he throws your way (mirror you look in each day)
6. Sword of the Spirit—God's Living Word (toothbrush)

I came up with these simple everyday items so I could "put on the armor" easily. I teach/speak on "the Armor of God" at conferences, and yet I've gone days without being spiritually aware, prepared, or thinking twice about getting dressed adequately for the daily battle.

Feelings are powerful *but* they don't have to be overpowering. Put on the armor of God and contemplate right away how the Helmet of Salvation is there to protect your thoughts because salvation by the blood of the Lamb is yours to claim. Think on the hope of who *He is* and why He came. Think about what it means to be a believer in Christ Jesus.

I love how author and speaker Chad L. Bird explains, "How do you know that you're a Christian?"

> Not because your heart is good and pure, but because the heart of Christ pulses for a love for you that will never end. Not because your deeds are righteous, but because He has been righteous on your behalf and clothes you with that righteousness. Not because you have lived for Him, but because He has lived and died and

risen for you. Not because you asked Him to be your Savior, but because while you were yet a sinner, Christ died for you, chose you, called you, and baptized you as His own beloved child. [80]

When I let God's Word seep into my heart and think about how He loves me for who I am and not for what I do or don't do, I'm relieved and thankful. So relieved. Satan is the "father of lies" and he is a "prince of darkness" that "masquerades as an angel of light." So, his strategy is to take dark and evil things and *package them* as light and good things and to take evil things and *package them* as good and virtuous things. When researching the plots and lies of the Enemy of our Souls, I came across a devotional titled *A Father's Heart Ministry*. Author Russ Walden writes:

> The Father says today turn a deaf ear to the accuser. Your affirmation comes from Me and not from what others think or what they do. My favor is upon you, says the Father. My favor is a shield that protects and safeguards you in every area of your life. Your blessing and promotion are not based on your intelligence or doing everything right. I am the God who makes you prosper even in the midst of mistakes and errors and miscalculations. If others look down on you or don't take you seriously, they are not discounting you, they are discounting themselves from the things I have purposed to do in your life.
>
> Take the accusations against you and make them a point of ascension in your life. Refuse to be distracted by your critics. Instead of responding to what they are saying, respond to what I am saying. See yourself as I see you. Believe what I say about you and not what others or what circumstances says about you. You will either believe and respond to what I say of you or what others say but you can't do both. You cannot honor God and fear man. Turn to me and I will turn to you with an avalanche of blessing. Be bold

---

[80] Kevin DeYoung, and C. L. Bird, "So How Do I Really Know I'm a Christian?," thegospelcoalition.org, June 4, 2015,
https://www.thegospelcoalition.org/blogs/kevin-deyoung/so-how-do-i-really-know-im-a-christian/, viewed August 28, 2021.

enough and determined enough to take a risk and move forward believing that I am with you and will not leave you or forsake you. I will bring you to promotion and My plan for you will come to fruition and fulfillment even as you have asked.[81]

Understanding the voice of God over the lies of the enemy is crucial. Be wise and choose what you think on for as Proverbs 23:7 speaks: "For as a man thinks in his heart, so is he . . . ," followed by Ephesians 4:23: "Be constantly renewed in the spirit of your mind, having a fresh mental and spiritual attitude." The more you meditate on the right things, the less trouble you're gonna have with Satan trying to control your thoughts. That's how it works: The more we focus on God, the less often the devil can defeat us. We can walk in peace knowing that while everything isn't good, God always is. He is not surprised by what's happening, and He's always on the move with a plan of redemption. Nothing is wasted with Him. And of course, He understands if you hate wearing a mask or that you hate that others aren't more sensitive in wearing one, Lord have mercy.

By the way, Rhonda called me back and we had a wonderful conversation. She wasn't mad at me. (Isn't it crazy how our minds imagine the worst scenario first, especially with someone we care about?). Life is hard, people are hard, and our minds can be such a mess. Choose what you think on and resist the enemy's lies, and you'll be surprised to see the changes of peace and joy that enter into your life.

Note: I decided bangs wouldn't be a good look for me.

---

[81] Russ Walden, "The Father Says Today:: August 21st, 2020," Father's Heart Ministry, https://fathersheartministry.net/the-father-says-today-august-21st-2020/, viewed August 27, 2021.

42
GETTING TO THE OTHER SIDE

"The Lord himself goes before you and will be with you; He will never leave you nor forsake you. Do not be afraid; do not be discouraged."
— **Deuteronomy 31:8 (NIV)**

"I HONESTLY DON'T THINK I CAN MAKE it through another day. I just don't."

Ever feel like that? There's a storm in your life and it's of hurricane proportions; so you feel you just might not make it. The Bible tells the account of Jesus commanding the disciples to get into a boat to go to the other side of the lake, but " . . . suddenly, behold, there arose a violent storm, (of hurricane proportions), on the sea, so that the boat was being covered up by the waves . . . " and Jesus was sleeping. (Matthew 8:24).

Maybe the storms in your life are failing finances, or a failing marriage, and then, to top it all off, you have health issues. But wait, there's more! There are the everyday concerns of Covid-19 and the next election with all its drama. You *feel* overwhelmed like you might even drown. Or perhaps you have a burning pain in your heart because your child is addicted to drugs and then there's your aging parent who can't remember who you are anymore. You're going through so much and, "Where's Jesus in it all?" you ask.

What's interesting is that Jesus knew about the storm before they got on the boat. He's God; He knows everything and is never surprised by our circumstances. Remember, Jesus gave orders to cross to the other side of the lake (Matthew 8:18). He knew there would be a storm with intense waves and winds. He also knew that the storm wouldn't keep them from their destination. He knew that "in the middle" there would be difficulties, but when He declared, "We're going to the other side," all the forces of darkness could not stop Him from getting to the other side. In the same way, when God makes a promise of redemption and restoration for "*All* things to work for the good," He's not moved by the winds. He's not worried by the storms in your life because *He knows* there will be storms on your journey through this life. He controls the universe *and* He cares about every single detail of your life. "God will perfect everything that concerns you" (Psalm 138:8 NASB). You will get to the other side.

Like me, maybe you're flailing from *so* many changes surrounding you that you're simply and desperately trying to remain stable. You might *feel* consumed by these fiery trials. Your feelings are valid, *but* the truth is you'll come through. He sees. He knows. He cares. The Lord speaks a promise from Isaiah 43:2: "When you go through deep waters, I will be with you. When you go through rivers of difficulty, you will not drown. When you walk through the fire of oppression, you will not be burned up; the flames will not consume you." And perhaps what you're going through is not about breaking you but about the breakthrough you've been waiting for. God often uses bad things for a later good. I thank Him for that truth all the time.

I've also found that's it's true that a good walk with a good friend helps when you've been in your pajamas three days with no shower. When I called to cancel my walk with my friend, Alyssa, I said I wasn't feeling well. She sent a text back which read, "Are you actually 'for real' sick or are you just stuck?" I waited a bit and then replied, "I'm stuck." Mental anguish is rough, and it affects you physically, too. The best medicine can simply mean going outside, walking, and talking to someone who you can be "for real" with.

Where are you looking to satisfy your deepest desires and longings? John 4 tells of the woman at the well with whom Jesus spoke. She had been with five different men and was currently living with a man who was not her husband. Jesus didn't give her a lecture on morality. He spoke to her about her thirst. Someone shared the following quote with me referring to John 7, and I wish I could find or remember who they are: "Christ enters the 'Tuckered Towns' of the world, stands at the intersection of 'Worn-Out Avenue,' and 'Done-In Street' and compels, 'If you are thirsty, come to Me! If you believe in Me, come and drink!' For the Scriptures declare that rivers of living waters will flow out from within."

Only Jesus can satisfy that ache in your heart. If you're eating the junk food of the self-centered life, you'll never be satisfied. God is in the filling business, and He wants to satisfy your deepest desires. Jesus can fill your emptiness. Another dose of good medicine I would recommend is inviting a couple or small family into your home for a meal or dessert. I am trying to do this every Sunday evening, and I'm calling it "church." Barbra Streisand sang, "People Need People," and it's *so* true. We need each other to encourage one another, share our stories or hurts and our hopes, and we need to listen. You can have church anywhere. When church stops being about us, it can be about God again. Church is meant to crush our selfishness, and church without God does none of that. Often our evangelism becomes winning people to our doctrine or our denomination instead of reaching the people next door who have no direct access to freedom in Jesus. Our job is not to judge but to let others know it's not about rules but about a personal relationship with Jesus. His grace and mercy, not rules and regulations.

I love the *Chronicles of Narnia* by C. S. Lewis. In the second book of the series, *Prince Caspian*, there's a wonderful illustration of how Aslan, the main character in the series, portrays the character of Jesus. There's a scene where Aslan meets and comforts Susan; he's all powerful but also gentle and compassionate. Aslan appears mysteriously to the four children to show them the way they should go in order to help Prince Caspian, but because of her doubt, Susan is the last of the group to see Him. When she must greet Aslan, she's crying. I expect that Aslan will reprimand Susan for her lack of faith, but instead He says, "You have listened to your fears, child. Come, let Me breathe on you. Forget them. Are you brave again?" Susan responds, "A little." He doesn't scold but instead breathes His peace into her heart and soul. This is so like God because as we read in 2 Corinthians 2: 3, the Father of mercies and God of all comfort longs to do the same for us.

People need God desperately and not in a Pollyanna or Christianesy way, "it's all for a reason," sort of way (that's not in the Bible). Jesus came to save the lost by letting them know they are loved right where they are at and not where they should be. You and I need to be the church, not merely go to church (which is oddly difficult right now anyway). We need to love unconditionally no matter if the person believes like us, looks like us, or shares the same opinions.

Unless we acknowledge that we are the sinners, the sick ones, and the lost sheep for whom Jesus came, we do not belong to the "blessed" who know that they are poor and inherit the Kingdom. Do you ever try and appear righteous before God and others with your performances? I have and it's exhausting. It's a dangerous zone to get your assurance from wealth or status. Realize *this*, that "they" are you and me, wretched, pitiably poor, and so often blind. Isaiah 64 lays things out clearly when we begin to think, *I'm doing really well here*. "We're all unclean and all our righteous acts are like filthy garbage." It's what Jesus did on the cross that cleans us up and sets us free.

I need Jesus but I need, or more accurately, want others to

change, too. Yet, only God can change a heart, and when there's a heart change there's behavior change. Oh, but there's that place when you know the only change that will happen is if you ask God to change you. So, I've cried in the middle of a dark living room and asked God to forgive me, to change and mold and make me to be more like Him. I chose not to ask Him to change the other person, but instead I knew the only real solution was that my heart be changed. And still, I'd cry, "It's not fair," but God gets it. I often don't understand why a particular heartache is happening, but it isn't always for me to understand. Know the answer to the question "Can God be trusted?" And He can because of His grace and comfort to meet us right where we're at. Humble yourself by swallowing your own pain and pride and look at Peter 5: "Humble yourselves under God and He will lift you up in due time and then cast all your care upon Him, for He cares for you."

There are some religious organizations who spend a lot of time telling people what they need to do and not enough time telling them who they are in Christ. Trust who God says you are because you've accepted what He's done for you.

Briefly and succinctly, Jesus emphasized the *rock* foundation of the Christian Life. And in so doing, He wants us to respect one another and take care of one another; He wants us to fuss over, be concerned with, comfort, and forgive one another until the day we die. He recognizes that we all go through storms, but we will get to the other side and He promises to *redeem* all and everything we go through. Encourage that friend who needs to know this truth. Encourage yourself, too. If you aren't quite able right now, text a sincere friend and let them know, "Hey, I'm stuck." God will provide who and what you need. And always be mindful that these three things last: "faith, hope, and love; and the greatest of these is love" (1 Corinthians 13:13 NIV).

I'll see you on the other side.

Therapeutic Gentleness

43
UNTIL WE MEET AGAIN

"And if I go and prepare a place for you, I will come again and will take you to myself, that where I am you may be also."
— **John 14:3 (ESV)**

> We waited with anticipation and hope for Azariah to enter the world. Now in the operating room, we were unable to see anything but a huge blue curtain surrounding us. But then, we began to hear the most precious sound . . . his first little cry! While the doctors checked him over, he expelled a few more cries. Tears were streaming down our faces as we still lifted up prayers of healing for our baby. Then the doctors called Nathan over to see Azariah. I held my breath and tried to turn my head to see what was going on. And then . . . Nathan began to sob and I knew . . . I knew God had chosen, in His sovereign plan, not to grant the miracle we had so desperately desired.
>
> — Facebook post from October 24, 2016

MY HEART WAS RACING as I read Rissa's post. Like so many others, I had been following her pregnancy journey, knowing that a miracle was needed for the multiple abnormalities the doctors had forecast for their baby. Rissa, Nathan, and their two little girls held on to hope to the Creator of us all and to the prayers of others—such as myself—waiting in hopeful expectation for the healthy arrival of Azariah John, who would be delivered October 20, 2010, at thirty-four weeks.

The post continued:

> My heart felt broken into a million pieces with a heaviness I had never known. My baby, oh, my sweet baby boy. And then just when I felt like the pain was overtaking my body, I cried out the name of Jesus and peace began to flood my heart and consume my soul. I felt God's presence in such a mighty way. The love of Jesus was holding all the broken pieces of our hearts right in His capable hands. Azariah was brought over to me and was laid right on my chest. His heart rate was about forty beats per minute. The doctors were still working to put me back together and then stitch me up so I couldn't move like I wanted. As soon as I laid eyes on sweet Azariah, I immediately fell in love. I wanted to tell him so many things . . . but I found myself just taking in all his little features. Tenderly I lifted his hand into mine and kissed all his fingers, the lack of oxygen causing them to be cold to the touch. Our baby weighed a healthy seven pounds, four ounces, but with all the other complications he was slipping away. Nathan and I began to weep out loud. We told Azariah how much we loved him as we watched him take a small breath in. Time was going too fast.
>
> The doctors had finished sewing me up and needed to move me onto another bed. The neonatologist took a quick listen to Azariah's heart rate. It was now down to twenty beats per minute. Before they moved me over, I touched his face one last time, stroking his cheek while telling him that he was fearfully and wonderfully made, and Mommy loves you, Azariah, so much. Nathan then scooped him up from my chest into a soft blanket and Azariah was now safely snuggled in his earthly Dad's arms. I was transferred over to the bed next to me as the doctor listened once again to Azariah's heart rate and I laid there, I heard seven words no parent ever wants to hear a doctor say . . . "I can no longer find a

heartbeat." Thirty-one precious minutes together, that was how long our sweet baby boy was alive on this Earth. Nathan was holding Azariah in his arms as he took his last breath and passed from this world, straight into His heavenly Father, Jesus.

More than a month earlier, Rissa and Nathan had been presented options to spare their baby's life from the first appointment and then again when the results of their amniocentesis came in and confirmed their baby's terminal diagnosis.

Rissa posted on September 8:

A whole team of doctors met with us. They asked if we wanted to continue on with the pregnancy given the diagnosis. Yes, Nathan answered for us immediately. Yes, he is our son. We both broke open and sobbed. We would fight for his life no matter how long he would be with us.

They had a peace knowing God *is* greater. They knew God was aware and had a plan and would never leave them. God's peace kept them moving forward in hope, and inspired hundreds of others who followed their story to pray and hope along with them.

As Nathan and I let go, we wept for our son, for what might have been. Our hearts hurt so bad we could barely breathe... Oh, how we wanted him to live. Oh, Azariah. *but*... to know that at that very moment, Azariah was being held in the arms of Jesus, whole and complete, looking up into His eyes, feeling nothing but love ... it brought our hearts such *joy*. Through the intense pain and suffering, the Lord provided Himself as a refuge for us to run to and a rock upon which we could stand. Even though in that moment God chose to take from us, we will continue to bless His name, we will worship Jesus because He is enough. Leaving the hospital yesterday with empty arms was one of the most excruciating moments in our lives. Nathan was so sweet to help me in the car so gently. Once he got in, he reached for me, and we held each other and cried so hard our bodies ached. I know the Lord was grieving alongside of us and was holding each of our tears in His hands.

The outpouring of love, sympathy, and "thank you for sharing your life with us" soon streamed all over Rissa's Facebook page after she shared her journal post (along with several photos) only four days after the birth/death of Azariah John. They took their experience of loss to bless others because they're the kind of people who've realized, "Life isn't all about us." They understood that sharing their journey would help others face seasons of heartache and loss, and that the love that God was giving them would be given to others through their story.

"Mary" posted, "If you want to live a deeper, more intentional life and heal some of your own hurts and maybe even connect a little, read the story and watch this amazing video about Rissa, her husband, and their amazing children. We are humbled by this incredible family and how they've honored and praised Jesus through it all."

Rissa's post concluded:

Today Nathan and I planned the funeral for our sweet baby boy, something we never planned to do. We met with an amazing team of people who helped us through an extremely difficult process. It's our prayer that Azariah's memorial service brings glory to the Lord as we celebrate his short but powerful life. Nathan and I would personally like to invite each of you to attend Azariah's memorial service this Saturday, October 29, 2010. By your love and outreach, you have touched our lives by choosing to walk with us through this difficult journey and so we'd be honored by your presence. Azariah has a story to share and that story is just beginning . . .

No one quite knows the ache of this mother's loss or that of the family, but perhaps no one quite understands the peace they are experiencing despite the loss. Rissa wrote me, "It is a blessing to have you share Azariah's story. It fills my mama heart to overflowing and also, to be chosen by the Lord to carry Azariah and walk through this difficult season as a way to minister to others, while heartbreaking, is so humbling and an absolute honor."

I know, right? Grab that tissue.

Many of us have experienced the desperate isolation and cold darkness that Job describes in his memoir. These seasons of life without the light of understanding or any sense of God's presence test our faith in an invisible shepherd. In his book, *While Shepherd's Watch Their Flocks*, Dr. Timothy Laniak writes, "My wife and I journeyed through such deadly shadows for several years when our children were young. Faced with disabilities and the resulting shift in our life's direction, we entered *tsalmavet* (deadly darkness). The light we longed for did not dawn as we expected. Only slowly did we reemerge from this valley as sobered believers and humbled leaders. When a friend recently explained the devastating impact a family tragedy was wreaking on their spiritual life, I couldn't respond like Job's friends. I simply said, 'Welcome to the darkness. There are more questions than answers in this place. But you'll find good company among those who understand how little we understand, but who still hold on to God's hand.'"[81]

Rissa is holding on to God's hand and God is holding on to Azariah.

But ... I want to understand, at least on some level, yet God tells us in Isaiah 55:8, "My thoughts are not your thoughts, nor are your ways My ways."

I know, right? You can scream, *Why!*

I'll say it again, "This Earth experience is hard." But wait, it's not our home. There is hope ahead, there is a light, and whatever challenge you're facing, it won't last forever. You're not alone. Our challenge in dry and dark times is to respond in simple faith, to believe that the unseen Divine Shepherd is with us in our unlit valley. We wait in hope until eventually light begins to push the night away. As Job said, "He reveals mysteries from the darkness, and brings *tsalmavet* into the light."

Sometimes we're given a mountain of great magnitude, only to

---

[81] Timothy Laniak, *While Shepherds Watch Their Flocks: Forty Daily Reflections on Biblical Leadership* (London, UK: Higherlife Development, 2009).

show that it can be climbed because others are watching, to see if God is real in those dark and scary places. Others need to know that they, too, can face the challenge of the steep incline and jagged rock circumstances. Rissa and her family showed that here was a greater purpose to their loss; it was their testimony of how they handled the loss, the way they still hoped and could even plan a funeral days later.

They didn't grab the nearest numbing agent and escape the pain with a substance or other distractions. They felt and are feeling the pain and they're allowing us to share it with them. But know this, there will be a day when they'll see their baby again and this allows us to hope, to believe that all the sorrows and troubles we go through will not be wasted, however dark it is, there is always hope, always some light. Oh, yes, we will see the babe again and "that" day, oh, what a day it will be. "Not only so, but we ourselves, who have the first fruits of the Spirit, groan inwardly as we wait eagerly for our adoption to sonship, the redemption of our bodies" (Romans 8:23, NIV).

Of course, Rissa, Nathan, their girls, family, community, and all wanted their baby to live. We hoped, against all hope (we pleaded and prayed), right along with them that a miracle would take place, but when it didn't, we did not think any less of God, but more of how He was able to sustain and bring a whole community of people together to love, cry, rejoice, and mourn.

Let's weep with those you weep and cry with those who cry, and at the end of the day let's all be able to say, "Blessed be the name of the Lord." Life is not a guarantee of what we want. It is a journey. What God gives us is the certainty that at the end of this life, our own lives and our relationships do not end. Oh, what a day that will be, what a brilliant *light* of joy and glory awaits.

44
I'M KEEPIN' IT REAL, JAMMERE

"Do to others as you would have them do to you."
— **Luke 6:31 (NIV)**

"Hey, Debbie, this is Jammere. Can you bring me a pizza?"

"Are you messin' with me again, Jammere, or are you being real?"

"I'm not messin' with you, Debbie. I'm being real. I need pizza."

"Is your dorm room clean; are beds made?"

"Yes, indeed, Ma'am."

"All right, I'll be at the dorms in thirty minutes with pizza."

I met Jammere, Daveon, Ray, Brian, and Juvontae while at Kmart buying a laundry basket. (When you continually throw an empty one down the stairs, it eventually becomes plastic art that no longer holds laundry.) While purchasing my basket at the service desk, I noticed Jammere being served while his "homies" waited for him off to the side. Living in a town of just barely seven thousand folk, populated mostly by Scandinavian Hoo-ha, it's fun to discover why others might come to live in International Falls, Minnesota, "the Icebox of the Nation."

"Are you guys part of the basketball team at the community college?" I asked.

"Yes, Ma'am," they replied.

I learned their names, asked where each one was from, and took a photo. I assured them I would be at their first game of the season the next day. When I got home that evening, I wanted to post the photo and their names, but when I went to the Voyageur men's basketball roster the names they gave me didn't match with what I saw in the team photo. It took several texts before they knew they couldn't "play me."

The decision to bring pizza to the dorm for Jammere and the gang was because I knew it was yet another opportunity God had given me to have fun and bring His *joy*. There have been Christmas times I have felt alone, with or without family, but there always seemed to be someone God brought along who had food, hope, and a full cup of laughter, which made all the difference.

"Oh, boy, is there joy!" I've been saying that phrase aloud for fun when I get frustrated. It helps remind me that no matter the challenging situation, season or person, there is always a place for joy. This Earth experience is tough. It's not our home. It's why God came down to Earth, off His throne as a wee babe, named Jesus. He came so we could have life. He came so we'd have hope and purpose. He came because He loves us so much and wants us home with Him in every season . . . forever in heaven. "I'll be home for Christmas," is for real because of Jesus.

Because of Jesus, I have a relationship with God and I hear Him speak. Not because I have to, but because I get to. It is why I read the Bible. It's how we hear God, which is that stirring in our hearts, that peace within, the hope inside that tells us things will get better, and His Word prompts us to share this hope with others. There is a God who "gets us," and He will never leave us.

Scripture verses don't magically help me; God does. It's how relationships develop because we take the time to get to know someone, not just by sharing, but by listening. Reading the Bible and memorizing

Scripture also help me to hear God's voice. Sometimes it's hard to discern the voice of the Holy Spirit rather than what my feelings are saying. Often my feelings are so strong, I think I should be led by them. A good question to ask is, "Am I reading the Bible to get to know God better or because I think it's my own personal self-help book?" Author and teacher Chad Bird explains it well. "Jesus is not a life coach, a personal trainer, or a cheerleader on the sidelines of life. He is the Lord of the storms of life. He rules the winds and the waves. He comes to us in the midst of our fear and hopelessness to say, "Take courage, it is I; do not be afraid."[82]

We are led by God's love for us and by His love for others. Years ago, I had a problem with credit card debt, and I needed freedom in this area, to get right with God and my husband in taking responsibility for my spending. I would use credit cards from individual companies (mostly clothing catalogues) because, c'mon, they give such great incentives and perks. J. Crew clothing store (which I call, "J. Covet") was a card I liked to use often. Yet eventually I paid off that debt, so with my next billing statement I discovered I had a positive credit. At first, I thought to spend it, but the better choice was to call J. Crew and ask them to give me a refund check. So, I called the company. I was put on hold for a while and explained my situation to the catalogue salesperson who then transferred me to their credit card department. A man named Grant came on the line and was ready to assist me. Of course, he asked me if I just didn't want to leave my credit balance on the card. I did not. We finished the conversation and I hung up the phone but then immediately I had a very strong prompting that God wanted to me pray for Grant. I did. Then God said, "Call Grant back." That's weird, I thought (it's so weird). What are the chances I'd even get this Grant guy back on the phone? I wrestled with the logic

---

[82] Chad L. Bird, "God Is Not a Personal Trainer," July 25, 2021," Instagram post, https://www.instagram.com/chadlbird/, viewed August 28, 2021.

of this request but finally I obeyed and called J. Crew back.

This time the wait was even longer as I was transferred from the catalogue company to the financial department dealing with credit cards. I prayed for Grant while I waited on hold but because it was taking so long, I thought I should probably hang up. I had obeyed, I prayed. Besides, I didn't even know what I was supposed to tell Grant *or* how I was supposed to connect with him personally. Finally, a lady came back on the line who said, "Go ahead, Ma'am, Grant will help you." My heart was beating like crazy. This was incredible. God brought Grant back to me and while I was a bit panicked, I also had a peace come upon me, and I knew what I was supposed to say.

"Ah, yeah, hey Grant, this is Debbie with the refund check thing which I just spoke to you about a little bit ago. I know this seems strange, but when I got off the phone with you, God wanted me to pray for you, and I did. But then He told me to call you back and tell you something. This is it, Grant: "I don't know if you know Christ, but He knows you and He wanted me to let you know *right now* how very much He loves you."

Grant was quiet for a bit (and I'm sure stunned, too) and then he said, "You just confirmed something for me. Thank you." I really can't remember anything after that but when I go off the phone this second time, I was quiet, too, for the wonder of it all and then I prayed again, repeating one phrase over and over: "Bring Grant back home, Jesus. Bring him back home to You." I had this sense in my spirit that Grant had walked away from God, but God hadn't walked away from him. I am certain someone was praying for Grant to come back to Jesus, to "come home" and I had the opportunity, blessing, and joy to let Grant know how much God loves him. Wow.

So, it was God's voice again that led me to the dorm on a Monday evening with our son, Peter, who was eighteen years old at the time. Jammere and the other players were waiting for me on a snowy December evening at the dorm entrance. We delivered pizzas and chocolate milk. We prayed before we ate (and Jammere was firm with the guys about everyone removing their hats as a show of respect), and then we talked and listened to each other, with much laughter. It was fun. There was a stirring of hope and a promise of "next time."

I want joy and I want to bring joy . . . and hope. Hope is the good news of God's transforming grace *now* and not just the hope of heaven. He promises us in 2 Corinthians 5:17 that in *Him* we are new, the old life is gone and a new one is here. Everyone needs to hear this message of Good News and I believe what is needed is a good round of laughter from God to prevent us from taking the world too seriously.

God's laughter, His loving act of salvation, began in Bethlehem. If I want to know what a person really believes, I don't just listen to what they say, but I see how they live. I look for the fun. I think we all hope there is something beyond the stress and evil in this world. I know there is. The best way for someone to know the hope and love of Christ is to live in a way that shows who He is. Shouldn't our faith shape the way we live, talk, and love in our everyday lives with everyday people and everything in it? Do we have a divine sense of humor that sees through people and events into the unfolding plan of God?

People in general do not have a problem with Jesus. It is the religious systems that we build around Him that people often find so annoying. We can get out of balance so quickly. Everyone in . . . love and grace. Everybody out . . . you're a wretch, a sinner. But's it both. God is love. God is holy. Because God is holy, He must punish sin. But because He is love, He didn't want to punish us. On the cross He accomplished both, the holiness and the lovingness of God. He satisfied the holiness by serving the sentence for sin by dying on the cross when He was sinless. Jesus proved His love for us in the same act. We are all in the sinners' club, and we all need to be in the Savior's club.

Jesus is God. He is this gift of hope, the Christmas miracle, an undeserved gift of peace, but a gift that we make a decision to receive or reject, which really is the decision to trust.

Are you for real, God? Will you really make all things new? Hope says I no longer need to be worried about my failings because I am not a failure because of them or because of my feeble lack of faith. The questions should no longer be: Can I do it? Am I able? Can I overcome my bad attitude, laziness, grudges, and resentments? The only question is: Is Jesus Christ able? Can my Savior, the Lord of my life, revive my wearisome spirit and transform me at Christmas as He transformed the world through His birth in Bethlehem?

The answer is *yes!* He is the great Transformer who not only rescues us but redeems us, too. It's such a great gift, I hope you know.

So maybe you need to begin each season (at Christmas especially) to look for the Jammere characters and others you can bless to find and give the hope in everyday life, for there is joy, fun, and laughter. Bring it to others the gift you've accepted, that Jesus is for real, and He's not messin' with you.

45
EMBRACE YOUR INNER LOSER

> *"But thanks be to God! He gives us the victory through our Lord Jesus Christ."*
> — **1 Corinthians 15:57 (NIV)**

"**W**ELL, LET ME HUG YOU. I'm a hugger."

Jill waited in line to talk after my last speaking session at a retreat, and, as with anyone I first meet, we hugged. She was shaking so much I didn't know if she'd be able to speak.

"I just wanted you to know that your openness about anxiety attacks and depression helped me. I could relate to everything you talked about and especially the part on how God knows and loves us even when we're frozen with fear. I was so nervous to talk to you, but I just had to thank you," Jill said.

"Of course," I said. "I'm so glad to meet you."

When I got home, I found Jill on Facebook and requested her friendship. She made a big deal that I wanted to be her friend. Silly, I know, but that was many years ago, and since that time Jill and I have developed a very kindred friendship. She has traveled way out of her way to hear me speak at various events in Minnesota, and if I could say I had a "groupie," Jill would be it. The thing is I'm her "groupie," too. We are in the same group—both broken but made beautiful through Christ. We aren't "enough," but that's okay because He is. Every person can experience being loved in their brokenness because through Christ we are made whole.

True peace comes through understanding that we're all lovely losers without Jesus. To be clear, the biblical truth is "Love Never Fails" (1 Corinthians 13:8) rather than "Love wins." Actually, sin wins all the time unless there is repentance with Christ's forgiveness. Musician and author Jason Gray has a song called "Blessed Be" that explains what I'm trying to communicate:

> *"Losers, all the lovely losers*
> *who never thought you'd hear your name*
> *Outside, always on the outside*
> *empty at the wishing well, but time will tell*
> *Blessed Be the ones who know that they are weak*
> *they shall see the kingdom come to the broken ones."*[83]

My son, Marco, came up with the concept to "embrace your inner loser." I liked the phrase almost immediately because I understood the premise, that we are all *lost* without Christ, each facing our own insecurities. The solution to our problems can't be found within ourselves; we are the problem. Jesus is the solution. It is okay to admit our weaknesses. We need to recognize it's a losing battle trying to perform and be "good enough," hoping that we've earned our way into God's good graces. We cannot earn someone (Jesus) dying for what we did—our sins. So, let go of trying to perform being "enough." It's exhausting and you can never hold up long enough anyway.

My husband, Dan, is still not super keen on this directive to

---

[83] Jason Gray, "Blessed Be," posted by TheMistyFrog, April 26, 2010, https://www.youtube.com/watch?v=qT5dh3JqasA&list=PLWGpwN1QcNZfqWJt RW7_p8ICHcAp5beBE, viewed August 28, 2021.

"embrace your inner loser." He says, "I felt like a loser all my life in the broken trailer house I lived with a broken family. I don't want to hear how I need to embrace that." I understand what he means, too, when you feel like you're "on your own" and life's successes are all up to you because of a dysfunctional home, poverty, and you've rarely heard any positive affirmations, so it's not really looked at as encouraging sentiment. I get that, but the idea here is not about an insignificant nobody but a somebody whom God loves dearly, a somebody who's a sinner. Again, Charles Spurgeon, who's a master of "nailing it down" says this: "When God accepts a sinner, He is, in fact, only accepting Christ. He looks into the sinner's eyes, and He sees His own dear Son's image there, and He takes him in."[84]

I have had mentors throughout my life. One of those was my mentor Barb, who one year used her book *Inner Virtue, Outer Expression* to guide me through nine months of meeting together once a week. It was the chapter and understanding of true humility that really helped me. "True humility is not a denial of your positive attributes. It isn't a humble person who says, 'I'm not good at anything.' This is an expression of pride which says, 'Look at poor me. I just must have special consideration because I'm so weak. Please pity me . . . treat me well.' True humility is not thinking less of yourself but thinking of yourself less."

Snap! That definition of humility was a revelation to me. Barb gave me assignments to work on areas where I needed to surrender. I discovered that I had pride in areas where I believed the praise belonged to me rather than God. Of course, He lovingly straightened me out and Barb was there, too, and guided me. Be confident in the gifts God has given you rather than feeling bad about what you don't have. Happy and free people are humble people. And happy and free

---

[84] Charles Spurgeon, "Charles Spurgeon Quotes," http://christian-quotes.ochristian.com/Charles-Spurgeon-Quotes/page-3.shtml, viewed August 28, 2021.

people also know that self-care and pampering oneself have a place, too. No one ever said having a spa day or getting a manicure/pedicure was a bad thing, and if they did, I think they're wrong.

But back to my most lovely "loser" friend Jill who was looking for happiness, joy, and peace. She thought maybe she would find it by following the good church girl path, but it did not fill the ache and loneliness in her heart. She grew up attending church as something that was expected and she heard that Jesus had died for her sins, but Jill didn't understand the importance of a personal relationship with Him. She attended youth groups and Bible camps, and during her journey she would meet Jesus at a crossroads. But she was trying to live her life to please people and doing what she thought she needed to find happiness.

The church scene and people weren't cutting it, so Jill found friends who accepted her as she was. At age seventeen she began drinking, smoking, and stealing as a part of her everyday life. In her last years of high school, she lived a double life. Church Girl, who did the things that others expected to please them; and Party Jill, who told lies, partied hearty, and did what was ever necessary to fit in. By nineteen, Jill was a full-blown closet alcoholic.

Jill said, "There was a part of me that desired to have God and a part of me that didn't." She attended Bible college for a short time, and she later started attending a large church in Minneapolis, because she figured she could just fade into the crowd.

Jill continued to go home and party with friends on the weekends. Yet, she kept feeling something drawing her to church. On New Year's Eve in 1991, her friends all bailed on her and she found herself alone with nothing to do, so she decided to go and listen to the Lundstrom Family Singers who were in town. She sat in the back of the church hoping not to be noticed. The message that night touched her heart, yet she didn't go forward at the invitation to receive Christ as Savior. Nevertheless, Londa Lundstrom noticed her sitting in the back and talked with Jill and then prayed with her to accept the Lord into her life.

A seed was planted, and a slow change was initiated. Jill went back to church not only Sundays but Wednesdays as well, and God brought new people into her life who loved her even though she tried hard to push them away. These friends presented Jesus on a personal level, not just "that guy" from the Bible stories.

Slowly, Jill grew closer to Jesus, and she even traveled to England on a mission trip. But afterward, her mom was killed in a car accident. Jill and her mom had had a turbulent relationship and the week before the accident they had an argument over the phone, and Jill hung up on her. The grief was great. After the funeral Jill moved back home where she turned back to alcohol rather than to God.

Eventually, Jill began realizing it wasn't God who had left her. She walked away from Him. She began reading her Bible and although she wasn't consistent at first, God honored her efforts. Her eyes were opened to the idea that being a Christian was so much more than being a good person. In five years, she met her husband and their love brought them a daughter. Of course, she's faced trials since then, like we all do, but she knows that Jesus has always been by her side or carrying her as needed.

Part of Jill's journey, a few years ago, was being diagnosed with clinical depression, and she soon entered what she calls "a very dark season." But through a different medication and a new friend, things changed.

Jill wrote: "God brought me a friend who was a speaker and she understood me, someone whom I could relate to, who had walked the journey I was on. She spoke things to my heart that could have only been from Him, things I hadn't shared I was struggling with, yet the things she spoke went straight to my heart. She was encouraging, and as she talked I listened, and she reminded me where my hope was found. This speaker shared Lamentations 22–24, which pretty much summed it all up: 'Because of the Lord's great love we are not consumed, for His compassions never fail. They are new every morning; great is your faithfulness. I say to myself; the Lord is my portion; therefore, I will wait for Him.'"

That speaker girl was me, Debbie Griffith.

I love this story and Jill. I love how she continues on in her journey just like I do—failing, falling, but then getting back up, knowing we are loved and redeemed. It's so important not to just read God's Word, the Bible, and think its power is for someone else or that any one verse brings magical healing. Reading what God says and promises is about faith in trusting God's character with the hope He promises. Knowing the Bible is one thing, but knowing the Author is another.

I love people. I love Jill and I am so thankful God brought her into my life. In the years I've known her, she has lost more than eighty pounds and is now a REFIT instructor which is an exercise program where "mom-type" woman dance to positive music. She leads worship at church and most recently received the honor of performing a couple's wedding. Jesus is her Savior, but also a very real friend. Jill knows she's the daughter of a King and embraces her inner loser or, better put, her inner need, the part we all have inside of us that knows there is more to life than what we see now. God isn't wasting time thinking about all the trouble He has with us or how awful we feel about where we are with ourselves and our troubles. God loves us unconditionally.

Everyone wins when you believe and trust in who God says He is and what He has done for you. You are no longer lost but found by Christ and you know from Him you are ever so lovely and worth the price He paid for you. He never sees you as a loser but only sees your need and that you're His child who He wants to unconditionally love. Think on that.

Another powerful revelation that God revealed to me was through Moses' journey in the desert. He was questioning and searching for the direction he should go. The Lord spoke to him through a burning bush. How crazy is that? God speaks in love, but He was direct when He told Moses, "Get to Egypt, get my people and *go!*" And when Moses asked, "What should I say to the people when they ask me Your name?" God got right to the point and didn't spend time telling Moses all the things He was. God simply said, as shown in Exodus 3:14, "Tell My people I *am* has sent me to you!" *Okay, whatever that means*, Moses might have thought, but God was revealing to Moses that I *am,* meant *everything*!

God *is* saying, "What you need, I *am!* I *am* your navigator, speaker, provider, comforter, your hope, future, and strength. *I am everything you need* when you need it."

Sometimes God lets you hit rock bottom so that you will discover that He is the rock at the bottom. The devil knows your name but calls you by your sin. Jesus knows your sin but calls you by your name.

Embrace your inner loser and accept that God is sufficient to fill in the blanks for your insufficiencies. This Earth is not our home and the Earth struggles are hard, but in it all God promises to fill us with His goodness; when we are ever so weak, He is ever so strong. God is a Redeemer and no matter how awful you feel about yourself, He sees the potential beauty He created you to be.

We all fall short of the glory of God right now—all of us. Accept the fact that you'll never be enough to cure yourself. The sooner you realize it's not about you and that it's all about Him, the sooner you'll understand who you are and what your purpose is until you're Home with Him. You'll enjoy the uniqueness of who you are and others. You can receive God's forgiveness and work on forgiving yourself for what He's already promised to forget. When this happens, you'll be living in His grace which you so desperately need, and you'll be better equipped to extend His grace to others. I desire to *obey God's Word* and hope that all people I come in contact with can know the grace of God, the peace and joy I have despite my moral failings and mistakes and despite awful circumstances and people. I have received His forgiveness and cleansing. Real change didn't happen in me as a result of being told I needed to change. Real change happened as a result of knowing I was fully known and fully loved by Jesus.

We are in this world together as lovely losers, fully known and loved by Jesus. "Jesus loves me"; sometimes saying this out loud will help you take the steps you need to be strong, especially when you're feeling defeated, lost, and not so lovely. Try it and say it aloud for yourself: "Jesus loves me, this I know." He will always be available, drawing you to Him with unfailing kindness and everlasting love. Embrace who you are in Him. You're a sinner (and such a lovely one), saved by His grace and given full forgiveness. Embrace *that* and walk forward unafraid.

Below is a prayer I pray aloud from Brennan Manning's book, *The Ragamuffin Gospel,* and when I do, I almost always cry:

> Lord Jesus, we are silly sheep who have dared to stand before You and try to bribe You with our preposterous portfolios. Suddenly we have come to our senses. We are sorry and ask You to forgive us. Give us the grace to admit we are ragamuffins, to embrace our brokenness, to celebrate Your mercy when we are at our weakest, to rely on Your mercy no matter what we may do. Jesus, help us to stop grandstanding and trying to get attention, to do the truth quietly without display, to let the dishonesties in our lives fade away, to accept our limitations, to claim to the gospel of grace, and to delight in Your love. Amen.[85]

---

[85] Brennan Manning, *The Ragamuffin Gospel,* (Colorado Springs, CO: Multnomah Books, 2015), 144.

Pray the prayer, cry out to God, and share your heart. He's listening and He's aware of every single detail of your life (and your heart) and He cares for you more than you'll never know until eternity with Him. Embrace your inner loser. Yes, share that you're weak because 2 Corinthians 12:9 tells us to boast about our weaknesses, so that God's strength can work through us forever and ever, *Amen*.

46
GOD IS NOT MAD AT YOU

*"For it is by grace you have been saved, through faith—
and this is not from yourselves, it is the gift of God."*
— **Ephesians 2:8 (NIV)**

I MET WITH A COUNSELOR. I needed to. And it was better than I expected. I talked. A lot. The counselor listened. She had questions, too. I answered.

Afterward, she pushed her chair back and gave me some solid counsel and encouragement. I took it. I can't stop thinking about her words to me: "Debbie, you came in completely open and honest. You're not guarding secrets. You're not hiding, and because of your transparency you told me much more than you probably realize." Being honest helps us to really heal, and from that we can better come alongside others to help them heal. We are only as sick as our secrets. When we bring our burdens into the light, the darkness no longer has power over us.

Sharing my brokenness publicly allowed other wounded birds to flit my direction, and I continue to receive messages, cards, and emails of love and encouragement, along with people sharing their own stories, asking, "Can I tell you my secrets?"

"Of course," I would say. "Tell everything to Jesus, too, because He already knows. We can't hide from Him. He's not mad at you, but rather heartbroken over anything that hurts you. He always has a way for you to be blessed and restored."

I had been traveling some difficult and dark roads the thirteen months beginning in 2016. Much of the rough terrain has had to do with the deep ache of broken relationships or loss of a family member or friend. And during this grieving time, I let go of some titles that made me feel "important," such as being a director of a theatre company and spokesperson for a foundation helping young women who had been enslaved.

I then heard from a No.1 radio station that my short feature, *Everyday Matters*, would be dropped from their programming. Sheesh. I felt like I was being stripped of worth and purpose. Of course, this wasn't true, but I felt like it.

Then when I thought, *Surely, I'm coming to the end of this dark road*, I began to have physical pain, as one of the rods in my back started to pinch a nerve near my left shoulder and I could not find relief. In 2003 I had had scoliosis back surgery and doctors said I could later have problematic pain from the rods as I aged. But *really* . . . now? I started to think I could empathize with Job.

But unlike Job, I made a really stinky choice, which involved concocting and drinking an adult beverage (and not a VFW drink size, as my sister-in-law later pointed out) and then driving two miles, in my pajamas, to the McDonald's drive–thru to get a Big Mac.

This stinky choice landed me in the "cop shop" wearing an orange jumpsuit.

I was a wretch. I was a mess. I was ashamed. I knew better, but I wanted to feel better. I wanted to numb my pain. But the numbing never lasts and if it does, it's a problem. I've watched Brené Brown give her "TED Talk" on the power of vulnerability a zillion times. Brené shares her own breakdown, but she shares what she learned in counseling and in her research.

There's this super truth Brené gives, saying, "We can't numb those hard feelings without numbing our emotions. We cannot selectively numb. So, when we numb, we numb joy, we numb gratitude, we numb happiness. And then we are miserable, and we are looking for purpose and meaning, and then we feel vulnerable, so then we have a couple of beers and a banana nut muffin. And it becomes this dangerous cycle."[86]

Wisdom speaks through the experiences of others, but we have to be willing to share and be honest about ourselves to really be of use to anyone, especially God. Our breaking point can be our release date. The more we depend on God, the more He can do through us. But sometimes we go through brokenness before we enter God's blessings.

I didn't plan on breaking, but I did. Instead of hiding my brokenness and pain, or living in shame, I made phone calls, wrote messages, and sent emails. Then I wrote an essay on my pain, shame, and brokenness because I knew there was grace, love, forgiveness, and redemption. I brought my story to the light. I went public. And while I purged, I met with a counselor. Healing began and in April 2017 in Northern Minnesota, when the snow was almost melted, my sorrow, too, was melting.

I think when God begins to really use us, He gives us some type of pain, a thorn in our flesh, as he did Paul. We don't actually know what Paul's "pain" was, but somehow, I think it was mental and not physical.

When I read Paul's second letter to the Corinthians, I can almost hear him yelling, "Enough already with this pain, Lord! Take it away, *now!* I. Can't. Even." Over and over Paul asked God to remove the thorn that was tormenting him, but God said no. God told him, "My grace is all you need, it is sufficient right NOW, and as you get to really know Me, you'll see that I work best when you're weak so I can be strong."

---

[86] Brené Brown, "The Power of Vulnerability," TEDtalksDirector, January 3, 2011, https://www.youtube.com/watch?v=iCvmsMzlF7o, viewed September 7, 2021.

I know it's crazy, but I agree with Anne Lamott who writes in her book *Hallelujah Anyway* that Paul had to see his thorn as a gift: "He had to want to be put in his place, he had to be willing to give God thanks for this glaring new sense of humility, of smallness, the one thing anyone in his right mind tries to avoid. Conceit is intoxicating, addictive, the best feeling on Earth some days, but Paul chose instead submission and servitude as the way to freedom from the bondage of self. Blessed are the meek."

As my heart thaws, I hear God speak to me: *Debbie, anything good you do has nothing to do with you. I am the One who is good. When you see yourself doing anything good, it is only because I have wrestled with you to get your flesh under subjection long enough to allow My glory to shine through.*

That's it, isn't it? It's about Him and what He does through us. Nothing is wasted. He's God and we're not.

I continue to ponder the counselor's words about transparency. God fully knows us and still fully loves us. He doesn't need our performing. He needs our hearts, our obedience, and our brokenness. I know what it is to perform or pretend, but as I age and experience life I see no benefit in playing this charade. When I let God into my head space and heart, I have peace and security. Performing doesn't come into play when I know whose girl I am. I'm God's Girl. This secure Debbie isn't spending time worrying about herself because with my confidence I'm freer and my desire is to serve others. When life is hard or I'm in a hard place I tell someone instead of pretending that everything is fine. People may be inspired by your successes but more so by your failures so they know they're not alone.

It's important to remember that God is not mad at you when you fall. He is heartbroken over our bad choices and sins. We can't hide from Him. God's grace is always there when we turn to Him. His gentleness with forgiveness helps us take the steps in the right direction and walk down the road of healing where there's no condemnation or shame.

So, look up to the light and be honest. It's okay. I get it. Cry if you need to as it helps cleanse. Even your anger has a place if you don't set up camp there.

Let Christ breathe new life into you. C. S. Lewis was spot on when he wrote, "Look for yourself, and you will find in the long run only hatred, loneliness, despair, rage, ruin, and decay. But look for Christ, and you will find Him, and with Him everything else thrown in."[87]

You must lean into your life. You must recognize that if it's admitting you have a problem that scares you, it's because you know how good recovery could be, but you don't want to heal because then you'll regress again. If it's opening up to love that scares you, it's because you know how deep your heart could hold someone, and you don't want to let them in and then lose them. If you fear starting a new job or beginning a company or leaving the monotony of the life that was all but chosen for you, I get it. Because you know that there's a whole new existence on the other side—one you might fear and don't want to be responsible for messing up, if you actually step out and "go for it."

God is for us just like the Bible is for us today. The Apostle Paul wrote in 2 Corinthians 5:17, "If anyone is in Christ, they are a new creation. The old has passed away; behold, the new has come."

Live like you believe you are a new creature in Him. Live like you know you're unconditionally loved and there's a specific purpose for you by the specific way God created you. God is good and He wants the best for all whom He formed in His image. Day by day, with honesty and transparency, you'll find the sufficient grace and strength you need. Healing and wholeness will be the gift to yourself and others because, in our brokenness, we are made beautiful. I have never regretted being transparent and honest. It's time. God is not mad at you. Step up and step into the light.

---

[87] C. S. Lewis, "C. S. Lewis Quotes," https://www.brainyquote.com/quotes/c_s_lewis_714959, viewed August 29, 2021.

47
BECOME LIKE A LITTLE CHILD

"Then He said, 'I tell you the truth, unless you turn from your sins and become like little children, you will never get into the kingdom of heaven.'"
— **Matthew 18:3 (NLT)**

WHEN BROOKES IS ON the cover of *Fortune* magazine, I want to be quoted that I saw it coming.

Ever since he was three and could talk, Brookes knew just about everything about lawn mowers. One of the first things he would ask a person was what kind of lawn mower they owned and how it was working for them. If you asked Brookes what kind of lawn mower he had, he would very directly say, "Fisher Price."

Brookes was eight the summer he started a neighborhood lawn-mowing business, our lawn included. In August, Brookes knocked on our door and reported: "Debbie, I was biking around the neighborhood and noticed your lawn needs mowing. Are any of your boys home?" I wasn't sure, so Brookes followed me into the basement and we found our oldest of four, Marco.

"Hey, Marco, you know you need to cut your lawn out here,"

Brookes reprimanded. Marco agreed, but said he didn't have the time, which is the answer Brookes was waiting for. "Well, you know, I cut lawns. Debbie, would you please just let me?"

"Can you do this, Brookes? Is your mom okay with this?" A quick phone call from Brookes to his mom confirmed he was good to go. I had to run errands, but I told Brookes if he needed anything to go into the house and ask Marco. I smiled as I watched this "little man" begin mowing, but as I was pulling out of the driveway, Brookes stopped, turned, and said, "I gotta ask Marco about your lawn perimeters and find out where the boundary markers are." Who is this child? Lawn perimeters and boundary markers—is there such a thing for a simple lawn as we have?

Just last week Brookes saw me and said, "Can I please mow your lawn, one last time, before it snows? I don't want the money, I just wanna cut the grass."

I love this kid. His tenacious and his sweet spirit, along with his childlike faith, continues to impress and bless me *and* others.

Ah, children. I love our four sons, but, oh, there was the season when someone would remind me to "Enjoy your kids while they're young . . . they grow up so fast." My thought was always, "Good, I can't wait." But *now*, I remind other moms with, "The days are long, but the years are short."

The funny thing is my dream was to be a Broadway star. I always thought I'd get married so I could have a husband to support me as I auditioned for shows, but I never really dreamed of having babies. Of course, I have four, and I now see how God knew me better than I knew me. My children continue to teach me more about love, sacrifice, simplicity, battles, tears, and the joy of loving someone so fiercely you'd give your life for them. *And* now I do get to travel and perform on stage, and many of the stories I share are these of being a wife and mom, and the blessings and lessons I've learned.

When the disciples asked Jesus the question about who is the greatest in the kingdom of heaven (Matthew 18), Jesus drew a distinction between the elite and the ordinary in the Christian community. He called a little child to Him whom He set among them. Then He said, "In truth I tell you, unless you change and become like little children you will never enter the kingdom of Heaven. And so, the one who makes himself as *little* as this little child is the greatest in the kingdom of Heaven."

The kingdom belongs to people who aren't trying to look good or impress anybody, even themselves. They're not planning on how they can call attention to themselves, worrying about how their actions will be interpreted or wondering if they will get gold sticker stars for their behavior. Jesus gets us. He loves us, and we don't need to worry about faking it or trying to pretend that we get it. So, let's stop trying to appear "so spiritual" because that gets exhausting, then we hold a pity party by thinking that no one loves us, the "poor nobodies," and that can pretty much wipe us out. Know the truth: God loves His kids just as we are.

The child doesn't have to struggle to get herself in a good position for having a relationship with God. She doesn't have to be creative in explaining her position to Jesus. She doesn't have to create the right look for herself, and she doesn't have to achieve the "right" spiritual feeling, or be an über intellectual. All she has to do is happily accept the gift of God's love.

When Jesus tells us to become like little children, He is inviting us to forget what lies behind. Whatever we have done in the past, be it good or evil, great or small, is irrelevant to where we stand with God today. It is only *now* that we are in the presence of God.

The meaning of living in the present and not looking back is wonderfully illustrated by a Zen story about a monk being pursued by a ferocious tiger (and again this story and insight I share from Brennan Manning). The monk raced to the edge of a cliff, glanced back, and saw the growling tiger about to spring. The monk spotted a rope dangling over the edge of the cliff. He grabbed it and began shinnying down the side of the cliff out of the clutches of the tiger. Whew! Narrow escape. The monk then looked down and saw a quarry of jagged rocks five hundred feet below. He looked up and saw the tiger poised atop the cliff with bared claws. Just then, two mice began to nibble at the rope. What to do?

The monk saw a strawberry within arm's reach, growing out of the face of the cliff. He plucked it, ate it, and exclaimed, "Yum! That's the best strawberry I've ever tasted in my entire life." If he had been preoccupied with the rock below (the future) or the tiger above (the past), he would have missed the strawberry God was giving him in the present moment. Children do not focus on the tigers of the past or the future but only on the strawberry that comes *in the here and now*.[88]

Whatever past successes might bring us honor, whatever past "I'm so ashamed" makes us want to hide, all have been crucified with Christ and exist no more except in the deep recesses of eternity, where "Good is enhanced into glory, and evil miraculously is established as part of the great good."

For the disciple of Jesus, "becoming like a little child" means the willingness to accept oneself as being of little account and to be regarded as unimportant, but to be sure, *not* insignificant. The little child is a symbol of those who have the lowest places in society, the poor and oppressed, beggars, prostitutes, and tax collectors—the people Jesus often called the "little ones" or the "least."

Jesus's concern was that these little ones should not be despised or treated as inferior (Matthew 18:10). He was well aware of their feelings of shame and inferiority, and because of His compassion, they were, in His eyes, of extraordinarily great value. As far as He was concerned, they had nothing to fear. The kingdom was theirs. "There is

---

[88] Brennan Manning, "Strawberries and Monks and Tigers, Oh My!", January 26, 2012, https://journeyonword.com/2012/01/25/strawberries-and-monks-and-tigers-oh-my/, viewed February 19, 2022.

no need to be afraid, little flock, for it has pleased your Father to give you the kingdom (Luke 12:32)."

Jesus gave these "little ones" a privileged place in the kingdom and presented them as models to would-be disciples. They were to accept the kingdom in the same way a child would accept her allowance. If the children were privileged, it was not because they had merited privilege, but simply because God took pleasure in these little ones whom adults may have despised. The mercy of Jesus flowed out to them wholly from unmerited grace and divine love.

I want to live life like a child of God, like Brookes does, like we all need to. When we trust God's great love then we can operate in life with confidence and security. He gives us gifts and ways to love and help others, and, when done, it all comes into a full circle of love. So, I will continue to share my gifts of storytelling and encouragement, not because I get paid to do so, but because I love to do so.

That summer Brookes continued to scout out neighborhood lawns with grass that needed cutting simply because he loves to mow. Take a deep breath and release and rest in the Father's love for you, His child, and then go out and bless others with what He's given you to do, every day.

48
THE BEAUTY OF GOD'S 'GRACE'

"Peace I leave with you; my peace I give you.
I do not give to you as the world gives.
Do not let your hearts be troubled and do not be afraid."
— **John 14:27 (NIV)**

LET ME INTRODUCE YOU TO GRACE.
She bikes to my door to take a walk and talk. She's a firefly of light and love, with shining blue eyes and freckles, accompanied by the sweetest and softest of voices.

Grace explains her journey with Hodgkin's lymphoma as well as her trust and relationship with God. Her faith is beautiful and her outlook on life refreshing. The day we took our walk is in stark contrast to the battle with darkness I had over the prior days. It is God's gift to me. It's when Love puts shoes on and walks with you, and at the time of our meeting she was a fourteen-year-old girl with cancer.

Grace was currently in treatment and transplants, driving three hundred miles every three weeks in between sports, school, and youth group. I would say she's an angel, but, even better, she's a daughter of the King, created in His image and she's living authentically, with purpose.

On our walk we talked about the hard places of cancer, the fear, the throwing up that glues her to the bathroom floor, the waiting, and all the people she's met and the type of experiences that make you think this girl to be much older than fourteen. She is clearly making a difference in the lives of so many. She literally is taking her cancer as an assignment from God.

On our walk I told her, "Gracie, God only chooses a very special few for very special journeys, like the cancer walk." She takes her face in her hands and says to me: "Oh. My. You get it. I mean, you really get it." Her angel voice does state that, "Cancer sucks," but she also adds, "Most people don't understand how I could have any joy or a hope at all, but I do, I really do."

When we sat in my living room for another hour, I asked if I could take more photos of her because I want to remember how she lit up my room.

We talked about taking the hard things in life as a class and how to be good students in it. When it was time for her to go, I asked if I could pray for her. She quickly responded, "Of course. May I pray for you, too?"

Certainly.

I can hardly wait for Sunshine to come into my home again. Grace is her name, which fits her perfectly. On Facebook I posted Gracie's photo and a tribute. I did it four days after our time together, because it was hard to gather all that light and share it with mere words and a photo.

Gracie attended the same church as me, so I knew her, but not as deeply as after our walk on that magical Monday afternoon. Within hours of the post, I had more than one hundred people acknowledging and commenting on the impact Gracie had made on their lives.

It was true. She was different. She was allowing God to use her in a way that was supernatural.

The evening of "Let me introduce you to Grace," I started to get a cold and I began to feel like absolute crap. I shuffled throughout the house, upstairs and down, whining aloud with my hoodie on and announcing, "I don't feel good. I feel like crap." I began to have really bad nausea so I made another announcement about how nauseated I was, saying, "I think I'm going to throw up."

I asked all members of the family who were home to stop what they were doing and individually pray for me. My husband did, as did two of my sons. They prayed according to the memo I had given a couple years earlier on *how* to pray when one feels like crap.

You see, most times when we're not feeling well and we ask someone to pray for us they begin with, "Dear God, I pray Debbie would feel better . . . " *Wait What?* I don't want to *feel* better; I want to BE better. I want to be healed and done with "it." My family knows "how" to pray, but still Joey said, "Mom, I don't feel like praying, but I will."

"Okay, that's all I need, Joe."

After Joe prayed, I went to the bathroom and lay on the floor. I was miserable and knew the throwing up part was coming. It came. I would feel better for about ten minutes until the next round came and then I'd heave again. This went on for about an hour.

Finally, I was able to roll into bed. Twenty minutes later my husband, Dan, crawled in and I said, "Please pray again, but this time for Gracie." As I lay on the bed, I realized this little bout with sickness wasn't about me, it was about *Gracie*. It was about praying and asking God to be with and heal *Gracie* and I knew, quite certainly, that I would be better in the morning. My assignment for that evening was to pray for Gracie's healing and to experience the loneliness and sick that comes with cancer on a bathroom floor.

Prayer works, but only if you actually pray. Often on Facebook we see someone asking for a prayer and then a thread of comments that lovingly say, "praying" and I always think, "Are you?" I mean, I see the thread, too, and if I write the word "praying," it means I see the request and I care, but unless I intentionally write out a prayer and pray aloud right at that moment, I'm not likely to pray later on. Instead, I'm likely to scroll around to look at Jamie's wedding plans or Hope's new baby, and I totally forget about praying for Annie, who so desperately needs it.

My night of sickness in knowing *how* to pray for Gracie certainly impressed me to actually pray, not just intend to. I drifted off to sleep, thanking God and praying for Gracie.

Recently, someone sent me a post on Instagram that read, "A key to success is playing the hand you were dealt like it was the hand you wanted." I had to really think if there was truth to that. Yes, I might not have wanted what was dealt, but "here it is," so what am I gonna do with it? My choices—scream, cry, complain, and hide, or make the best of the situation and find the lesson and blessing in it. *That* is exactly the conversation Grace and I had. We can let experiences change us for the better or ruin us. Character more often is developed in crisis when we stop focusing on the hurt and search out a good that can come from the hurt.

During my recovery of scoliosis back surgery in 2003, I was miserable, yet I don't regret what I went through. I remember lying on the floor in the bathroom, for what seemed like days, unable to eat or poop, but yet I seemed to have no problem dry-heaving into the toilet. Fear crept in and I thought I might never make it up off the floor and care for my young boys again.

I needed faith, which is another way of having confidence that God IS and God cares. So, I said the simplest of things lying there on the bathroom floor: "God, I choose to receive the peace You give and not the fear I feel." You "see," He tells us that He has peace to give from John 14:27: "Peace I leave with you. My peace I *give* you. I don't give as the world does. Don't be troubled or afraid."

Once I said and believed, I received. My feelings were still crappy, *but* I had peace and the hope that I would get better. And I did.

Gracie and I talked about this kind of peace. It's something you know and not something you feel. What you know is that it will pass and you will get off the floor. It's faith to believe God is good and a Redeemer who will use our experiences and pain to be a blessing to someone else because hope is the belief things will get better. Despair is the opposite of hope, and it brings the fear that you'll never be well and you'll always be stuck on the bathroom floor.

So yeah, I definitely wouldn't use the word *thrilled* to describe the hard places in life, but oddly, I would say I am thankful. There is a sweetness and nearness of God's grace that is hard to explain. And when I am willing to honestly share my heart, it reaches into the lives of others in a deeper way that I could imagine and they reach into mine.

"The times when I have felt strong, self-sufficient, and good are the times when I have been furthest from God. The times when I have felt closest to God are those times when I have felt the weakest, when I have failed miserably, when I have been flat on my back." So says my friend Tullian in a tweet posted around the same time I was meeting with Gracie.

I know I am not alone, even though there are feelings of it. I am so thankful for His peace in the midst of life's harder climbs. You have been assigned a difficult mountain to climb to show others it can be moved.

Pastor, author and speaker, Paul Tripp puts it well. "You see, the character of a life is not set in two or three dramatic moments, but in ten thousand little moments. The character that was formed in those little moments is what shapes how you respond in the big moments of life."[89]

---

[89] P. D. Tripp, "Trading One Dramatic Resolution for 10,000 Little Ones," February 9, 2022, https://www.desiringgod.org/articles/trading-one-dramatic-resolution-for-10000-little-ones, viewed February 14, 2022.

Receive the peace God has to give and keep on keeping on. God's got you. You might not know a Gracie Girl like I do, but you can know grace, and walk forward in courage with God's strength, moment by moment, every day.

CRAVING
SELF-CONTROL

49
WE'RE ALL ADDICTS

"My conscience is clear, but that does not make me innocent. It is the Lord who judges me."
— **1 Corinthians 4:4 (NIV)**

WE WERE ALL GUILTY.
We sat in a circle facing one another, looking at our hands or the old junior high chalk board, *anywhere* but at each other for fear of making eye contact and being seen. Yet, we knew why we were there waiting for Sue, "the Cussing Sailor Counselor," to enter the classroom. We had all been ordered to attend a DUI class and Sue was our instructor for that day.

What we knew about each other is that we all had experienced some jail time, worn orange, and been fingerprinted, and the news of our guilt had been shared rapidly in our small town as soon as our photos and names were posted on the roster.

When Sue walked into the room, she wanted to get down to business. Teach us what we needed to hear with no messin' around. I liked Sue. She was my treatment counselor and after the first few sessions we had covered a lot of ground, including the back history she had with my husband's mom, who had brought Sue into treatment decades ago. I marveled at the fact she could use the F-bomb so effectively to make a point, and honestly, it was impressive. She helped me explore my relationship with alcohol and what being an addict was all about.

I knew a little bit about being an addict in my own personal life, maybe not specifically to alcohol, but I was an addict to feeling good when I wanted and how I wanted. Many times, I want to experience only what's pleasurable without thinking of others or any negative consequences. The flesh wants what it wants, when it wants it, and sometimes it seems God stands in the way.

In Christianity we call it having an idol, which is anything we seek, pursue (idolize) above God. It might be shopping, eating, exercise, status, money, career, you get the idea. It's the time when the enemy of our souls can creep in and tell us what feels good to hear. "God is a killjoy. He is in the way," or "He doesn't even exist. Do what feels good to you. Be your own god."

It really doesn't take much faith to believe in God—evidence of His creative design is everywhere. You need faith to believe God is *still* good when your circumstances are not. The conundrum of yelling at God for letting us down, and in the same breath assert He doesn't exist. Don Miller's book *Blue Like Jazz* is really the first place I heard my problem described so accurately: *"No drug is so powerful as the drug of self. No rut in the mind is so deep as the one that says I am the world, the world belongs to me, all people are characters in my play. There is no addiction so powerful as self-addiction."* And Don adds, *"I discovered that my mind is like a radio that picks up only one station, the one that plays me: K-Don, all Don, all the time."* [90]

And I thought I hear the same tune, different station: *"W-Deb, all Deb, all the time."*

---

[90] Donald Miller, chapter on self-addiction, *Blue Like Jazz* (Nashville: Thomas Nelson, 2003).

I'll always be walking on the road to recovery in trusting who God says I am and believing in faith that God is always good even when I'm not. But we can't kill what we don't confess. When I received my DUI, I deserved it. I was guilty. But here's the *good news* of the Gospel; when we admit and confess our sins and guilt, God forgives us and gives us a clean slate. We can get back up and move forward, and in so doing we are able to help others, too, get back up after falling.

Might I recommend the book *Grace In Addiction* by priest, author, and former alcoholic John Z. It's a solid attempt to bridge this divide between the church and Alcoholics Anonymous, both being in the business of bringing hope to the hopeless. It's about bringing the unexpected good news of AA out of the basement and into the pews—and beyond. We're all addicts in one way or another, there's some other "thing" that's vying for our attention that trips us up in ways we never wanted or imagined. *Only grace* can lead us on the path. John writes: "Grace is the hope that seeks us out when we are at our worst. It looks forward to the long, hard road ahead. Grace is not worried, even if everything falls apart and everything goes wrong. It is the love of God that does not let go. It brings good out of bad, and it sees hope where there is none. Grace always gives another chance. Grace waits. It stands when you have fallen; it leaves the door open. Grace stays awake for you when you can't keep your eyes open for another minute, even though you know you should."[91]

So, there I was in an all-day DUI class, ready and ordered, with others, to learn the seriousness of driving while intoxicated. Sue needed no introduction and was ready to dive into the charts of statistics and models of vital organs, but before she could begin, I interrupted her. "Ah, Sue, can we please go around the circle, and each share a little of our stories and how we got here?" She rolled her eyes. She wasn't having

---

[91] John Z, *Grace in Addiction: The Good News of Alcoholics Anonymous for Everybody* (Charlottesville, VA: Mockingbird Ministries, 2012).

it. But I continued, "There are only nine of us here and I think it would be helpful if we could just listen and connect to one another." Sue sighed, and in her gravelly sailor voice said, "Debbie, we don't have time. We've got an awful lot of material to get through."

"Oh, but it won't take long. I think it's really important, and so I'll begin."

Of course, Sue was right. It did take longer than expected... because of me. *Because* I had to interrupt every single person to ask more questions. I wanted to know more and connect deeper. We needed to hear each other's stories. It's okay to be scared. It's okay to feel pain and cry or scream or both.

You see, DUI Debbie was still kinda in shock and embarrassed by what she had done and with that, I had some shame. So, it really comes down to humility and accepting what Christ is offering. I think sometimes the hardest part is forgiving ourselves and admitting how weak we are. None of us in class, "Circle Time," needed to stay ashamed. We had showed up. We were taking responsibility and learning things to help in our journeys ahead. More significantly, we were learning to be vulnerable and honest in sharing our pain.

This is what makes "group" and AA and other treatment programs so effective. We're able to connect with others who are struggling and needing accountability and hope. Three years before my DUI in spring 2014, I bought the book *Grace In Addiction* at a Mockingbird Ministry Conference in NYC (which is a brilliant read with wit and wisdom). I met the author, John Z at the conference and introduced myself as a possible alcoholic.

I shared a lot in a short amount of time (or maybe too much time, I know myself). After listening to my story, the author, John Z, said, "Ah, thanks for sharing, but I don't think you're an alcoholic." After reading the book I see what he means. My human frailty, my need to numb pain and not always with alcohol, was problematic. The wisdom of the book offers great insight to all of us fallen earthlings and nails the amazing power of God's grace in a way that AA doesn't. Below is an excerpt from the book, which was like an "Aha" moment for me:

> There is often talk in meetings about two kinds of humans: "alcoholics" and (normal) "Earth people." The two conceivably cannot make heads or tails of each other. Alcoholics understand alcoholics, and Earth people understand Earth people. The alcoholic may find that she has a lot in common with a drug addict or even a gambling addict, but she has nothing in common with those people out there who don't struggle with the problem of personal powerlessness and the compulsive behavioral meltdowns that accompany it. This view is naïve.
>
> Traditional Christian theology, in contrast, understands the universalities that unite and define all people. The Church teaches that addiction displays, in fact, the true nature of what it means to be a human being living in a fallen world. The bridge between the alcoholic and the nonalcoholic is called sin, and faith affirms that the alcoholic has no greater need for God's grace than the "Earth person" does, even if the circumstances in one case appear to be more dire. Both people will die, and both people need love. The same is true for both men and women, people of different races and ages and cultures—it's universal. Is the cancer patient who feels "fine" really any less sick than the depressed person who cannot get out of bed? We are all equal in sin and personal powerlessness, and although some manifestations may be more destructive than others, to obsess over one particular expression of sin is to misinterpret the data. For this reason, church leaders would do well to recall Christianity's notion of the bound will. The fruit of this idea is a compassion borne out of a stark honesty about the human condition.[92]

Isn't that good? It makes me think about another man named Paul, the apostle, who says in Romans 7:18–20 (NLT), "I know that nothing good lives in me, that is, in my sinful nature. I want to do

---

[92] John Z, *Grace in Addiction*.

what is right, but I can't. I want to do what is good, but I don't. I don't want to do what is wrong, but I do it anyway. But if I do what I don't want to do, I am not really the one doing wrong; it is sin living in me that does it."

Another human who understands the grace of God, falling, failing and getting back up is my friend Tullian and every time I try and say his last name, Tchividjian, I come with a new way of pronouncing it if only to entertain myself because of its uniqueness and my "gift" of phonetics. Anyway, almost every single post he shares on Instagram (my go-to in Social Media Land) is something I "heart," and make a comment on and/or share with others. What you see below is from a post Tullian shared on December 4, 2020, and obviously he understands, too, "We're all addicts," and it's Christ who will guide us through recover and bring us full redemption. Tullian writes:

> We tend to think that those who are in Recovery programs are weak, and those of us who aren't are strong. After all, we have not succumbed to the destructive demon of addiction like they have. But that is a lie. The truth is, we are *all* in Recovery. We all have unhealthy relationships with something that we depend on to soothe the pain—to make us feel strong and important and in control. Your substance abuse problem may not be alcohol, but it may be getting approval. Your addiction may not be getting high, but it may be getting attention. It may not be sex, but it may be shopping. It may not be food or nicotine, but it may be financial security or fitness. In other words, we are all jacked up people living in a jacked-up world with other jacked-up people. And that means that there are two types of people in this world: people in Recovery who admit that they are in Recovery and people in Recovery who deny that they are in Recovery. But there is no one who is *not* in Recovery. And this means that those who admit it are the "strong" ones. The "weak" ones are those who don't. There's failure, loss, regret, addiction, and the amazing grace of God. But the one point

that I wanted to make loudly and clearly was that it is not enough for local churches to have Recovery ministries. The church must begin to see itself AS a Recovery ministry. If it doesn't, it will continue to fail in connecting the deep realities of God's amazing grace to the dark regions of human need."[93]

And there we are and there we go. We're living in a world that's not our home, but we have the hope of eternity with Him someday where all is good, all the time, and we are perfected. And it's only through Christ, who can save us from ourselves, from death, and bring us this eternal hope.

Right now, we journey along with others where we all need each other's grace and love. God commands us that *above all things*, "Love one another." These words to an addict (or any sort of human) can be some of the most soothing and healing: "I love you whether you're using or you're not. I love you whatever state you're in, and if you need me, I'll come and sit with you because I love you, and I don't want you to be alone or to feel alone."

Russell Brand, English comedian, actor, and radio guy, has a lot to share—he has some great insights in addition to being entertaining. I came across this quote from him when I was reading through my journal and trip to see Uncle Peter (which I covered in chapter 38). "It is difficult to suffer the selfishness of a drug addict who will lie to you and steal from you and forgive them and offer them help. Can there be any other disease that renders its victims so unappealing?"[94] Yet, I will still hold on to hope because God is real and I know prayer works, but some days are desperately dark.

But I digress. Let's go back to the DUI class. The morning hours were long and the only part I really enjoyed was group-sharing time.

---

[93] Tullian Tchividjian, "Real Recovery Post," December 3, 2020, Instagram, https://www.instagram.com/p/CIWrSx5nov_/, viewed August 30, 2021.
[94] Russell Brand, *Russell Brand: My Life without Drugs,* https://www.fellowship-hall.com/2018/08/russell-brand-my-life-without-drugs/, viewed Feb.14, 2022.

I mean, have you seen the diagrams on how alcohol can wreck your liver? It's pouring poison down the hatch. It was in the first half of the day that we had filled out pages of a personal questionnaire and now, after break, Sue handed back our results and her assessments. We sat in our seats, quiet, no one looked up, but I knew we're all thinking the same thing. *How does Sue know that I'm in denial?*

So, Girlfriend Barb barked out what we all were thinking, "How can you tell we are addicts in denial?" Sue's deep voice explained, "I've been an addict. I've been in denial, and I've done this for years." Enough said. We are all addicts. Oh, the Spirit is willing but how weak my flesh. It's not me trying harder but me flat out surrendering daily, moment by moment. Lord, hear my prayer.

The last half of the day and the final part of class was to watch these horrific real-life videos where family members have agreed to let a team follow their tragedy and recovery of a member in a DUI accident. Wow. You can't look at the screen the entire time. It's so awful. Afterward, I wanted to say something sassy to break the ice like, "I dunno about the rest of you, but after *that*, I could use a drink." I keep my mouth shut.

What I did instead was stand up and ask; "Hey, I'm giving out hugs. Who wants one?" It seemed everyone was "in" and ready to receive. We concluded with one big group hug, and I exchanged information from a few of my new friends. I hugged Sue, too, and reminded her I'd see her next week. Then I walked down the three flights of stairs and outside to where my bike was (not yet having my driver's license back), and pedaled home. It was an April day in Minnesota and only forty-two degrees, but the sun was smiling, and I was, too.

It'd been a good DUI Day. I biked home thinking about love, hope, and forgiveness (and did I really want to risk damaging my kidneys?), but also about the connections I'd made with some of the loveliest addicts I'd ever meet, myself included.

50
I WANNA BE POP-U-LAR

"May God grant you out of the rich treasury of His glory to be strengthened and reinforced with mighty power by the Holy Spirit Himself indwelling in your innermost being and personality."
— **Ephesians 3:16 (ESV)**

I LOVE BEING LIKED. I think it's safe to say I am not in the minority. Social media alone reveals that a lot of time and effort goes into managing an image that makes you irresistible, adorable, fun, wise and witty, on-trend, yet authentic.

Success cannot be defined by my "likes" or "shares," or whether my quotes end up on artsy, cool plaques and posters. But to be honest, why wouldn't every speaker-girl person want this kind of exposure? Duh, it's being popular, and popularity is the drug of choice to convince you of your worth and value or that your message must be on point. Our culture gets it. Look at the lyrics from the musical *Wicked* where Glinda, the Good Witch, sings:

"La, la
We're gonna make
You pop-u-lar!

When I see depressing creatures
With unprepossessing features
I remind them on their own behalf
To think of
Celebrated heads of state or
Specially great communicators
Did they have brains or knowledge?
Don't make me laugh!
They were popular! Please -
It's all about popular!
It's not about aptitude
It's the way you're viewed
So it's very shrewd to be
Very, very popular
Like me!"[95]

    Is being smart, knowledgeable, or accomplished the guarantee of success? Nope. It's not about seeking the approval of others. Popularity requires being savvy and shrewd, among other things, but at what price? What is the message you want people to really hear? What do people need to hear?

    I decided to do a little research. I had a free weekend, so I spent a large amount of time on Instagram stalking every amazing woman blogger, communicator, and speaker-girl person I could find who had experienced a good dose of fame and popularity. I was broad in my search and didn't limit myself to just Christian "types," even though I guessed I'd fall into that category. It wasn't long before I found it necessary to break and bolster myself. I accomplished this by opening the freezer and passing my spoon from one pint of gelato to another

---

[95] Kristin Chenoweth, *Wicked*, July 29, 2009, words and lyrics by Stephen Schwartz, https://www.youtube.com/watch?v=0x6VTnjGHjU, viewed September 3, 2021.

until all three pints were consumed in a five-hour span.

Now, don't get me wrong. These women warriors (Paula White, Jen Hatmaker, Priscilla Shirer) are amazing people, and, besides their external beauty, they are beautiful in the way that they honestly share their wisdom and wit. I've learned a lot from their transparency, but that weekend it wasn't their words of wisdom as much as the "wow" of how they presented themselves on social media.

I looked at their outer décor and wondered, "Does she diet, and which ones has she tried? How often does she highlight her hair? Is that really her dog, and are those her children or just props? How real is she?" But they are real people with real heartaches and hopes, too, and most are sincere about their insecurities. It all has a certain "cost" being popular because the larger the audience, the larger amount of love, but it also brings a larger amount of judgment too.

The Instagram women I looked at were of all ages, shapes, and sizes, but when I compared myself to them, I never measured up. Now a person could look at my social media photos and say, "Shut up, Debbie, you should talk." I can clean up nice, but the past few years my real, everyday look has been a hooded sweatshirt covering my head, sweat pants, no makeup, with teeth that haven't been brushed. Trust me. I have witnesses and documentation to prove it.

By the time I finally stopped my inquest on Monday, I was depressed. I'm sure it would have helped if over the weekend I'd gotten out of my loungewear pajamas, but heck, I still made some meals, did some writing, and I did the laundry.

But as I was sorting socks and peeling potatoes that rainy Monday afternoon, I thought about the purpose of all Christian Speaker-Girls. Why do we travel and share God's love? I think the consensus would be similar: Everyone needs to know God created us for a unique purpose, and He loves us right where we are, not based on what we do but what He did. We all make mistakes, but we are not mistakes and we need to know we're not alone and we're lovable despite the unloveliness of life. However, if the questions went deeper and more specific to my fellow Speaker-Girls, we'd begin to see that while we all may claim to be Christians, we all have differences, some that are quite significant when it comes to a biblical worldview, which, I am now finding, makes some of us more or less popular than others.

But one fine day as I was again scrolling through Instagram Land, I saw a post from my friend, Liza (we've met maybe twice but you know how some internet friendships can be the best). She just happens to be stunningly beautiful and a pastor's wife with five children and two are newborn twins, *but* she also has had heartaches and heavy trials. I applaud her for her bold and truthful posts, which I know don't make her popular among some of her Christians friends. Yet, Liza posted something I think is helpful to all of us and something I'm continually trying to get from my head to my heart. She wrote:

> How do you know who you really are? Do you look inside yourself to discover your identity? Or do you look to the Bible for God to tell you who you are? What if when you look inside yourself you find you are a homosexual, or a man instead of a woman? Or you're someone who really deserves that money you took from the office account. Or that you're really in love with your secretary or your yoga instructor. If we lose an external authority for our identity, then we lose an external Savior. If you define yourself, you must save yourself. To a sinful human ear, "You don't get to define yourself" sounds like bad news. But heard by and acknowledging they're a sinner, "You don't have to define yourself" is wonderful, freeing, and comforting news. . . . The same Lord who defines you can save you. The heart is deceitful above all things. Look instead to Jesus, Who can tell you honestly who you are and then save you."[96]

(FYI: "Follow you heart' is not good advice. It's not in the Bible. See Jeremiah 17:9.)

---
[96] Liza Koch, "Identity in Christ," April/May 2021, Instagram, https://www.instagram.com/lizatkoch/, viewed in 2021.

I appreciate Liza letting me share this insight, which she learned from Nick Lannon from his podcast episode, "Stand Firm," where Nick stated, "If Jesus isn't giving you your identity, then He isn't saving you either."

It's totally freeing to understand the message of the cross, which is to recognize that all of us are sinners, but through Christ we have our salvation, along with the opportunity to be confident knowing who we are in Him. Our true identity is found in Him because He created and knows best how we operate. Jesus is the *best* (because He's God but also because He knows what it is to be human because He was). Jesus is the perfect love we all need, but He's not always popular. He reminds us in John 15:18, "If the world hates you, keep in mind that it hated Me first," which is to say that when someone says, "Debbie, is that what you really think or believe about adultery? I mean don't you think Janice deserves to be happy when her husband is such a jerk?" If I answer the question by saying, "It's not what I think about adultery (no matter the circumstances) but what Jesus thinks and says." I often see this expression, on their face, which reads to me, "Yeah, whatever, you're so intolerant," and I'm sure to have lost popularity points with them. It does matter most what *Jesus* says. And what is real tolerance anyway? I would say that real tolerance is treating one another with respect regardless of our different opinions or beliefs.

I thank God that He's not merely tolerant of me but *loves* me, the Debbie Girl, as I am. Sometimes, I'll whisper to myself (as if it's God speaking to me), "Debbie, I love you." I need these words from Him when I feel unlovable because I'm depressed and don't leave the house or shower. I know too, I'm not being completely honest by saying, "I don't feel well," when it's merely depression and I can't explain why or feel I can tell anyone about it. What's to be depressed about, Debbie? I know, right? So, this freedom comes when I believe *He* loves me despite myself. Understanding God's grace then frees us to face our addiction and sin. God paid a high price for our freedom and pardon, and He is not persuaded by our moralism, our good intentions and greater self-effort, only the realization of our need for *His* finished work on the cross. *This* is the message I try and bring to others whether on my couch or on stage in front of an audience. Of course, it's not my job to convict people, but I've certainly tried to play the role of God in someone's life and "just let them have the truth" but if there's no love then I'm simply noisy and irritating. Love is the answer and God through the Holy Spirit can do any and all convicting that needs to be done.

When I was charged with a DUI, I was so encouraged by the immediate grace from honest friends who shared how they had gotten behind the wheel intoxicated but never got caught. Others saw it as an invitation to share their embarrassing personal struggles. Yet, there would not have been real healing without facing my problem, and taking responsibility and the consequences. Despite forgiveness there are consequences to sin, and there is never true peace when we are disobeying God. He loves us enough to teach us a better way.

I had the privilege of hearing Fleming Rutledge speak at a conference in New York City in 2017. She was one of the first women ordained in the Episcopal Church (1975) and her book, *The Crucifixion: Understanding The Death of Jesus Christ*, is a masterpiece. I have not read all of it, but what I have read is profound. She's beautiful and popular, but I don't think she knows or cares.

Rutledge was born in 1937 and wears her bobbed white hair like a crown. She focused on why Jesus came and says this about popularity: "Paul had discovered something that the church can never forget: our work is not to repackage the Gospel in ways that will make it more appealing or popular. Our mission is to preach Christ crucified; Christ risen; Christ incarnate; Christ in His body the Church; Christ in the blessed sacrament of the altar; Christ in the mighty Word read, proclaimed, and obeyed; Christ the Lord and Savior of all. We preach Christ crucified. God will take care of the rest."[97] I couldn't write notes fast enough on the message she gave.

Isn't that good? Sometimes I think we try and take our own sufferings and struggles and think, *I can relate to Jesus*, but it's the other way around. God came as man, in Christ, so He can relate to us. There is no way we can "relate" to Jesus's necessary death because we are the necessity that caused the death.

I am a work in progress, but I know I'm justified by faith. I know that God is always good even when I'm not. Maturity and becoming Christlike (and free) take time and big helpings of grace. I am sure we can all point to people who are kinder or better than those who profess Christ. The good news is God looks at our hearts and how much we trust Him for His finished work and the unfinished work He has yet to do in us. The good news is, He never stops loving us despite our pitiful lack of trust in our most challenging times. C. S. Lewis likewise always seems to have the best advice, in this case: "Be weird. Be random. Be who you are. Because you never know who would love the person you hide."

My desire is to be able to walk in the grace God gives me in spite of myself and share that Good News with others. God gets us. He loves us. He wants us to be free to enjoy life and the peace He offers. When He died, every sin we committed was in the future, so we know even when we sin tomorrow, we are forgiven. I think this is why I can sing along with Glinda in part . . .

"My tender heart
Tends to start to bleed

---

[97] Fleming Rutledge, "The Raising of the Crucified One," https://mbird.com/podcasts/the-raising-of-the-crucified-one-fleming-rutledge/, viewed February 14, 2022.

And when someone needs a makeover
I simply have to take over
I know, I know exactly what they need."[98]

Yes, I know exactly what we all need, too, Glinda. We need unconditional love. I's not about having followers who make you popular, but about following the One who sets you free.

---

[98] Kristin Chenoweth, *Wicked*.

51
SINNERS & SAINTS: LIFE IS SHORT

"So, if the Son sets you free, you are truly free."
— **John 8:36 (NLT)**

IF YOU'RE SERIOUS ABOUT JESUS, can you be serious about having fun?

I'm here, serious about Jesus and serious about having fun and being free.

Where are you at?

Billy Joel was one of my favorite artists growing up. He has this song; "Only the Good Die Young," which was on my favorite album, *The Stranger*. I can still belt out most of the lyrics:

"They say there's a heaven for those who will wait
Some say it's better but I say it ain't
I'd rather laugh with the sinners than cry with the saints
The sinners are much more fun . . ."[99]

We are all sinners no matter how well we behave, and choosing intentional sin against what God asks certainly can be fun; it's just that

---

[99] Billy Joel, "Only the Good Die Young," *The Stranger*. https://www.youtube.com/watch?v=q6yQ14TGB8U, viewed September 3, 2021.

the consequences are not. God is not in the business of destroying our joy and giving us instructions to drown our parties. He just loves and knows us well enough to know that there are boundaries so we don't end up as slaves to sin. Yep, sin can be fun, but there is always a payback. A lot of times God isn't saying we can't but just to wait or to have balance with a particular activity.

Sometimes we partake in what we know to be a bad choice, a sinful choice because it helps us hide who we are. We put up this front to keep people from getting too close because we're afraid that if they really knew us, they would run.

We don't have to pretend to have it all together with Christ who loves us with no conditions. He knows our spirit and flesh all the way through, and He will never leave or abandon us. That's freedom in Christ. That is what Christians mean when they say, "Let go and let God."

"What a God we have and how fortunate we are to have Him! Because Jesus was raised from the dead, we've been given a brand-new life and have everything to live for, including a future in heaven—and the future starts now! God is keeping careful watch over us and the future. The Day is coming when you'll have it all—life healed and whole" 1 Peter 1:3–5 (MSG).

Well, I'm "in." How about you? It sounds great; it sounds perfect.

Christianity is the only religion where God is living now and be active in our lives. He loves the liars, cheaters, addicted, and immoral. He loves you and me. God offered a gift of a clean slate of forgiveness we shouldn't refuse, because to refuse blocks real hope and freedom.

Mark Twain had it right: "Heaven goes by favor. If it went by merit, you would stay out and your dog would go in."[100]

There are a lot of Christians who share about finding their purpose, finding encouragement, finding a way to step forward from the

---

[100] Mark Twain quote No. 1351625, https://quotepark.com/quotes/1351625-mark-twain-heaven-goes-by-favor-if-it-went-by-merit-you-wou/, viewed Feb. 14, 2022.

past. I am one of those Christians who share about finding that kind of hope in this life. But I am also the Christian gal to not only share the Good News that through Christ we have forgiveness of our sins and the hope of heaven, but that there are ways to find fun in the everydayness with everyday people like me and like you.

When accepting the love and forgiveness of Christ, we have a new self in Him and we're irrevocably bonded to our brothers and sisters in the family of God. We're not still here to make the most of it. We're still here to let others know that while we were yet sinners, Christ died for us and Planet Earth is not our final destination.

Paul instructed Titus, who was an early Christian missionary and church leader, a companion and disciple of Paul the Apostle, to teach good sound doctrine and to teach people to live right so they might be identified as true Christians. More than ever now, people are leaving the church because they have observed pretend or "fake" Christians who tell others what to do but do not do it themselves. Those who don't "walk the talk" are the hypocrites who do such damage in trying to represent Christ. We don't need to defend Christ. He's perfect and we aren't. We need to walk in love, live humbly, and share that it's only by God's grace that we can move forward with our messy mistakes and judgmental attitudes, and apologize for the times we open our mouths and try and speak as God.

The Bible version I most often read is the Amplified Classic Version, "The Everyday Life Bible," with commentaries throughout this Bible, by Joyce Meyer, are extremely insightful. Titus 2:1 says, "As for you, Titus, promote the kind of living that reflects sound doctrine." Joyce shared some thoughts concerning this Scripture in the Bible commentary, which I find very insightful:

> The way you live, it's very important. When you put a Christian bumper stick on your car, wear jewelry with the cross on it, or shirts with Scriptures and go to church, people watch you and they look for authenticity.

Wearing a bracelet with the letters "WWJD" was a fad at one time. The initials stood for, "What would Jesus do?" Wearing a bracelet is nice, but what is inside a person should match what they promote on the outside. How would you like it if you saw a grocery store sign and when you went inside you found hardware? You would be aggravated because what was advertised was not what was offered. I believe the world feels the same way about people who advertise Christianity through bumper stickers, jewelry, T-shirts, and church attendance but do not live the life showing Christ has changed them from the inside out.

The Bible is filled with encouragement on how to live well. It teaches us how to think, talk, and act, as well as where and who we spend your time with and how we manage our money. The Bible also teaches us not to be anxious and fearful or out of balance in any area. What good does it do to have a "Jesus loves you" bumper sticker on your vehicle and then break the speed limit, refuse to wear a seatbelt, and park in handicapped parking spaces when we are not handicapped?" [101]

I am guilty of breaking all three examples and maybe that's why I never put a "Christian" bumper sticker on my car.

I encourage you to step "outside yourself" and examine your lifestyle regularly so you're the kind of person who makes people better, and not bitter, by being around you. The way you live sincerely each day represents how you live your life by what you say you believe. Humble people who know God's grace are better able to give grace to others and that can make all the difference in someone wanting to be a Christian like you.

It's easy to love those we agree with, those who do us no harm, who don't need anything from us, and those who don't offend us. It's so much harder when love has to put shoes on—when we have to walk in those words. Who needs your love today? Each person you

---

[101] Joyce Meyer, T*he Everyday Life Bible: The Power of God's Word for Everyday Living* (New York: Faith Words, 2018), p. 2020.

come in contact with today needs love.

John 13:35 (NIV): "By this everyone will know that you are My disciples, if you have love for one another."

Jesus calls us to be tender with one another because He is tender. He invites us into an identity that isn't measured by what we do, who we marry, our achievements, our trophies and awards. Success is made by whose lives we influence. That is how we'll be remembered. We will be remembered by how we treated others. That is our legacy. The real party, where real life begins, is in heaven. And quite honestly, it is "happily ever after."

In the meantime: "I recommend walking in the freedom of God's forgiveness and having fun. There is nothing better for people in this world than to eat, drink, and enjoy life. That way they will experience some happiness along with all the hard work God gives them under the sun" (Ecclesiastes 8:15).

So, until the day we are all having an absolute blast in heaven, let's focus on the good we have here. Let's love one another, express compassion, and have fun. There will be tears, but there can be a whole lot of laughter, too.

Jesus is friend to us all, the Sinners and the Saints, and we have the hope to experience the wholeness of who He created us to be for evermore.

52
ONE STEP AT A TIME

> *"May the God of hope fill you with all joy and peace*
> *as you trust in Him, so that you may overflow*
> *with hope by the power of the Holy Spirit."*
> — **Romans 15:13 (NIV)**

TRANSPARENT. THAT'S WHAT I WANNA BE. Being transparent is the only thing that has brought me true peace and freedom; transparency has helped me to understand and empathize with others, too.

I've come to understand that Jesus doesn't need me to "get fixed" before coming to Him, but simply to humble myself before Him, with all of my garbage laid out and unhidden. Christianity is a "Come As You Are" Party. He tells us in 1 Peter 5:6–7 to "Humble yourselves, therefore, under God's mighty hand, that He may lift you up in due time. Cast all your anxiety on Him because He cares for you" (NIV).

God is basically telling us to come as we are. Not when we are perfect or even necessarily going in the right direction, but as we are, humbly and fully before Him. This can be scary, but it's scarier to hide. God knows. He sees everything. Besides, we're only as sick as our secrets.

It's hard. It's one thing to humbly reach out to God who doesn't condemn us, but another thing to reach out to others and ask for accountability, especially when we feel we might be judged.

I always feel ashamed and start questioning myself . . . again. *Debbie, how is it possible that alcohol even became an issue for you after God gave you the opportunity to be heard on the radio and then have a speaking ministry? C'mon, you're even heard in Norway! Really, Debbie!*

Really, what? Oh, you mean that the radio feature, Everyday Matters, *is heard in Norway? I know . . . right!? No? Oh, you mean the issue I sometimes have with liking vodka and cranberry juice a little too much. Right. Gotcha.*

How is this possible? Because I got bruised by loneliness, rejected, discouraged, uncertain, ashamed, or focused so much on past failures that I couldn't see anything else.

In his book, *The Ragamuffin Gospel*, the late author and speaker Brennen Manning asked the same question that I asked, "How is it possible that I became an alcoholic *after* I got saved? Because the Christ-encounter did not transfigure me into an angel. Because justification by grace through faith means I have been set in right relationship with God, not made the equivalent of a patient etherized on a table."[102]

Manning's answer comforts me.

I've come to realize that laying my own junk and struggles on the table sincerely helps others much more than does a pat answer followed by a Scripture verse. I think a lot of harm is done by "Christians" or "the Church" when we're not willing to get real about our struggles.

And I get it. I get why we don't share more of our junk. It's be-

---

[102] Brennan Manning, "Problems of Alcoholism," *The Ragamuffin Gospel* (Colorado Springs, CO: Multnomah Books, 2005).

cause it's so nasty and we know we should know better, and the "judgment" of the well-meaning individual is just too much for us.

A young woman I mentored wrote me after a session we had: "I know what God has to say about the choices I'm making. I know what the Scriptures say, so why can't I just be obedient and follow? I'm so frustrated with myself."

My reply was as much to her as to myself. "We all have our crap. We're all sinners in need of grace. The enemy knows your struggles, too, so he is always going to try and mess you up and try and destroy you. 1 Peter 5:8 (NLT) says, "Stay alert! Watch out for your great enemy, the devil. He prowls around like a roaring lion, looking for someone to devour." Yep. The devil is not out and about to just frustrate, irritate, and annoy you; he's out to devour and destroy you.

It's helpful to find a community of believers who struggle and are simply trying to live free of addictions, hang-ups, and junk. We are all scrambling to find love and fill the ache of our hearts, whether it's a substance, another person, or running so scared we don't stop to think and let God or anyone else in.

I told the gal I was mentoring, Sam, to find a project or activity that involved helping others. It helps when the temptation comes, and it will come. I said to check into attending some AA meetings, not because you're an alcoholic, but because it's a group of honest people working toward freedom.

Frederick Buechner, writer, poet, and theologian and Presbyterian minister, makes a great point: "I do not believe that such groups as Alcoholics Anonymous are perfect any more than anything human is perfect, but I believe what goes on in them is far closer to what Christ meant His church to be, and what it originally was, than much of what goes on in most churches I know."[103]

---

[103] Frederick Buechner, *Wishful Thinking: A Theological ABC* (New York: Harper & Row, 1973).

I don't mean to knock down any church, church program, or denomination, I am the church, but there's truth here. I *hate* that I had to ask for help, and like my friend, Sam, I get so frustrated with me . . . being me. *Blecchh!*

Yet, God knows me and you, and despite all of our junk He loves us completely. He loves you completely. We experience real freedom because that empty ache in our hearts can only be filled by having a relationship with Christ, accepting Him as our Lord and Savior. But just because we have freedom in Jesus doesn't mean we have freedom from problems, but it does mean there's hope when we walk with Him.

Hope is the happy anticipation that something good is going to happen. When we have hope, we can have faith, which is trusting in something we cannot see. We choose to trust God who to us might feel very distant, yet we know He's "there" and He'll never leave us. He has the strength and grace for us to carry on. His grace of hope and strength is new every morning (thank God) and for many of us in difficult seasons, it's a moment-by-moment experience in receiving this grace, so we can simply take one more step and move forward without complete despair.

"The hopes of the godly result in happiness, but the expectations of the wicked come to nothing" (Proverbs 10:28 NLT).

It would be nice if there were a smart phone app for our issues such as "Snap Sin" or "Insta-Free," and by merely typing in the correct code or verse we could be rid of our entire pile of poo.

Have you ever gone to the "Google Doctor?" I have and I did not experience the peace God promises after I Googled, "reddish rash on wrist" and discovered it might be some rare form of a crazy cancer. There aren't "click here" links that will solve the ache in our hearts and make everything feel better.

Faith is not believing that God exists. The devil believes in God. Faith is believing God is still good when the circumstances are not.

When there's a stress downpour, faith wavers because we worry God is not trustworthy or able to handle the storm that's raging.

"I'm drowning over here, Jesus. Do you see me?"

Isaiah 43:2 (NLT) comforts us with, "When you go through deep waters, I will be with you. When you go through rivers of difficulty, you will not drown."

Jesus had no romantic notion of the cost of discipleship. He knew that physical and emotional pain, the loss of a loved one, failure, loneliness, rejection, and betrayal would sap our spirits. He knew that the day would come when faith wouldn't offer reassurance or comfort, and that prayer would lack any sense of reality or progress.

He knew.

And because He knows, He'll never condemn us for our feelings. Instead, He understands. He picks us up and walks with us through it all. Sometimes He carries us.

OK, so maybe there's no storm and it's not even raining, but there's this annoying drip-drip-drop, and it's lonely. I've been "there." I was a single mom for two weeks because my husband was out of town, and our four teenage sons just needed me to be the mom who does mom stuff, like laundry, cleaning, and cooking. I was feeling weak and lonely, and I wasn't having fun. I began to lament and tried to share my heart with my oldest son, but he finally said, "Mom, don't you have a friend you can talk to?"

I stopped talking.

I have lots of friends, but when you don't let anyone in for a while, you decide it's too much work to "lay everything out there" because "you should know better," so you end up retreating into your "I'm so alone" hole and think how good a cocktail (or two) might help.

God is aware. I was lonely. It was my third son, of the four, who helped take me away from my party with Pity. Joey, was fifteen at the time and he let me pick a movie to watch with him. I picked *Pride and Prejudice*. I know. Halfway through the movie we had to stop so he could go to bed and I asked, "Joe, will it always be this way?"

"What, Mom?"

I was referring to a bruise on my face that just wasn't disappearing as fast as I had hoped. Deeper down I wondered if this season of wait and lonely weirdness would ever leave?

"Mom, it will always be that way. It will never change." And then he grinned. "Of course, it's gonna be fine. It's just a bruise. It's not a scar. You know that. Why do you even ask?"

Because I just needed to hear, "It will get better. There's hope." There's always hope. Yes, I'm talking to you, too. It will get better.

However, be aware that the enemy of our souls, the devil, wants to destroy our hope and faith in God with his two favorite words—forever and never.

Satan tells us the negative things in our lives will *never* change and will *forever* be the way they are. He tells us we will *never* get what we want and we'll *never* experience the freedom or healing we desire. He says the way we are right now will stay that way *forever*.

Lies.

The devil is a liar. Lies create fear in our hearts, and they are untrue because sooner or later, everything changes. The truth is, God is always good. Circumstances and people often are not. Ecclesiastes 3:1 (NIV) reminds us; "For *everything* there is a season, and a time for every matter or purpose under heaven."

OK, so that was a season I'd been in, and maybe you're there now, and . . . I've always thought a season was like four months, but what if the season is four years, or longer. Sometimes we want God to put us back on track in a mere two weeks or less because we've finally decided we need to make a change. But suppose it's been twenty years of making unhealthy choices? How then can we expect that in two weeks everything will be set right?

We must take one step at a time, receive God's fresh grace each day, and eventually we'll get better. When we fall, we just get back up. There is hope of restoration and redemption.

There's redemption for *everyone*. Salvation is by *grace*. God's Riches At Christ's Expense (G-R-A-C-E) and it is for *everyone who wants it*.

I think we'll all be surprised by who makes it "in" heaven and who does not. Being a pastor, priest, missionary, or Christian speaker is not a sure thing. There will be sinners (like you and me) standing in front of the throne of Jesus and set free and fully forgiven simply because we chose to let Jesus into our lives. We did nothing to earn it.

I think we'll see people like my friend, Sherry, with guilt and remorse, who I sat and grieved with over her three abortions because at the time she felt there were no alternatives. My theatre friend, Ryan, who never fully kicked his drug habit, but who never forgot Jesus loved him. Jessica thought she had to prove herself so she lied and sacrificed her integrity, but by receiving God's grace she'll be "in" too. They will all be "in" because they let go and let God move in. They received what they could never earn.

They received real love.

Remember that there's no sin or offense God can't forgive. There's no pit so deep that He can't reach down and lift us up. He isn't surprised when I commit to abstain from alcohol, only to buy a bottle of Tito's (more than once) one night and pour it all down the drain in the morning.

He is right there with me with no condemnation. There is always the temptation to think, *I can handle my issues* or *I can get away with this*. But the truth is, I need to bring my junk to the light. Hidden sin will always have power over us, but once exposed to light we can step forward and begin healing.

Tell a trusted friend you need help and then get help. Later on, you'll be able to help and understand someone who is sitting in a pit of despair and shame as you once were. It's so wonderful when we're able to take this deep sigh of relief and say, "The monkey is off my back, the pesky one who's so heavy and constantly chattering, the one we never thought we'd be free from." And if you're carrying someone with an addiction problem, it's time to take that bundle off your back and give them to God. Detach in Love in an Everyday Matter feature that aired on the radio:

"Everyday Detach in Love" Sunday Matters

Loving someone who has an addiction problem can be very challenging. I remember hearing the story of a woman who was married to an alcoholic and every night her husband would come home drunk, collapse on the floor, and fall asleep. And every night this woman would somehow get him up and put him to bed. She became worn out and frazzled from rescuing her husband. A friend suggested she attend Al Anon and there she learned about "Detachment." The next night when her husband came home drunk and fell asleep on the floor, she simply put a blanket over him and left him there. She loved him by covering him but by not picking him up she was detaching. She did not rescue him. She created a loving boundary and let go.

Sometimes love calls us to let go completely. It can be a scary and uncertain time but God will guide you always (Isaiah 55:11). And He'll often send others to help who've been through a similar trial. Reach out. You are not alone . . . everyday.

Detachment is experiencing our feelings without allowing them to control us. We step back and look at things objectively. We let go and accept what we cannot change. We detach from the choices others make, knowing that their spiritual work is not ours to do. We choose how we will act rather than just reacting. We step away from harmful cravings. Detachment is a deep breath of peace and patience in response to unexpected anger. We can listen without losing ourselves. With detachment, we see our mistakes honestly, make amends, and start afresh. Detachment allows us to be in the world but not of it. It frees us to lead our lives with grace.

Are you listening? Jesus is speaking. Hear His voice: "You are forgiven. Today is a new day, with fresh grace. You have new mercy every morning."

And by receiving God's forgiveness, you have washed your robes and made them white by the blood of the Lamb. (Revelation 7:14).

> Here we are—the whole lot of us who so wanted to be faithful, but who at times got defeated, beat up by life, and bested by trials, wearing the bloodied garments of life's tribulations, but through it all clung to faith." Again, the wisdom of Brennan Manning: "Because salvation is by grace through faith, I believe that among the countless number of people standing in front of the throne and in front of the Lamb, dressed in white robes and holding palms in their hands (Revelation 7:9), I shall see the prostitute from the Kit-Kat Ranch in Carson City, Nevada, who tearfully told me that she could find no other employment to support her two-year-old son. I shall see the woman who had an abortion and is haunted by guilt and remorse but did the best she could face with grueling alternatives; the businessman besieged with debt who sold his integrity in a series of desperate transactions; the insecure clergyman addicted to being liked, who never challenged his people from the pulpit and longed for unconditional love; the sexually abused teen molested by his father and now selling his body on the street, who, as he falls asleep each night after his last 'trick,' whispers the name of the unknown God he learned about in Sunday school.
>
> "But how?" we ask.
>
> Then the voice says, "They have washed their robes and have made them white in the blood of the Lamb." My friends, if this is not good news to you, you have never understood the Gospel of Grace. We were tempted to sin and then fell into it, but through it all we held on so tightly to our faith in Christ.[104]

---

[104] Brennan Manning quotes, https://www.goodreads.com/author/quotes/27405.Brennan_Manning, viewed February 14, 2022.

We come as we are, completely transparent, and receive this crazy unconditional love He has for us. This is Good News, the Gospel of Grace and something to celebrate. Let's raise "a glass of hope" and carry on in faith together. Life is a battle but our Commander in Chief promised us victory. Onward and upward, Christian Soldiers. Let us carry on, one step at a time.

53
SEASON FINALE: ORANGE IS THE NEW BLESSING

> *"See, I am doing a new thing! Now it springs up;*
> *do you not perceive it? I am making a way*
> *in the wilderness and streams in the wasteland."*
> — **Isaiah 43:19 (NIV)**

I HAVE EMBRACED THE COLOR ORANGE like nobody's business. I like the color. It's a good color on me, and I'm saying this even after I have had to wear orange *in jail* for a February 28, 2017 DUI arrest.

It was surreal that my three-mile roundtrip/road trip to the McDonald's drive-thru landed me in jail. A quickie review from earlier: I was sitting in my driveway with the vehicle running eating a Big Mac in my pajamas when the officer knocked on my window. What followed was a breathalyzer test that landed me in jail for a three-hour wake-up call and one that would allow me to enter into an eight-month season now known to me and others as "Orange is the New Blessing."

God is wherever you are. He has never left me and I have experienced His grace and *love* in my life like nobody's business, especially at a time where I had no business getting behind the wheel after drinking a homemade cocktail. And even after all these years of following, knowing, and sharing the love of Jesus, I am still often surprised that He is never surprised by our mistakes or failings. He shows up with redemption and hope in every way possible, especially in times when we don't deserve it.

My attorney at law, Dan Griffith, also happens to be my husband. His grace now and then is an example of what "for better or worse" looks like. Because I am somewhat of a prankster, with shenanigans up my sleeve, my cute husband (my nickname for him) thought perhaps I had found a way to prank call him from the jail, but, unfortunately, it was all too real.

After the initial shock wore off, and the admission of guilt and sorrow brought forth not only healing and support, we were advised that we could challenge the charge with a legal argument to have the case dismissed on constitutional grounds. But had I known that it would be eight months of canceled court dates and rescheduling, I don't know if I would have "fought" the fight.

I remember the time in June when we had to reschedule the court date, based on the fact that my husband could no longer be my attorney and a witness at the same time, and I felt the hope in me slowly exit. A new date was set in August so that all parties (my new attorney, the city attorney, two police officers, the judge, and the DOT attorney from Minneapolis) could attend. As the meeting was adjourning, I silently left the chambers and biked to the nearest church because I was so angry and sad.

St. Thomas Catholic Church is conveniently next door to the courthouse *for such times as this*, I thought. My memory is that I crawled into the sanctuary, even though my legs worked, and I knelt and cried in the pew while a student was practicing "How Great Thou Art" on the piano. God was there because He is wherever we are.

So, I continued biking and praying, and even when the court date was moved, again, from August 24 to October 16, I had God's peace to hope and wait. *But then* . . with only four days remaining before the final hearing, I sat in a law office with Dan and another attorney, pushed my chair back, and declared I had made the decision to plead guilty and no longer contest the matter.

What? Who does that? Why? Yep. After eight months of biking and asking people for rides, I made this decision. I made it with a peace that only God can give. And I came to understand that it was not about winning, it was about waiting.

So, I paid the fines, took a twenty-question written test at the DOT, went to the license bureau and within twenty-four hours I could drive again. Now, granted, thirty days after the February 28 arrest I could have done the same thing, but at that time it was not the plan or God's best for me.

I can name specific and clear blessings that came from the eight-month season run of "Orange is the New Blessing," which ended up being a nonfiction story I wrote and entered in a writing contest and . . . won. But the real victory was all the lessons and love received from God and others that are yet still flowing.

One clear blessing at that time was that our eighteen-year-old son, Joey, was my chauffer who drove me *every* place I needed to be if I was unable to bike. He brought me to ladies' retreats, where I was booked as a speaker-girl, and we indeed made some special and fun memories. But probably most significant was that he was not only my driver, but my company when I needed to be with my dad, who was in the ICU at the hospital 250 miles away for two months. Joey's steadfast companionship, comfort, and humor, and lack of complaining, was medicine only God knew I would need in the month of September 2017.

A blessing came, too, in my decision to work at the local Mexican restaurant. Without the DUI, I would have chosen another summer employment option. Previously, I had worked as a managing artistic director each summer in Moorhead, Minnesota, where I lived in a rented home, but a year prior I had let go of that position. My substitute-teaching earnings, along with the majority of speaking events, ended in summer, so the three-block biking trek to Barajas Mexican Bar and Grill to work proved to be the perfect fit. The experience was far more about people than chips and salsa. I love people.

Many people made an impact in the way I journeyed through the season of orange, and I am amazed at how much I learned about others and myself. It was big news for a small town and the initial embarrassment in being known as a teacher, speaker, and radio gal with my ministry, *Everyday Matters,* makes for good gossip, especially when your name and photo on the jail roster can be sent as a screenshot throughout the community quickly and efficiently (the girls' hockey team was the first to send a group text).

Yet, the number of private messages and calls allowed others to share their own stories, knowing they were not alone. Three days after the incident, I entered the high school to substitute teach, and I was met with incredible support by both students and staff. On one white board was the message from a student who wrote, "Plz be nice to the sub today." A counselor in the school office patted my arm and said, "It could have happened to any of us. We're all behind you."

When we take personal responsibility for our actions, rather than blame or play victim, we can help and identify with others on a new level because we all make mistakes. It's how we choose to get up or stay down, which determines character. "Jesus didn't take the wheel this time," was the most common joke I heard, but the winner goes to a student who said to my youngest of four sons, "I guess Everyday Beer Matters?!" My sweet son David defended me, but I told him, "That's the best line yet. It's hysterical."

Probably the biggest challenge after the initial, "I own this story; it's not gonna own me" proclamation, was walking through and living my story humbly. So there I was, known and in the spotlight as an accomplished individual, married twenty-six years with four sons, and now I have a spotlight on one evening of a bad choice I made, which landed me in the role of DUI Debbie. I was a fifty-year-old server girl and I wore my orange work T-shirt proudly, but it's not like all my sunshine orange enthusiasm hasn't been met with some cool tones.

Yes, I love people and my Christian "family," but people can be unlovely and Christians can be weird, even when they don't mean to be. "Why did you choose alcohol over Jesus?" was a question asked. It was a phone call the day after, and I couldn't answer because it seemed like such a weird question. I didn't choose vodka and orange juice over Jesus. I chose alcohol on that Tuesday evening as a way to stop the pain from a rod pinching a nerve in my back, along with the pain of some other unpleasant life events. My spirit knew what was best, but my flesh is weak and my flesh won.

I also had a loving and well-meaning friend write, "I'm praying as you go back 'into the world' that you would represent Jesus well. After all, you are certainly not the only person to let Jesus down . . . and still go on to be used greatly by God." Yeah. It bugged me because I've always thought, "But I don't represent Jesus well. He represents me well. His grace covers me. I fall down. I get back up and by *Him* in my life and ME taking responsibility, for what I do, others will *see Him* and not me. His grace in my life represents me *so* well.

Of course, people were disappointed in me with what happened or maybe even embarrassed, but was Jesus disappointed in me? I think ten years ago I might have thought He was, but I didn't understand His grace as I do now. Our sins grieve Him, but He knows us, so He's not surprised or shocked when we fall. He sees and knows us completely and loves us anyway. I disappointed people, but with Jesus I was safe, I was good.

I repented and I needed to. I changed direction, which is what Acts 3:19 (AMPC) talks about simply and brilliantly: "So repent, change your mind and purpose; turn around and return to God, that your sins may be erased, blotted out and wiped clean so that times of refreshing may come from the presence of the Lord." Remember this, "guilt" says you did something wrong and "shame," on the other hand, says that *you are* something wrong. I confessed I was guilty and then took a big scoop of His grace and walked forward forgiven and free. And there's no shame in that at all.

I also chose to do a six-week outpatient program to understand more clearly why, in the last five years, I was choosing alcohol as a "let go" release, more often than not. I had always gone to a Christian counselor or professional psychiatrist for help, but having a treatment counselor who freely used the F-bomb to make a point brought new insight into my life, too. I also remembered from my mentor Barb from years past, that to walk humbly through life is the best route. Barb had even written a book where she shared her wisdom: "The truly humble person recognizes their strengths and weaknesses, and so rather than a concentration on yourself, humility leads you to look around you for opportunities to encourage and help others."

I had some idea, but did not imagine how sharing my story would be such a blessing to *me*, while encouraging others, too. There was the ladies' retreat where Joey drove me to speak, and a gal afterward handed him a note (unsigned), which read, "Thank you for being so open about your life. If cool Speaker Girl has this kind of 'stuff' in her life, maybe my battles aren't so shameful."

I am trying to live in sincere humility every day, and perhaps even more so because of this season that I entered into and am now coming out of. This Earth experience is really hard, but it is not our home, our final destination. However, what happens here can wake us up and change us to really live while we're still *here*. I'm a better "me" because of what happened, but no matter what, I will always try to "Live, Love & Laugh" (which is something that seems to be embroidered on pillows and painted on plaques) through each challenge or adventure. (I don't want one of those pillows or plaques. It's written on my heasrt.)

Laughter will always be one of the best medicines . . . *ever*. And I always get people grinning when I tell how I asked the female officer in jail if I could keep my orange socks. It's a great prop.

Even that evening, I knew God would use my experience as a blessing (and a lesson) if I allowed Him to. His grace always does that.

In October 2017 as we looked for a new vehicle for me to drive, I insisted it must be orange. Embrace the good of who God is in *all* of your seasons and in the different directions you take. God *is* here, waiting to make creative, redemptive use of what has happened. He is always on the move. He isn't wasting time thinking about all the trouble He has with you, or how awful you feel about where you are with your troubles and yourself.

Jesus gets us, knows us, and loves us unconditionally. I got to experience His grace and love in such a surprising and beautiful way with a matter that burst, bright orange, into my life for eight months that was a game changer.

Orange is the New Blessing turned out to be a great season run. The finale was worth the wait. But stay tuned, as I know there are other adventures, I will be going on and sharing. God's not finished with me (or you) yet. God bless us as we journey together in all the different colors of each season we find ourselves in.

"Are you tired? Worn out? Burned out on religion? Come to Me. Get away with Me and you'll recover your life. I'll show you how to take a real rest. Walk with Me and work with Me—watch how I do it. Learn the unforced rhythms of grace. I won't lay anything heavy or ill-fitting on you. Keep company with Me, and you'll learn to live freely and lightly."
— **Matthew 11:28–30 MSG**

Griffith Family 2022

Peter, Marco, Rachel, Debbie, Dan, David, Joey.

Looking at the picture of all of us Griffith folk, at the park right in front of our house in 2022 or at the City Beach in 2010 (International Falls, Minnesota), makes me happy. I love us. Perhaps you see a happily posed family and perhaps, you too, love us. But to be sure, we aren't always happy, and we don't all think alike or agree on big subjects like politics, the pandemic, church, or media/entertainment. Yet, we do agree that God is love, and we love one another. People who love one another have disagreements and situations or confrontations that aren't always poised and happy, but we can walk in love, agreeing to disagree, and we can give forgiveness. It's a dangerous trap when we compare our insides with other people's outsides. We all are messy because life is messy, and we're sinners in need of God's grace.

Debbie & Dan 2010

Joey, David, Marco, Peter 2010

The Earth experience is hard, but God is always good even when circumstances or others are not. He's a Redeemer of all things. Whew. While we are all living "here" on earth, let's be mindful of 1 Peter 4:8, "Above all things, have intense and unfailing love for one another, for love covers a multitude of sins, forgives and disregards the offenses of others."

www.ingramcontent.com/pod-product-compliance
Lightning Source LLC
Chambersburg PA
CBHW031610160426
43196CB00006B/83